AUTHORITARIAN SOCIALISM IN AMERICA

Authoritarian Socialism in America, Edward Bellamy & the Nationalist Movement

ARTHUR LIPOW

UNIVERSITY OF CALIFORNIA PRESS
BERKELEY / LOS ANGELES / LONDON

All quotations from the Bellamy manuscripts
by permission of the Houghton Library.

University of California Press
Berkeley and Los Angeles, California
University of California Press, Ltd.
London, England
© 1982 by
The Regents of the University of California
Printed in the United States of America
1 2 3 4 5 6 7 8 9

Library of Congress Cataloging in Publication Data

Lipow, Arthur.
  Authoritarian socialism in America.

  Bibliography: p.
  Includes index.
    1. Socialism—United States—History. 2. Nation-
alism—United States—History. 3. Bellamy, Edward,
1850–1898. Looking backward. 4. Authoritarianism.
5. Collectivism. I. Title.
HX86.L73   320.5′31′0973   79-65763
  ISBN 0-520-04005-8   AACR2

To Anne

CONTENTS

PREFACE

The use of the term "authoritarian socialism" in the title of this book raises many theoretical and political questions which require an explicit statement of the author's standpoint. The starting point of this study is the belief in socialism as a revolutionary and democratic idea: one opposed to the bureaucratic new class societies throughout the world which call themselves "socialist" in order to mask their class-exploitative nature. It is an idea equally opposed to modern-day capitalism, with its powerful internal authoritarian and bureaucratic statist tendencies, tendencies which are greatly accentuated by its deadly rivalry on a world scale with its dictatorial opponents.

The identification of socialism with state ownership of the economy per se, an equation made not only by opponents of socialism but by many who call themselves socialists today as well, has nothing in common with this idea of socialism. This is not only a moral distinction but an important social and political one as well. The sine qua non of socialism is political democracy combined with public ownership of the means of production, under the most extensive possible system of democratic workers' control, including trade unions free of state intervention. To the idea that state ownership of the means of production in itself constitutes any kind of socialism, whether as the result of being imposed from the top down by a bureaucratic elite or having evolved peacefully out of capitalism by the steady bureaucratic statification of existing society, I would counterpose the question of *who*—what class—"owns" the state, which in turn owns or controls the economy. For the working class, the propertyless majority in any modern society, there can be only one answer. Without political democracy there can be no workers' state, no socialism, whatever the various apologists for totalitarianism may say: without democracy in a statified economy the outcome must inevitably be the emergence of a state and party bureaucracy constituted as a new ruling class, as the experience of Russia, China, Cuba, or a wide variety of similar social formations demonstrates. There can be no "economic democracy" apart from political democracy.

In short, there can be no socialism, nothing worthy of the name, which does not include the widest and most popular forms of democracy and political freedom. It is a goal which is inseparable from the means to attain it. No benevolent elite or dictator can hand it down. Only through a movement from below involving the conscious and active participation of the overwhelming majority of the people is it possible to realize the aim of democratic socialism.

This is not a popular point of view. Many on the contemporary left would find themselves uncomfortable with it, if not openly scornful, as they search for yet another, possibly less brutal, example of "socialism" among the many national variations of bureaucratic collectivist society throughout the world, or as they cling to the deeply rooted idea that a statified economy is somehow "progressive." It cannot be popular either with those socialists, many of whom proclaim themselves adherents of a democratic socialism, or of social democracy at any rate, who see in the on-going piecemeal bureaucratic statification of capitalism the realization of their ideal of socialism and thus converge in their views of what socialism is, or might be, with the more moderate apologists for totalitarianism.

The very need to make this point, indeed the need for a study such as this one, points to the political, theoretical, and moral crisis of socialism in the modern world. For if socialism can be equated with the statification of the economy and, however reluctantly and inconsistently, with its imposition from above by a totalitarian party (for the "good of the people") then it is possible to regard it as only moral fastidiousness or sectarian dogmatism to quarrel with the totalitarian dictatorships whose "progressiveness" lies in the undoubtedly non-capitalist nature of their rule. The roots of this viewpoint go back a long way in the history of the socialist movement, antedating the rise of Stalinism. It is the purpose of this study to examine one of the more important expressions of these antecedents in the authoritarian ideas of Edward Bellamy and the Nationalist movement. A generation after *Looking Backward* appeared, Bellamy's British counterparts, Beatrice and Sidney Webb, became out-and-out apologists for Stalinism. Like Bellamy, Sidney Webb had dreamed in the 1880s of locking up the working class in an industrial army.* Many years later the self-described proponents of a bureaucratic socialism found Stalin's version of their ideal Fabian prison for workers an eminently desirable and practical realization of their kind of socialism.

The Government Organization of Unemployed Labour (London, 1886).

I must take note too that the view of democracy and socialism stated here is not a popular one among many, if not most, of the present generation of liberal academics. Or, more precisely, its premise is unacceptable to those of them who have argued with great persistence that democracy is neither possible nor desirable; that rule by benevolent elites over the incompetent masses is the most that can be hoped for and that democratic socialism, which is to say, democracy itself, is utopian. The contempt for democracy of much of the American New Left in the 1960s and 1970s was first learned from this source, although it quickly found, in its rejection of capitalism, a more powerful model on which to base its arguments. For the liberal proponents of "elitist democracy," a phrase which testifies to the degradation of the idea of democracy in modern liberalism, the concerns of this study can have little meaning. There is no place here for a theoretical answer to this point of view, except to take note of it as a symptom of the moral and political decay of American liberalism, and in this respect an illustration of the argument of this book concerning the connection between a political current such as that represented by Edward Bellamy and the origins of modern bureaucratic liberalism at the turn of the century.

But if a theoretical answer to both of these points of view is not possible here, a practical political one is readily at hand. As this book was being completed, the Polish working class rose up once more to challenge its Communist Party rulers and the latter's Russian masters. The outcome of their struggle is yet to be decided, although its historical importance is clear enough. If the Polish workers are successful—a success which would require a revolutionary struggle for state power and the spread of the working-class fight for freedom to the rest of Eastern Europe and to Russia itself—the result will be a democratic socialism in the sense used here and a magnificent example of what the working class in motion can do, demonstrating that only in a mass struggle from below is it possible to form a truly democratic social order. This conception of socialism is at the heart of Marx's idea of revolutionary socialism and it stands counterposed to the authoritarian socialism of Edward Bellamy, whose vision of an industrial army of labor the Polish workers would easily recognize. If the reader wonders then what I mean in the following pages by a movement from below, by an independent working class struggling for its own emancipation and democratic self-rule, I would point to the fight of the Polish workers. Even if defeated in the short

run, that struggle will inevitably break out again: the system of totalitarian rule cannot be reformed; it will not evolve into democracy but must
be overthrown in revolutionary action. Upon its ultimate success, in the
face of the combined opposition from both sides of the Cold War, the
very future of mankind depends.

I want to acknowledge the help and encouragement given me by
many people, some of whom read the original doctoral dissertation or
various early drafts of this book, and who argued with its ideas as they
were in gestation or shared with me their knowledge and insights into
various aspects of this topic.

There is, first of all, my long time friend and comrade, Hal
Draper, at whose suggestion I first undertook this study, and whose
ideas about the "two souls of socialism" and study of Marx's political
ideas in *Karl Marx's Theory of Revolution* have provided a focus for this
study and a guide to my understanding of socialism in the present-day
world. About American liberal reform I learned most of all from Sam
Haber, whose study of progressivism and scientific management led me
to many of the Bellamyites and helped me to understand more clearly
the antidemocratic historical origins of modern bureaucratic liberalism. I
learned much too from Lewis Feuer, Michael Rogin, and Seymour Martin Lipset, and was greatly encouraged and aided by Kenneth Bock and
Nathan Glazer, who served as the Chairman of my dissertation committee. Ernest Haberkern and Richard Broadhead read one of the drafts of
the present book, as did David Brody, all of whom made valuable suggestions which contributed to the final product. I owe a particular debt
to Paul Goodman, not only for necessary moral support, and for the
sharing of his knowledge of American history, but for some very hard
work in helping me to shape the final manuscript. And last, but not
least, there has been the support over the years from my wife, Anne,
and my children, Jenny, Stephanie, and Nick.

add Fromm

INTRODUCTION

"We are not among those communists who are out to destroy personal liberty, who wish to turn the world into one huge barrack or into a gigantic workhouse. There certainly are some communists who, with an easy conscience, refuse to countenance personal liberty and would like to shuffle it out of the world because they consider it a hindrance to complete harmony. But we have no desire to exchange freedom for equality. We are convinced . . . that in no social order will personal freedom be so assured as in a society based upon communal property."[1] Thus wrote the editors of the *Journal* of the Communist League in 1847, under the direct influence of the founders of modern revolutionary democratic socialism, Karl Marx and Frederick Engels. Their description of another type of socialism, an authoritarian, antidemocratic creed, could as well be applied in our own age to the various totalitarian collectivist ideologies which claim the title of "socialism. "

This is a study of one such authoritarian current within the history of the socialist movement: the political and social ideas of Edward Bellamy (1850-1898), author of the late nineteenth-century American utopian novel, *Looking Backward*, and of those who were inspired by its message to found the "Nationalist" movement. At the heart of this inquiry is a distinction that Hal Draper has made between "the two souls of socialism":[2] democratic revolutionary socialism based on a mass working-class movement, fighting from below for the extension of democracy and human freedom, versus the many varieties of "socialism from above" which have led in the twentieth century to movements and state forms in which a despotic "new class" rules over a statified economy in the name of socialism. This division runs through the history of the socialist movement, antedating the rise of Stalinism which, in those movements outside Russia, concentrated in itself tendencies already present within the socialist movement. Bellamyism is one such tendency, and in the history of authoritarian socialist ideas it occupies an important place.

1. *The Communist Journal* (1847) in D. Ryazoff, ed., *The Communist Manifesto of Marx & Engels* (New York: International Publishers, 1930), Appendix E, p. 262.
2. Hal Draper, *The Two Souls of Socialism* (1961).

The significance of Bellamyism, however, goes beyond this and even beyond its important role in the history of the American socialist movement during the formative period of the 1890s, for it not only foreshadowed later totalitarian collectivist ideologies but it was also a precursor of the bureaucratic statist or "corporate" liberalism which, more and more in the twentieth century, converges intellectually and politically with the antidemocratic currents represented in authoritarian socialism. The author of *Looking Backward* had much in common with modern liberal seers who, in the wave of the future syntax pioneered by Anne Morrow Lindbergh, announce the inevitable demise of democracy and fatalistically proclaim the advent of a "postcapitalist," "technetronic" society, an "industrial state," or, more bluntly, of a "new slavery." In this vision of totalitarian liberalism, the new order silently invades capitalism, carried forward by the inevitable tide of bureaucratization and technological complexity. "Ideology"—politics—fades along with the strife and disharmony it once engendered. As bureaucratic administration spreads, democracy withers away and the managers are free to manage those below them. These bold voices of the new liberalism are only echoing Bellamy's late nineteenth-century views in their belief that democracy is neither practicable nor desirable because all important decisions in "modern" society are beyond the competence of all but a tiny ruling elite.[3] It goes almost without saying that "socialism"—in this case understood as the democratic rule of the people—is relegated to the cloud-cuckooland of all utopias.

This study of Edward Bellamy's ideas, then, is an attempt to understand the intellectual roots of the authoritarian side of both the socialist tradition as well as that of bureaucratic liberalism in America. Henry Steele Commager long ago argued that the 1890s were the watershed of contemporary American society. And even in the last decades of the twentieth century we still live very much in the shadow of the political and economic ideas and institutions which took form in the period of transition from an older, rural America to the America of large-scale

---

3. For examples of this genre see Clark Kerr et al., *Industrialism and Industrial Man* (Cambridge: Harvard University Press, 1960); Zbigniew Brzezinski, *Between Two Ages: America's Role in the Technetronic Era* (New York: Viking Press, 1970); John Kenneth Galbraith, *The New Industrial State* (Boston: Houghton Mifflin, 1967). Kerr uses the phrase "new slavery" while Galbraith's book owes, by his own admission, a large intellectual debt to James Burnham's *The Managerial Revolution*. For Galbraith's view that democracy and hence socialism are impossible in the modern world, see *The New Industrial State*, pp. 103–104.

industrial capitalist enterprise and the bureaucratic capitalist state. Edward Bellamy's genius lay in his ability to respond to the rapid disintegration of established patterns of American life in the 1880s and to foresee in the breakdown of the old order one potential line of development, and thus to fashion a utopia that celebrated the inevitable triumph of a bureaucratic statist socialism. It was a vision which appealed to Bellamy's contemporaries as well as to many more millions of people in America and abroad in later years for whom an ordered collectivism was preferable to the chaos of anarchic, planless capitalism.

Published nearly one hundred years ago, *Looking Backward* has been read in every generation since it first burst into the consciousness of the American people. Yet, although widely read, extensively commented on by writers on American history, and correctly regarded as one of the most influential works in modern American social thought, *Looking Backward* has always lent itself to greatly varying and contradictory interpretations. In the 1890s some praised Bellamy's vision as the culmination of the American dream of freedom, while others damned it because it abolished democracy and personal liberty. In the 1930s, the great crisis of American capitalism rekindled enthusiasm for *Looking Backward* among liberals and radicals who testified to its influence on their political development and hailed it as one of the most important expressions of the democratic spirit in American thought.[4] More recently, when the dream of an efficient technocratic society has become a totalitarian reality, a book once hailed as democratic now seems to some critics an expression of "totalitarianism." Still, for the most part, Bellamy's message continues to be seen as that of a "man of good hope," an expression of "socialist humanism," and the embodiment of "democratic" socialism.[5] Certainly, over the years it has been this last view of Bellamy which has been predominant.

Although these contradictory reactions are to a degree merely a reflection of changing intellectual fashions, Bellamy's ideas and the utopian vision in *Looking Backward* do pose a puzzling problem of historical interpretation, one which transcends the immediate circumstances of their reception at the end of the nineteenth century. Paradoxically, Bella-

---

4. See for example John Dewey, "A Great American Prophet" (1934).

5. The term "totalitarian" is used by John L. Thomas in his Introduction to *Looking Backward* (Cambridge: Harvard University Press, 1967), p. 61; Daniel Aaron, *Men of Good Hope* (1951). For the characterization of Bellamy as messenger of socialist humanism see Erich Fromm's Foreword to *Looking Backward* (1960).

myism itself manifested the tension between the two souls of socialism and it is because of this, in part, that modern readers have failed to understand either its content or its place in the history of American social thought.

As a novel, *Looking Backward* was a consciously contrived political tract which combined a savage indictment of laissez faire capitalism with a detailed alternative portrait of a new collectivist society which neither employed the methods nor sought the goals of working-class socialism. Its indictment of the cruelty and inhumanity of industrial capitalism inspired many of its readers to think about social alternatives to capitalism. But at the same time it appealed to others who feared democracy as much as they hated the overweening power of the new industrial-financial ruling class and who saw in Bellamy's utopia the model of an authoritarian, bureaucratic form of socialism. Thus Bellamy's political views simultaneously stimulated not only an emergent democratic socialism in the 1890s but also an antidemocratic collectivism which was to come to full maturity in the twentieth century.

The popular response of Bellamy's contemporaries to *Looking Backward* was phenomenal in an age addicted to the dogmas and harsh doctrines of social Darwinism. *Looking Backward* sold by the hundreds of thousands and its ideas were widely discussed and debated in the 1890s. It quickly became the ideological foundation of an organized political movement. "Nationalism" consciously appealed, with considerable success, to educated middle-class people, especially to the "new" propertyless middle class, and to displaced professionals and intellectuals.

Many contemporary observers were puzzled by the popularity of Bellamy's ideas. The eminent political scientist, Franklin H. Giddings, early in 1891 exclaimed that "there has been no more curious phenomenon in recent times than the wholesale hypnotizing of clever literary people by Mr. Bellamy's dazzling vision." Giddings believed that those so fascinated by Bellamy's anticapitalist doctrine would soon recover their senses and "resume their intellectual self-direction."[6] But the response of Bellamy's admirers and followers was hardly the irrational matter Giddings thought it to be. The source of Bellamy's "hypnotic" appeal lay in his ability to express the frustrated expectations which many middle-class persons experienced in the 1880s and 1890s. A future under the reign of a plutocracy

---

6. Franklin H. Giddings, "The Ethic of Socialism," *International Journal of Ethics* 1 (January 1891): 242.

looked grim. Equally foreboding was a radical democratic movement of workers and farmers spawned by industrial capitalism which further undermined their precarious but still privileged position. Bellamy's non–working-class socialism was the perfect alternative.

The Nationalist movement that *Looking Backward* inspired adopted a name to distinguish its politics from the several varieties of socialism based on the working class and the labor movement. The Nationalists claimed to speak for all classes and not just workers. Though they sympathized with the workers' conditions they feared them and held the organized labor movement in contempt. Seeing themselves as the representatives of an organic nation, transcending classes and "politics" as the expression of narrow class interests, the Nationalists made the absorption of class conflict and politics into the body of the organized bureaucratic socialist state their primary goal.

Looking Backward and the Nationalist movement were truly a major launching point for that "intellectual pursuit of collectivism" which played a role in the politics of American socialism as well as in the emergence of modern liberalism before the First World War.[7] Yet, with few exceptions, the traditional portrait of both Bellamy and the Nationalists in most studies of American reform has failed to comprehend the actual content, much less the significance, of their political and social views. On the most critical point, historians have perpetuated the myth that Bellamy's views were "democratic." And those who permit themselves to recognize his authoritarianism cannot fit it into the liberal-progressive framework which has dominated American reform historiography and have retreated in confusion from the theoretical and substantive questions which Bellamy's political views pose.[8]

The traditional view of Bellamy and his followers presents them as the anti-Marxist democratic forerunners of the native-born, English-

7. See James Gilbert, *Designing the Industrial State* (1972) for an analysis of "collectivist" currents, including Bellamy, in the emergence of the new liberalism in response to "industrialism." Gilbert notes the links between Bellamy's politics and the "varieties of collectivist thought that followed some years later," but does not trace the connections in detail.

8. The major treatments of *Looking Backward* and of the Nationalist movement are to be found in the following: Marie Louise Berneri, *Journey Through Utopia* (1950); Sylvia E. Bowman, *The Year 2000* (1958); John Hope Franklin, "Edward Bellamy and the Nationalist Movement (1938): 739–772; Arthur E. Morgan, *Edward Bellamy* (1944); Howard Quint, *The Forging of American Socialism* (1953); John L. Thomas, "Introduction" to *Looking Backward*; Elizabeth Sadler, "One Book's Influence: Edward Bellamy's *Looking Backward*" (1944): 530–555; Robert L. Shurter, "The Writing of *Looking Backward*" (1939): 255–261.

speaking, socialist movement that began to crystalize in the 1890s and came to maturity after 1901, with the founding of the Debsian Socialist Party.[9] On a broader canvas, the Bellamyites are portrayed as one expression among many, albeit an important and influential one, of the new democratic spirit of opposition to laissez faire capitalism that swept the middle classes between 1890 and 1912, giving birth to both the populist and progressive movements with their commitment to state intervention in the economy as a way of "democratizing" economic and political power.

Bellamy's and the Nationalists' relationship to the nascent socialist movement as well as to the broader current of middle-class reform was far more complex. The traditional portrait conceals as much as it explains, obscuring the meaning not only of Bellamyism, but of the entire spectrum of political ideas that are loosely and misleadingly lumped together on the "left," under the rubric of the "reform tradition."

This approach is at the heart of the misreading of Bellamy and his doctrine as "democratic" by Vernon Louis Parrington, John Dewey, and Howard Quint, among many others. Only historical sleight-of-hand can sustain this view. Parrington's well-known essay on Bellamy and the method underlying its construction formed the model.[10] In *Looking Backward*, Parrington writes, Bellamy drew "the outlines of the democratic society of the future," while the sequel, *Equality*, written ten years later, "supplied a justification and commentary" on his earlier views.[11] For evidence, Parrington quotes liberally from passages in which the term "democracy" is used, though of course the use of the word "democracy" proves nothing in itself. Some of the most reactionary, antidemocratic movements and figures in the nineteenth and twentieth centuries have felt compelled to describe themselves and their views as "democratic."[12]

In fact, Bellamy did not at the outset of his political career justify

9. See Quint, *Forging of American Socialism* ch. 3 et passim.

10. Vernon Louis Parrington, *The Beginnings of Critical Realism in America*, vol. 3, *Main Currents in American Thought* (1930): 302–315.

11. Ibid., p. 304.

12. See, for example, J. Salwyn Schapiro's *Liberalism and the Challenge of Fascism* (1949), ch. 13 for a discussion of Louis Napoleon's use of the term democracy to describe his plebiscitarian dictatorship. Schapiro's discussion of Carlyle and Proudhon, as "heralds" of fascism provides an invaluable insight into the beginnings of the decline of bourgeois liberalism in Europe and the appearance of authoritarian socialist currents at the end of the nineteenth century. Another important example is provided by Bernard Semmel's account of Robert Blatchford in *Imperialism and Social Reform* (1960), ch. 12.

his views as democratic and the *word* itself never appears in *Looking Backward*. Only in *Equality*, a book written ten years later, after a decade of intensive political activity which had a profound effect upon him, did Bellamy use the term. By mixing up passages from the two books, Parrington could prove what *had* to be true: that Bellamy was a genuine American democrat. It is a method which others have not hesitated to follow.[13] So powerful is the hold of the progressive frame of mind, a kind of American version of the "Whig interpretation of history", that it simply never occurred to Parrington and most of those who have followed in his footsteps, which is to say most of the historians of American liberalism and reform, to ask why Bellamy never cared to use the term "democracy" in his first and most important attempt to set forth his views, and why, ten years later, in *Equality*, which Bellamy rightly considered his political testament, the term is used repeatedly and with great emphasis. Imprisoned in the ideology of progressivism, which is to say of modern liberalism, it has been impossible for most commentators to recognize that Bellamy avoided the term and the idea of democracy because he and his audience had soured on democracy, fearing majority rule would lead to working-class rule, a fate which they dreaded as much as the final triumph of the new plutocracy.[14] Only a few writers have permitted themselves to see the overwhelming evidence that Bellamy's

13. Parrington, *Beginnings of Critical Realism*, pp. 302–315; cf. Quint, *Forging of American Socialism*, pp. 91–92, in which Quint, in the manner of Parrington, mixes together quotations from different periods of Bellamy's political development. The citations demonstrating, according to Quint, that Bellamy advocated "political democracy" (p. 92) are taken from the second phase of Bellamy's (and the Nationalists') political development.

14. "Democracy" in this period is used, of course, both to refer to the Democratic party and its politics as well as in the modern sense of rule by the majority. That the distinction in usage was clear may be seen in Francis Parkman's letter (W. R. Jacobs, ed., *Letters of Francis Parkman* [Norman: University of Oklahoma Press, 1960]). "I use the word democracy in its general and not in its party sense,—that is in the same sense in which it is used in French" (vol. II, p. 69). At the same time it was also used, perhaps most frequently, with the party. See, e.g., Jonathan Norcross, *The History of Democracy: Considered as a Party Name and as a Political Organization* (New York: Putnam's Sons, 1883), and Ransom H. Gillet, *Democracy in the United States: What It Has Done, What It Is Doing, and What It Will Do* (New York: D. Appleton and Co., 1868). Nevertheless it isn't likely, nor strictly speaking is it relevant in any case, that Bellamy's nonusage of the term stemmed from his fear that it would be associated with its narrow party use. The case for the conservative Bellamy's repugnance for its "radical" meaning is quite strong; when he does use it—very infrequently—it is in the romantic, Rousseauian sense of "unitary democracy." The same ambiguity may be found in the European context. See the discussion of this problem in Hal Draper, *Karl Marx's Theory of Revolution*, vol. I, *State and Bureaucracy*,

views changed greatly during the 1890s toward a less authoritarian version of socialism, but for want of an adequate conceptual framework have failed to see the significance of this change and to understand its larger meaning.[15] What is true of Bellamy the individual is doubly true of the treatment of the Nationalist movement, and is ultimately even more important precisely because it represented more than a single individual's views. The Nationalist movement was, in its inception, a symptom of a new authoritarian middle-class reaction against capitalism, paralleling those which appeared in Europe toward the end of the nineteenth century. The Fabian socialism of the Webbs provides one of the clearest examples of such a trend: Bellamyism was in every sense the American kissing-cousin, albeit an independent invention, to the bureaucratic socialism which the Webbs propounded.[16] The United States was not immune

---

pp. 84–87 (New York: Monthly Review Press, 1977), and also Jens A. Christophersen, *The Meaning of Democracy as Used in European Ideologies from the French to the Russian Revolution: An Historical Study in Political Language*, 2nd ed. (Oslo: University of Oslo, Institutt for Statsvitenskap, Skrifter, nr. 5, 1968). After 1890, the term democracy tends to be used in its philosophical sense and becomes much more widespread; it is picked up by the very same conservatives who shied away from it, and by the "Progressive" era, of course, *everyone* becomes a "democrat"—that is, given the upheaval of the period, the radicalization of politics, the old tory repugnance for the term is no longer politically viable and just as in the case of suffrage restriction, the reactionary antidemocratic political reforms of the period are instituted in the name of "direct democracy." (See my unpublished paper, "Progressivism, Plebiscitarianism and Direct Democracy," American Historical Association, 1973.)

15. Several writers, notably Franklin and Bowman, notice this change in Bellamy's viewpoint but given their view of Bellamy as a democrat and their inability to grasp the idea of anticapitalist collectivist ideologies which are at the same time antidemocratic—i.e., Bellamy's—they are unable to pursue the implications of this insight. Bowman grasps the historical context, the impact of Populism upon Bellamy, and in many ways hers is by far the most useful treatment of Bellamy.

16. The most valuable account of the early Fabians, one whose analysis parallels our own with regard to the Bellamyites, both as to their politics as well as the peculiar appeal which the anticapitalist collectivist doctrines had to the newly emerged "educated" middle classes, is Eric T. Hobsbawm, "Fabianism and the Fabians, 1884–1914" (Ph.D. diss., Cambridge University, 1948). See also Hobsbawm's article, "The Fabians Reconsidered," in *Labouring Men* (1964), ch. 14, for a summary of his argument, one which, however, backs away considerably from his earlier and far more accurate perception of Fabianism as a peculiar anti-working–class collectivist ideology which impinged upon the labor and socialist movements. Bernard Semmel's *Imperialism and Social Reform* is essential for understanding the extremely reactionary nature of Fabianism. For Germany, where middle-class anticapitalist movements did not, for the most part, impinge on the left, and were closely associated with the various currents of political antisemitism, see Paul Massing, *Rehearsal for Destruction* (1949), and Herman Lebovics, *Social Conservatism and the Middle Classes in Germany, 1914–1933* (1969).

from such "foreign" currents, and Bellamyism was not merely a genial, democratic humanitarian philosophy because of its native origins and resolute opposition to laissez faire capitalism.

Of the minority of Bellamy scholars who have correctly identified the authoritarian, antidemocratic nature of Bellamy's utopia, some resolve the problem this poses to their own understanding of American intellectual and political history by viewing it as a sport, without roots or connections in any established tradition. Others argue that Bellamy was a true democrat who had a "mistaken" notion of democracy. And some dismiss Bellamy's authoritarianism and his vision of a barracks socialism with the remark that only a "modern" mentality, sensitized to the horrors of totalitarianism, could read into Bellamy's attack on democracy anything more than a minor personal quirk. Thus, Daniel Bell smugly assures us that despite the "revulsion" which a modern reader must feel for Bellamy's specific plan, it was only the "indigenous home-spun made in Chicopee Falls vision of . . . [a] religiously minded New England journalist." Happily, Bell observes, it was this vision "rather than Marxian dogmatics of organized socialism which introduced this idea of socialism to millions."[17]

The failure to describe Bellamy's views correctly or to analyze the significance of an authoritarian socialist ideology which played such an important role in American thought stems from causes more fundamental than Bell's type of crude anti-Marxism. Encased in the dominant liberal reform tradition, most historians have simply ignored the antidemocratic, elitist ancestors of modern-day liberalism, of which Bellamy was only one. Only in the last ten years or so have a few historians, whose views diverge sufficiently from the prevailing liberal consensus, whether to the right or the left, broken through the ideological barriers erected by generations of liberal historians to discover the strong antidemocratic elements in modern bureaucratic or "corporate" liberalism.[18]

17. Daniel Bell, "The Background and Development of Marxian Socialism in the United States," in Donald Drew Egbert and Stow Persons, eds., *Socialism and American Life* (1952), vol. 1, pp. 220, 269.

18. In addition to James Weinstein, *The Corporate Ideal in the Liberal State*, (Boston: Beacon Press, 1968), and Gilbert, *Designing the Industrial State*, the more important "revisionist" histories of American liberalism include Gabriel Kolko, *The Triumph of Conservatism* (New York: The Free Press of Glencoe, 1963); Arthur A. Ekirch, Jr., *The Decline of American Liberalism* (1955); Charles Forcey, *The Crossroads of Liberalism* (New York: Oxford University Press, 1961); Richard Hofstadter, *The Age of Reform* (1955). The term "corporate" liberalism is not an entirely felicitous one, although not all of these authors use the

To do so, these writers, some of the most insightful of whom are conservative in outlook, have been forced to challenge the assumption which is the bedrock of most American social reform historiography, of the "progressive" version of American history. This is the simple-minded but very American equation of all critics and opponents of lais-sez faire capitalism and advocates of state intervention with the genu-inely democratic and anti-authoritarian reform currents, including both its liberal and socialist wings. Historians of late nineteenth- and early twentieth-century American political and social movements have only barely begun to grasp the point that antipathy to bourgeois society and in particular hostility to laissez faire doctrine does not necessarily mean a commitment to democratic values or institutions.[19] For those who oper-ate within this naive framework, the particular characteristics of currents such as those exhibited by Bellamy and the Bellamyites—an anticapital-ist collectivist vision combined with deep hostility to democracy and individualism—appear as an impossible contradiction, if indeed they are recognized at all. Such a current is simply far too anomalous to allow its correct classification, much less a systematic attempt to solve the puzzle it poses. Thus not only Bellamy's utopia and the Nationalist movement but also much of the history of socialism and social reform in America have been misunderstood or distorted. To an astonishing degree, espe-cially for those who should be able to look backward from the vantage point of the second half of the twentieth century, the history of liberal-ism and of "reform" ideas in America is still treated as a study of the collective ideology of what Daniel Aaron has termed the "men of good hope."[20] Under this rubric Aaron includes Brooks Adams, because of his

---

term or share the concept. *Bureaucratic* or administrative liberalism describes, far better, I think, the essential characteristics of this current in modern American liberalism. An important account of the development of the bureaucratic liberal ideology beginning with Woodrow Wilson, Charles Beard, Herbert Croly and other administrative reformers is to be found in Dwight Waldo, *The Administrative State* (1948), while Samuel Haber's *Efficiency and Uplift* (1964) deals with the interpenetration of scientific management ideology, and progressive political thought. The most important study of the post–Civil War intellectual background to the rise of elitist, antidemocratic liberalism may be found in George M. Frederickson, *The Inner Civil War* (1965). Frederickson correctly ties Bellamy into the strain of conservative, antidemocratic "reform" thought (pp. 225–228).

19. For a representative example of the standard progressive-liberal view see Sidney Fine, *Laissez Faire and the General-Welfare State* (1964).

20. Daniel Aaron, *Men of Good Hope;* see also Charles A. Madison, *Critics and Crusaders* (1947).

trenchant criticism of bourgeois society. That Adams also hated democracy and the labor movement, preached imperialism, was both a racist and anti-Semite, ended his life as an advocate of an imperial dictatorship, and generally advocated views which can probably best be described as "proto-fascist," in the words of his most perceptive biographer, can hardly stand discussion in Aaron's treatment.[21] Little wonder that Bellamy emerges in Aaron's pages, Parrington style, as an advocate of democracy, whose authoritarian scheme is at worst an ill-considered aberration.

Yet, as this study will show, not only did Bellamy regard the politics of Nationalism as the alternative to democracy, but, most important of all, far from being an individual peculiarity, Bellamy's ideas about democracy, the abolition of universal suffrage, the relationship of the individual to the state, and the role of the working class, were well within the main currents of post–Civil War reform thought.[22] It is a current which, however, has simply vanished down the memory-hole to which all such non-progressive ideas have been relegated, with few exceptions, by American liberal historians.

How little Bellamy's political views were peculiar to himself and the Nationalist movement should be clear merely from the fact that *Looking Backward* was only one of a number of middle-class authoritarian utopian fantasies published after 1880, most of them inspired by the success of *Looking Backward*. This recurrent "literary quest for utopia" in late nineteenth-century America has not been satisfactorily dealt with, and the substance of their complaints against the political and economic system and the prescriptions which these utopian concoctions offered has been largely ignored or misunderstood.[23]

---

21. Charles Beringause's biography *Brooks Adams* (1955) provides an important antidote to Aaron's portrait of Adams.

22. See Frederickson, *The Inner Civil War* on the conservative political reformers. Also useful is L. L. Bernard and Jessie Bernard, *Origins of American Sociology: The Social Science Movement in the United States* (New York: Russell and Russell, 1965) which for whatever it lacks in analysis presents, unintentionally, the strong antidemocratic streak in reform thought, especially the impact of the Comteans.

23. Allyn B. Forbes, "The Literary Quest for Utopia," (1927):179–189, gives forty-nine as the number of such books published between 1884 and 1900, but there were many, many more than this. The most recent study, Kenneth Roemer, *The Obsolete Necessity: America in Utopian Writings, 1888–1900* (Kent, Ohio: Kent State University Press, 1976) deals with over 160 such utopian novels. Both Forbes' article and Roemer's treatment are useful, but lack any theoretical framework to deal with the outcroppings of utopian literature and deal with them in an uncritical way, particularly with their political ideas. Robert Shurter,

Consider, for example, *Looking Backward*'s predecessor, *The Diothas* (1883), by John MacNie, which expresses a revulsion against "pluto-cratic" capitalism and hostility to mass democracy in terms very similar to Bellamy's.[24] Like the author of *Looking Backward*, MacNie offered a dream of a new social order that would end the evils of party politics, offset the threat of misrule by the proletarian mob, and bring law and order from above in place of the anarchy which unnatural "class rule" and "selfishness" had spawned in America. Similarly, although not cast in the form of a novel, Laurence Gronlund's immensely important and influential introduction to "modern socialism," *The Cooperative Common-wealth*,[25] projected, as part of its author's attempt to "Americanize" a foreign, "German," socialism, a sketch of an ideal socialist society whose authoritarian outlines anticipated the spirit and many of the arguments of *Looking Backward*.

Just as Bellamy's utopian views were not an isolated expression of a lonely dreamer, so Bellamyism was a genuine part of the American reform political tradition—not despite, but *because of* its authoritarianism and ha-tred of democracy. A number of intellectual currents within the post–Civil War reform movement shared a disdain for the doctrines of laissez faire and social-Darwinist rationalizations for the power of the new capi-talist ruling class. They did so not only from an antisocialist and anti-working class standpoint, but from one that was increasingly hostile to liberal democratic values and institutions, a stance that became more

---

"The Utopian Novel in America, 1864–1900" (Ph.D. diss., Western Reserve University, 1963) is more valuable for the material it presents as well as for its author's ability to do more than summarize the plots. Vernon Louis Parrington, Jr., *American Dreams*, 2nd ed. rev. (New York: Russell and Russell, 1964), is a pedestrian account of utopian novels. By far the most useful is Margaret Thal-Larsen, "Political and Economic Ideas in American Utopian Fiction, 1868–1914" (Ph.D. diss., University of California, Berkeley, 1941).

24. Ismar Thiusen [pseud., John MacNie], *The Diothas; or a Far Look Ahead* (New York: Putnam and Sons, 1883). There were persistent allegations that Bellamy plagiarized *Looking Backward* from MacNie's book. Bellamy had met MacNie and there are a few similarities, including some idea about a national service. But the charge of plagiarism is quite flimsy since MacNie's utopia is little concerned with an indictment of capitalism and his ideal society is a kind of modern handicraft economy in which all work is done in the home for profit. And in any case, one could on the basis of the unoriginality of most of these productions make the same charge about any one of them. *Looking Backward* is a work of genius (of a kind) and whatever elements it shares with other utopian works is simply of a generic sort.

25. Laurence Gronlund, *The Cooperative Commonwealth* (1884).

prominent as the century drew to a close. American Positivism, which had a long and consistent history of reactionary political and social views, one that antedated the Civil War, and whose influence was quite widespread among intellectuals, is only one such example. David Goodman Croly, leading Comtean and father of the future editor of the *New Republic*, Herbert Croly, advocated a "government *of* the people, and *for* the people, but not *by* the people." "Government by counting noses is . . . a preposterous government." "We do not believe in Democracy nor in universal suffrage."[26] In the coming positivist order, "education, character, and efficiency," and "selection instead of election" must be the basis of the rule of a new civil-service elite. "This is the first step toward the Positivist conception of government."[27] Lester Ward, whose antidemocratic collectivist notions were drawn from the American Comtean tradition; Henry Demarest Lloyd, who echoed Croly's views almost word for word; Francis Parkman; Henry and Brooks Adams; Mark Twain; and assorted Mugwump reformers in the last decades of the nineteenth century also contributed to this current of conservative reform.

Reacting strongly to the consolidation of industrial capitalism after the Civil War and believing that the social and economic ills of the new system were becoming more intense, conservatives bent on reforming capitalism—saving the system from itself—adopted more and more statist and bureaucratic ideas. Using organic metaphors borrowed from native American Hegelians such as W. T. Harris—and even from Spencer himself—they rejected the atomistic individualism of Manchesterian Liberalism and groped for some new basis for harmonizing the individual with society or the State.[28] Elisha Mulford, a prominent representative of this tendency, asserted that "The Nation" must be viewed not as a collection of individual atoms whose individual wills were to be added up in order to arrive at the social good, but rather as an organism with a will and purpose of its own. Selfish individualism—the pursuit of private interests—did not and could not serve the organic Nation but was a fatal disease which would destroy its fundamental and necessary unity.[29]

26. "C. G. David" [pseud., David Goodman Croly], *A Positivist Primer* (1871), p. 63.

27. Ibid., pp. 103–104.

28. Herbert W. Schneider, *A History of American Philosophy*, 2nd. ed. rev. (New York: Columbia University Press, 1963), pp. 277–399.

29. Elisha Mulford, *The Nation: or Foundations of Civil Order and the Political Life in the United States* (Boston: Houghton Mifflin, 1882).

Other reformers, adopting the idea of civil-service reform as a means of ending corruption, pushed beyond it as a narrow panacea and saw it as a way of attaining rule by the nation's brains and moral elite over the rude democratic mob.[30] Administration by experts would replace politics and partisanship. Government would reflect the needs of the entire nation rather than the push and pull of selfish class interests. Seen as the forerunner of the wing of Progressivism associated with Herbert Croly and the *New Republic*, it was certainly not accidental that the conservative-turned-Progressive and President-to-be, Woodrow Wilson, first made his mark as a young scholar with an important essay setting forth the importance of elevating "administration" over mere politics.[31]

Clearly revealed in these ideas for reform is a turning away from democracy—even of the limited sort which the American followers of John Stuart Mill advocated in the belief that the "best" would continue to rule and property would be secured despite the entry of the property-less working classes onto the political stage through the extension of the suffrage. Writing in 1888, the same year *Looking Backward* made its appearance, the American novelist and reformer, Albion Tourgée, observed that "among those claiming to represent the most highly cultivated and intelligent classes, especially of the Eastern and Middle States, the general trend of sentiment is in the direction of admitting the failure of republican institutions, and the acceptance of modifications and limitations thereof which will restrict the privileges of the many and enhance the power of the few."[32] The abolition of universal suffrage, the dissolution of political parties, and the suppression of "politics," together with the substitution for them of a new class of bureaucratic administrators, which Bellamyites were to make the keystone of their program, had ideological roots in this conservative political reaction against liberal democratic values and institutions.

Thus Bellamyism was no isolated outcropping of authoritarian, antidemocratic ideas. Rather, it was a collectivist variation upon the conservative reform theme. By adding not only opposition to capitalism but a conception of a society organized into "one huge barrack," Bellamyism emerged as a new and distinctive political strain—an American vari-

---

30. Ari Hoogenboom, *Outlawing the Spoils* (1961). See also John Sproat, *The Best Men* (1968), for an excellent account of the conservative nature of Mugwump reform.

31. Waldo, *The Administrative State*, p. 304, fn. 2.

32. Albion Tourgée, *Letters to a King* (Cincinnati: Cranstone and Stowe, 1888), p. 28.

ant within a broader species of middle-class anticapitalist collectivist ideologies which under the usual label of "state socialism" sprang up
throughout the capitalist world at the end of the nineteenth century. As
in the case of the early Fabians in Britain, Bellamyism, for similar historical reasons, appeared as part of the "left" rather than the "right"
despite the antipathy of its founders to the working-class movement and
to democracy.[33] To examine the meaning and significance of Bellamyism, in its proper historical context; to search for the real Edward
Bellamy and to understand the nature of his ideas and the complex
course which they took; to examine the authoritarian soul of socialism in
order to better grasp the meaning of a genuinely democratic socialism, is
the task of the chapters which follow.

33. Hobsbawn, *Fabianism and the Fabians.*

1 ORIGINS OF A UTOPIA

I regard the suffrage of ignorant classes of men, black or white, as a nuisance and a danger. . . . Universal suffrage is, as I think, the most dangerous enemy of liberal government, and the source of all the dangers which threaten the United States.

* * *

I have always declared openly my detestation of the unchecked rule of the masses, that is to say of universal suffrage, and the corruption which is sure to follow in every large and heterogeneous community.[1]

Francis Parkman: 1873

You may easily suppose I hate all shades & forms of republican government, . . . I am doing what every good citizen ought to do—trying my best to win you & the rest of the rising generation over to an honest & saving loathing for universal suffrage.[2]   Mark Twain: 1877

That the horrors of the Paris Commune were not repeated here is only because the pestilential spirit was not so deeply rooted as there. Give it time and let it alone, and it will lift its red hand with the savage ferocity with which it struck Paris.[3]

Allan Pinkerton: 1878

There are, indeed, those in America—and the number is at present growing— who ask if democracy is not a failure; they see the voters of our cities bought and sold; they see offices put up at auction, legislation obtained by corrupt means. They think this is due to the ignorance and corruption of the people, and therefore they desire from good motives to restrict the ballot. . . . The fact cannot be denied that a growing class in America desire to restrict the suffrage, to have less frequent elections, to take power from the people.[4]

"Democracy," Encyclopedia of Social Reform, 1897

Edward Bellamy was the first critic of laissez faire capitalism in America advocating a collectivist alternative to find a large and enthusi-

1. Wilbur R. Jacobs, ed., *Letters of Francis Parkman* (Norman: University of Oklahoma Press, 1960), Vol. II, pp. 69, 81–82.
2. Dixon Wecter, ed., *Mark Twain to Mrs. Fairbanks* (San Marino: Huntington Library, 1949), pp. 208–209.
3. Allan Pinkerton, *Workers, Communists, Tramps and Detectives* (New York: G. W. Carleton, 1878), p. 79.
4. W. P. D. Bliss, ed., *Encyclopedia of Social Reform* (New York: Funk & Wagnalls, 1897), p. 495.

astic audience. Though historians have therefore assigned Bellamy and *Looking Backward* a key role in making socialism "respectable," Bellamy vehemently denied that he preached socialism.[5] His enthusiastic native-born English-speaking middle-class audience recognized that here was a conservative anticapitalism: a socialism for the middle classes which was an alternative to the radical working-class socialism of the Paris Commune and the notorious International. Socialism was a revolutionary and democratic attack on property rights from the propertyless workers and, in an America where the doctrine of laissez faire dominated, even the schemes of the farmers to regulate the railroads and trusts were regarded as socialistic.

To the conservative eye the expansion of the working class inherent in the growth of large-scale industrial enterprise together with the existence of universal manhood suffrage posed a direct threat to private property, the very foundation of American society. Thus Richard Ely, addressing himself in 1883 to "friends of law and order," wrote that the social democrats "have two distinguishing characteristics. The vast majority of them are laborers, and, as a rule, they expect the violent overthrow of existing institutions by revolution to precede the introduction of the socialist state. I would not, by any means, say they are all revolutionists, but the most of them undoubtedly are. The tendency of their popular writings is revolutionary. They are calculated to accustom the thoughts to revolution, and to excite the feelings of laborers to such a pitch as to prepare them for risking all in battle."[6]

Fear of mass democracy and universal manhood suffrage came to the surface in part as the result of the development of an organized national labor movement during and after the Civil War, accompanied

5. Howard Quint, *The Forging of American Socialism* (1953), ch. 3. See also Daniel Bell, "The Background and Development of Marxian Socialism in the United States," in Donald Drew Egbert and Stow Persons (eds.), *Socialism and American Life* (1951), vol. 1, pp. 269–271.

6. Richard T. Ely, *French and German Socialism in Modern Times* (New York: Harper & Bros., 1883), p. 204. See also "German Socialism in America," *The North American Review* 128 (1879): 372–387, 481–492 for one example of the fear of socialism. The latter warns of the existence of the nucleus of socialist organizations "which, if at any moment swelled by numbers and stimulated by industrial depression, might burst upon us as a mighty torrent, perhaps too powerful to stem at the outset, and calculated to threaten the best social and business interests of a country vast in extent of territory and fairly destitute of military protection" (p. 384).

by an unprecedented wave of strikes.[7] The "labor question" replaced the
issue of slavery as the focus of American politics. In 1871 the Paris
Commune reinforced the apprehension of the "respectable classes" that
the workers constituted a danger from below to their safety and to
the stability of society. Throughout the 1870s the specter of the Commune—its destruction of property, the "proof" that there existed a
powerful and nefarious "International" which had directed the Paris uprising and whose tentacles reached out to America—began to haunt conservative Americans.[8] The fear of a proletarian uprising took on flesh-
and-blood reality with the great railroad strikes of 1877.[9] Previously
isolated though ominous, conservative opinions now blossomed forth
into a fullblown antidemocratic reaction inspired by massive assaults on
property and the breakdown of "law and order" restored only by the
U.S. Army. The Commune had surely come to America, some thought,
when bands of strikers and their sympathizers fought pitched battles
with the militia and an elected municipal government in St. Louis
yielded its power to the organized strikers under the leadership of the
Workingmen's Party of the U.S.[10]

Though the strike was suppressed, the franchise gave workers
another route to power through a mass political movement. In response,
a chorus of voices expressing antidemocratic sentiments swelled in the
two decades following the Civil War. Two generations earlier the abolition of the property qualification for voting had democratized the suffrage in America. Conservative resistance was easily swept aside in the

7. See David Montgomery, *Beyond Equality* (1968), on the rise of the national labor
movement during and after the Civil War and of the response to it by radical Republicans
and others.

8. George L. Cherry, "American Metropolitan Press Reaction to the Paris Commune," *Mid-America* 32, no. 1 (January 1950): 3–12. After the assassination of Garfield, the
Weekly Iowa State Register (Des Moines) wrote that "for ten years the snake of the Commune
has been trailing its insidious poison through the lower orders of society in this nation. . . .
It grew up first in the dark and noisome places of New York City. . . . One particular
political party [The Greenback Party], a fungus growth of that part of the public mind
which grew morbid during the late hard times, has aided perhaps unconsciously but none
the less wrongfully and criminally in popularizing its wrongs and condoning its crimes."
("America and the Commune," July 8, 1881, quoted in Fred E. Haynes, *Third Party
Movements Since the Civil War* [Iowa City: 1916], p. 145.)

9. Robert V. Bruce, *1877: Year of Violence* (New York: Quadrangle, 1970). On the
use of the militia and the army to suppress strikes see the important article by Robert
Reinders, "Militia and Public Order in Nineteenth-Century America," pp. 81–101.

10. David T. Burbank, *Reign of the Rabble* (1966).

1820s and 1830s because few perceived immediate dangers. The United States was still a nation of farmers; urban artisans had long enjoyed the franchise and a mass electorate had existed despite the property qualification without threatening law and order or private property. Only in Rhode Island—the most industrialized and urbanized state in the Union with a large working-class and immigrant population—did violent conflict accompany the democratization of the ballot in the 1840s.[11]

Repeatedly, however, in the decades following removal of the suffrage barrier, the course of American political development generated fresh anxieties that a democratic suffrage was dangerous to the conservative establishment. The emergence of political machines, especially in the polyglot cities, displaced from a position of leadership elites accustomed to presiding over municipal government. The sudden eruption of the Know Nothing Party in the mid-1850s demonstrated anew the dangerous volatility of an electorate that momentarily abandoned established parties and "respectable" leadership for those exploiting the nativist frenzy. After the Civil War, widely publicized urban corruption and scandal on an unprecedented scale, the Greenback and free silver movements, and the experience of black suffrage in the South provided additional evidence to the conservative classes that democratic suffrage was a menace to the continued existence of capitalism itself.[12]

No one registered these doubts more explicitly than Mark Twain, who discovered in the 1860s a paradise on Hawaii because there only men of property could vote. Twain's political ideal was Louis Bonaparte's dictatorship over the French "canaille" which he celebrated in

11. See Chilton Williamson, *American Suffrage from Property to Democracy, 1760–1860* (1960), pp. 282–285, 292–295 on the antisuffrage reaction. Also Marvin E. Gettleman, *The Dorr Rebellion: A Study in American Radicalism, 1833–1849* (New York: Random House, 1973).

12. The best single account of this reaction is in Clifton K. Yearly, *The Money Machines* (1970), ch. 1. Important intellectual figures who proclaimed their disillusionment with universal suffrage included not only Parkman, but James Russell Lowell (*Democracy and Other Addresses* [Boston: 1887], pp. 8–40), and Laurence Godkin (*Unforeseen Tendencies of Modern Democracy* [Boston: Houghton Mifflin, 1893]). Of special interest, because they were the views of a reformer, is Washington Gladden, "Safeguards of the Suffrage," *The Century Magazine* 38 (1889): 621–628. J. B. Harrison's *Certain Dangerous Tendencies in American Life* (Boston: Houghton, Osgood & Co., 1880), like Gladden's article, recognizes the impossibility of abolishing universal suffrage and advocates its restriction—the course which the reformers actually followed in this and the "Progressive" era, in the name of purity.

Innocents Abroad (1869).[13] Six years later Twain anonymously proposed in the *Atlantic Monthly* to end rule by the unfit masses by abandoning universal suffrage.[14] In 1880, Henry Adams in his novel, *Democracy*, and John Hay in *The Breadwinners* in 1884 joined in a caustic attack on democracy and on the labor movement. Similarly Francis Parkman proclaimed "The Failure of Universal Suffrage" in *The North American Review*.[15] In New York City in 1878, the Tilden Commission proposed to restrict the suffrage, and although such proposals were not put into practice, except in the South, the same ends were reached indirectly through personal registration laws and other reforms in the electoral system before the end of the century.[16]

The strike of 1877 touched off some of the most explicitly antidemocratic sentiments. Federal Judge Walter Gresham confessed in 1877 that "all honest, thoughtful men know that the ballot must be restricted, and I suppose that can be done only through blood. . . . Our revolutionary fathers . . . went too far with their notions of popular government . . . . Democracy is now the enemy of law and order and society & as such should be denounced." United States Senator from Missouri,

13. A. Grove Day, ed., *Mark Twain's Letters from Hawaii* (New York: Appleton-Century, 1966), p. 106; *Innocents Abroad* (Hartford: 1869), pp. 157–58.

14. "The Curious Republic of Gondour," *Atlantic Monthly*, October 1875, pp. 461–63. There is a powerful resemblance, politically and personally, between Twain and Bernard Shaw. Both were thoroughgoing cynics and haters of democracy and, of course, brilliant artists. The way in which Twain's antidemocratic views have been systematically covered up and/or excused as the jest of a clown parallels the treatment given Shaw. In Twain's case, it is part and parcel of the liberal historiographic tradition discussed in the Introduction, in which all critics of society, all haters of sham and hypocrisy, are "good" and hence "democrats"—which would make Carlyle the outstanding democrat of all time, a position which at least one modern biographer has attempted to sustain. The attempt of Philip Foner to deal with Twain's hatred of democracy, as part of Foner's contribution to "people's history," is both hilarious and instructive. (*Mark Twain: Social Critic* [New York: International, 1958], pp. 86–87.) See also Justin Kaplan, *Mr. Clemens and Mark Twain: A Biography* (New York: Simon & Shuster, 1966); Kaplan deals with this aspect of Twain's ideas quite capably—see pp. 154, 168, 214—but makes little out of them. The best treatment of Twain in many respects is still Van Wyck Brooks, *The Ordeal of Mark Twain* (New York: E. P. Dutton, Dutton Paperback, 1970), who correctly labels Twain's views as those of Twain's own contemporaries among the "privileged classes who feared the suffrage in the hands of the propertyless workers" (pp. 137–138).

15. *North American Review* 127 (July-August 1878): 1–20.

16. On the Tilden Commission see Samuel Haber, *Efficiency and Uplift*, pp. 99–101. The effect of personal registration laws and other attempts to restrict the suffrage is analyzed in Walter Dean Burnham, *Critical Elections and the Mainsprings of American Politics* (1970), ch. 4.

George Vest, agreed: "Universal suffrage is a standing menace to all stable and good government. Its twin sister is the commune with its labor unions, etc.," he wrote. The *St. Louis Post* affirmed the conclusion that "universal suffrage is played out."[17]

In the decade after the upheavals of 1877, industrial conflict on a still greater scale became a chronic feature of American experience. Some 130,000 workers participated in 477 strikes in 1881; five years later over 600,000 engaged in over 1500 work stoppages.[18] In an address to the National Education Association in 1885, one speaker warned of "the impending conflict between labor and capital, and the onward strides of socialism and communism. A mob spirit is abroad in the land. Perchance it is only a spark, but that spark, being essentially contagious and progressive, must be extinguished, or it will soon become a mighty conflagration."[19] Lyman Abbott, who was to become an apostle of the social gospel, expressed the apprehensions of many in the same year:

> On one side of a narrow valley capital is concentrating its forces, small in numbers, compact in organization, powerful in equipment, and not always either scrupulous in its means or generous in its spirit. On the other side labor is concentrating its forces—an increasing host, loose in organization, but with a discontent in its heart which a great disaster might easily convert into bitter wrath—armed by modern science with fatally efficient equipment for destruction, and officered by leaders often both unscrupulous and daring. Every morning paper brings us the report of some strike or lockout, which is like the shot of a single picket along the line; and now and then we are startled by a riot such as that at Cincinnati, Chicago or Cleveland, which is like a skirmish between the advance guards. *Who* can tell that the next skirmish may not bring on a battle?[20]

Then in 1886 the Haymarket "riot" in Chicago brought swift and brutal repression; there would be no Paris Commune in the Hog Capital of the World.

These events shaped both Bellamy and his audience. Bellamy powerfully indicted American capitalism as the source of social injustice which unleashed the dangers of mob rule. But he insisted that one need

---

17. Quoted in Robert Bruce, *1877* (1959), p. 317.

18. *Historical Statistics of the United States, Colonial Times to 1947* (Washington: U.S. Dept. of Commerce, 1961), p. 99.

19. J. E. Seaman, "High Schools and the State," in *The Journal of Proceedings and Addresses of the National Education Association* (New York: 1886), p. 175.

20. "The Danger Ahead," *The Century* 31 (November 1885): 51–59.

not embrace a radical socialism if one rejected capitalism. Instead Bellamy offered a collectivist alternative to working-class socialism which substituted bureaucratic order from above, government by an elite which abolished universal suffrage and imposed military discipline on the unruly workers. He explained to his literary mentor and fellow Nationalist, William Dean Howells, that "I may seem to outsocialize the socialists, yet the word socialist is one I could never stomach. It smells to the average American of petroleum, suggests the red flag and all manner of sexual novelties, and an abusive tone about God and religion. Whatever German and French reformers may choose to call themselves, socialist is not a good name for a party to succeed with in America."[21] In a series of notes written after *Looking Backward*, in preparation for the sequel, *Equality*, Bellamy affirmed the conservative genesis of his collectivist utopianism: "When I came to consider what could be radically done for social reorganization, I was helped by every former disgust with the various socialist schemes."[22]

Bellamy appealed to middle-class readers shaken by the unpredictability, violence, and widespread suffering endemic to the new industrial capitalist society, where both capitalists and the workers threatened those in the middle. Caught by the conflicting pressures of urbanization and rapid changes in the occupational structure, the middle-class family sought to become a protective island against the forces of change; but whatever psychic security it could provide was at best temporary as new generations were forced to seek their way in a world increasingly dominated by large capital.[23]

Economic developments in mid-nineteenth–century America profoundly altered the social structure and affected the composition of the middle class. Although in 1870 the United States was still largely rural— roughly three-fourths of the population lived in rural areas or towns of less than 2,500 population—the majority of the work force was made up of wage earners. After 1870, the concentration of capital and the technological and organizational changes that accompanied the rise of large-scale industry resulted in the decline of the propertied middle classes and the development of a *new* middle class. By 1910 the old, entrepreneurial

21. Bellamy to Howells, June 17, 1888, Bellamy Papers, Houghton Library, Harvard University (henceforth Bellamy Papers).
22. Ibid., Notebooks, Bellamy Papers.
23. Richard Sennett, *Families Against the City* (1970).

middle class, whose independence had been thought the foundation stone of the American social order, became a minority within the middle class as a whole. Salaried elements, especially in large businesses and corporations, outnumbered them. (See Chapter Five.)

The pioneer popularizer of socialist ideas in America, Laurence Gronlund, immediately grasped the fact that Bellamy had succeeded in casting anticapitalist ideas in an idiom which would appeal to this fragmented and anxious middle class, especially to the "educated" among them. Gronlund temporarily withdrew his own book, *The Cooperative Commonwealth*,[24] to help promote sales of *Looking Backward*, whose radical antiworking-class and antidemocratic message he fully shared.

Yet, despite Bellamy's intent, *Looking Backward* had a complex and ambiguous influence that went far beyond the precise doctrines of Nationalism as they emerged in the first few years of the movement. Before Bellamy, explained Eugene V. Debs, who evolved from a conservative trade unionist in the 1880s into the leader of American working-class socialism by 1900, one could "count all the American Socialists on the fingers of one hand." The publication of *Looking Backward* at the beginning of 1888, however,

> had a most wonderful effect upon the people. He [Bellamy] struck a responsive chord and his name was upon every tongue. The editions ran into the hundreds of thousands and the people were profoundly stirred by what was called the vision of a poetic dreamer. Although not an exposition of scientific Socialism, Bellamy's social romance, *Looking Backward*, and its sequel, *Equality*, were valuable and timely contributions to the literature of Socialism and not only aroused the people but started many on the road to the revolutionary movement. . . . Thousands were moved to study the question by the books of Bellamy and thus became Socialists and found their way into the Socialist movement.[25]

Debs here insightfully stresses *Looking Backward*'s function of impelling persons who were groping for some alternative to the dominant ideology of American capitalism along the road to the democratic socialist movement which emerged with the founding of the Socialist Party at the beginning of the twentieth century. However, given the advantage of hindsight and without Debs' need to affirm the native American geneal-

---

24. Morgan, *Edward Bellamy*, p. 389.

25. Eugene V. Debs, "The American Movement" (1904) reprinted in *Writings and Speeches of Eugene V. Debs* (1948), p. 89.

ogy of the socialist movement, one can see that Bellamy and his followers travelled along two roads. Overlapping, parallel, and often hard
to distinguish at times, one led to the reconstuction of capitalism through
the organization of a mass, popular movement from below. The other
led to a bureaucratically organized and authoritarian collectivist society
to be reached as well as to be ruled from above by the agency of a new
elite.

Looking Backward: Conservative Utopia

In outline, Bellamy's story concerns Julian West, a member of the
wealthy leisure class of Boston, who falls into a hypnotically induced
sleep in 1887. Awakening, he finds that he has slept through the twentieth century to the year 2000, where all of the social problems which
seemed so vexatious and menacing in 1887 have vanished. Above all, the
"labor question," the struggle between worker and capitalist that had
plagued America in the 1880s, and which was so frightening and uncomfortable to Julian West and his class, had been permanently solved.

The new society which replaces the old laissez faire capitalist order
is not the product of revolution or social cataclysm—as the revolutionary
socialists had predicted, and as the middle classes had feared—but the
natural evolutionary outcome of the very society in which Julian West
had lived. Tendencies within the competitive order, although largely
invisible to people in 1887, had transformed America into an orderly
society based on cooperation and social harmony.

In the new collectivist society, the state owns all property except
personal possessions. Each citizen receives an exactly equal stipend from
the state, no matter how difficult the job, or how high the position.
Equality of reward assures an absence of classes and class distinctions.[26]

The central institution, around which all economic and political
activities revolve, is the "Industrial Army." All men and women are
members of the army from the age of twenty-one until retirement at
forty-five. At retirement, the citizen is freed from productive work and
is free to pursue further education and leisure, while receiving the same
stipend as when a member of the industrial army.[27]

Bellamy's utopia is organized precisely in the same way as a mili-

26. Edward Bellamy, *Looking Backward, 2000–1887* (1917), pp. 72–75.
27. Ibid., 95–109.

tary bureaucracy, except that its aims are not war but scientifically organized production of the nation's goods and services. All promotion is by merit from the rank of private. Merit is defined by ability, proficiency, and the spirit of willingness exhibited on the job. Officers of the army determine promotions.[28]

Each special trade is organized within one of ten departments. The highest ranking generals command each department. These "ten great officers" form the council of the "general in chief," the president of the entire industrial army, that is, of the nation.[29]

All officers of the guilds, the heads of the departments who comprise the president's cabinet, including the president himself, must have passed through each of the grades of the industrial army. Absolute equality based on merit is the rule.

> It is simply by the excellence of his record as a worker that one rises through the grades of the privates and becomes a candidate for lieutenancy. Through the lieutenancies he rises to the colonelcy, or superintendent's position, by appointment from above strictly limited to the candidates of the best records. The general of the guild appoints to the ranks under him, but he himself is not appointed, but chosen by suffrage.[30]

"Suffrage" is restricted to the retired workers who remain "honorary" members of the guild. Retired workers of the industrial army vote for president, who must be chosen from among the generals who head the ten departments.[31] The industrial army has no vote.

Within the ranks of the army, there is no internal organization nor are there any democratic rights—no more than in any army or efficient bureaucracy. The workers, the actual members of the industrial army, may not vote for their leaders or managers, nor exercise any control over the guild, the department or the president. Suffrage for the rank and file of the army, Bellamy explains, would be "ruinous to the discipline of the guild," for among other things, it would "tempt candidates to intrigue for the support of the workers under them."[32]

While the "efficiency of industry requires the strictest discipline in the army of labor," justice and considerate treatment are assured to the workman "by the whole power of the nation." Should an official act either with "churlishness" or "rudeness" to members of the public, or

28. Ibid., 98–99.   29. Ibid., 148, 151–154.   30. Ibid., 153.
31. Ibid., 153–154.   32. Ibid., 153.

abuse his position of power over workers in any way, members of a judiciary punish him. Judges are not elected but appointed from above by the president from among the ranks of the retired.[33]

Significantly, while members of the "technical professions," the engineers and the architects, are part of the industrial army proper and are eligible for the presidency, members of the "liberal professions"—doctors and teachers, artists and men of letters, who have obtained release from their term of industrial service, do not belong to the army. Instead they serve in an auxiliary corps whose members may vote for the president, although they may not themselves hold that office.[34]

The organization of the nation as an "industrial unit," that is, around the industrial army, does away with local and state governments, and dispenses with the need for representative bodies of any kind. In place of government there is the administration of the industrial army: "Almost the sole function of the administration now is that of directing the industries of the country. Most of the purposes for which government formerly existed no longer remain to be subserved. . . . The only function proper of the government which still remains is the judiciary and the police system."[35] For all practical purposes, the industrial army is the state.

A vaguely constituted congress meets once every five years, and then only to accept the report of the outgoing president.[36] "It is rarely that Congress even when it meets considers any new laws of consequence, and then it only has power to commend to the following Congress, lest anything be done hastily," Julian West is told. "If you will consider a moment, Mr. West, you will see that we have nothing to make laws about. The fundamental principles on which our society is founded settle for all time the strifes and misunderstandings which in your day called for legislation."[37]

Thus, without controversies of substance, there is no need for representative bodies to legislate. Politics, politicians, political parties, representation, and representative bodies are gone. All decisions are matters of mere administrative technique which can and must be made by administrators and experts, the bureaucrats who head the industrial army, who are familiar with the problems of production. Such a system

33. Ibid., 167–168, 169.   34. Ibid., 126.   35. Ibid., 169.
36. Ibid., 155–156.   37. Ibid., 169.

could never have worked a century earlier, Julian West explains: "The demagoguery and corruption of our public men would have been considered, in my day, insuperable objections to any assumption by government of the change of the national industries. We should have thought that no arrangement could be worse than to entrust the politicians with control of the wealth-producing machinery of the country. Its material interests were quite too much the football of parties as it was."[38] By the year 2000, however, "all that is changed. . . . We have no parties or politicians, and as for demagoguery or corruption, they are words having only an historical significance."[39]

Not only, then, is there no workers' control nor are there trade unions in what some historians have called a model democracy, but there is no democratic control of any kind. Any person who wishes to alter the "fundamental principles" upon which Bellamy's collectivist society is based, or who questions the management of the non-elected bureaucracy, will find no meaningful channels by which opinions can be represented, nor permanent associations formed, such as a party, for the purpose of making their ideas known or for carrying out changes. In brief, the exclusion of "politics" from this utopia means the abolition of all democratic public life in which citizens can actively participate. Bellamy does discuss in detail the arrangements which will be made to guarantee the freedom of the press, allowing any individual or groups of individuals who have a point of view in common to bring their ideas before the "public," in order to influence "public opinion."[40] But without parties, elections, and representative bodies, there cannot be, either in logic or in fact, a "public opinion." At best, then, this provision testifies to the residual power of the forms of democracy, if not its substance, over Bellamy's mind.

The "politics"—if indeed it may correctly be called that—that Bellamy's utopia does allow for is of a peculiar variety. Because the members of the industrial army are interested parties, Bellamy argues, they cannot be allowed any role in making the decisions affecting their lives. Instead the retired members, presumably disinterested, choose leading officials from among those generals who have risen through merit to the top of the hierarchy. But they too, like the members of the work force, have a limited role. With the exception of a plebiscite every five

38. Ibid., 45.   39. Ibid.   40. Ibid., 133–136.

years, and certain duties associated with their own guilds, even the
retired have no other opportunity to participate. In "no previous form of
society," Bellamy explains in a critical passage, has there been "a body of
electors so ideally adapted to their office, as regards absolute impartial-
ity, knowledge of the special qualifications and records of candidates,
solicitude for the best result, and complete absence of self-interest."[41]
This stress on the absence of "self-interest" and the importance of impar-
tial expertise is fundamental in Bellamy's political thinking.

The one check upon the power of the officers of the army is the
judiciary. But it is not elected but appointed from above. Moreover,
the jury system has no place in the year 2000 because "no conceivable
motive but justice could actuate our judges."[42] Nor are there law
schools or lawyers, for there is no law, only a "few of the plainest and
simplest legal maxims" which apply to the changed state of affairs. The
judges "are simply widely informed, judicious, and discreet men of ripe
years."[43]

Of particular importance to grasping the inner meaning of
Bellamy's hatred of capitalist society is the conception of legal procedure.
The private who claims injustice at the hands of an officer may appeal to
the lower judges, whose decision must be final. In the rare cases in
which an individual is actually accused of a misdeed, there is no right to
a defense lawyer. Indeed, there are none to be had. As the narrator
explains, "It would not seem reasonable to us, in a case where the only
interest of the nation is to find out the truth, that persons should take
part in the proceedings who had an acknowledged motive to color it."[44]
But this lack of a defense lawyer, Bellamy explains, will be of no great
import, for if the accused is a criminal "he needs no defense, for he
pleads guilty in most instances." If, however, the accused is perverse or
antisocial enough to deny the charges against him, and is found guilty,
then the penalty is doubled. "Falsehood is, however, so despised among
us that few offenders would lie to save themselves."[45] Trial by jury is
done away with, and the accused is expected upon pain of double penalty to confess to the charges leveled against him. The judges, like the
officers in the industrial army, are not responsive nor responsible to the
people.

41. Ibid., 134.   42. Ibid., 166.   43. Ibid., 167–168.
44. Ibid., 164.   45. Ibid., 165.

These are, in outline, the essential components of Bellamy's plan for a collectivist utopia. Even by the most generous standard, there is no democracy to be found in it. Universal suffrage is abolished, for it would interfere with the discipline necessary to the running of society, and there are no mechanisms or opportunities for the individual to change or affect public policy.

In one respect, however, Bellamy shows tender concern for individual rights: the right of the consumers to obtain the goods they desire. How, it is asked, can a small minority be assured that it can obtain the articles for which there is no general demand? Might not "an official decree at any moment . . . deprive them of the means of gratifying some special taste, merely because the majority does not share it?" "That," the spokesman for the new order very solemnly agrees, "would be tyranny indeed,"

> and you may be sure that it does not happen with us, to whom liberty is as dear as equality or fraternity. . . . The administration has no power to stop the production of any commodity for which there continues to be a demand. . . . Again, suppose an article not before produced is demanded. If the administration doubts the reality of the demand, a popular petition guaranteeing a certain basis of consumption compels it to produce the desired article. A government, or a majority, which would undertake to tell the people, or a minority, what they were to eat, drink, or wear, as I believe governments in America in your day did, would be regarded as a curious anachronism indeed. Possibly you had reasons for tolerating these infringements of personal independence, but we should not think them endurable. I am glad you raised this point, for it has given me a chance to show you how much more direct and efficient is the control over production exercised by the individual citizen now than it was in your day, when what you called private initiative prevailed, though it should have been called capitalist initiative, for the average citizen had little enough share in it.[46]

Thus, on the one hand, forced self-incrimination of accused persons is not regarded as tyrannical in Bellamy's world while interference with the right to consume the goods of one's choice could be indignantly rejected as a major infraction of "liberty." Apart from what it says about the absurdity of regarding Bellamy's socialism as "humanistic" and "nonmaterialistic" this facet of Bellamy's thought provides an insight into the nature of Bellamy's popular appeal.

46. Ibid., 149–150.

Looking Backward and the Nationalist Movement

Within a year of its publication in 1888, the sales of *Looking Backward* began to soar—to the surprise of the publisher and the delight of the author. By 1889, it had already sold some 200,000 copies. By the end of the century, it had sold more copies than any other book published in America except *Uncle Tom's Cabin.*[47]

In 1888, a group of retired army officers attracted by Bellamy's military solution to the labor problem formed the first "Bellamy Club." A short time later the membership expanded and the First Nationalist Club of Boston was founded.[48] *The Nationalist*, published by the First Club, became the official periodical of the new movement. Clubs began to spring up throughout the country and the constitution and declaration of principles of the First Boston club became the model. By the end of 1890 there were 158 Nationalist clubs in twenty-seven states. Sixty-five were in California and sixteen in New York City. The peak of the movement was reached in early 1891 when there were 165 clubs chartered. The continued spread of the movement and the "Bellamy craze" seemed to have no limits. But by 1894 most of the clubs had disappeared and the Nationalist movement had been absorbed into the newer currents to which it had helped give birth.[49]

Bellamy welcomed the organization of the clubs, but played no active role in the movement at first. He displayed a sympathetic interest in its progress, speaking for the Boston Club and contributing occasional articles to *The Nationalist* and other, more popular, periodicals. With the demise of *The Nationalist* in 1891, however, Bellamy established the publication of his own Nationalist periodical: *The New Nation*. During three and one-half years, its columns were devoted to the exposition and application of the ideas of Nationalism which had been propounded in *Looking Backward*.

Bellamy's entrance into the field of active politics, marked by the publication of *The New Nation*, coincided, not accidentally, with the emergence of the People's Party. *Looking Backward* had itself reached many of the same farmers who moved through the Farmers' Alliance and

47. Morgan, *Edward Bellamy*, pp. 252, 148.

48. Quint, *The Forging of American Socialism*, pp. 79–80.

49. Ibid. See also Everett McNair, *Edward Bellamy and the Nationalist Movement, 1889–1894* (Milwaukee: Fitzgerald, 1957), chs. 2–7, for a detailed account of the activities of the clubs.

the Grange to the formation of the People's Party. As an expression of the same discontent which gave rise to Populism, the members of the Nationalist Clubs, eager to translate their ideals into reality, flowed into the Populist movement.[50] After some hesitation, Bellamy supported the People's Party and *The New Nation* became a voice for Eastern Populism. In urban centers, particularly in Massachusetts, New York, New Jersey, Ohio, and California, the Nationalists became the urban wing of a party whose base was largely western and southern, and agrarian. In California, the Populist movement, rural as well as urban, owed a great deal to the prior Nationalist agitation and Nationalists played an important role in the party. When Ignatius Donnelly met Bellamyites who were Massachusetts delegates to the Populist convention of 1891, he is reported to have said: "Edward Bellamy—whom not to know is to argue one's self unknown."[51] Bellamy and the Nationalists particularly welcomed the provisions of the Omaha platform of 1892 which called for the nationalization of the railroads and telegraph. To the Nationalists these were the first installments of the new society pictured in *Looking Backward*.[52]

As the depression of 1893 deepened, and as the Populists became more afflicted with the "free-silver" panacea, Bellamy became disillusioned with Populism. In 1894, *The New Nation* suspended publication for financial reasons, and the original Nationalist movement no longer had any organ—although Wayland's *Coming Nation*, which proclaimed itself to be in the Bellamy tradition, continued to be published until 1901.[53] Bellamy, as always in ill health, retired from active political life in 1894 and, after returning to Chicopee Falls, began work on the sequel to *Looking Backward*, *Equality*, which was published in 1897, shortly before his death.

The decline of the Nationalist clubs in 1894, the growing "free-silver" panacea among the Populists, and the fusion with the Democratic Party in 1896, foiled the hopes of the anticapitalist reformers for a new movement. Disillusionment with political action was rife. Political failure produced new panaceas designed to create a noncapitalist social order without the need for popular, organized, political participation from below: Communities, plebiscitarian "direct-democracy" devices, bureau-

50. Quint, *Forging of American Socialism*, p. 101.
51. Morgan, *Edward Bellamy*, p. 278.
52. Quint, *Forging of American Socialism*, p. 220.
53. Ibid., pp. 175–209.

cratic and elitist schemes for "non-partisan" socialism, and even—quite inevitably—the formation of an American version of the Fabian Society, all appeared during this period.[54]

These tendencies culminated in the formation, in 1897, of the Social Democracy of America. Bringing together the remnants of Debs' American Railway Union, the adherents and members of the various communitarian experiments, especially the Ruskin colony, publishers of the *Coming Nation*, and the assorted native-American socialistic clubs which were remnants of the Bellamy movement, the Social Democracy was from the start split into two irreconcilable factions. In one wing stood the colonists who felt it impossible to build a political movement and were convinced of the corruption of the mass of non-believers. More important, they were hostile to a socialism based upon the working class and labor movement. Instead, they proposed to build socialism in one western state. In this wing of the S.D. of A. were most of the utopian-communitarians as well as many of the early supporters of the National-ist clubs who had broken with Bellamy over his political involvement with the Populist movement which was too "political" and thus inconsis-tent with the bureaucratic, antidemocratic vision of a collectivist society imposed from above which Bellamy had first proposed in *Looking Back-ward*. Among this group was Eltweed Pomeroy, leading Nationalist and advocate of "direct legislation," as well as Laurence Gronlund, whose political views had become so antidemocratic by the end of the 1890s that, perhaps following the lead of the Webbs in England, he preferred to call himself a "collectivist" and not a socialist. More clearly than anything else this shift in terminology reveals the degree to which the existence of two irreconcilable roads had become clear to those most deeply involved in the movement.

If Gronlund, Pomeroy, and the communitarians represented one tendency in the birth period of the Socialist Party, Debs personified the other. By the time of its first convention, in 1898, the Social Democracy of America was irrevocably split. While the majority continued to search for a New Jerusalem, the minority, which included Debs, favored inde-pendent political action and pointed itself toward the building of a working-class socialist movement. With the parting of ways, the minor-

---

54. Ibid., chs. 8–11. A detailed and politically sensitive account of this period may be found in Ira Kipnis, *The American Socialist Movement, 1897–1912* (1952), chs. 1–6.

ity organized itself into the Social Democratic Party (SDP). Composed mostly of native-born, English-speaking Americans, the Social Democratic Party became the most significant element in the formation of the new Socialist Party.[55] Bellamy himself did not live to see the divergent path taken by the American socialists who had found socialism through *Looking Backward*.

Edward Bellamy: Anomic Utopian

Edward Bellamy's life and intellectual development provides the key to the sources and content of the anticapitalist views and the bureaucratic socialist utopia sketched in *Looking Backward* and help us to grasp the reasons for the positive response which it received.[56]

Not long after *Looking Backward* had begun to receive wide acclaim, Bellamy attempted to suggest that the very writing of his utopia as well as the great "discovery" of the solution to the labor question through the industrial army had been largely unintentional.[57] Yet, not only was the elaborate authoritarianism of *Looking Backward* a reflection of conservative antidemocratic ideas which came to the surface after the Civil War, but it was also the culmination of a long concern with social questions on Bellamy's part, a concern which had led him repeatedly to search for utopian solutions to the anarchy and isolated individualism of capitalist society. Moreover, Bellamy's authoritarianism expressed a deep need in Bellamy's psychological make-up, one that led to the denial of individual personality and the idealization of an all-embracing organic state. Thus Bellamy's psychology, class origins, career expectations, and location in

55. Quint, *Forging of American Socialism*, ch. 9.

56. In addition to Morgan, *Edward Bellamy*, and Bowman, *The Year 2000*, both of which provide a wealth of information about Bellamy's personal background, John L. Thomas's introduction to the John Harvard Library edition of *Looking Backward* (Cambridge: Harvard University Press, 1967) provides an unusually subtle and insightful account of Bellamy's intellectual, but not political, development and of his fictional writing before *Looking Backward*. See also Jackson Wilson, "Experience and Utopia: The Making of Edward Bellamy's *Looking Backward*," *Journal of American Studies* 11, no. 1 (1977): 45–60; Wilson makes a number of important points but does not consider Bellamy's ideas in their historical context. His argument that Bellamy's utopia was rooted in "his unwillingness or inability to confront the industrial city and its proletarian labor force" and hence is "conceived not in hope or in expectation but in nostalgia" is difficult to sustain. On a number of other aspects of Bellamy's personal development, especially his use of *Eliot Carson*, Wilson offers rare and often persuasive insights.

57. Bellamy, "Why I wrote *Looking Backward*" (1890), reprinted in *Edward Bellamy Speaks Again!* (1937), pp. 199–203.

the structure of late nineteenth-century society enabled him to articulate the reactions of large segments of middle-class America to the problems arising out of industrialization and the concentration of wealth. Bellamy's class situation and experience were typical of an important, new, and growing stratum of the population: an educated middle class which was neither entrepreneurial nor working class.

Chicopee: Microcosm of the Future

Born exactly at mid-century, Bellamy grew up and lived his entire life in Chicopee Falls, a small Massachusetts village which had been united into the larger town of Chicopee in the year of Bellamy's birth. Nearby lay Springfield, already one of the more industrialized cities of the Northeast. Both Bellamy's father and paternal grandfather had been Baptist ministers. On both his mother's and father's sides of the family there had been many ministers, including Joseph Bellamy, a noted Calvinist theologian and friend of Jonathan Edwards. Bellamy's own family seems to have been financially well-off: in his youth Bellamy travelled extensively in Europe and to the South Seas. In short, for over two hundred years, Edward Bellamy's family had been a solid part of the native-born New England middle classes.[58]

Until early in the nineteenth century, Chicopee Falls had been a small agricultural village. Because of its water-power resources, Boston capitalists located textile factories there and rapidly transformed the village into an industrialized company town. Primary investment was in large-scale, highly integrated cotton mills. By 1850, as Vera Shlakman has shown, the town of Chicopee was "modern in every sense of the word." Chicopee Falls had passed almost overnight from a rural community into an advanced modern industrial town. This rapid development had significant consequences for the local middle classes: "There was no smooth economic progression from stage to stage—artisan or merchant to manufacturer; craftsmanship to mass production; partnership to corporation. This town did not grow into an industrial community; it suddenly found that it *was* one."[59]

The local Yankee middle class played little active role in the devel-

58. Morgan, *Edward Bellamy*, pp. 9–17.

59. Vera Shlakman, *Economic History of a Factory Town* (1934), chs. 1–3. See also John Michael Cudd, *The Chicopee Manufacturing Co., 1823–1915* (1974), and Michael H. Frisch, *Town Into City* (1972).

opment of the town. Yet, the initial period of investment by absentee Boston capitalists generated a period of modest growth for the middle class. Between 1866 and 1873 a number of small manufacturing businesses and retail establishments were founded. However, they were dependent to a very large degree upon the prosperity of the cotton mills, which meant that very early the Chicopee Falls middle class was swept up into the national and world market economy and became sensitive to business fluctuations far beyond their own immediate circumstances.[60]

Even as Chicopee's traditional local middle class reached its peak in the 1870s—just as Bellamy was entering his early twenties—it came face to face with forces which diminished its power and prestige and which forecast a further decline. First the invasion of the Irish working and middle class threatened its dominance.[61] By the 1870s the older Yankee working class had been replaced with a permanent class of workers of French-Canadian and Irish extraction. From 1860 to 1890, numerous strikes and other symptoms of class conflict came to western Massachusetts. Attempts to establish a union organization were uniformly unsuccessful due to a combination of employers' resistance and the workers' own organizational weaknesses.[62]

By the mid-1880s the sagging fortunes of the local middle class appeared irreversible. This decline involved not only the economic position of the middle class as a whole, but also a loss of social status of the older, Yankee middle class.[63] Of this period of decline, Shlakman writes:

> While it is true that the merchants multiplied, we do not find that there arose from their ranks leaders of business enterprise such as flourished—in small numbers it is true—in the earlier years of the life of the town. We find that as the town grew in size, and as new large scale investment poured in, the local business men were overshadowed by the weight of the big corporations and the sheer numbers of the workers. . . . The result of these conditions was the recession of the social and economic position of the most vigorous section of the middle class, increasingly apparent by the end of the nineteenth century.[64]

By the 1890s all of the ills of modern urban life afflicted Chicopee: social disorganization, spreading slums, and a rising crime rate. When Chicopee formally became a city in 1891, the new charter "brought with

60. Shlakman, *Economic History*, pp. 168–169, 176–177.
61. Ibid., pp. 176–177, 182.   62. Ibid., ch. 8, p. 206–207.
63. Ibid., 209–210.   64. Ibid., p. 210.

it the inauguration of ward politics [and] the rise of political machines which utilized the votes of conflicting nationalities to achieve power."[65]

Early and intense industrialization made Chicopee a prototype which foreshadowed the fate of countless other communities whose middle classes found their social dominance shattered by the rise of industrial capitalism. Present before Bellamy's eyes as he grew up in Chicopee Falls were all the elements of the drama experienced by millions of Americans. Bellamy's circumstances thus prepared him to become the interpreter of the changes transforming the conditions of a threatened and declining social class.

The older middle class was rooted in a stabler mercantile-agrarian order. Industrialization, however, speeded up the tempo of change. The newly rich possessed little culture and even fewer moral scruples. To many middle-class persons it seemed that an unrestrained pursuit of wealth corrupted the American dream of individual success and independence. The "passion for sensual pleasures," wrote the twenty-three-year-old Bellamy in the *Springfield Daily Union* in 1873, is like a "malaria" in the atmosphere of society,

> perceptible as a subtle poison to persons of delicate taste, and sufficiently obvious to those of coarser organs by eruptions as unmistakable [as] the pustules of small-pox. It has worked down from the richer classes to the poorer, from capitalists to the smaller tradesmen and the day-laborers, exciting their envy of the physical indulgences which money can command and stimulating them to seize these gratifications whether they can afford them or not. It is not, perhaps, so much to be wondered at as deplored that this should be the effect of the lavish display of this luxurious side of life by the more opulent, which is continually flaunted in our faces.[66]

In the new economic order, the older middle-class virtues and values were shuffled aside: success went to those who could break free of the chains of tradition and Christian morality and claw their way to the top.

The corrupt new political system paralleled the developments in the business system. The factories brought to the cities and towns a flood of immigrants speaking strange tongues and carrying their foreign customs with them. Above all, industrialization created a growing class

---

65. Ibid.

66. "Wealth and Sensual Pleasure," *Springfield Daily Union*, February 24, 1873, p. 2.

of permanent wage earners whose struggles against capital became increasingly bitter. The periodic depressions which paralyzed the American economy after the Civil War wiped out small businessmen by the thousands and drove farmers to the wall. The drift from a simpler agrarian republic to complex industrial nation terrified many. An uncertain future surely lay ahead for many middle-class Americans.

Personal Background

The outlines of Bellamy's personal development suggest a deeply troubled and lonely person, unable to find a material or psychological foothold in a world which was being transformed by industrialization and concentration of wealth. He reacted sharply against the commercialism and competitive spirit of the new order, but his notebooks reveal an intense but thwarted desire for material success and power. At the age of twenty-two Bellamy confided to his notebook that what "angers me most is not that I am put off for a week or a day or a year from wealth and position, but that it is in the power of foolish men with whom I deal to delay me about a whole life's work."[67] Bellamy's resentment and feelings of failure were intensified by his inability to enter the two professions which seemed to offer the best opportunity for advancement outside business itself.

Bellamy had been fascinated as a child by military life.[68] The Civil War had a profound effect on the imagination of Americans who saw in the marshalling of great armies and the way in which during wartime petty concerns had been put aside a model for overcoming the disorder and anarchy of American society.[69] But the dream of a military career was shattered when Bellamy was rejected by West Point because of poor health. He then attended Union College for a short while, but again because of his always precarious health was forced to leave before graduation.[70]

Returning to Chicopee Falls after a year of study in Germany, Bellamy took up the study of law for two years in nearby Springfield, and in 1871 he opened a practice in Chicopee Falls. His first case was also his last. The eviction of a widow for failure to pay her rent con-

67. Notebooks, February, 1872, Bellamy Papers.
68. Mason A. Green, "Edward Bellamy," pp. 9–10.
69. Frederickson, *The Inner Civil War*.
70. Bowman, *The Year 2000*, p. 19; Morgan, *Edward Bellamy*, pp. 118–120.

flicted too strongly with his conception of an honorable calling. Bellamy expressed his lifelong hatred for the legal profession and the crass spirit of commercialism which pervaded it in an unpublished fragment of an autobiographical novel, *Eliot Carson:*

> The principle of the profession that the lawyer is morally irresponsible for the ends he is employed to further, that his duty is only to his fee, is the survival of the Swiss Musketeer's principle that his loyalty was due only to the keeper of the money chest. In all other professions and occupations this barbarous principle is cut out. In the so-called liberal profession of law alone it is still professed by personally honorable men.[71]

It was undoubtedly a shattering experience for the twenty-one-year-old Bellamy. His journal for this period reveals how his failure to find a satisfactory place troubled him, though he tried to hide his sense of hopelessness: "I have had not a few disappointments in this life, already become an old story, and yet do not find my self-confidence one whit abated. Although no man would appreciate more keenly the rewards of fame or ignominy of public contempt, yet neither of these is essential to my mental ideal."[72] In the end, Bellamy recognized that "the feeling of utterly isolated and necessarily self-dependent personality is peculiarly developed in my mental constitution."[73] "I ought to take the spoiling of my life more quietly," he reflected bitterly in *Eliot Carson*. "It is the general fate, like death. What use to repine? It is the law of society."[74] Turning like so many other young, educated persons to journalism, Bellamy found employment during the 1870s on the *Springfield Union*. It is clear, however, that he did not relish his new role: "Another week of slavery," he confided despairingly to his notebook.[75] He preferred to write novels and in the late 1870s was able to give up the daily routine of newspaper work to devote himself to writing fiction. His second published novel, *Dr. Heidenhoff's Process* (1880), drew critical acclaim from William Dean Howells, who predicted that Bellamy might become the Hawthorne of his age.[76]

Undoubtedly of great importance in the development of Bellamy's political and social attitudes was a year which he spent in Germany, in 1868-1869. In later years he recalled

71. Eliot Carson, Bellamy Papers.
72. Notebook, Bellamy Papers, August 1871.
73. Ibid.   74. Ibid.   75. Ibid., probably early 1870s.
76. Morgan, *Edward Bellamy*, p. 62.

how much more that background of misery impressed me than the
palaces and cathedrals. . . . I distinctly recall the innumerable de-
bates, suggested by the piteous sights about us, . . . as to the possibility of finding a great remedy for poverty, some plan for equaliz-
ing human conditions. . . . So it was that I returned home, for the
first time aroused to the existence and urgency of the social problem,
but without as yet seeing any way out. Although it had required the
sights of Europe to startle me to a vivid realization of the inferno of
poverty beneath our civilization, my eyes having once been opened,
I had no difficulty in recognizing in America, and even in my own
comparatively prosperous village, the same condition in course of
progressive development.[77]

Bellamy was particularly impressed by the powerful, efficient
armies of Europe, especially Germany's.[78] His lifelong fascination with
the army, his disappointed hopes for a military career at West Point, now
focused on the efficiency of the Prussian army and from it the model of the
industrial army was drawn. Echoing an article by Von Moltke, Bellamy
explained in 1875 that the superiority of the Prussian Army to the American was due to the way in which the former selected its officers from the
ranks, "any of whom showing military aptitude receives a government
education." Rather than fill West Point and Annapolis through an "Aristocratic" system of "appointments from civilian life, we ought to have an
arrangement by which promising young soldiers and sailors already in
service might receive a training they had developed a taste for." Here in
Von Moltke's model of a rationally organized modern mass army Bellamy
found his bureaucratic model of socialism in which merit rather than birth
would be the basis for leadership.[79]

In two lectures delivered to the Chicopee Village Lyceum probably
not long after his return from Europe, Bellamy took the first tentative
steps toward formulating his ideas of social reconstruction. The vast in-
equalities of wealth and the "general subjection of the poorer to the richer

77. Quoted by Green, "Edward Bellamy," Bellamy Papers, pp. 22–23; the date
given is 1884 but it seems clear this should read 1894, after the publication of *Looking
Backward* had made its author reflect upon the sources of his political and social views.

78. James T. George, "Edward Bellamy and the Nationalist Movement," Divi-
sional Honors, Amherst College, 1938, pp. 29–30, based on interviews with Bellamy's
widow and daughter.

79. "Von Moltke's Criticism on Our Army," *Springfield Daily Union*, August 3,
1875, p. 4; see also "The Swedish Civil Service," *Springfield Daily Union*, November 21,
1877, p. 4, as evidence of Bellamy's Mugwump-type concern with efficient bureaucratic
organization of government.

classes," he asserted, constitute an element of "barbarism" in modern society.[80] The common people have never before "achieved such power as they now possess" and in their discontent lies not only the hope of society, but also its greatest danger. The masses may "tear down better things than they can build up. . . . world experience has woefully proved, that the course of human progress may be turned backward and the laborious civilization of ages be annihilated."[81] Anticipating the message of *Looking Backward*, Bellamy declared that "there is then enough in the world to support all in abundance if it were equally divided. If the burdens of life as well as the pleasures of life were apportioned equally among all, then should none labor beyond moderation, and none be utterly idle. This is the social condition which justice demands, and to which a reform in the interests of justice will lead us back."[82] To achieve this goal it was necessary to banish "the fell power of gold from the earth, [and] bring back the Golden Age." Reacting defensively to his audience, Bellamy denied that his views were those of a socialist. Yet, he asked, why should demands for reform be identified with a term which "in the minds of most men" is "synonymous . . . with ignorant presumption and fanatical atheism?"[83] Bellamy admitted to his audience that he was unable to offer them hope, but the need to search for a solution which was preoccupying him through the years was not forgotten:

> Gentlemen, if you expect from me this evening a theory of Socialism, if you expect a minute description of the institutions of that new world of whose peace and liberty and happiness I have told you, you will be disappointed. It is an undiscovered country, no community of men ever essayed its Elysian climes, no human foot has ever trod its shores. But I know that it exists—the faith of humanity points to its existence—and we must find it. I see the countless difficulties which envelop the task, but I feel this to be the great problem of humanity, propounded by the sphinx-like fates, which we must solve or perish. For the toiling masses of the world are already fiercely questioning the right to exist of a society which is founded on their subjection. The atmosphere is rife with revolution. Society in its present form will not long exist. Whether shall succeed it an anarchy, a chaos to which organized slavery were preferable, or an era of a more perfect liberty and happiness than the world has ever known, the rich fruition of the garnered hope of the ages, depends on the

80. Second Lyceum Talk, Bellamy Papers.
81. First Lyceum Talk, Bellamy Papers.
82. Second Lyceum Talk, Bellamy Papers.   83. Ibid.

action or inaction, the folly or the wisdom, of this generation of whose eternal responsibility we must bear a part.[84]

In *Looking Backward*, written over fifteen years later, Bellamy found the undiscovered country of his youth and revealed to the world the "minute description" of an alternative to the social anarchy engulfing America. Throughout the intervening period, however, Bellamy remained concerned with social and political issues, frequently expressing his views in the editorial columns of the *Springfield Daily Union* and, indirectly, through the medium of an historical novel, *The Duke of Stockbridge*,[85] dealing with Shays's Rebellion. Scattered in these writings as well as in the private notebooks to which Bellamy committed his inner thoughts and sketched plots for short stories in which the disharmonies and anxieties of modern life are overcome, were the seeds of Bellamy's utopian prophecy.

Running through Bellamy's *Springfield Daily Union* editorials is a powerful current of middle-class resentment and envy at the corrupting effect of great wealth on the morals and politics of American society in the 1870s.[86] The conspicuous consumption of the rich results in the "common curse of inordinate social ambition and ungoverned desire of fine living and the luxury of wealth, passions which, with all its compensating blessings, a democratic state of society unquestionably tends to aggravate."[87] "As our overgrown fortunes multiply," Bellamy complained, "there is a wasteful prodigality of luxurious display and self-indulgence which is utterly unseemly, which is both morally and economically bad; which springs from the grosser natures of men; which burglarizes and debauches society."[88] Worst of all, such exhibitions of wealth "have much to do in embittering the poorer classes against the richer, in fanning the fire which is burning so hotly in the hearts of many of our labor reformers and their followers."[89]

---

84. Ibid.

85. Edward Bellamy, *The Duke of Stockbridge: A Romance of Shays' Rebellion*, ed. Joseph Schiffman, (Cambridge: Harvard University Press, 1962). Although badly flawed by a conventionalized romantic plot, Bellamy's story of the uprising in Western Massachusetts is an often moving and sympathetic account of the grievances of the debt-ridden farmers.

86. These editorials and other of Bellamy's contributions to the *Springfield Daily Union* (hereafter *SU*) have been identified by Sylvia Bowman (*The Year 2000*, pp. 350–375).

87. "Are We a Marrying People?" *SU*, August 14, 1873, p. 4.

88. "Luxury and Extravagance," *SU*, July 7, 1873, p. 4.   89. Ibid.

Bellamy reacted to the scandals of the Grant era in typical Mug-wump fashion. Decrying the "monstrous grab game . . . wherever a clutching fist can be thrust into the spoils," he declared that "the worst feature of this whole matter is that a class of men has come to the front with whom office holding is a profession—a means of support and en-richment; . . . It is their trade, their business and very likely their gam-bling capital. They go for it by every possible artifice, and when they get it, they make the most money out of it they can, and by any means within reach, without regard to moral considerations. They are an una-voidable nuisance under all kinds of government; perhaps our kind gives them a ranker soil to sprout in."[90] Here the hatred of politics and politi-cians and the implicit wish to find a replacement for them which per-meates *Looking Backward* is apparent.

Not surprisingly, the "labor question" and the growing menace of socialism on the part of discontented workers increasingly preoccupied Bellamy during the 1870s. Denouncing Charles Bradlaugh, the English reformer, as a "socialist," Bellamy warned Americans that Bradlaugh was the wrong sort of reformer, one who desired the "commune" in England.[91] In America the virus of radicalism had also begun to appear: "There is a vague discontent with the present state of affairs, a chafing under the restraints of society and a disposition to disregard the rights of others that is neither American nor manly and that too often finds ex-pression in indiscriminate acts of violence and crime. This feeling is largely the outcome of the pernicious communistic teachings of dema-gogues and so-called social reformers, whose chief object is to tear down the present fabric of society." Fortunately, however, Bellamy admitted, "these teachings are not openly accepted by the masses" although "the ideas find unconscious lodgment in many minds, and spring up and bear evil fruit when least expected." But it was necessary to be on guard, "the times are critical and we need all our sturdy Anglo-Saxon sense to enable us to pull safely through."[92] Strikes were another sign of social disorder. And although Bellamy would not deny the right of striking "when . . . it is the only redress" to a "crying injustice," still it was a "lame and

90. "Serbonian Bogs," *SU*, April 7, 1874, p. 4; "The Head and the Tail Changing Places," *SU*, April 3, 1874, p. 4.

91. "Two Types of Reformers," *SU*, September 25, 1873, p. 4.

92. "Crime and its Causes," *SU*, February 19, 1874, p. 4.

blundering instrument." "The strike injures society for the sake of individuals. It repudiates a contract with the community to injure persons indirectly interested in that contract." The ideal solution would be a plan for workers and employers to "adjust" their disputes. "Meanwhile, . . . a man's labor . . . is a debt to society which it is strictly dishonest to repudiate," and Bellamy counseled "strikers to act with much circumspection, as becomes those who do evil that good may come. Strikes may be justifiable, but the presumption is against them."[93] Bellamy could hardly have been expected to have sympathized with the often violent strike of 1877: he called for the "crushing" of the riot and the arrest of the "mob" and derided those persons who in places such as Pittsburgh had welcomed the destruction of the railroads' property.[94]

On the surface, then, Bellamy's social and political views were consistent with the response of many conservative middle-class reformers of the period. Appalled at the excesses of wealth and the many injustices of capitalism, finding politics the corrupt province of self-interested professionals, fearing the social chaos which an unruly mob of workers might create at any time, the new breed of reformer began to search for an orderly society that would reconcile capital and labor, purify politics, and put people like themselves at the center of affairs once more. Yet, as the youthful Lyceum address revealed, together with the impressive "romance of Shays's Rebellion," *The Duke of Stockbridge*, there was a more radical side to Bellamy's political views which the ordinary independent, mugwump reformer did not share. The message of his novel of Shays's Rebellion is in part a cautionary one, designed to prevent rather than glorify the organization of the poor against the rich. But at times Bellamy's hatred of the power of the propertied and his sympathy for the downtrodden farmers whose hopes of a better society had been trampled in the post–Revolutionary War era, overwhelms the conservative message and seems more like a call to arms. But an even more radical element in Bellamy's thought and make-up was his reaction against the egoistic, atomized individualism of the age and the assertion of the need for a new type of community that would submerge selfish individualism into an organic social order.

93. "The Ethics of Strikes," *SU*, April 15, 1875, p. 4.
94. "Who Has Got to Pay?" *SU*, July 25, 1877.

Solidarity and Communion: The Loss of Self

Three years after Bellamy acknowledged his sense of deep failure arising out of career disappointments, he wrote *The Religion of Solidarity*, a statement of his personal philosophy which contained the core of the social outlook later embodied in *Looking Backward*.[95] As an expression of Bellamy's inner anguish, it provides the clearest evidence of the kind of psychological motives underlying the radical anti-individualism of his authoritarian utopia.[96] Bellamy was conscious of the importance of this document and of its relationship to the message in *Looking Backward*. In 1888, the year of the novel's publication, he wrote that *The Religion of Solidarity* represented "the germ of what has been ever since my philosophy of life. . . . By this time I begin to feel that this is my ripe judgment of life."[97] He asked that it be read at his funeral.

The central theme of *The Religion of Solidarity*, which also permeates the socialism of Laurence Gronlund as well as the ideology of the Nationalist movement, is the desire for *communion:* the powerful expression of a yearning to immerse the individual personality in an impersonal, infinite universe, thereby escaping the anxiety of individual existence.[98]

The loss of "personality" and individual identity, Bellamy maintains in *The Religion of Solidarity*, is the precondition of a genuine communion with the universe. The personality of the individual is not the "ultimate fact," but is rather "a mere temporary affection of the universal."[99] To personality and individual identity, Bellamy counterposes the concept of "solidarity":

95. Edward Bellamy, "The Religion of Solidarity," reprinted in Joseph Schiffman, ed., *Edward Bellamy: Selected Writings on Religion and Society* (1955), pp. 3–57.

96. Morgan, Bowman, and Schiffman agree that it is the central document necessary for an understanding of Bellamy's psychological and social thought. Morgan, an uncritical admirer of Bellamy, correctly notes "we may well assume that Bellamy's interest in military organization was an expression of his craving for a religion of solidarity, and for an efficient method of doing the public business" (Morgan, *Edward Bellamy*, p. 323). For a fuller exposition of Bellamy's philosophical views see Arthur E. Morgan, *The Philosophy of Edward Bellamy* (1945).

97. Schiffman, "Introduction," *Edward Bellamy: Selected Writings on Religion and Society*, pp. 26–26.

98. See Erich Fromm's discussion of the authoritarian character and the ideological appeal of totalitarianism to the lower middle classes in *Escape from Freedom* (1941), chs. 5 and 6, and the discussion in Chapter 7 below of the communion theme and the applicability of Fromm's theory.

99. "The Religion of Solidarity," in Schiffman, ed., *Edward Bellamy*, pp. 13–14.

> The opposition in human nature of the two ideas of solidarity and
> personality may be . . . illustrated by describing as an expression of
> the former the sense of the sublime, of the grand, or whatever may
> be called the instinct of infinity, and on the other hand as an expres-
> sion of the personality, the desire of being circumscribed, shut in,
> and bounded, the aversion to value limitations . . . what may be
> called the instinct of finity.
>
> . . . the instinct of finity to its opposite seems synonymous with
> pettiness, with infinitesimality, suggestive of a mean, base, and nar-
> row scope, a low-lying sensuous atmosphere.[100]

As for individualism, Bellamy argues that the "tides and tempests
of the soul" do not arise within the individual personality as some men
vainly imagine but "come from the uttermost parts of the universe."[101]
Thus he emphatically rejected the "claim of the personality of the soul
and its sufficient self-comprehending consciousness."[102] From his own
experience, Bellamy testified that "unconsciousness of personality or impersonal consciousness does not imply a vague and shadowy mode of
being, but rather a stronger, intenser pulse of feeling than is obtainable
in the most vigorous assertion of personality."[103] For Bellamy, then,
"Individuality, personality, partiality, is segregation, is partition, is con-
finement, in fine a prison, and happy are we if its walls grow not
wearisome ere our seventy years' sentence expires."[104]

Bellamy's rejection of individual existence as the ultimate fact, and
his explicit wish to escape the self, to merge personality in the infinite,
has an almost nightmarish quality: "Who has not often felt in sudden
shocks of feeling as if the sense of personal identity, i.e., sense of his
connection with his particular individuality, were slipping from him?"[105]
But it is precisely this experience—"losing our personal identity"[106]—
which is the essence of the "religion of solidarity." The significance of
the individual personality is that of "an atom, a grain of sand on a
boundless shore, a bubble in a foam flecked ocean."[107] Only to the
extent that men attain communion with the impersonal universe and cast
off their individual identities, do they realize their higher natures and
achieve that solidarity with other souls that ends isolation.

In place of the anxiety and loneliness of personal existence and the

100. Ibid., p. 14.   101. Ibid., p. 9.   102. Ibid., p. 8.
103. Ibid., p. 9.   104. Ibid.   105. Ibid., p. 17.
106. Ibid., p. 19.   107. Ibid., p. 6.

lack of any organic relationship between persons, Bellamy hoped to see
the development of a "universal solidarity." Rather than the pettiness of
individuality, the "prison" within which the higher part of man is
caught, he yearned for the "sublime, ecstatic, impersonal emotions, transcending the scope of personality, manifested by human nature."[108]

What this contrast between the merely personal emotions and the
grander "impersonal" emotions—between "personality" and "solidarity"—meant in *The Religion of Solidarity* Bellamy revealed in a passage
directly foreshadowing *Looking Backward*'s authoritarian message. The
combination of the inner yearning of the individuality for solidarity, and
the proper "physical" setting for its realization, would produce results
more remarkable than mere psychic unity, or physical unity alone, "as
when the inspiration of martial music, combining with the instinct of
nationalism (which is one of the soldierly forms of solidarity), the heart
of the soldier melts in a happy rapture of self-devotion. He is impatient
to throw his life away and rejoices in his body as a sacrifice which he can
make for his country, even as the priest rejoices in a victim for the altar
of his god."[109] In Bellamy's model society of the year 2000, the army
provides the key to "solidarity," substituting the impersonal motivations
of a bureaucratic order for the mean and base motives which stem only
from the individual's selfish personality, thereby providing the psychological dynamic for the system.

Communion and "Unitary Democracy"

The counterposition of individual personality to the state of organic
solidarity lends itself, when placed in the framework of evolutionary
thought, to the idea that progress in society can be understood in terms
analogous to those applied to nature. Progress, thus, logically consists of
the impersonal evolution away from the individual, the anarchic and the
unorganized state of affairs, toward a complex, differentiated, and organized (or "cooperative") society, just as in nature the more highly organized and developed forms of life tend to replace the simpler and less
resistant organisms. This organicist conception was also at the heart of
Laurence Gronlund's rejection of the laissez faire order, and of his view
of socialism. Essentially, the argument turns social Darwinism on its
head by drawing attention to the increasingly collectivist nature of soci-

108. Ibid.   109. Ibid., p. 21.

ety as an alternative to the stress on the positive role of individualistic effort.[110]

In Bellamy's *Religion of Solidarity* these two elements—the individual and the collective—are presented as irreconcilably in conflict. Once Bellamy had discovered the collectivist conception of evolution in the 1880s, the way was clear to *Looking Backward*. There the contradiction is resolved by the conception of evolution from individualism to solidaric society, that is, by the dissolution of individual personality and its submergence in the collective.

Within the framework of this evolutionary outlook, with its stress on the collectivity as opposed to the individual, the term "democracy" tends to become identical with total organization and with the maximization of social control. If historical and social developments are seen as the product of an impersonal evolution then there can be no role for the thinking, conscious, acting, human agent. Progress is the inevitable future; historical alternatives do not exist. This organicist conception of an evolutionary development postulates as its ideal outcome a society of perfect harmony and solidarity, with each of its constituent parts functionally arranged in relation to all other parts. Intermediate and non-centralized relationships are excluded; they are, in fact, antithetical to the health of the social organism.

The resulting conception is one that the conservative sociologist Robert Nisbet has termed the tradition of "unitary democracy."[111] Its principal strategy aims at

> the sterilization of old social loyalties, the emancipation of the people from local and regional authorities, and the construction of a scene in which the individual would be the sole unit, and the State the sole association, of society. Hence, the rising stress on large-scale bureaucracy: to provide new agencies representative of the *whole* people for the discharge of powers and responsibilities formerly resident in classes, parishes, and families. Hence, the increasing administrative centralization of society to reduce in number and influence the intermediate social authorities. Hence the growing stress upon standardization: to increase the number of cultural qualities shared by the people as a whole and to diminish those shared only by fractions of the population. . . . State and individual were the two elements of the unitary theory of democracy. The abstract individ-

110. Cf. Richard Hofstadter, *Social Darwinism in American Thought* (1955), ch. 6.
111. Robert A. Nisbet, *The Quest for Community* (1953), pp. 251 ff.

ual was conceived as the sole bearer of rights and responsibilities. The State, conceived in the image of people who lay incorruptible beneath the superstructure of society, would be the area of fraternity and secular rehabilitation. All that lay between these two elements— guilds, churches, professions, classes, unions of all kinds—were suspect for their fettering influence upon the individual and their divisive consequences to the people's State.[112]

This Rousseauean conception of "democracy" underlies Bellamy's counterposition of individual personality to the state of solidarity. Individuals can only exist as a collection of atomized units within the state, and whatever stands between the individual grain and society is antithetical to social order and the higher individuality of non-personality. Antidemocratic and nonpluralist, it leads to the vision of an ant-heap society in which the submersion of the individual is the highest good. In one of his notebooks, probably written before the publication of *Looking Backward*, Bellamy explicitly makes the connection between the yearning for communion and the political and social movement toward a new kind of organic community which culminates in "democracy": "The democratic and cosmopolitan movement of modern times is favorable to the development of the religion of solidarity. The former destroys in order castes and traditional corporations of all sorts, reduces society to individuals, thus preparing the way for the conception of all existence under the sole aspect of the one universal and the many individuals."[113] And in another notebook entry, probably not long before *Looking Backward*, Bellamy asked, "What is the democratic idea? It is the recognition of the solidarity of the race in the alphabet of the religion of the whole."[114]

For Bellamy, thus, the anxiety of human existence arising out of the isolation of the individual in the anarchic society of laissez faire capitalism, is resolved by the creation of a "unitary democracy." This involves, however, not the expansion of the individual's ability to determine his own life fate, but rather the absorption of the person into society. By the reduction of society to its individual atoms the way is prepared for the total integration of the individual into a truly harmonious system; gone are the obstructions of personal selfishness and individual self-regard, arising out of membership in groups or associations mediating between the individual and society.

112. Ibid., pp. 252, 263.
113. Notebooks, Bellamy Papers.   114. Ibid.

How central this idea was to Bellamy's thought may be seen in newspaper articles which he wrote in the 1870s for *The Springfield Daily Union* in which Bellamy discussed the advantages of cooperative housekeeping. This was an idea which was to occupy a prominent position in the plan for a collectivist society developed in *Looking Backward*. In these articles Bellamy advocated this system because, his sympathetic biographer Bowman admits, "he had decided that eating in common would develop esprit de corps, check the tendency to form cliques, and increase social pressures."[115] Here is a concrete application of Bellamy's yearning for communion, in the form of a proposal for the elimination of family dining to check the partiality it produced.

Thus a unitary democracy meant for Bellamy not only the destruction of intermediate public institutions and association together with universal suffrage, but also the elimination of individual privacy and those institutions which touch immediately upon the individual's personal development. In private relations, and through institutions such as the family, loyalties other than to society or the state develop, giving rise to individuals motivated by their mere personal or individual interests. The "cliques," not being subject to the pressure of society, are the source of desires and motives at variance with the total harmony of society and are thus a symptom of the very anarchy and disorganization against which Bellamy rebelled.

Somehow, Bellamy felt, the hindering effects of individuality and personality would have to be overcome in order to avoid the anarchy which was "worse than slavery." This could only be done by a new solidaristic social order.

Private Utopias

His private notebooks and published short stories reveal that well before the writing and publication of *Looking Backward*, Bellamy had begun to look for new social arrangements which would eliminate strife and conflict and achieve the perfect communion for which he expressed such a deep yearning in *The Religion of Solidarity*. For the most part this side of Bellamy's development was confined to these private notebooks, although a few of his published stories hinted at his concern with solutions to these problems.

115. Quoted in Bowman, *The Year 2000*, p. 291.

Bellamy's outline for "A Reorganization of Society to Extinguish Sorrow," contained in one of his unpublished pre–*Looking Backward* notebooks, proposed to supplant the family tie by the impersonal organization of the state. Like his proposal for cooperative eating, his plan aimed at the elimination of an institution which he saw as standing between the individual and perfect communion. His plan, he wrote, was "based on the observation that certain affections of men, women, and children are the causes of nearly all their sorrows, the chiefest of all causes of sorrow and the most piteous being parental love. It is not deemed that much happiness comes to parents from the cultivation of tenderness of this relation, but it is believed that the anxiety and sorrow that spring from its indulgence tenfold exceed the happiness."[116] Therefore, Bellamy concluded, it was necessary to arrive at some social arrangement which would modify and restrict parental love. While mothers would still nurse their children, they would be

> relieved of nearly all other care of them, and fathers shall have no intimate relations with them. At an early age they shall be educated in kindergartens, their education and corrections shall not be determined by their parents, but by the State, consulting with the youth. As the provision for the care and maintenance of the child is to be made wholly by the State, the parents having no responsibility for the child will be without one of the chief inducements to devoted guidance. The only object of Nature in parental love is to provide for children's welfare. Society having been arranged to provide for that better than the parents possibly could, the parental love is but an effete survival, an aching root of a tooth no longer useful. The fraternal and sisterly tie and all family ties also loosened as consequence of discontinuance of family life. Play for the sentiment thus expressed found in a vast increase of intellectual and artistic sympathy, and in cultivation of the sense of the universal life in God.[117]

Here is an excellent illustration of the process whereby Bellamy translated his personal feelings into proposals for social reform. Bellamy's self-hatred, and his desire to escape from the burden of personal existence into an impersonal community where feelings no longer would trouble one, led him to search for a new society free of familial loyalties with their individualistic consequences. Thus he wrote in his notebooks of "a future and wiser society" which would "discourage the growth of the affections, recognizing as indisputable that more misery results from

116. Quoted in Morgan, *The Philosophy of Edward Bellamy*, p. 75.
117. Ibid.

excess of affectional development than from deficiency. The affectional natures, however, not to be repressed but devoted to nature, the eternal, the ideal!"[118]

The idea of a society based on perfect solidarity and communion plays a central role in one of Bellamy's published short stories, *To Whom This May Come*. The Zoroastrian inhabitants of a South Sea Island are discovered by a visitor from the outside to have lost the power of speech; yet they can communicate perfectly with each other because they can fully read each other's minds. With no secrets, unable to conceal their selfishness, the new society is a totally harmonious one.[119]

Genetic Utopias

In notes written in 1878, Bellamy outlined a story to deal with the idea of the "breeding of superior souls"—and a plan for a future society in which the state would regulate, through an "enlightened sort of stock raising" the future of the race. Along the same line, Bellamy's notebooks contain the outline of a plot entitled, "stirpiculture Fantasy—A story of the future, representing a society in which the state has taken hold of the subject of procreation, and has regulated matrimony on the principle of the improvement of the species."[120] In the published "A Love Story Reversed," Bellamy portrayed an ideal society in which marriages were arranged according to the theory of natural selection. His expectation was that the result would be a great improvement in the character of the race.[121]

Bellamy revealed the assumptions which underlay these attempts at utopia-building through eugenics in an outline for a story:

> In stirpiculture story of coming race . . . relate how pessimism had so theorized on the evil condition of the race that suicide was the fashion, and a school of thugs was established. The most cultured of the race also as a solemn duty took life whenever they could out of sheer compassion. A convention called which declares that the pessimists are right as the world stands, but that if men were physically, morally and mentally what they ought to be, life would be enjoyable. They also decide that none of the reforms, political or

118. Notebook 7, Bellamy Papers.

119. In Edward Bellamy, *Blindman's World and Other Stories* (Boston: Houghton Mifflin, 1898), pp. 389–415.

120. Morgan, *Edward Bellamy*, p. 159.

121. In Bellamy, *Blindman's World*, pp. 192–236.

social, which have been agitated since the beginning as means of ameliorating the race, have any chance of success until men are more moral and intelligent. The experiment of stirpiculture is attempted. Hope is born again among men. They see a future for the race and devote themselves with enthusiasm to the new cult.[122]

The fundamental assumption in this passage, and the one which makes Bellamy's thought at one with the older utopian tradition, is the idea that a better social order can be created only by the action of an agency outside of society and the operation of its laws, upon the mass of mankind. For reasons not necessarily of their making—force of circumstances, education, or even biological infirmity—the mass of men are imperfect and corrupt and therefore can play no role in the transformation which is to lead to their emancipation; they must be emancipated from without—"from above"—by some external agent. It was this necessarily authoritarian viewpoint that Marx rejected in all utopianism. For Marx, the domination of man over man could only be ended as the result of the process of self-emancipation in which men transformed themselves and made themselves fit for self-rule as they transformed society.[123] In the utopian perspective, in contrast, men in the mass would remain the objects of history, instead of becoming its subject.

In Bellamy's utopian view, human nature itself had to be altered first in order for political and social changes to take place: there was no dialectical interaction of these factors. Whether at the level of biology or of character, an external force had to be brought to bear upon the recalcitrant human material. In the case of Bellamy's eugenic utopias, the agency of change alternated between a philanthropic state and a dedicated "cult" or elite. Implicitly, the agent had to transcend the bonds which society and circumstances had fastened on most men, making them incapable of self-liberation. Moreover, these agents could have no particular self-interest to serve.

The successful quest for a utopia hinged upon the discovery of a *deus ex machina*—an agent which brought some special means to bear upon individual men or upon their society and thus accomplished the desired changes. The tool or means could be biological (eugenics), psychological

---

122. Quoted in Morgan, *Edward Bellamy*, p. 159.

123. For a brilliant discussion, from a Marxist standpoint, of the authoritarian nature of utopian thought see Sidney Hook, *From Hegel to Marx* (New York: Humanities Press, 1950), ch. 8, and the contrasting democratic, revolutionary view expressed in Marx's Third Thesis on Feuerbach, see pp. 288–289.

(conditioning), educational (special schools) and the agents of change might be a benevolent state, an elite, or even an impersonal, self-activating and suprahuman one, such as evolution or technology, as in *Looking Backward*. The permutations and combinations are virtually infinite. All these varieties of utopia have in common the assumption that since the mass of men cannot emancipate themselves, they must, if the world is to be improved, be freed by powers from above.[124] Both Bellamy's proposed reform of the family and his program of eugenics clearly fell within this utopian—which is to say, authoritarian—framework.

Given these characteristics of Bellamy's utopian premises, it is clear that no conception of social change through popular action could enter into his thinking. Any notion of political action or the formation of a social movement as a means to bring about the desired change was foreign to the impulse that sparked Bellamy's dreams, inasmuch as the attainment of goals through mass political or social action would involve the masses acting on their own behalf. But Bellamy believed that ordinary people were, with very few exceptions, not capable of arousing themselves to such a task, of overcoming their innate "selfishness" in the interests of harmony. Organized political action in fact (by demagogues or others) would be quite impossible, then, as well as dangerous. An unpublished manuscript of Bellamy's carried this hostility to politics and change from below to its logical conclusion: the abolition of politics altogether, and the substitution of a trained elite for popular control. In this utopia, a forerunner of *Looking Backward*, Bellamy wrote,

> There were no popular elections. . . . No one under the age of forty
> was eligible for public office. The men most eminent in their several
> professions . . . constituted a class of eligibles, from whom the gov-
> ernors were chosen by lot in order to avoid all possibility of emula-
> tion or self-seeking, and rendering pride in office absurd . . . No
> taxes. Everything is the state's. For each high office only those
> eligible who had served in the lower offices, familiarity with affairs
> being here required.[125]

Here Bellamy explicitly introduced a central theme of *Looking Backward*: the substitution of "administration" and bureaucratic control for politics and political conflict. In the socialist movement struggling to be born in the 1890s, this rejection of politics provided the focus for all of the many

124. Hal Draper, *The Two Souls of Socialism*.
125. Notebook, Bellamy Papers.

kinds of socialists who opposed the idea of building a socialist movement based upon movement from below. It was a struggle that was resolved only with the formation of the Social Democratic Party and the subsequent founding of the Socialist Party. It is this theme too that tied Bellamy's anticapitalism to Gronlund's socialism.

The Two Souls of Edward Bellamy

Looking Backward was the culmination of a private odyssey and a long process of personal political development and did not, as Bellamy himself half-thought at first, represent a total break with his earlier career. Publication meant that the private search for utopia had entered a new phase however. By making his personal troubles public, by linking his own situation, anxious and isolated, with that of millions of others, Bellamy was transformed—or transformed himself—from a private, tortured individual into a political figure and the spokesman for a political movement. The deep ambivalence with which Bellamy approached his new role is perhaps best revealed by the fact that he at first proposed to his publisher, Ticknor, that the novel be issued anonymously.[126] In a later letter, however, underscoring the growing confidence that he felt, he told Ticknor that he wished *Looking Backward* to be published under his own name.[127] Thus ideas born of a utopian desire to change mankind from above launched Bellamy into a public role and ironically, together with the popular response which his tract stimulated, subjected both the utopian and his ideas to pressures out of which a more democratic set of ideas and movement were to emerge.

Bellamy's several contradictory versions of how *Looking Backward* came to be written and his description of his motives provide clear evidence of this process. From the very first moment that *Looking Backward*'s phenomenal success brought him to the public eye, Bellamy proclaimed on every occasion that he harbored no previous connection with, or even sympathy for, any radical socialist sect or organized reform group of any kind. Bellamy presented himself to the conservative classes whom he hoped to win over to his scheme as a proper God-fearing middle-class American, not tainted by foreign—socialist—ideas or infected by any of the other perverse and dangerous notions which the

126. Bellamy to Ticknor, August 11, 1887, quoted in Green, "Edward Bellamy," pp. 60–61.
127. Ibid., October 1, 1887.

middle-class American associated with any opposition to capitalism. To the prominent reformer and writer and fellow Nationalist Thomas Wentworth Higginson, Bellamy made it clear that the new movement must be safely in the hands of men of "position and education" with intellectuals like themselves helping to form public opinion. "We shall take this subject up out of the plane of the beer saloons and out of the hands of the blatant blasphemous demagogues and get it before the sober and morally minded masses of the American people. Not until it is presented to them by men they trust will they seriously consider it on its merits."[128]

When asked by the editors of *The Nationalist* in 1890 to explain how he had come to write *Looking Backward*, Bellamy reiterated that he had had no connection with radical sects or reform organizations, nor, he confessed, had he "any particular sympathy with undertakings of the sort." Bellamy denied that he had written *Looking Backward* with the conscious intention of "attempting a serious contribution to the movement of social reform." Rather, "the idea was a mere literary fantasy, a fairy tale of social felicity. There was no thought of contriving a house which practical men might live in, but merely of hanging in mid-air, far out of reach of the sordid and material world of the present, a cloud palace for an ideal humanity."[129]

Only when he had discovered that the idea of a military organization of society was "not merely a rhetorical analogy for national industrial service, but its prototype,"[130] he told the readers of *The Nationalist*, did he hasten to share it with others. His discovery, he admitted, "led to a complete recasting, both in form and purpose, of the book I was engaged upon. Instead of a mere fairy tale of social perfection, it became the vehicle of a definite scheme of industrial reorganization."[131]

Thus Bellamy tried to convey to his audience the sense that *Looking Backward* had been written almost by chance. Yet even in this description, the utopian reform impulse which had animated him in designing a new social order was clear. The fact that the utopia suddenly became a practical scheme through the discovery of the "prototype" of the new collectivist society does not alter its essential continuity with his previous attempts to find a solution to the chaos and anarchy besetting American

128. Quoted in Schiffman, *Edward Bellamy*, p. 138.
129. "Why I Wrote *Looking Backward*," p. 199.
130. Ibid., pp. 201–203.   131. Ibid., p. 202.

society. From reform at the biological level Bellamy had turned to reform of the social circumstances which formed men and guided their actions.

In a second account, written in 1894, after the Nationalist movement had subsided, Bellamy stated that he had indeed begun the writing of *Looking Backward* in 1886, "with the definite purpose of trying to reason out a method of economic organization by which the republic might guarantee the livelihood and material welfare of its citizens on a basis of equality corresponding to and supplementing their political equality." In sharp contrast to his earlier pose, Bellamy in 1894 sought to trace the creation of *Looking Backward* to his lifelong concern with social problems. Autobiographically, he chronicled the impact which industrialization had had upon the middle class and his own career.[132]

These two contradictory versions of the genesis of *Looking Backward* reveal the ambivalence with which Bellamy undertook the role of social prophet. The contrast underscores the degree to which Bellamy was unconscious of his motivation in writing *Looking Backward* and explains the initial reluctance he displayed in taking an active part in the movement launched by the success of his book. In understanding Bellamy's personal ambivalence, it is possible to see the reasons for the two conflicting stages of Bellamy's political career following the publication of *Looking Backward*. Its success took him by surprise, launching Bellamy on a voyage which altered both the dreamer and the dreams themselves.

132. "How I Wrote *Looking Backward*," pp. 223, 217–218, 202.

2 UTOPIANISM IN THE AGE OF INDUSTRIAL CAPITALISM

There will be no tyranny or dictation—no control of the individual by the individual—no disciplining by monastic rules and regulations—no violation of individual will for the pretended good of the community—no subjection of man to arbitrary systems;—but liberty and independence—the satisfaction of all legitimate tastes and inclinations, with variety and change in order—unrestricted personal freedom, when it does not degenerate into license—free choice in occupations and social relations—no sacrifice of the individual to the mass—and adaptation of the social Organization to Man.

Albert Brisbane: *A Concise Exposition of the Doctrine of Association, or Plan for a Reorganization of Society,* 1844

Bellamy's utopianism marked a sharp departure from earlier utopian thinking in America. A generation before Bellamy wrote his tract, communitarians such as the Brook Farmers and Albert Brisbane constructed bucolic visions that capital and labor could harmonize in one great Association of Producers that would preserve both individualism and freedom while extirpating the egotistical, anti-social "individualism" of capitalist society. Such a peaceful revolution was necessary, the organ of the American Union of Associationists argued in 1846, to prevent the productive classes, "maddened by the constant contrast of their own want, care, toil, with their employer's wealth, leisure, ease," from leaguing together "in an outbreak of destructive radicalism such as earth has never seen."[1]

Chronic, violent industrial warfare made such predictions ominously real after the Civil War. Intensified fears of violence from below reshaped utopian thinking. Like the earlier utopians, Bellamy assumed that only a benevolent elite could rescue the laboring classes, so cruelly deformed by capitalism, from their own propensity to thoughtless violence and destruction and from the merciless exploitation of capital. But

---

1. *The Harbinger,* 3 (June 13, 1846; December 5, 1846), pp. 14–16, signed by William H. Channing. Reprinted in Henry W. Sams, ed., *Autobiography of Brook Farm* (Englewood Cliffs, N.J.: Prentice-Hall, 1958), pp. 187–191.

the earlier utopians, despite their belief that human nature in the mass must be transformed from above, held fast to a vision of a new and freer social order in which human personality would flower, not subordinated to some "pretended good of the Community" nor in which people would be denied the freedom to rule themselves. The leadership of an elite was seen as only a temporary stage of tutelage over the masses—an "educational dictatorship," as it were—until people were ready to assume individual responsibility for their own lives. Bellamy, however, broke with this vision. The new utopianism insisted on permanent discipline, order, and organization imposed on the unruly working class with an iron hand from above. Neither democracy nor the liberal individualism of Owen or Brisbane had any place in the new order. Instead of reorganizing society so that a humane, democratic individualism might flourish within the context of a cooperative society, the new utopians proposed to immerse the self in the larger social organism. Thereby they offered to an individualism grown impotent a vicarious sense of power, one that could no longer be found in the old and fading social order based on individual ownership of small property.

The new direction in utopian thought registered the traumatic impact of social disorder in industrial America. Above all it adjusted middle-class socialism to the new reality: the existence of a permanent class of propertyless proletarians, increasingly organized in unions militant in defense of their interests, and failing to give deference to their betters among the middle class. Such a working class had only been emerging in the decades before the Civil War, when the older brand of utopians began pondering the future. The distant fears of liberal thinkers from Jefferson to Tocqueville, no less than the early utopians, that industrialization and concentration of wealth would create a dangerous class of proletarians without a permanent stake in society had become in Bellamy's own lifetime a frightening reality for the middle class. As in England with the Fabians, and in Germany the various expressions of political antisemitism among the middle class, a strain of anticapitalism counterposed to both proletarian socialism as well as to capitalism began to emerge toward the end of the nineteenth century. In an age of industrial warfare the new society could not be brought into existence by model communities based on agricultural and handicraft production or through the gentle persuasion of workers and capitalists. For Bellamy utopia required the application of discipline, military organization, and the elimination of democracy.

Bellamy's utopia was thus more realistic and practical than earlier schemes. It offered not only a well-formulated plan detailing the precise structure of the ideal society that was to replace capitalism, but also provided a theory of how it was to arrive. This theory, as much as the specific sketch of the new bureaucratic order, was the reason that Bellamy's tract had such an impact upon the nascent radical and socialist movement of the 1890s. *Looking Backward* promised a happy ending that would avoid either a revolutionary bloodbath or a plutocratic dictatorship. Paradoxically, this happy outcome would be the necessary and inevitable result of the very tendencies toward organization which seemed so full of menace to the middle class. Bellamy recognized, to use Louis Filler's words, that "the future was with organization"[2] and it was upon the organizational demiurge that the New Jerusalem for the middle class was to be built. Organization was to be the salvation of the middle class rather than its undoing. Organization in the form of the trust, the corporation, and the omnicompetent State, collectivist and bureaucratic all, would end the anarchy of laissez faire capitalism and give to every individual, not just to those who were capable of self-organization, a place and a function in the social organism. In this way, *Looking Backward* offered an impotent, unorganized middle class threatened by organization from above and below a way out. His solution to this dilemma provides a key to the meaning of *Looking Backward*'s ideas, a clue for understanding the source of its appeal and the inner meaning of the Nationalist movement.

The Cooperative Commonwealth of Laurence Gronlund

Bellamy's authoritarian socialism was no isolated sport. Laurence Gronlund's "Anglo-Saxon Socialism," worked out in *The Cooperative Commonwealth* in 1884, prefigured the response to capitalism and the solution offered later in *Looking Backward*.[3] Gronlund's book was an im-

2. Louis Filler, "Edward Bellamy and the Spiritual Unrest," *American Journal of Economics and Sociology*, (April 1949): 244–245.

3. Laurence Gronlund, *The Cooperative Commonwealth* (1884); 2nd ed. rev. and ann. (1890). I have used the first edition as the basis of all references in this chapter, except where otherwise noted. Gronlund's other books were: *Ça Ira* (1887); *Our Destiny* (1891) (first serialized in *The Nationalist*); and *The New Economy* (1898).

portant landmark in the emergence of the native-American socialist movement. Selling over 100,000 copies in fifteen years[4] (most of them after the publication of *Looking Backward*), read by Debs and thousands of Nationalists and populists, *The Cooperative Commonwealth* exerted enormous influence among these circles because of its rejection of the class struggle and its espousal of a peculiar brand of socialism-from-above: one that differed in particular details from Bellamy's, but harmonized with the spirit of *Looking Backward*'s anticapitalism. Like Bellamy's, Gronlund's brand of socialism had been consciously refurbished for American consumption. It had been filtered through "a mind Anglo-Saxon in its dislike of all extravagancies and in its freedom from a vindictive feeling against persons who are from circumstances what they are," Gronlund boasted. Gronlund frequently invoked the name of Marx, but it is clear that his ideas were more a curious mixture of the authoritarian doctrines of Comteanism and Lassalleanism than any recognizable part of Marx.[5]

4. The figure of 100,000 may be found in *The Coming Nation*'s obituary for Gronlund (October 28, 1899). In 1887 Gronlund claimed that it had already sold some 50,000 copies, but this seems exaggerated. ("Le Socialisme aux Etats-Unis," *Revue d'Economie Politique* 1 [1887]: 109–124).

5. On Gronlund's influence and the characterization of him as a "Marxist" see Arthur Mann, *Yankee Reformers in an Urban Age* (1954), pp. 154–155, and Quint, *The Forging of American Socialism*, p. 28. Solomon Gemorah, "Laurence Gronlund's Ideas and Influence, 1877–1899" (Ph.D. diss., New York University, 1965) is a very useful but politically naive treatment of Gronlund's ideas. See also Richard Hofstadter, *Social Darwinism*, p. 114. Gronlund's advocacy of dynamite (euphemistically called "vril" in *The Cooperative Commonwealth*) was attacked by Washington Gladden in his book, *Applied Christianity* (1886), pp. 73–74, and in the second edition of *The Cooperative Commonwealth*, Gronlund hedged his views without at the same time actually disavowing them (rev. ed., 1890, p. 302). Quint terms Gronlund an "ethical idealist." Gronlund's impact on William Dean Howells and other middle-class intellectuals during the 1880s is discussed by George Arms, "Further Inquiry into Howell's Socialism," *Science and Society* 3 (Spring 1939): 245–248. Howells gave the first edition of *The Cooperative Commonwealth* a very favorable review (*Harper's Monthly* 76 [April 1888]: 801–803). Brooks Adams was also greatly influenced by Gronlund, according to Arthur F. Beringause. Beringause traces Adams' "aristocratic state socialism" in which "the state should become a giant corporation run on business principles" to Gronlund's as well as Bellamy's influence (Beringause, *Brooks Adams*, p. 287). Debs read and reviewed *The Cooperative Commonwealth* for the locomotive fireman's journal, according to Ray Ginger (*The Bending Cross* [1949], pp. 71–72). The relationship of Gronlund's work to Bellamy's political views is very much in dispute. Quint states that Bellamy had "undeniably" been introduced to some of the main facets "of scientific socialism" by Gronlund. No evidence is cited for this conclusion and it would seem that Morgan is correct in concluding that Bellamy had not read Gronlund before writing *Looking Backward* (Morgan, *Edward Bellamy*, pp. 62, 242, 372). Bellamy's own attitude toward Gronlund and his denial of having read *The Cooperative Commonwealth* may be found in a letter to Howells

Although at the time of *The Cooperative Commonwealth*'s publication, Gronlund had been a prominent member of the Socialist Labor Party, he apparently resigned from the SLP around 1890 to become an active Nationalist. Gronlund did not limit his organizational efforts to the Nationalists, however, but attempted to organize an "American Socialist Fraternity," a conspiratorial society made up of young academic intellectuals who would prepare themselves to help bring about the collapse of capitalism and the initiation of the coming collectivist social order.[6] With the decline of the Nationalist clubs after 1894, Gronlund travelled throughout the country attempting to organize an American Fabian society—an effort which came to very little in the end. Active in the formation of the Social Democracy of America in 1897, Gronlund wrote its chief piece of propaganda, a pamphlet, "Socializing a State," as well as a book, *The New Economy*, in which he advocated the Social Democracy's scheme to establish socialism in one state.[7]

Gronlund thus played an important role in the nascent American socialist movement of the 1890s and his ideas had an especially strong impact upon the Nationalist movement. His own political course was in keeping with the vision set forth in his works. The formation of the Social Democratic Party, which marked a critical break with the uto-

----

(June 17, 1888, Bellamy Papers) in which Bellamy raises objections to various aspects of Gronlund's scheme but admits that "there are certainly many resemblances between our suggestions, some of them remarkably close . . . on the other hand there are broad and essential differences." Not surprisingly, none of the differences mentioned by Bellamy deal with Gronlund's antipathy to democracy and his radical anti-individualism. A special British edition of *The Cooperative Commonwealth* was prepared by Bernard Shaw and was favorably reviewed by Annie Besant in *Our Corner* (September 1, 1885): 162–167. For Engels' offhand reaction to *The Cooperative Commonwealth*, see Marx and Engels, *Letters to Americans* (1953), pp. 146–147. Eduard Bernstein refused to review it, telling Engels that when he had finished Gronlund's chapter on "The Sphere of the State," one of the most virulently antidemocratic sections of the book, he realized that "the fellow has translated word for word whole pages from Lassalle" (Bernstein to Engels, September 24, 1884; in the Marx/Engels Archives of the International Institute for Social History, Amsterdam).

6. Information on Gronlund's life and background is sparse. See Solomon Gemorah, "Laurence Gronlund's Ideas and Influence" (1965); *The Dictionary of American Biography* 8, (pp. 14–15); the *National Cyclopedia of American Biography* 2 (p. 199); Quint, *Forging of American Socialism*, ch. 2 et passim; David T. Burbank, *Reign of the Rabble*, pp. 195–197 on Gronlund's role as "Peter Lofgreen" in the St. Louis railroad strike and takeover of the municipal government by the Workingmen's Party.

7. Quint, *Forging of American Socialism*, pp. 317–318; "Socializing a State," in *Three in One: A Trinity of Arguments on Socialism* (Chicago: The Social Democracy, n.d. [c. 1898]).

pian/authoritarian elements then extant within the native radical movement, found Gronlund, consistent with his pure Nationalist-style socialism, firmly opposed to the building of a socialist organization committed
to the expansion of democracy and based on the conscious movement of
the working class.[8]

Gronlund's idea of socialism and his analysis of capitalist society
rested upon an organicist theory of the state and society. Turning
Spencer's later ideas on their head, Gronlund attempted both to refute
the arguments of laissez faire capitalism and to establish a sound theoretical basis for his own anticapitalist doctrine. Spencer's postulate of society
as an organism, Gronlund argued, undermined Spencer's own earlier
individualistic premises. If society is an organism, then as it matures it
will be increasingly interdependent, cooperative and highly organized: it
is collectivism not individualism which is the natural outcome of evolution. Thus limiting the powers of the state is inconsistent with Spencer's
own organicist premises.[9]

Capitalism, Gronlund argued, was only a transitional age, one inferior to both slavery and feudalism because it lacked the social "unity"
which bound men together. Capitalism had destroyed this unity and
represented an era of "anarchy, of criticism, of opposition," that would
have to be succeeded by a new age of unity, socialism.[10] Socialism
represented true "Social Order" against "Social Anarchy."[11]

The evolutionary concentration of capital and the growing power
of the centralized bureaucratic state would end the anarchy of capitalism.
In the new age of unity, socialism, "everybody will again feel a dread of
living for himself only. We shall have *Corporate Responsibility*, *Equality*,
Freedom, all three combined in INTER-DEPENDENCE, SOCIAL COOPERA-
TION."[12]

The idea of the state as an organism was to be understood literally:
"It is not that the State merely resembles an organism, but it, including
with the people all the land and all that the land produces, literally IS an

8. Quint, *Forging of American Socialism*, pp. 317–318. *The New Economy* represents
Gronlund at his most extreme pitch of authoritarian, antiworking-class doctrine.
9. Gronlund, *The Cooperative Commonwealth*, pp. 79–81. I have retained all of Gronlund's abundant use of italics and his habit of capitalizing phrases or sentences he wished to
emphasize. See Hofstadter, *Social Darwinism*, pp. 114–115 for a discussion of Gronlund's
critique of social Darwinist thought.
10. Gronlund *Cooperative Commonwealth*, pp. 98–99.   11. Ibid., pp. 54, 52.
12. Ibid., ch. 3, passim, p. 98.

organism, personal and territorial."[13] Society and state are distinctive spheres only under the unnatural order of capitalism. Under the cooperative commonwealth, the state will become society, for it will then embrace the whole people. Government may be abolished, but the state can never disappear: "To dispense with the State would be to dissolve society."[14]

Like any organism the state is characterized by a functional division of labor between its various parts. In a fully developed state, each person plays a necessary and important role in its functioning. Capitalism is anarchic because of the undeveloped nature of the state. The capitalist "stomach" is gorged, while the "brains" and "hands" are starved. Under socialism, however, there would emerge "the fully developed State; the State that has incorporated in itself not only all social activities, but also the whole population; the State where every citizen is part of the Administration . . . a real, integral part, performing his share of it in the place where he is put; a State, where, . . . everyone is a public functionary, where therefore all State-help is really and truly Self-help."[15]

The freedom of the individual thus lay in his subordination to the state, which would be the embodiment of the new unity. In the new unity the individual personality, the "self," would become the manifestation of the social collectivity. The Cooperative Commonwealth, Gronlund proclaimed, would see the "upbuilding of the Organism of Humanity." Along with organized humanity there would emerge a new Religion:

> The Coming Religion will make us feel that we are here for the sake of Humanity. . . . it will make holiness consist of identifying ourselves with Humanity—the redeemed form of man—as the lover merges himself in the beloved. Individualism: the deception that we have been born into this world each for the sake of himself, or family friend or kindred. *Selfness* will be acknowledged to be the satanic element of our nature.
>
> We therefore more than doubt, we deny [Lester] Ward's proposition that individual happiness is the end of human life. . . . The end of the individual existence is to further the evolution of Humanity.[16]

The implication of this view, which Gronlund developed in greater detail in his Nationalist tract, *Our Destiny*, is that the "progress of humanity" is identical with the maturation of the social organism and can be

13. Ibid., pp. 80–81.   14. Ibid., p. 81.   15. Ibid., p. 128.
16. Ibid., p. 277.

measured by the increasing subordination of the individual to society. The complete subordination of the individual to the state is the goal of human existence: it *is* the realization of socialism for Gronlund.

The goal of communion is thus an all-important element in Gronlund's collectivism. The desire to escape from the self, to lose one's individual existence in communion with the higher and more powerful social organism is a sure sign of progress toward the cooperative commonwealth. The loneliness of human existence, the extreme fragmentation of human relationships in a society of contract, are to be replaced by a new community—one of a peculiar kind in which men do not become better able to develop their individual capacities and freedom in and through their association with others in a community of individuals, but instead become a subordinate part of the whole and give up their independence and individual personalities.[17] "Selfness," the "satanic" element of human nature, is exorcised.

The Cooperative Commonwealth is the outcome of the inevitable organic evolution of society. "Extend in your mind Division of Labor and all the other factors that increase the productivity of Labor," Gronlund asked his readers. "Apply them to *all* human pursuits as far as can be; imagine manufacturers, transportation and commerce conducted on the grandest possible scale, and in the most effective manner; then add to Division of Labor its *complement:* CONCERT; introduce adjustment everywhere where now there is anarchy; add that *central regulative system* which Spencer says distinguishes all highly organized structures, and which supplies 'each organ with blood in proportion to the work it does' and—behold the COOPERATIVE COMMONWEALTH."[18]

In the new order the domination of the capitalist will be replaced by the domination of the "brains"—the managers—who will receive material benefits commensurate with their high position. The distinction between mental and manual labor, the division between the brain and the hand, between managers and managed, the very basis of class society, is to be extended and deepened in the cooperative commonwealth, rather than abolished. In short, a new class, based on brains and education, will emerge: "socialism" requires their domination and it was to such elements, indeed, that Gronlund explicitly appealed.

Gronlund's socialism is thus bureaucratic, authoritarian, and anti-

17. Cf. Fromm, *Escape from Freedom*, chs. 5 and 6.
18. Gronlund, *Cooperative Commonwealth*, p. 102.

democratic—a species of "managerialism" differing little in intention from the totalitarian realities of the twentieth century. The capacity of the individual for intelligent insight and understanding of social relationships and the functioning of the social order—the capacity for "substantive rationality" which is the basis of the liberal democratic and Marxist belief in the possibility of self-rule—is clearly ruled out by Gronlund's organic-functionalist theory. Gronlund pointed to the rule of a new class of bureaucrats and proposed a theory of socialism that identified it with the progressive functional rationalization of society, that is to say, with the bureaucratic and collectivist elements within capitalist society.[19] This view of socialism, based on the extension of the division of labor and the permanent subordination of the working class, constituted the central theoretical premise of the authoritarian socialism launched by Gronlund and Bellamy.

Perhaps the most remarkable aspect of *The Cooperative Commonwealth*, especially from a modern standpoint, is the explicitness with which Gronlund spelled out the antidemocratic meaning of his theory. Unlike Bellamy, Gronlund used the term democracy, but gave it a meaning which the most reactionary opponents of democracy would have found unobjectionable.[20] The socialist administration of the future state, Gronlund told his readers, would be made up solely of "competent and *qualified* functionaries," whose interests, happily, would be "entirely coincident with their duty."[21] This arrangement is the very essence of "democracy." Recognizing the validity of the objection that such a definition of democracy was little more than a notion of "good" or efficient administration, Gronlund asserted that if by democracy one means the "perpetual town-meeting," then *"we must find another name for the Administration of Public Affairs under the New Social Order."* In the Cooperative Commonwealth, "the plan of counting heads will . . . be wholly unsuitable. If our public affairs *now* have altogether outgrown that primitive plan, how

19. For a discussion of "substantive" and "functional" rationality, see Karl Mannheim, *Man and Society in an Age of Reconstruction* (1940), pp. 52–56.

20. The title of the chapter on the "Administration of Affairs" in the first edition of *The Cooperative Commonwealth* was changed in the revised edition, six years later, to "A Democratic Commonwealth," although the substance of the ideas remained unaltered. The need to legitimate his ideas by the rhetorical use of "democratic" terminology reflects the shifting character of the socialist movement brought about by the same popular political upsurge, particularly populism, which also led Bellamy and the Bellamyites to adopt both the terminology and, to a degree, the substance of a more democratic viewpoint.

21. Ibid., pp. 168–169.

much more when 'public affairs' will mean all affairs with industrial affairs in the foreground?"[22] The socialist administration of the future will do away with such "primitive" ideas as voting and it will not require the expansion of democratic control from below. Implicitly, if the system of head counting was primitive, even under capitalism, then in the framework of Gronlund's evolutionary organic theory, the progressive substitution of the rule of experts and the usurpation of political control from the people were all progressive steps into the socialist future.

Yet, Gronlund insisted, the administration of the new order could legitimately be called democratic because democracy was "that form of administration where *no one* of the public officers *is at any time the master of the situation;* where, consequently, none of the public affairs can at any time be conducted with a view to private or class interests."[23] There cannot be, by definition, any private or class interests in the fully developed state; their existence could only signify the immaturity of the social organism. In the mature state, the Cooperative Commonwealth, "the whole population" will be incorporated into society. "It will destroy classes entirely. And with classes will go all 'rule.' "[24] Every individual will become a "public functionary" and cease to be a private person.[25] Between the individual as public functionary and the mature state there can be no intervening associations to mediate between the individual and the state. As long as each individual performs his proper function there can be no conflict over social decisions.[26] Without conflict, and with no choices to be made between alternative policies, there could be no function for democratic political machinery in Gronlund's scheme. Just as the health of the body must be attended to by expert physicians, so the well-being of the social organism must be determined scientifically, not politically. From this point Gronlund arrived at his final definition of democracy—one that he reiterated throughout each of his books on socialism and Nationalism: "The 'whole people' does not want, or need any government at all. It simply wants *administration—good* administration. That will be had by putting everyone in the position for which he is best fitted and making everyone aware of the fact. *That is what Democracy means: it means 'Administration by the Competent' "[27]* (my emphasis).

This definition of democracy as control over the State by an elite of

22. Ibid., p. 169.   23. Ibid., p. 162.   24. Ibid., p. 167.
25. Ibid., p. 128.   26. Ibid., pp. 255–256.   27. Ibid., p. 167.

administrators composed of the "competent," combined with the vision of the Cooperative Commonwealth as the culmination of the bureaucratic rationalization of society, completed the edifice of Gronlund's American-style socialism. It was, plainly, not a plan which had anything in common with any conception of democracy, much less of democratic socialism. The abolition of government meant, for Gronlund, nothing less than the abolition of democracy itself. The reduction of politics to a matter of technique, to "administration" by an elite, and the definition of democracy in terms of a lack of any intermediate associations, plays a critical role in the ideas of Bellamyism and thus in the section of the socialist movement that Bellamy and Gronlund helped to inspire and lead.

In providing a "fancy sketch" of the socialist administration of society, Gronlund introduced another element which was to play an important part in the ideology of the socialist movement of the 1890s as well as in the birth of progressive era political reform.[28] Recognizing the need for some check on the managers, Gronlund provided for a system of plebiscitary or sham democracy which was consistent with his belief that the majority cannot and ought not to interfere in the running of society. Laws promulgated by the elite, Gronlund explains, are to be submitted to the people to be accepted or rejected. "Rather than representation there will be the referendum."[29] "We claim that this feature represents the function which the people are fitted to perform and which it is every way expedient they should perform. They are peculiarly fitted to perform this function of ratifying, or rather of vetoing measures . . . while they are peculiarly unfitted with that which they are now constitutionally invested: that of selecting the men of whose qualifications they can know nothing for offices the duties of which they are ignorant. The people should leave the framing of laws to the wisest and most competent."[30]

This completely passive, plebiscitary, "polling democracy" conception of democracy is buttressed by Gronlund's understanding of "public opinion." With representative bodies abolished, the Board of Adminis-

28. This "fancy sketch" is, of course, the utopian architect Gronlund's attempt to lay down a plan to guide the enlightened elite, particularly the "Anglo-Saxon" who "does not want to help demolish before they know something about what is to replace the old." (Advertisement in *Ça Ira* for the first edition of the *Cooperative Commonwealth*.)

29. Ibid., p. 175.

30. Ibid., pp. 175–176. "Talent, genius and intellect," Gronlund proclaims, "will in our Commonwealth have their due influence, what they never had before" (p. 268).

trators will "form a working body, not a talking body. The people in their organic capacity will watch, stimulate, and control them, but not meddle with details. Their agents will have been put into the positions they occupy, because they know better than anybody else how to contrive the means and execute the measures demanded. They will administer the Nation's affairs as a pilot directs and handles a ship, but the direction of the Ship of State will be indicated by Public Opinion."[31] However, this public opinion cannot be formulated by permanent political parties because such parties are not compatible with the health of society, although temporary associations, if they are truly temporary, are possible.[32] Behind Gronlund's prohibition of permanent political parties—an idea which crops up in the course of the Nationalist movement and which expressed a long-standing American view of the "dangers of faction"—was the vision of a society of atomized individuals, permitted to come together temporarily on the condition that they dissolve once more into their original state.

Yet, even these "temporary" parties that Gronlund would allow are irrelevant because under the Cooperative Commonwealth, as befits a perfect organism, there would be no differences of opinion permitted. "The great need of the age is to organize, diffuse and assimilate that which is known," Gronlund explained. When this task is accomplished, "we shall again reach a substantial agreement of opinion as to this universe in which we live, what it means, and what, therefore is the part we ought to play in it. The anarchy of opinion of this transitory age is an enormous evil. Unity of opinion is the normal condition of the human intellect; *it is just as natural for healthy men to think and believe alike, as it is for healthy men to see alike*"[33] (my emphasis).

With this totalitarian notion of complete unity, Gronlund's organic evolutionary theory of society comes full circle. The yearning for communion, the fear of individual isolation, the desire to escape the anarchy of the present for the comfort and organization of the collective future, all weave together in Gronlund's utopia. Politics and free association, democracy itself, are all clearly irrelevant in a society in which all men naturally think alike. "Genuine freedom," Gronlund asserts, is "interdependence." "Instead of being a crowd, not able even to keep our streets

31. Ibid., p. 178.   32. Ibid., pp. 159–160.   33. Ibid., pp. 255–256.

clean, we shall have *organization;* instead of gregariousness we shall have association; instead of everybody pursuing his individual petty interests absolutely indifferent, and often hostile, to the interests of Society, everybody will instinctively be conscious of himself as a being who, *of course,* considers the social welfare in his every act."[34]

The foundation stone of Gronlund's theory of socialism and his hatred of democracy—as for all authoritarian currents within the socialist movement—is the idea that the workers as a class are incapable of self-emancipation and must be freed from above. The subordination of the "hands" to the "brains" in the Cooperative Commonwealth is one which the workers themselves desire. Undoubtedly reflecting the Lassallean influence in the Socialist Labor Party, Gronlund found the organized workers have "*always* been willing to acknowledge that some were wiser than themselves" and that when they "hit upon the right leaders, they have been willing to thrust their whole collective power into their hands."[35] In 1898, after a decade of class conflict, during which the forces for the emergence of both the modern trade-union movement and the Socialist Party had matured, Gronlund was driven into a rage by the workers who had begun to believe falsely that they could do without "their true superiors," the men of "ability."[36] Even Bellamy, whose earlier view of the workers' capacity for self-organization had been the same as Gronlund's, was now the object of his scorn because in *Equality* Bellamy had enjoined the workers to "Do for yourselves that which is now done by the capitalists." But that "is precisely what they cannot do," Gronlund fumed.[37] Marx's dictum, "still a law to his disciples," that the emancipation of the working class must be accomplished by the workers themselves, was fundamentally unsound and both Bellamy and Marx (who he now lumped together) simply did not understand the need the workers have for dictation by their superiors.[38]

With the working class incapable of acting for itself, how would the Cooperative Commonwealth come about and what would be the role of the workers in the process? Gronlund's answer was to formulate a theory of the inevitable, inexorable evolution of the social organism into socialism. Socialism was merely the sum total of the collectivist tendencies at

34. Ibid., p. 265.   35. Ibid., p. 170.
36. Gronlund, *The New Economy*, p. 96.
37. Ibid., p. 345.   38. Ibid., pp. 96–97.

work in society. Rather than the product of human choice and struggle, socialism would arrive, if not exactly from above, then from behind the backs of mankind. He had not, Gronlund admitted, written *The Coopera-tive Commonwealth* to "show that the socialist system is a good system." On the contrary, his point was to demonstrate that "society is moving irresis-tibly toward socialism . . . that we are going to have the socialist State whether it is good or bad, and that every active individual in our country is, consciously or unconsciously, working to that end, in some way."[39] In one form or another the emerging socialist movement of the nineties held to this fatalistic theory (for practical purposes identical to Bellamy's own), identifying socialism with the self-collectivization and statification of capi-talism and as a result found itself in a practical and theoretical dilemma that had important consequences for the development of the movement and for their ideas about what constituted "socialism."

Gronlund's organic evolutionism saved him from the contradictions of such a fatalistic theory and allowed him to explain the need for a socialist movement and, indeed, the role of his own book. "Though society is truly an organism," Gronlund explained, "the evolution of society does not take place precisely like the growth of plants or animals. The former is the result of efforts *consciously* put forth; the progress of men requires the cooperation of men." If society is an organism which evolves consciously, then it is the heroes, the great men, who are the brains of the social organism who will guide the transition to the new order.[40] The socialist movement then must be made up of a dedicated elite whose task it will be to prepare for the revolution as it "grows itself" and then "when the decisive moment has arrived act on the masses, as the power acts on the lever."[41] It is the "passion" of the working class which will provide the power to overthrow the old regime; and the trade unions are of special importance because "it is these organized labor battalions that are to form the lever by means of which the new ideas are to move society."[42]

Here, then, is the culmination of Gronlund's theory of the coming of the cooperative commonwealth. Socialism will be introduced from above by a determined minority led by the "brains" of society. It is not, nor can it be, a movement of the majority: only the self-elected minority

39. *The Cooperative Commonwealth* (2nd rev. ed.), p. 239.
40. *The Cooperative Commonwealth* (1884), pp. 262–263.
41. Ibid., pp. 10–11.   42. Ibid., pp. 271, 273.

can introduce socialism.[43] The working class is to be the battering ram, the passive instrument in the hands of the "effective minority." It is, to use Hal Draper's succinct phrase, a "socialism from above based upon a mass movement from below,"[44] and as such constitutes an important example of one variant in the long tradition of the authoritarian side of the socialist movement.

In practical terms Gronlund's views led him not only to the Nationalist movement which was organized at its inception along the elitist lines his theory pointed to. At the same time that he found himself in the Nationalist movement, which provided a new and broader audience for a new edition of *The Cooperative Commonwealth*, Gronlund began to organize his "American Socialist Fraternity." A circular written by Gronlund to attract young college men to this cause conveys fully the practical meaning of the reactionary, authoritarian, "ethical socialism" contained in Gronlund's views:

> The thought of becoming an effective force in our country's development should, surely, be a fascinating one to a young man of education. May I but get the ear of a small number of men, who admit that some generous *social* object (besides the occupation by which they gain their living) should constitute *their real life-work*! I wish to persuade them, *first*, that Socialism, under the auspices of the intelligence of the country is *providentially destined* to be our future social system (not the socialism which is in the interest only of the weak and inefficient, but that which will create *glad* and *willing obedience* in all—ORDER, and thus is even more in the interests of the competent.) *Next*, that they should form the *American Socialist Fraternity*, a private organization of intimate friends, that they may, as instruments in the hands of the Power behind Evolution realize this Socialism.
>
> Think only of the tremendous power there is in organization, in *unity*, especially when joined to a strong belief that 'the stars in their courses are fighting for us,' and you will share with me the conviction that a thousand young men, in the different centers of our country, can, by a persistent pull, IN CONCERT, in the course of, say, twenty-one years, convert our people, particularly when they start in this decade, in which, being on the threshold of the

43. Ibid., p. 266; in the 1884 edition, Gronlund saw the actions of this dedicated elite as insufficient to bring socialism to the United States. But by 1890, in the revised version of *The Cooperative Commonwealth*, he became more optimistic: "Give socialists such a minority and the future of every civilized country will be theirs!" (p. 294, rev. ed.).

44. Draper, *The Two Souls of Socialism* (1961).

twentieth century, we may reasonably expect to witness a revival of thought like unto that of the 'forties.

I lay stress on the word 'private,' and mean thereby that the fact of membership shall not be known outside this fraternity; this, principally, in order that no one's influence and usefulness may be jeopardized and lost to the cause.[45]

It would be too easy to dismiss Gronlund's ideas, as Engels did, as merely the revival of the old and discredited utopianism of the earlier part of the nineteenth century.[46] What was new in Gronlund's anticapitalist doctrine was that the development of large-scale industrial capitalism with its increasingly collectivist character had brought into existence an educated middle class without property, for whom such ideas were ready-made and to whom Gronlund could openly appeal, as later totalitarian ideologies were to do with such success. Gronlund's socialism from above, combined with the similar, but independently formulated, notions of Edward Bellamy, played a critical role in shaping the ideology of the American socialist movement that was coalescing in the 1890s. As the expression of a new anticapitalist ideology that held up as its ideal a bureaucratic, rather than democratic, collectivist society, a bureaucratic utopianism, appealing to elements in the middle classes who felt that there was no longer any place for them within capitalist society, these ideas and the organized current which they stimulated assume a significance which transcends the immediate circumstances of their origin.

The Bureaucratic Utopia: Looking Backward

Every utopia is an attempt to find a solution in the imagination to problems perceived in the author's own world. The particular form and content of the imaginary world, the idealized society, tell us at least as much about the author himself and his relationship to his own society as about the ideal itself. Moreover, the details of the desired new order, drawn as it must be from contemporary reality and set in opposition to it, offer signposts along the road leading to the future. Bellamy's indictment of capitalism and his theory of the arrival of the new collectivist society provided that direction for the nascent socialist movement. By examining in detail the terms of his indictment and the theory contained

45. The Folwell Papers, Box 35, University of Minnesota. See the discussion and excerpt from this same document in Joseph Dorfman, *The Economic Mind in American Civilization*, vol. 3, *1865–1918* (1949).
46. Engels, *Letters to Americans*, pp. 146–147.

within it, it is possible to grasp the larger political and social meaning of Bellamy's utopian tract; to go beyond an understanding of it as a mere literary production and thereby to be able to comprehend the practical translation and role of its ideas in the politics and organization of the Nationalist movement.

Capitalism as Disorganization

Bellamy's brilliantly presented image of capitalist society at the end of the nineteenth century as a coach, jolting along a rutted road, succinctly conveys his view of life under the competitive order.[47] Those who ride on top of the coach serenely observe the scenery, and their position protects them from the mud and the dust. Below are the straining masses of men who are driven by Hunger to pull at the coach and to serve the needs and whims of the passengers on top. When the coach must be pulled over a rough stretch, or up a steep hill, those on the top shout encouragement to the men straining at the ropes below, offering the consolation of a better life in the hereafter to the toiling masses as compensation for their poor, bitter lot in this world. In time, the distance between those on top and those below increases because the former imagine they are of a "finer clay" and that their position, therefore, is the consequence of some inherently superior quality.

The parable of the coach is Bellamy's version of the social-Darwinist catch phrase, "the survival of the fittest." But the values of the laissez faire ethic are reversed. Not only does the smooth ride of those on the top depend upon the unrewarded and unremitting toil of the workers who are forced by circumstance to work in the mud of the road, but the moral qualities which enable them to climb to the top and to keep their seats are shown to be in keeping more with brute nature, than with individual talent or moral worth. In addition the ability to reach the top and to remain there can depend upon an accident of birth, for position can be inherited, and need not be earned. The ruling class, moreover, also performs no useful function, contrary to the self-justifying claims of social Darwinism. The riders are purely parasitical. The characteristics they believe mark them off from the common herd are not the product of their inherent worth as individuals, but merely pass into their possession as the result of the suffering of the masses, whose labor makes it possible for them to devote themselves to self-cultivation.

47. *Looking Backward*, pp. 3–5.

Yet, for all its advantages, sitting on top of the coach is precarious. With each shake, men tumble from the very top down to the road where they must immediately take up the burden or starve. Here is a society in which a man must "plunge into the foul fight,—cheat, overreach, supplant, defraud, buy below worth and sell above, break down the business by which his neighbors fed his young ones, tempt men to buy what they ought not and to sell what they should not, grind his laborers, sweat his debtors, cozen his creditors. Though a man sought it carefully with tears, it was hard to find a way in which he could earn a living and provide for his family except by pressing in before some weaker rival and taking the food from his mouth."[48] If Bellamy's era was the age of individualism, then the New Jerusalem would be the age of "concert."[49] In the former, the individual exists only as a part of an "unorganized throng of men," finding "a place for himself anywhere he chose if he were strong enough."[50] For the weak, brute nature leaves no useful role to play. Its law is eat or be eaten. In the age of concert, by contrast, "everybody is part of a system with a distinct place and function"[51]

Capitalism to Bellamy is laissez faire capitalism: individualistic, entrepreneurial capitalism, with the state consigned to watch over the contenders, and the economic system is only the expression of the human instinct of selfishness. Such a system of "unorganized and antagonistic industries was as absurd economically as it was morally abominable":

> Selfishness was their [capitalism's] only science, and in industrial production selfishness is suicide. Competition which is the instinct of selfishness, is another word for dissipation of energy, while combination is the secret of efficient production. . . . Even if the principle of share and share alike for all men were not the humane and rational basis for a society, we should still enforce it as economically expedient, seeing that until the disintegrating influence of self-seeking is suppressed no true concert of industry is possible.[52]

For Bellamy, as for Gronlund, the antipodes of modern society are disorganization or anarchy versus organization or "combination." Only in a collectivist society could the higher, nonselfish characteristics of mankind prevail.

It is important to recall here the ideas in *The Religion of Solidarity*, for it is clear that underlying Bellamy's conception of the competitive order as the embodiment of selfishness is the theme of communion

48. Ibid., p. 226.   49. Ibid., p. 122.   50. Ibid., p. 143.
51. Ibid.   52. Ibid., pp. 198–199.

expressed in that document. In *The Religion of Solidarity*, Bellamy sought to find a solution for the unbearable feelings of isolation and impotence not by reasserting individualism, but by blotting out individual personality through communion with an impersonal universe. In *Looking Backward* it is the age of concert, the age of organized society, which provides a place and a function for every individual. The metaphysical yearning had found an economic and social form in which to express itself.

Just as Bellamy had stressed the impersonal character of the universe that was to overcome the narrow selfness of the individual, the mere personal identity, so he now looked to the impersonal bureaucratic order of his utopia in which to find communion, to lose the self. The judicial system, in which the accused person feels internally compelled to confess his transgressions, and in which no third party, the hired defense lawyer, can be allowed to come between the accused and the state in order to act as the agent for the accused criminal's purely personal or private interests, is a critical illustration of Bellamy's solution to the problem of attaining "solidarity," or in our terms, *communion*. In the relationship between the accused person and his accuser, society, no barriers of a purely private or personal sort can be allowed to remain: even the accused feels morally compelled to place society's interests above his own.[53]

53. Bellamy's lifelong interest in jury reform and in abolition of the advocate system along with the presumption of innocence, an interest which is reflected in articles written for the *Springfield Union* during the 1870s (see the discussion in Bowman, *The Year 2000*, pp. 230–232), and embodied in *Looking Backward*, was consistently carried forward in his Nationalist period. An examination of articles which Bellamy wrote for *The New Nation* provides additional evidence for the conclusion stated here. Bellamy complains that "there is no civilized land in which technicality and legal finesse are permitted to delay, confuse and defeat the administration of law in criminal cases as they are in the United States." The root cause of these delays (and the resulting frustration which leads to lynching) is "the admission of the mercenary motive into the administration of law by the toleration of advocates hired by prisoners and interested, not in the furtherance of justice, but the acquittal by all and any means of the accused persons who hire them. . . . He [the private advocate] is the officer and agent of the prisoner of the bar, who, if guilty, has every motive to defeat the purpose of the court." The solution—the same presented in *Looking Backward*—illustrates the translation of Bellamy's utopia into everyday political and social proposals: "No one . . . would wish to deprive an accused person of a fair defense, *but the cause of the people against the accused is certainly as important as that of the accused against the people*, and if a public prosecutor suffices to protect the interest of the people, surely a public defender, equally without private interest in the case, is all the accused can reasonably ask. . . . It should be his [the public defender's] business to present the prisoner's side in every case brought to the bar, without charge to the prisoner, *who should be allowed to have*

Only by thus obliterating one's "selfishness" can the self and society become one: the unit and the collectivity can at last be indissolubly welded together. In the terms of *The Religion of Solidarity*, the mere personality, that which makes the individual apparently unique, but only apparently, is made to reach the higher state of impersonal existence. This goal of perfect communion is achieved for society as a whole, of course, in Bellamy's utopia, by the device of the Industrial Army. As in Gronlund's socialism, Bellamy's collectivist utopia solves the problem of the relation of the individual to society by dissolving the former into the latter, completely and perfectly.

The terms in which the indictment of the competitive order is couched are equally revealing. Bellamy's utopia is no less hierarchically organized than the society of the coach: it is merely that a different and, for Bellamy, higher principle of organization provides the foundation for the new elite. The flaw in the competitive system, its jungle morality, is that there is no real relationship between reward and virtue, *real* virtue. Those at the top are a "plutocracy," that is, their only merit is the possession of wealth. Even if that wealth were gained by their own efforts, and not inherited, it only reflects their capacity for success in the "foul fight" of capitalist life. The competitive system places a premium on acquisitiveness and selfishness which is both morally wrong *and* industrially inefficient. In the words of Thorstein Veblen, who was deeply influenced by *Looking Backward*, the "pecuniary" virtues are rewarded, while the "industrial" or productive talents are ignored. For those with nonpecuniary intelligence or talents, success in this system requires that they subordinate these qualities to the worship of Mammon. If one cannot, as Bellamy could not, for ethical or circumstantial reasons, participate in the system of organized selfishness, one is displaced, functionless.

---

no other counsel in court." The result would be "that the presentation of the prisoner's case would be fair, temperate and adequate, but that no special pleading or devices would be employed to delay or defeat justice" (my emphasis). (*The New Nation* 2, no. 27 [July 2, 1892]: 419–420; see also vol. 2, no. 28 [July 9, 1892]: 494, and vol. 3, no. 17 [April 29, 1893].) This particular example is an excellent illustration too of our point that Bellamy's utopia contains signposts which indicate concrete social reforms that point to the author's concept of social progress under the existing system. In utopia, no private interests are to be allowed to interfere with "justice"; in real-life nineteenth-century America, it is progress to subordinate the interests of the individual to the state. Cf. the discussion of "unitary democracy" in Chapter 1, above.

Bellamy's indictment of commercialism—the rejection of pecuniary values, the vivid portrait of life in a "wolfish" society, and the denial of the "survival of the fittest" as a moral foundation for society— add up to a powerful critique of capitalism which deeply moved readers then and since. Yet, though Bellamy rejected capitalism and moved people with his moral indignation, his alternative was neither humanistic or democratic. For Bellamy's bureaucratic utopia, like his rejection of capitalism, expressed *ressentiment* in reaction to the values of laissez faire capitalism without a genuine transvaluation of its values.[54] Instead of envisioning a new order based on nonmaterialistic and democratic values, Bellamy only inverted the structure of reward, substituting a new principle of hierarchy, merit, in the place of the old pecuniary standards. The supposed essence of capitalism, selfishness, is not transcended but only suppressed through a system of mechanical, forced economic equality. Rather than the plutocracy, a new elite of talent would run society. This current is found, of course, among admirers of contemporary totalitarian societies who have no sympathy with the masses of people, despise democracy, and admire a social order which they believe rewards the nonpecuniary talents which capitalism denigrates. To use the formula which Marx applied to the "crude communism" of the early utopian socialists, Bellamy's collectivist utopia was only the "positive annulment of private property," rather than its "positive transcendence," i.e., humanistic communism. Like crude communism, Bellamy's utopia was "merely one form in which the vileness of

54. "Ressentiment . . . does not involve a genuine change in values. [It] involves a sour grapes pattern which asserts merely that desired but unattainable objectives do not actually embody the prized values. . . . one condemns what one secretly craves . . ." (Robert Merton, "Social Structure and Anomie" [1957]: 155–156). Bellamy's early railings against "luxury" and "extravagance" clearly fall within this psychological pattern. See also Svend Ranulf, *Moral Indignation and Middle Class Psychology* (New York: Schocken Books [paperback], 1964). Politically, Bellamy translated this into an insistence on exact equality of material reward and, of course, this in turn would reinforce the organic solidarity or communion which is at the center of Bellamy's utopia. Exact equality of reward, Bellamy explained, "is logically involved in the idea of extending the public or national administration over productive and distributive functions. It is an axiom that the state or nation in all its relations to citizens can be no respecter of persons. All public administration is invariably for the equal benefit of all persons. . . . Evolution toward . . . [the coming] order is strictly the evolution of the nation, the completer realization of the national idea, already so strongly rooted in the experience and sentiment of humanity" (*The New Nation* 2, no. 32 [August 6, 1892]: 498–499).

private property, which wants to set itself up as the *positive community*, comes to the surface."[55]

Bellamy's treatment of the working class makes clear his failure to transcend the class nature of the society he despised. If the concentration of capital posed a threat to the middle class from above, the "labor question" threatened to "devour society" from below. Throughout *Looking Backward*, strikes and class conflict between organized workers and business take the center of the stage as the major problem of the old society.

Although the struggles and suffering of the workers earn Bellamy's sympathy and are viewed as the natural result of the blindness, stupidity, and greed of the competitive system, the workers pose an enormous danger to society. Workers, Bellamy argued, "knew nothing of how to accomplish" the necessary changes. Moreover, "the eager enthusiasm with which they thronged about anyone who seemed likely to give them light on the subject lent sudden reputation to many would-be leaders, some of whom had little enough light to give."[56] The workers could only make "a sad mess of society. They had the votes and the power to do so if they pleased, and their leaders meant they should."[57] The result of their efforts would be a descent into social chaos.

The "educated classes" despised manual labor, Bellamy observed, for "manual labor meant association with a rude, coarse, and ignorant class of people."[58] Dr. Leete, the spokesman for the new society, wonders aloud to Julian West how the educated classes could consider "life worth living . . . surrounded by a population of ignorant, boorish, coarse, wholly uncultivated men and women." While the rich and cultured may have been objects of envy in the nineteenth century, in the twenty-first century, living as they did, surrounded by squalor and brutishness, "they seemed little better off" than the poor. "The cultured man in your age was like one up to the neck in a nauseous bog solacing

55. Karl Marx, *Economic and Philosophic Manuscripts of 1844* (Moscow: Foreign Languages Publishing House, 1959), pp. 99–101. "General *envy* constituting itself as a power is the disguise in which *avarice* re-establishes itself and satisfies itself, only in *another* way. . . . in the form of envy and the urge to reduce to a common level, so that this envy and urge even constitute the essence of competition. The crude communism is only the consummation of this envy and of this levelling-down proceeding from the preconceived minimum" (p. 100).

56. *Looking Backward*, p. 8.

57. Ibid., pp. 9–10.   58. Ibid., p. 177.

himself with a smelling bottle."[59] The workers, therefore, in Bellamy's view, were not only incapable of their own emancipation, but also a potential mob that might erupt under the pressure of social and economic exploitation. The consequences of their actions, however justified their grievances might be, could only be riot and ruin.

Given this idea of the working class as a brutish mass Bellamy was required to find a means of attaining a collectivist society without running the risk of unleashing the masses of workers as an independent force. Rather than socialism through political and social struggle from below, Bellamy had to discover the path to a collectivist society that would give the dominant position to the middle class. To educate and arouse that middle class was one of Bellamy's main purposes—a middle class he and others of like mind conceived as enlightened, cultured, and educated, and above all, disinterested.

In contrast to those middle class proponents of antimonopoly legislation, who looked to the resurrection of the golden age of free competition, Bellamy saw in the growing collectivization of American capitalism not only the possibility of more efficient production, but also of the transformation of laissez faire into a collectivist utopia. "The concentration of management and unity of organization" of the trusts provided the key to salvation for the middle class. From the imaginary vantage point of the year 2000, Bellamy observed that "the movement toward the conduct of business by larger and larger aggregates of capital, the tendency toward monopolies, which had been so desperately and vainly resisted, was recognized at last, in its true significance, as a process which only needed to complete its logical evolution to open a golden future to humanity."[60] All bitterness toward the corporation and those identified with it would cease as soon as people recognized "their necessity as a link, a transition phase, in the evolution of the true industrial system." The next logical step after formation of the trusts was for the Nation to take control of the economy.

> The industry and commerce of the country, ceasing to be conducted by a set of irresponsible corporations and syndicates of private persons at their caprice and for their profit, were entrusted to a single syndicate representing the people, to be conducted in the common interest for the common profit. The Nation, that is to say, organized as the one great business corporation in which all other corporations

59. Ibid., p. 126.   60. Ibid., p. 41.

were absorbed; it became the one capitalist in the place of the other capitalists, the sole employer, the final monopoly in which all previous and lesser monopolies were swallowed up, a monopoly in the profits and economies of which all citizens shared. The epoch of trusts had ended in the Great Trust. In a word, the people of the United States concluded to assume the conduct of their own business, just as one hundred odd years before, they had assumed the conduct of their own government, organizing now for industrial purposes on precisely the same grounds that they had then organized for political purposes.[61]

The transition to the new socialist order, therefore, would not be the consequence of a protracted struggle—certainly not any struggle on the part of the workers. There would be, happily, neither violence nor bloodshed. Nor would it require a conscious movement by a particular section or class of the population to bring about the new order. Instead, it would silently arrive, inevitably and inexorably, piece by piece, as the automatic consequence of the convergence of the collectivist tendencies within capitalism itself and the acceptance of the new order by members of all classes, high and low.

Bellamy's collectivist utopia was nothing more—nor less—than the sum total of the rationalization and bureaucratization of capitalist enterprise capped off by state ownership. Each step in that direction—the formation of a new corporation, the replacement of an individually run enterprise by one presided over by a professional manager, the creation of a new trust—were all steps toward socialism. Dr. Leete explains how the labor question was thus solved: "I suppose we may claim to have solved it. Society would indeed have fully deserved being devoured if it had failed to answer a riddle so entirely simple. In fact, to speak by the book, it was not necessary for society to solve the riddle at all. It may be said to have solved itself. The solution came as a result of a process of industrial evolution which could not have terminated otherwise. All that society had to do was to recognize and cooperate with that evolution, when its tendency had become unmistakable."[62] The logic of this theory pointed to the conclusion that Nationalism could be introduced without the consent, let along the participation, of the mass of people. It was preferable, of course, that the overwhelming majority assent to the changeover, as Bellamy hoped they would. Yet, the perversity of the masses, should that prove an obstacle, could not be permitted to stop an elite from imposing

61. Ibid., pp. 41–42.   62. Ibid., p. 35.

collectivism from above. However, Bellamy's emphasis upon the impersonal side of the evolutionary process shielded him for a time from having
to confront this conclusion. Bellamy recognized, albeit by the back door,
some possible role for deliberate human action in social transformation.
But, like Gronlund, he found himself caught in the contradiction of trying
to reconcile a fatalistic theory of social development with the belief that
men can make history. On the whole, however, from the beginning the
emphasis was on the automatic arrival of collectivism. A regular column in
Bellamy's paper, *The New Nation*, "The Nationalistic Drift," reporting the
latest mergers and combinations, as well as the latest moves toward municipal or national ownership of industry, demonstrated that it did not
matter whether these were the work of English municipalities or the
Russian Czar or Bismarck.[63] The title was self-explanatory: the new order
was emerging without the need for a conscious political and social movement, without even acceptance by the majority of people. Whether or not
the state which undertook to run industry was itself democratic was irrelevant. Once the process reached its logical conclusion, once the greatest
trust of all, the organism truly above class selfishness, the State, claimed
ownership, the perfect bureaucratic society would fully emerge, shorn of
commercialism and selfishness.

Despite Bellamy's stress on the automatic process by which the
new order would arrive, there is also a vague and contradictory reference, superimposed upon his basic theory, to a "national party" which
plays a role in the transition. Dr. Leete explains that the new party arose
to institute the new order once economic concentration had reached the
point when all but the most stubborn realized that a return to laissez
faire was impossible and impracticable. The National Party, however,
was neither a class nor a labor party:

> The labor parties, as such, never could have accomplished anything
> on a large or permanent scale. For purposes of national scope, their
> basis as merely class organizations was too narrow. It was not till a
> rearrangement of the industrial and social system on a higher ethical
> basis, and for the more efficient production of wealth, was recog-
> nized as the interest, not of one class, but equally of all classes, of
> rich and poor, cultured and ignorant, old and young, weak and

63. The following entry, quoted in its entirety, is typical of this column's content:
"The Freeland-Loomis Company, proprietors of the Continental Clothing house at Boston
and of many western branches, has been incorporated with a capital stock $300,000" (*The
New Nation* 1, no. 2 [February 7, 1891]).

strong, men and women, that there was any prospect it would be achieved. Then the national party arose to carry it out by political means. . . .[64]

The mission of the national party is to achieve the total integration of society and eliminate all disharmony. The name of the party itself, Bellamy explains, derives from the inclusion of *all* classes within its ranks and from its attempt to realize "the idea of the nation with a grandeur and completeness never before conceived, not as an association of men for certain merely political functions affecting their happiness only remotely and superficially, but as a family, vital union, a common life, a mighty heaven-touching tree whose leaves are its people, fed from its veins, and feeding it in turn. . . ."[65]

In short, the "party" would be an amalgamation of all classes and men of good will: a party above parties and, indeed, above "politics." In this way, every person united with every other person in an organic union, politics and strife would simply wither away, for politics and political divisions were assumed to be an expression of selfishness that the new collectivist society suppressed. *Any* party, therefore, not only a labor party, which set class against class, even the "producers" against the "plutocracy," would be incompatible with the kind of society Bellamy envisioned. For this reason, even the rich must join the work of reconstruction. By contrast, conventional parties raised the specter of class conflict that endangered the middle class and threatened to bring chaos. A classless party would thus save the middle class from destruction.

Following Bellamy's lead, the Nationalist clubs were not conceived of as "political" organizations, but seen instead as the first organized expressions of the ethical-utopian impulse which would in time inspire individuals from all classes to accept and work for the new order. Exactly what this work would be and what steps might be taken Bellamy did not specify. Once the Nationalists began to educate others, however, even in the gentlest manner, abusing no class of persons and speaking only in the most ethical tones, their efforts generated opposition and step-by-step they were pulled—despite the protests of many founders— into "politics." Once in politics, the contradiction between a political movement and the automatic collectivism of Bellamy's original theory became inevitable.

64. *Looking Backward*, pp. 206–207.
65. Ibid.

Bellamy's conception of the role of the collectivist tendencies within capitalism stands in sharp contrast to Marx's. For Marx the "socialization" of capital and the concomitant intervention of the capitalist state does not represent the abolition of the capitalist mode of production as such, but a basic contradiction within capitalism. The socialization of production, and the enormous rise in productive capacity of mature capitalism, merely provide the objective preconditions for socialism. The expansion of the state and the state bureaucracy into an organism "above society" and the ownership by the state of the means of production and exchange are not steps into socialism, but only the expression of growing class antagonisms within the framework of capitalist society.[66] Engels, in a comment applicable to Bellamy, notes the rise of a "spurious kind of socialism . . . that without more ado declares *all* state ownership, even of the Bismarckian sort, to be socialistic."[67] Socialism could not be established step by step *within* capitalism, as the mere "logical" summation of the collectivist tendencies in the organization of capitalism. Socialism required the formation of a conscious movement based upon the class struggle, the object of which would be the conquest of political power by the working class and the "establishment of democracy," by the "self conscious, independent movement of the immense majority, in the interests of the immense majority."[68] The workers could not be emancipated from above. Through the self-transforming revolutionary struggle necessary to reach socialism, the workers would become capable of establishing and ruling in a new social order in which the authoritarian social relations obtaining in capitalist society could be dissolved.

For Bellamy, every advance in organization, planning, and rationalization of production—that is, those tendencies most closely associated with the bureaucratization and statification of economic and political institutions—were tendencies unambiguously evolving into the kind of collectivist society he portrayed in *Looking Backward*. At the end of the evolutionary road would be the logical outcome—the "Great Trust"—a bureaucratic state organizing the economy and shutting out all forms of

66. Marx, *Capital* (Moscow: Foreign Languages Publishing House, 1959), vol. 3, p. 429, ch. 27; Engels, *Socialism: Utopian and Scientific*, in *Selected Works of Marx and Engels* (Moscow: Foreign Languages Publishing House, 1955), vol. 2, pp. 146–150. "The transformation, either into joint-stock companies and trusts, or into state ownership, does not do away with the capitalistic nature of the productive force" (p. 148).

67. Engels, *Socialism: Utopian and Scientific*, pp. 147–148.

68. "The Communist Manifesto," in *Marx-Engels Selected Works*, vol. 1, p. 44.

self-government. Implicitly, attempts at state intervention into the economy, the growth of state bureaucracy and state-owned enterprises, all of which removed the individual capitalist and the profit motive that hindered true organization, were steps toward the desired collectivization of society. Theoretically, then, Bellamy's view is very similar to Bernstein's revisionism or to the Fabians' view of socialism emerging step by step within capitalism, except that for Bernstein, at any rate, the process would not be automatic but dependent on the struggle of the working class. Nor did Bernstein envision the diminution of democratic political controls as did Bellamy.[69] Bellamy, as it were, stripped Marxism of its revolutionary democratic character and turned it to a kind of technological and organizational fatalism designed to avoid a mass movement and the democratic reorganization of society by the working class.

The Industrial Army: Model Bureaucracy

Bellamy thus did not casually overlook democracy and democratic controls in his utopian design. He consciously envisioned a bureaucratic social order emerging out of the trust and the state, and it was on this development that he pinned his hopes. Bellamy's socialism meant the bureaucratic statification of the economy and society. The most common criticism of Bellamy's utopia—that the central institution, the industrial army, which for all practical purposes is the state, introduces a "militaristic" note into an otherwise gentle utopia—misses the point entirely.[70]

Fundamental to Bellamy's choice of the army as a model for the structure of his collectivist society is its perfection of bureaucratic organization, absence of pecuniary motives, and efficiency. For Julian West, a military parade in Boston in 1887 pointed the way to utopia:

> A regiment was passing. It was the first sight in that dreary day which inspired me with any other emotions than wondering pity and amazement. Here at last were order and reason, an exhibition of what intelligent cooperation can accomplish. The people who stood looking on with kindling faces,—could it be that the sight had for them no more than but a spectacular interest? Could they fail to see

---

69. Bernstein based his argument for "evolutionary socialism" upon the passages quoted above from *Capital*. See Peter Gay, *The Dilemma of Democratic Socialism* (1950), ch. 8, esp. pp. 214–216. Gay's observation that "Marx and Bernstein could take the same idea and make it serve opposite ends" (fn. 1, p. 214) is of course applicable to Bellamy and to the entire tradition of bureaucratic socialism.

70. See, for example, Daniel Aaron's Comments in *Men of Good Hope*, pp. 110–111.

that it was their perfect concert of action, their organization under one control, which made these men the tremendous engine they were, able to vanquish a mob ten times as numerous? Seeing this so plainly, could they fail to compare the scientific manner in which the nation went to war with the unscientific manner in which it went to work?[71]

Bellamy seized upon the model of the military not only because it solved the labor question (who had ever heard of a strike in the army?), but because it exemplified the kind of relationship of the individual to the social organism that he desired. Moreover, it was a familiar model— especially in the post–Civil War years—by which to demonstrate the feasibility of replacing capitalist anarchy with a planned society run by an elite not motivated by the desire for personal gain but by honor and duty. "I confess," Bellamy wrote in 1890, "an admiration of the soldier's business as the only one in which, from the start, men throw away the purse and reject every sordid standard of merit and achievement."[72]

The modern military system was the "prototype" not only because it provided the sense of national unity, above and beyond class or party, but also because, Bellamy pointed out, it furnished "at once a complete working model for its organization, an arsenal of patriotic and national motives and arguments for its animation, and the unanswerable demon-stration of its feasibility drawn from the actual experience of whole nations organized and manoeuvered as armies."[73] These motives would impel the workers in the industrial army in the same way that they do the soldier. "The army of industry is an army, not alone by virtue of its perfect organization," Bellamy proclaimed, "but by reason also of the ardor of self-devotion which animates its members."[74] Unlike the capital-ist system, "diligence in the national service is the sole and certain way to public repute, social distinction, and official power. The value of a man's services to society fixes his rank in it."[75] Thus the values of the old order are turned upside down: the rewards of status, position, and power would go to those who really deserve them. Neither "wanton luxury" nor material need would continue to motivate men. These devices were,

71. *Looking Backward*, pp. 264–265.

72. Bellamy, *"Looking Backward* Again," in *Edward Bellamy Speaks Again!*, pp. 188–189.

73. Bellamy, "Why I Wrote *Looking Backward*," in *Edward Bellamy Speaks Again!*, p. 201.

74. *Looking Backward*, p. 76.   75. Ibid.

in any case, "weak and uncertain" insofar as they were relics of capitalist barbarism.[76] The industrial army would create a just relationship between virtue and one's position in society: "the honors and distinctions, the offices of rank and authority in the army of industry and in the nation, are allotted to men and women according to their comparative diligence or brilliancy or achievement, to the end that the fittest may lead and rule, and all be encouraged by the hope of honorable distinction to do their best."[77]

Democracy had no place in this model of social organization, no more than it could in the corporation, the trust, or the state. The individual was less and less capable of exercising reason and control in a complex industrial society, but "reason" would govern a society bureaucratically organized. The individual was sinking into impotence in the capitalist order, unable through free association with others to become more powerful. But by absorption into the impersonal collectivity of a bureaucratic society one could become strong vicariously, as a functional part of a "tremendous engine." Allowing the multitude to participate in the running of industry or to vote for those who would run the entire society would be inefficient, undermine "discipline," and mean that the "fittest" would not rule any more than they did under the prevailing system of universal suffrage.

The use of the army as his model reveals both the authoritarian character of Bellamy's utopian reform and his need for a convincing working model of the collectivist society he envisioned. If the workers and the vast majority were a brutish mass, there could be no question of forming a political movement out of them, nor of giving over to them the task of creating a socialist society. The new insitutions would not be created and shaped from below but would, of necessity, correspond to the plan laid down in advance by the utopian planner. Human nature, Bellamy made clear in *Looking Backward*, would not change under the new order. Only new motives, not dependent upon the profit motive, take the place of the old; the "good" side of human nature comes to the fore and the "bad" side, selfishness, is suppressed.[78] The model of the industrial army thus imposed external discipline, suppressing the in-

76. Ibid.
77. Bellamy, "Brief Summary of the Industrial Plan of Nationalism Set Forth in *Looking Backward* for Class Study," in *The Dawn* 1, no. 5 (Sept. 15, 1899): 3.
78. *Looking Backward*, pp. 45–46, 57.

eradicable selfish pecuniary motives in human nature, thereby avoiding democratic participation, which the discovery of the self-collectivization of capital had rendered unnecessary in any case.

Bellamy's utopianism thus translated into everyday politics quickly gave birth to an American variety of what Erich Fromm aptly terms "managerialism," or to use the parlance of the late nineteenth century, "state socialism." The political convergence of Bellamy's utopian spirit with the dry-as-dust bureaucratic reasoning of a Sidney Webb, can only seem an unfathomable paradox to those for whom "utopianism" is always associated with a libertarian spirit. Once, however, it is understood that both assume that the mass of men are incapable of self-emancipation and need not, in any case, be consulted because the plan for the new socialist order has already been carefully worked out by those who know what is good for the people, then all that remains is to find a device or technique to usher in the new order. It is preferable to have the consent, if not the participation, of the people, but it can be done without it if necessary. Whether by means of a philanthropic elite, by the permeation of Fabians and their ideas into capitalist institutions, or through the discovery, as in Bellamy's case, that organization brings the new order, there is no need for democratic politics. Walter Lippmann recognized in 1914 the common ground between the utopian and the "practical" reformer: "The bureaucratic dreams of reformers often bear a striking resemblance to the honest fantasies of the utopians. What we are coming to call State Socialism is in fact an attempt to impose a benevolent governing class on humanity. Oh, for wise and powerful officials to bring order out of chaos, end the 'muddle,' and make men clean, sober, and civic-minded. There is no real understanding of democracy in the State Socialist, for he doesn't attempt to build with the assent and voluntary cooperation of men and women. But he avoids the laborious and disheartening method of popular education, and takes satisfaction in devising a ruling class, inspired by him, as a short-cut to perfection."[79]

Inspired in part by Gronlund's *Cooperative Commonwealth* as well as Bellamy's *Looking Backward*, the last feeble manifestations of socialist colonies in the United States—Ruskin in Tennessee, Kaweah in California, as well as the ill-starred attempt by the remnants of the American Railway

---

79. Walter Lippman, *Drift and Mastery* (New York: Mitchell Kennerly, 1914), pp. 320–321. See Lippman's incisive analysis of the utopian mentality, pp. 318–319.

Union and the Social Democracy of America to colonize a state for social-ism—shared with the "managerial" socialists the belief that it was possible to "avoid the laborious and disheartening method of popular education" through the shortcut of building socialism in a single colony, as the nu-cleus of the coming society in the midst of the old. Both "state socialism," then, as well as the utopian colonies of the 1890s, were the legitimate offspring of Gronlund's and Bellamy's authoritarian socialism.[80]

The Corporation as Utopia

Bellamy's choice of the military as his model of the new collectivist society poses a question of some importance, given the later rise of social-ists who were to point to the corporation itself as the model of the perfect bureaucratic society. Such a conception was not incompatible with Bel-lamy's ideas and in fact, it will be seen, socialists and social reformers who were Bellamy's direct lineal descendants ideologically did adopt such a model even before the turn of the century.[81] It is a problem which takes on additional significance given the rise in the 1950s and 1960s of "neocor-poratist" liberals such as A. A. Berle, who was a fervent admirer of Bel-

80. On the utopian colonies and the S.D. of A., see Quint, *Forging of American Socialism*, chs. 6, 9; Kipnis, *The American Socialist Movement*, ch. 4. On Kaweah colony, see R. U. Hine, *California's Utopian Colonies* (San Marino, Calif.: Huntington Library, 1953), ch. 5. Bellamy personally was consistently hostile to the idea of establishing socialist colonies, pointing out the need for a "national" solution. The reasoning of the procoloniza-tion faction, which may be found in the pages of *The Coming Nation*, nevertheless began with Bellamy's own premises. If the trust was an almost-socialistic institution within capitalism, then a real cooperative enterprise owned by the producers themselves had to be regarded as a genuine step into socialism—a nucleus of the coming order. The idea of capturing an entire state in the West for socialism was simply the extension of this idea of outflanking capitalism. As an idea it reappears, of course, in the Wobblies' slogan of "building the new society in the shell of the old" (and their association with proponents of scientific management), and the EPIC campaign of Upton Sinclair.

81. See James Gilbert's important study, *Designing the Industrial State*, for a discus-sion of some of the currents analyzed here. Gilbert insightfully notes that one of the major intellectual roots of the "collectivist" ideologies he is concerned with is Bellamy's *Looking Backward*. Gilbert finds it "difficult to demonstrate a direct link between Bel-lamy's Nationalist movement and the varieties of collectivist thought that followed some years later" (p. 23). The following section is an attempt to sketch in some of those links. However, Gilbert is quite correct to emphasize that "most important, Bellamy's famous book appears again and again as a kind of unconscious archetype in writings about the solution to industrial problems" (ibid.). Anyone familiar with socialist and reform litera-ture of the 1890s and pre–World War I period can only echo Gilbert's judgment: "Bella-myism" in this sense permeates "collectivist" ideologies, liberal and socialist, as well as, of course, antisocialist.

lamy, and many others who proposed the reorganization of society around the existing corporations as a kind of "non-statist socialism."[82]

Bellamy, of course, did regard the corporation and the trusts as collectivist institutions leading toward socialism. In *Looking Backward*, Bellamy even speaks of the Nation organized as the "corporation" and "the great trust." But in the 1880s, the corporation or the trust were still too much imbued with the commercial spirit and dominated by the individual capitalist, rather than the professional manager, to allow Bellamy to adopt them wholeheartedly as his model. Yet Bellamy was groping in that direction in the 1890s, impelled by the inner logic of his identification of socialism with the collectivist and bureaucratic tendencies with capitalism. Thus he wrote that "the working principles of the National plan [are] already in partial operation in contemporary industry, politics, and society."[83]

The basic premise of all "technocratic" and corporatist thought, from Veblen, who was one of Bellamy's intellectual heirs, to Burnham and the neocorporatists such as Berle, is that as the result of the separation of ownership from actual control, those who run the corporation, the managers, are free of the "profit motive." The capitalistic side of the enterprise supposedly only acts as a brake upon the managers' desire to serve society through full production of superior products. While Bellamy recognized that the professional manager or administrator in business was coming to play a more important role, it was understandably difficult in the 1880s to conceive of the managers as an elite without commercial motives. The administration of the entire productive economy and the management of the work force, such as he had envisioned in *Looking Backward*, "involved the constant solution of problems of business administration on a far greater scale than they are presented by the affairs of the largest of our industrial or commercial syndicates, and that, as a matter of fact, the work of the epauletted administrators is done with an exactitude and fidelity unequalled in private business. Upon this administrative and essentially business side of the great modern military

82. Hal Draper, "Neo-Corporatists and Neo-Reformers," *New Politics* 1, no. 1 (Winter 1962): pp. 87–106. Berle's father was a Boston minister and a "friend and disciple of Bellamy" (Arthur E. Morgan, *Nowhere Was Somewhere* [1946], p. 9). For Berle's own conscious understanding of the relationship between the corporate collectivism he advocated, and Bellamy's ideas, see his Foreword to Edward S. Mason, ed., *The Corporation in Modern Society* (Cambridge: Harvard University Press, 1960).

83. Bellamy, "Looking Backward Again," pp. 183–184.

organizations the advocate of the practicability of Nationalism may properly lay stress."[84]

Even in *Equality*, writen in the mid-1890s, those who run the corporation are seen as the "private directors," who while not necessarily capitalists themselves, are not disinterested managers, but "more or less rascally" fellows, "who would be constantly trying to cheat the stockholders."[85] In order to attain the collectivist society, which Bellamy in *Equality* now called "public capitalism," it would be necessary to replace private directors with men responsible to the state.[86] Yet, given Bellamy's definition of Nationalism, and its underlying theoretical assumptions, the use of the corporation itself as the model for the organization of the new society, as well as a stress on the role of the professional managers or technicians as active agents of "collectivism" in opposition to the businessman, was only a matter of time. Indeed, many of the Bellamyite socialists of the late 1890s did in fact begin to draw these conclusions. "Technocratic" ideology was one of the major legacies of Bellamy's outlook.

The Coming Nation, founded by J. A. Wayland as the official newspaper of the Ruskin Colony in Tennessee, moved increasingly toward a conception of the corporation as the model of socialism—as a kind of nucleus of socialism within capitalism, without even the need for government ownership to make it "socialistic." Both under Wayland as well as under his successors, *The Coming Nation* proclaimed itself to be the advocate of socialism "as taught in Edward Bellamy's *Looking Backward.*" Herbert N. Casson, who had been the minister of the Lynn Labor Church in the early 1890s, and later became editor of *The Coming Nation* in 1898, left the socialist movement entirely to become a full-time scientific management expert and writer of books on sales efficiency. This connection between scientific management and a strain of bureaucratic socialism drawn from Bellamy is graphically illustrated in Casson's writings for *The Coming Nation*, while he described himself as still a socialist. Thus in the "Amateur Business Men" Casson wrote:

> In the Industrial world of today there are two kinds of business-men—AMATEURS and PROFESSIONALS.
> The Amateurs are those who believe in competition and the perpetual struggle for trade.

84. Bellamy, "What Nationalism Means," reprinted in *Edward Bellamy Speaks Again!*, pp. 93–95.
85. Bellamy, *Equality* (1897), p. 118.   86. Ibid.

> The Professionals are those who believe in the organization of industry, so that the extra labor and wastefulness of competition shall be avoided.

> The professional businessmen are composed of two directly opposite classes of people—monopolists and socialists.

> Both agree that competition is wasteful, unbusinesslike and out of date.

> Both have agreed that organization saves labor, time and money. The socialist has learned this by thought, and the monopolist has learned it by experience.

> But the difference between the two is that the monopolist desires to form trusts for PRIVATE PROFIT, and the Socialist wishes them for the PUBLIC WELFARE.

> . . . the Socialist is after all a more clearheaded and far-sighted businessman than even the monopolist.[87]

The professional managers (or engineers), whether they knew it or not, were the vanguard of "socialism," ushering in socialism, in the sense that these Bellamyite socialists understood that term: the bureaucratic collectivization of society. It followed logically that to the degree that corporations were run by professional managers, and the entrepreneurial element was excluded, the corporation became a socialist institution per se. But in 1899, while these ideas were clearly in the air, the development of the separation of management and financial-business control and the development of large-scale corporate bureaucracies had not proceeded far enough to allow even a Casson to leap directly to these conclusions. But Casson's socialism in *The Coming Nation* was unquestionably the logical extension of Bellamy's collectivist ideology.

The successor to Casson as editor of *The Coming Nation* was Corydon Ford, who with his brother, Franklin, introduced John Dewey to

87. *The Coming Nation*, no. 303 (March 11, 1899). See Arthur Mann, *Yankee Reformers*, pp. 95–97, on Casson as the minister of the Lynn Labor Church. Even before becoming editor of *The Coming Nation*, Casson's sermons were reprinted there regularly. In 1897, Casson spoke to his congregation of "the victories of socialism" and praised the monopolist as an "organizer" who was doing the "important and progressive work in the world." The plannist and efficiency strain in his thinking is very clear: "System is the mother of freedom. It is the methodological man who has the most time to himself. It is not slavery to be obliged to keep everything in its place" (*Coming Nation*, no. 201 [March 27, 1897]). For this connection between Casson and the scientific management movement I am indebted to Samuel Haber, whose own research into the political reform dimensions of scientific management turned up many of the direct links between Bellamyism and the subsequent "technocratic" thinking that I had only been able to guess at.

socialism.[88] As Lewis Feuer has shown, Ford's idea of socialism was that of a technocratic-intellectual elite, a "brains-trust," managing a collectivized economy.[89] Under Ford's editorship, the masthead of *The Coming Nation* carried the slogan: "Explain to folks that Socialism is Full Organization of Industries, so that all the people can own and control them. No one objects to organization." He repeatedly stressed the identity of organization with socialism. Under the heading of "Organization and Socialism One," Ford explained, "The highest cooperation means the highest organization, and it doesn't mean anything else. The synonym for Socialism is organism (organizationism); and the synonym for Socialist is organizationist."[90] Democracy, democratic control, and an active movement from below, meant no more to Ford than to Bellamy. All that counted was the rationalization and bureaucratic organization of industry. With perfect consistency, Ford concluded that Collis P. Huntington, the builder of a highly organized railroad empire, was in fact "much more of a Socialist than some of us who go by that name."[91] Thus, the idea of the "managerial revolution" by which James Burnham understood the negation of socialism, was seen by Ford as its very essence. Inevitably, the conclusion followed that the corporation was the model for the future socialist society. Here then, in this native socialism of Ford's, the "homespun" philosophy of the "village utopian," Edward Bellamy, came to its logical conclusion. Now the corporation had become the very model of socialism which Bellamy had been compelled to find in the military in 1888. From Ford's or Casson's standpoint the managers, no less than Bellamy's military, could perform their duties without mercenary motives.

By 1916, the bureaucratization of the corporation had proceeded far enough to allow another socialist, standing in the tradition which Bellamy and Gronlund had laid down, to avow that the modern corporation provided the model for the organization of a socialist society. In his book *America and the New Epoch*,[92] Charles P. Steinmetz, the "wizard of General Electric," described the coming socialist society under the head-

88. Lewis Feuer, "John Dewey and the Back to the People Movement," (October–December, 1959): 545–568.

89. Ibid., pp. 550–554.

90. *The Coming Nation*, no. 379 (Sept. 1, 1900).

91. Ibid. See also no. 400 (Jan. 26, 1900).

92. Charles P. Steinmetz, *America and the New Epoch* (New York: Harper & Bros., 1916).

ing of "The Future Corporation," for which, presumably, General Electric provided the model.[93] Even then, like Bellamy, Ford, and Casson, Steinmetz regretted that the development of the corporate soul was retarded because of the hangover of its capitalistic past. But he was optimistic that evolution would overcome all obstacles to corporation-style socialism. With genuine insight, Charles and Mary Beard understood *Looking Backward* as the "first utopia of applied science," which "naturalized socialism and baptized it anew in the name of business efficiency."[94]

The Burden of Freedom

Looking Backward was the consummation of Bellamy's quest for a society built on "solidarity," the evolutionary self-collectivization of capital, and the movement away from individualistic society toward organized society. The only way to rid man of selfishness, Bellamy discovered, was to rid him of self. Capitalism, for Bellamy, was, at its core, only an expression of the self-seeking and selfishness that in the vision of *The Religion of Solidarity* produced "individuality" and "personality." It gave an open license to the lower, ineradicable part of human nature. It placed a premium upon self-centeredness, the "partiality" of personality, and made a virtue of the unrestrained pursuit of self-interest. Capitalism's emphasis upon "individualism" produced social anarchy and disorder, not progress. The elimination of private interests became the foundation stone of Bellamy's ideal society. To Bellamy, reform through political or social conflict, through the organized form of self-seeking, could only signify that the old infection, selfishness, remained. The individual would be no better off, in Bellamy's view, than in capitalist society: lonely, isolated, and powerless. Men could live either in the capitalist jungle where the individual is a weak, isolated atom, prey for the strong and amoral, *or* in a society of "concert" in which the individual, still an atom, becomes powerful and banishes anxiety and loneliness by becoming a functional part of an all-embracing bureaucratic state.

Bellamy's *atomistic-collectivist* outlook was the mirror image of the atomistic individualism of the middle class, an individualism rooted in a way of life that was being destroyed by the concentration of capital and

93. Ibid., pp. 199–216. See the discussion of Steinmetz in Hal Draper, *The Two Souls of Socialism* (1961), and also James Gilbert, *Designing the Industrial State*, ch. 7.
94. Charles A. Beard and Mary R. Beard, *The Rise of American Civilization* (New York: Macmillan, 1930), vol. 2, p. 253.

which could visualize no way of reconciling individualism with collectivism, yet preserve the freedom of the person and the integrity of personality. For Bellamy, "utopia" lay in the reduction of society to its individual
atoms; but in order to make sure that the same selfishness, which was an
ineradicable part of individualism would not destroy society, the person
would be welded into a bureaucratic machine that eliminated all possibility of conflict.

The material equality of Bellamy's utopia was merely one more
device for wiping out the expression of individual differences, and not a
means for weakening privilege and strengthening the power of the individual. Bellamy's was no classless society: he designed a system based on
an inequality of power, with an elite of talent, rather than wealth, ruling
over the passive people. It is a classless society only in the sense that a
modern totalitarian society might be called classless: as an atomized society in which there are no significant intermediate associations which
come between the individual and perfect communion with society. Citizens become state functionaries. Membership in the industrial army replaces the free association of individuals by which an individual could
develop his personality. The absence of parties, politics, even of government—but not the *state*—means the absence of all mechanisms for self-
rule, which is to say, of democracy itself.

In Bellamy's collectivist theory, while the state owns the means of
production and exchange, and exercises complete authority over its citizens, the people do not in turn "own" the state. That is, in a society in
which there is no public life permitted, they are shorn of all effective
power to determine social and economic policy. For Bellamy, socialism
was equated with organization—and the highest form of organization,
the impersonal bureaucratic state, embracing all classes ("the Nation"),
was the highest form of socialism. Organization involved planning in
place of anarchy, efficiency in place of competitive selfishness, and suppression of conflict between the individual or group and society, in place
of class and political conflict.

The practical political and social implications of this supra-class
collectivist ideology were clearly revealed by the editor of the first Bellamyite organ, *The Nationalist*, who reported in an article appropriately
titled "The Democracy of Uniforms," the claim of a young Russian noble
that uniforms in the gymnasia of Czarist Russia produced a "democratic"

spirit among the youth of Russia.[95] The uniforms worn by the peasant lad as well as the son of the highest prince, prevented "that display of dress, that affectation of manner, that ostentatious superciliousness . . . productive of such pernicious results in Great Britain." *The Nationalist*'s editor concluded from this lesson in Czarist democracy: "Such would also be the effect of the national industrial army, with its distinctive uniforms and its humane discipline. Unlike a livery, which is a mark of servitude, a uniform is an honor and a token of equality. It replaces the false and extrinsic individuality sought through differences in dress and, approaching the intention of Nature, places all men side by side to show their real worth in the true individuality of personal traits and endowments, which are thus brought out and duly emphasized."[96]

For Bellamyites, "equality" meant the elimination of differences and the suppression of a selfish desire for material possessions. Bellamyites proposed forced equality not to equalize power, nor because of an ethical belief in equality—proving how little *Looking Backward*'s vision of a classless utopia transcended the boundaries of a class society. Bellamy's scheme thus served the needs of a class which felt itself powerless in the political and social struggle, incapable of collective action to protect itself from either the workers or capitalists, and, at the same time, envious of the wealth and display of luxury of the latter. Bellamy's middle-class audience found a compelling vision in his discovery that total organization from above would rescue those who could not help themselves.

95. *The Nationalist* 2, no. 2 (January, 1890).
96. Ibid., p. 74.

3 ORGANIZATION FOR THE UNORGANIZABLE: LOOKING BACKWARD AND THE CRISIS OF THE MIDDLE CLASS

The response to *Looking Backward*, Edward Bellamy testified, was "most general and enthusiastic" in the trans-Mississippi states, the newly admitted states, the territories and the far West[1]—that is, those areas outside the South where the populist movement, the chief expression of middle-class discontent in the 1890s, had its greatest support. In 1894, after the organized Nationalist movement had declined and many of the individuals involved in it had become active in the People's Party, Bellamy claimed that about half of the farmers' weeklies in the West "not only support the St. Louis Platform, but take every occasion to declare that the adoption of the whole Nationalist plan, with the industrial republic as its consummation, is but a question of time."[2] John D. Hicks notes that copies of *Looking Backward* were frequently offered by radical farmers' periodicals as premiums to prospective subscribers.[3] The People's Party convention in 1892 publicly acclaimed Bellamy while the various Nationalist periodicals and clubs were officially invited to participate in the founding of the new party. Yet, why should Bellamy's collectivist utopia have evoked such an enthusiastic response from people primarily concerned with saving small property from the onslaught of corporate capitalism? How did they understand the manifestly anti-democratic elements in *Looking Backward?*—if, indeed, they did. What was it in their situation that made it possible for Bellamy's message to touch them so deeply?

1. Edward Bellamy, "Progress of Nationalism in the United States," in *Edward Bellamy Speaks Again!*, p. 144.
2. Ibid.
3. John D. Hicks, *The Populist Revolt* (1931), p. 131.

The most obvious explanation of Bellamy's appeal is that the radicalized farmers of the 1880s and 1890s were experiencing a deteriorating economic situation and found in Bellamy's energetic indictment of the cruel and barbaric nature of capitalist society confirmation of their own hatred of the middlemen, the banks, railroads, and the corrupt politicians who served them. The successive crises in the agricultural economy throughout the last three decades of the nineteenth century profoundly stirred the victims to seek an explanation of their fate and a way out. One observer reported:

> People commenced to think who had never thought before, and people talked who had seldom spoken. On mild days they gathered on the street corners, on cold days they congregated in shops and offices. Everyone was talking and everyone was thinking. . . . Little by little they commenced to theorize upon their condition. Despite the poverty of the country, the books of Henry George, Bellamy, and other economic writers were bought as fast as the dealers could supply them. They were bought to be read greedily; and nourished by the fascination of novelty and the zeal of enthusiasm, thoughts and theories sprouted like weeds after a May shower. . . . They discussed income tax and single tax; they talked of government ownership and the abolition of private property; fiat money, and the unity of labor; . . . and a thousand conflicting theories.[4]

Looking Backward's indictment of iniquities of capitalist society touched a popular nerve. It condemned the plutocracy and it voiced outrage at the new economic and political system, and it offered an easily understood explanation which helped people to fill the need to "theorize upon their condition." The collectivist society it pictured, in the world of 2000 A.D., the harmonious, materially abundant and worry-free world, contrasted sharply with toilsome lives and hard times. Under the circumstances, Bellamy's orderly society had an obvious appeal. Its manifestly authoritarian character could be ignored or not fully grasped as people were carried away by the contrast between the dark present and the bright future. The vision of a bureaucratically organized collectivist society was not reflected directly in populist politics. Only in the Nationalist movement proper, which drew upon nonentrepreneurial middle-class elements for its early membership, was Bellamy's authoritarian utopia taken, as he had meant it to be, as an explicit blueprint for the future.

Agrarian radicals could be enthusiastic about *Looking Backward*

---

4. Elizabeth Higgins, quoted in Hicks, *Populist Revolt*, p. 132.

without adopting its perspective of an inevitable collectivized future because the problems of crop prices, credit, mortgages, and railroad rates
forced farmers to search for an immediate program of practical reform to
relieve immediate hardship. The long-run development of the great corporations and monopolies might bring utopia ultimately, as Bellamy
thought. But although they might find it pleasant to contemplate the
coming of the new order over the haze of more than one hundred years,
the hard-pressed farmers could not resign themselves to waiting for a
victory after they had themselves been vanquished by the trust. It would
have been difficult for them to summon up the same sense of optimism as
Bellamy's *New Nation* when it dismissed the resistance of small retailers to
the new department stores as "useless": "The small retail shopkeeper, like
the small manufacturer, is doomed. In the great cities he will soon become
as extinct as the fabled dodo. . . . But let him be comforted. The triumph
of his conquerors will be brief. As the mammoth store is bigger than his
shop, so is the nation bigger than the mammoth store."[5] Unwilling to be
comforted by history, farmers and small businessmen instead organized to
prevent monopoly from swallowing them up.

Thus of the several levels on which Bellamy's tract could be read,
Looking Backward's indictment of the horrors of "plutocratic" capitalism
has a strong claim, perhaps the strongest, as an explanation of Bellamy's
popularity. However, there is good reason to look deeper, to see whether
Bellamy's collectivist ideology with its explicit elimination of politics and
democracy, as well as its radical anti-individualism, did not find an echo
in some aspects of middle-class protest and reform in the 1890s.

The Dilemma of Liberal Reform

By the 1870s, the middle class found itself confronted by an extraordinary concentration of wealth and power which seemed to over-
shadow their own. Some suitable instrument was needed to restore to
the "producers" the power and independence that was being stolen by
the "plutocracy" and eroded by the new large-scale industrial society
that had come into being. The difficulty of creating such an instrument
and ensuring that once created it would be wielded effectively in *their*
interest posed the central dilemma for the middle-class reform movements throughout the last decades of the nineteenth century and early

5. *The New Nation* 1, no. 2 (1891), p. 21.

years of the twentieth.[6] Richard Hofstadter, in writing of the Progressive movement, defined the dilemma well: "The American tradition has been one of unusually widespread participation of the citizen in the management of affairs, both political and economic. Now the growth of the large corporation, the labor union, and the big impenetrable political machine was clotting society into large aggregates and presenting to the unorganized citizen the prospect that all these aggregates and interests would be able to act in concert and shut out those men for whom organization was difficult or impossible."[7] The changing conditions of American life made it necessary for members of a class whose everyday mode of existence was characterized by independence and individualism to seek a collectivist solution for their problems, and yet to act in concert was not only difficult but dangerous.

The root dilemma of the reform movement was that in order to counter the social and economic power of other classes and interests the middle class was required to turn to the state as a collective instrument to aid the unorganized individual—in the rhetoric of populism, to protect the "producers" and shore up small property against the onslaught of

6. The following discussion of middle-class reform draws heavily upon Richard Hofstadter's *The Age of Reform*, both for general inspiration as well as the main argument concerning the dilemma of organization which the heterogeneous middle classes faced. With many qualifications, Hofstadter's book remains one of the most important and seminal works on the reform tradition, largely because it was an attempt to break out of the sterile progressive historiographic tradition. One need not accept the more preposterous implications of Hofstadter's treatment of the populists—that there was a "straight line" from populism to McCarthyism, as some of Hofstadter's neoconservative cothinkers so crudely postulated during the 1950s—to be able to examine the "underside" of a lower middle-class protest against capitalism such as populism represented. Neopopulist critics such as Norman Pollack, *The Populist Response to Industrial America* (1962), and, most recently, Lawrence Goodwin, *Democratic Promise* (1976) have attempted with partial success to overturn Hofstadter's view of populism, particularly the charge of "anti-Semitism" (see Norman Pollack, "The Myth of Populist Anti-Semitism," *American Historical Review* 68, no. 2 [Oct. 1962]: 76–80). But even here it is an example of asking the wrong question. Instead of examining the nature of lower-middle–class anticapitalism, of which anti-Semitism is only one expression, an ideology in which the "producing" classes are counterposed to the "parasitic" capitalists and middlemen, examples of anti-Semitic stereotypes are counted. A brilliant but neglected article by Kenneth Barkin, "A Case Study in Comparative History" (1970): 373–404, draws attention to this aspect of populism. For a radical analysis of farmers' movements which supports, indirectly, Hofstadter's key point, the one argued in this chapter, about the organizational incapacity of these elements, see Michael Schwartz, *Radical Protest and Social Structure* (1976).

7. Hofstadter, *Age of Reform*, pp. 213–214 and chapter 6 passim.

monopoly. The state, they hoped, could become an instrument above classes. And yet there were grave dangers: a centralized state could be used against them by those better able to organize politically. The goal, therefore, was to take the state out of the hands of the capitalists and their servants and make sure, somehow, that it stayed out of their control, without at the same time setting the workers independently into motion, thereby giving over the state to them. Only by reforming the political system for the benefit of the unorganized citizen could this be achieved. Hence the characteristic demands of middle-class reformers in this period for direct legislation, direct primaries, civil-service reform, "non-partisan" administration: all devices aimed at supplanting or supplementing organized political parties, changes that were a political precondition for transforming the state into a "classless" instrument of the middle class.[8]

Thus the very inability to organize themselves and to institute reforms had led urban and rural middle classes to turn to the state to secure their interests against big capital. This contradiction was the essence of their dilemma. How to break out of this vicious circle was the continual problem facing middle-class reform politics in this period. To the degree that people found it difficult or impossible to organize themselves, they became disenchanted with organized politics, even with the idea of democracy. But this manifestation of the "populistic" mentality to which Hofstadter and other neo-conservative historians attributed so many of the ills of American democracy does not support the denigration of democracy and democratic movements. It only points, instead, to the limits of a democratic reform movement based primarily on the petty bourgeoisie. It is for this reason that in the politics and programs of the heterogeneous and atomized middle class, as Hofstadter correctly ob-

8. Ibid., p. 254–265 for a discussion of the meaning of direct legislation. See also Lipow, "Plebiscitarian Politics and Progressivism: The Direct Democracy Movement." S. M. Lipset writes of the lower-middle-class reform movement's demand for direct democracy: "On the political level they showed a strong distrust of parliamentary or constitutional democracy and were particularly antagonistic to the concept of party. They preferred to break down the sources of partisan strength and create as much direct democracy as possible through the introduction of the initiative and referendum, and through easy recall elections. Parties, politicians, big business, bankers, and foreigners were bad, only the people acting for themselves were good" ("Social Stratification and 'Right Wing Extremism,'" *British Journal of Sociology* 10, no. 4 [1959]: 26). Cf. Michael Rogin, *The Intellectuals and McCarthy* (1967), p. 197.

serves, the "complaint of the organized against the consequences of organization" is a constant refrain.[9]

After the Civil War, corruption without previous parallel permeated American political life. Politics increasingly became the province of professional politicians allied with the rising industrial capitalists; the older, established middle class found itself driven out. Efforts by the middle class to reform politics were frustrated at every turn by the "machine" and the "boss"—institutions that served the plutocracy yet

9. Hofstadter, *Age of Reform*, p. 214. On the neoconservative argument see idem, chs. 1–3; Daniel Bell, ed., *The New American Right* (New York: Criterion, 1953); and Edward Shils, *The Torment of Secrecy* (Glencoe: The Free Press, 1955). Rogin, *The Intellectuals and McCarthy*, is a devastating reply to this literature. The view taken in this chapter is based on an historical estimate of the middle classes' position in relation to big business, labor, its internal cohesiveness, degree of heterogeneity, economic role, etc. Whatever the ideals of the middle class, even if "democratic" abstractly, the attempt to actualize these ideals and at the same time to preserve small property forces them either to give up the ideals or to modify their content. In the case of populism, then, the ambiguity in their political program and the later "souring" of its tradition, stemmed not from the infirmity of democratic ideals or of mass democratic movements in general, but rather from the inherent weakness of a movement and program based on small property owners, especially an extremely heterogeneous and geographically dispersed grouping. The middle class is pulled toward socialism and toward the working class organized into its own party (which it was not, of course in the United States, then or now) to the degree that it sees no future for itself within the framework of monopoly capitalism, and it believes that a socialist reorganization of society offers them as individuals the chance to create a new, happier existence, free of the anxieties of middle-class existence, including private property itself. It is in this sense that one of the souls of American liberalism (and this is the positive side of the populist tradition to which Goodwin and others correctly point) is both democratic and "socialist": the striving for a democratic, rational society in which the individual may realize his potentialities. But as in the case of the populists and of the popular side of "progressivism," as long as that ideal remains within the limitations of the middle class, it constantly suffers defeat and produces solutions which are democratic in name only, hence the sham, plebiscitarian democracy of the initiative and referendum and the direct primary. When the situation of the middle class deteriorates and the working class fails to offer it an alternative, the need to find a way out grows, and it is here that "socialistic" movements of the right—i.e. anticapitalist collectivist ideologies which are also anti-working class and authoritarian—flourish. Thus the fascist movement gains its mass base among the lower middle classes by offering a kind of socialism: against big business, against big labor, for the "little man" who is crushed by both. (See Daniel Guerin, *Fascism and Big Business* [1939]). On the prefascist period see Massing, *Rehearsal for Destruction*; Lebovics, *Social Conservatism and the Middle Classes*; Peter G. J. Pulzer, *The Rise of Political Anti-Semitism in Germany and Austria* (1964). In the native-American fascism of William Dudley Pelley, this appeal for a middle-class "socialism" is central. Significantly—for what it demonstrates about the "left" and "right" appeal of Bellamy's collectivism—Pelley's call for a "Christian Commonwealth" (*No More Hunger*, 1939) offers as its centerpiece on the "iniquities" of "predatory" capitalism the well-known "Parable of the Water Tank" from *Equality*.

rested on the support of the growing numbers of propertyless urban voters. Reform organizations, as Ostrogorski demonstrated, were often captured by the very machine that they were intended to destroy, or else became the basis for a new machine and a new boss.[10] Even when after "herculean efforts," one prominent proponent of direct legislation pointed out, "good" men were elected to office, nothing was accomplished by forces of reform because "these men often failed to remain good."[11]

Such experiences produced despair and discouragement that honest men could ever win the political battle by the methods of organized politics. Many reformers openly expressed doubts about democratic, representative government. Henry Demarest Lloyd, half-liberal and half-socialist in the manner of Bellamy, expressed dramatically the conclusion many others had reached:

> Two classes study and practice politics and government: place hunters and privilege hunters. In a world of relativities like ours size of area has a great deal to do with the truth of principles. America has grown so big—and the tickets to be voted, and the powers of government, and the duties of citizens, and the profits of personal use of public functions have all grown so big—that the average citizen has broken down. No man can half understand or half operate the fulness of this big citizenship, except by giving his whole time to it. This the place hunter can do, and the privilege hunter. Government, therefore—municipal, State, national—is passing into the hands of these two classes, specialized for the functions of power by their appetite for the fruits of power. The power of citizenship is relinquished by those who do not and cannot know how to exercise it to those who can and do—by those who have a livelihood to make to those who make politics their livelihood.[12]

This feeling of being overwhelmed by the complexity of industrial capitalist society, of being incapable of affecting the course of events through politics—a feeling, in short, that participation in and even passive comprehension of politics was beyond the "average citizen"—underlies the "populistic" distrust of organized politics and political parties, and the proposals of Populists and Progressives for "direct democracy" by the unorganized citizenry as a panacea to cure the ills of American democ-

10. M. Ostrogorski, *Democracy and the Organization of Political Parties* (1902), vol. 2, chs. 8, 9, and 10.

11. John R. Haynes, quoted in Key and Crouch, *The Initiative and Referendum in California* (Berkeley: University of California Press, 1939), p. 425.

12. Henry Demarest Lloyd, *Wealth Against Commonwealth* (1894), pp. 519–520.

racy.[13] Others, following the line of thought indicated by Lloyd, rejected the idea of placing any more political burdens on the citizen. Rather than seeking changes in the political system or society that would allow the individual to participate more effectively in the political process, they looked to the creation of a strong executive power, a reformed civil service, and a "non-partisan" administration by specialists or at least by honest individuals able to rise above class or party. The sphere of "politics," their formula ran, was to be sharply delimited, and to be strictly separated from "administration."[14] Lloyd himself concluded that it was necessary to do away with democratic decision making and politics altogether and to substitute for them the rule of the educated experts.[15]

Bitter experience taught reformers that their attempts at sustained, organized, political action invariably resulted in failure because of the operation of a kind of "iron law of oligarchy." Rather than an abstract sociological theorem, however, it was a common-sense conclusion or feeling that was the sum product of many weary years of unsuccessful attempts to reform the political system and to put the "individual"—the honest middle-class man—back into the center of the political process.[16]

13. Cf. Hofstadter, *Age of Reform*, pp. 254–261.

14. On the "politics vs. administration" dichotomy, and its significance in the emergence of the statist liberal outlook, see Dwight Waldo, *The Administrative State*, ch. 1, esp. pp. 17–18, and Hofstadter, *Age of Reform*, p. 262.

15. See Lloyd's posthumously published collection of essays, *Man the Social Creator* (1906), esp. ch. 7 on the new spirit in politics. Lloyd proposed to do away with parties altogether, substituting "education" for election. He saw in the Boss and the Machine the prototype of the future political system—run "for" the people (pp. 170–173).

16. Robert Michels, in formulating his famous, if dubious, "iron law of oligarchy," drew very heavily upon M. Ostrogorski's treatment in *Democracy and the Organization of Political Parties* in order to provide comparative confirmation for his own study of the German Social Democracy. Ostrogorski's masterful account and analysis of the efforts of the American reformers, to whom he was sympathetic, to overcome the "machine" led him to conclude that in order for the "individual" to come into his own it would be necessary to eliminate political parties, and to substitute for them limited-purpose, temporary organizations. Yet, so convinced was Ostrogorski after his analysis of previous attempts to organize middle-class reform groups and parties that the middle class could not govern its own organizations if they allowed them to become *mass, democratic* organizations, that he advocated that these single-purpose, temporary parties themselves be organized on a thoroughly undemocratic, authoritarian principle:

> The adhesion of the citizen to a single issue organization will naturally be undivided and unreserved; limited to a particular cause, it will be more intense; his gaze fixed on the one object in view, *the adherent will follow the leader without looking to the right or to the left*. The subordination of the *ego*, which is the end of discipline and the basis of all association will be fully

Most historians, in attempting to place Bellamy in the context of American reform thought, have primarily stressed the important role of Bellamy's advocacy of an expanded social and economic role for the state.[17] This side of Bellamy's thought does, of course, provide a link to the contemporary programs of reform and explains the general appeal of his views to these elements. But it was Bellamy's special solution to the dilemma of those "for whom organization was difficult or impossible" as they faced the rise of collectivist institutions that provides an explanation of *Looking Backward*'s appeal that goes beyond the obvious. The feelings of impotence produced by their inability to alter or control political and economic events opened up such people to Bellamy's vision of a totally organized society. *Atomistic individualism in an age of collectivism and bureaucratization turned into its opposite: atomistic collectivism.* For the lonely crowd, whose instincts of individual virtue made all partial organization seem like a jail, only total organization from above could offer a utopia that would be bearable. It was Bellamy's genius in *Looking Backward* to have offered such a dream of the future at a time when the fortunes of the unorganized, individualistic middle classes seemed to be at their lowest ebb.

The New Liberalism and the Positive State

In advocating state intervention in the economy, either in the form of extensive regulation or outright ownership of monopolies, middle-class reformers broke sharply with the liberal tradition of laissez faire that, in theory at least, had been the cornerstone of the American middle-class political outlook. But by the late 1870s when industrial capitalism had already developed enormous strength, the old liberalism was no longer serviceable to the small entrepreneur, farmer, merchant, or manu-

---

exhibited here, and yet it will be for the citizen a sacrifice as easy as it will be little degrading. The absolute subordination of the *ego* is attainable only in an angel or an animal. . . . The new political method will enable the citizen to subordinate his ego as a man. It will never insist on the total deposit of his personality in the common stock. (vol. 2, p. 661; my emphasis)

Freely given loyalty, self-discipline without completely losing "ego," the exercise of individual intelligence, and the ability and willingness to replace or criticize "leaders," that is, the foundation stone of democratic organization, are thus in Ostrogorski's view impossible. "Democratic" and "organization" are contrary terms; therefore, at best only the fragmenting of groups can guarantee to the "individual" his liberty. Cf. C. Wright Mills, *The Power Elite* (New York: Oxford University Press, 1955), p. 308, on "political belonging."

17. E.g., Parrington, *Main Currents in American Thought*, vol. 3, pp. 309–312.

facturer. As Vernon Louis Parrington observed, "The great principle of *laissez-faire* that had proved so useful in the earlier struggles against aristocratic paternalism, had become a shield and a buckler for the plutocracy that was rising from the freedom of a let-alone policy."[18]

Into the old bottle of liberalism new wine was poured: for the old laissez faire policy, the new liberalism substituted a kind of middle-class collectivism. The farmers and other sections of the entrepreneurial middle class, Lewis Corey writes,

> demanded legislation to avert the doom of small property. The state was to *regulate* the freedom of enterprise and competition *to assure freedom of enterprise and competition;* to limit the rights of property in the interest of small property. This was a formidable shift on the part of the middle-class radicals. *They now urged limitation of the economic freedom which they formerly believed was sufficient in itself to realize the economic equality of a society of small producers.* Where formerly they demanded abolition of all political privileges, they now wanted them restored in the interest of the small enterpriser.[19]

To the degree that any departure from the laissez faire, any encroachment by the existing state upon the rights of private property, or any measures taken to soften the harshness of economic life, were seen as "socialist," then in this sense the new statist liberalism was a kind of socialism for the middle class.[20] It was a period of social ferment and political groping, a period in which both modern liberalism as well as the native socialist movement were being formed, and it was inevitable that the line between the two was often very indistinct. Individuals, especially in the 1890s and the early years of the twentieth century, crossed from one to the other quite freely and unconsciously, and many, like Henry Demarest Lloyd, were as much part of the new liberalism as they were socialists. From the standpoint of the native socialistic radicals, the major problem in the crucial decade of the nineties lay in differentiating socialism from statist liberalism.

18. Ibid., p. 283.

19. Lewis Corey, *The Crisis of the Middle Class* (1935), pp. 129–130. See also Arthur Ekirch, *The Decline of American Liberalism*, chs. 10–11.

20. *The Coming Nation*, founded by J. A. Wayland, who was later to found *The Appeal to Reason*, was the main expression of populistic socialism. Beginning in 1894, every issue carried a box in the upper lefthand column entitled, "Webster's definition of Socialism." It read: "Socialism—A more precise, orderly and harmonious arrangement of the social arrangements of mankind than that which has hitherto prevailed." With this kind of definition, anyone who favored state control—even a Bismarck—was a "socialist."

Once this popular equation of socialism with any incursions into the sacred rights of private property or challenges to the shibboleths of social Darwinist doctrine is recognized, then it is possible to understand, in part, the reception accorded *Looking Backward*'s collectivist message by elements still strongly rooted in small property. Socialism of this sort held less terror for the small entrepreneur or farmer than the juggernaut of triumphant plutocratic rule. Even Bellamy's projection of an all-embracing state that would own all property could be accepted as one possible outcome of the very politics they were advocating. From the vantage point of the 1890s, who could be so bold as to predict with certainty that *any* small property, especially the small farm, would be able to resist the superior power of big business and modern technology? If the choice were between the government of the plutocracy and state ownership, it was obvious which was preferable. And, to a degree, one could correctly read into *Looking Backward* the idea that the new society would be something like a joint stock company in which all would be shareholders.[21] Bellamy himself described his utopia as "one vast business concern," in which every citizen would be an equal partner.[22] Thus, the entrepreneurial elements who were turning to the state for protection against monopoly capital could regard Bellamy's ideas with favor, and believe that their own program was a kind of socialism. Indeed, that was what many who called themselves socialists told them, and, even more important, that was what their enemies called it.

However, despite the interpenetration of middle-class reform politics, and especially the politics of the "new liberalism," with those of the emerging socialist movement, Bellamy and the Nationalists as well as other middle-class socialist groups of the 1890s were more than variant strains of statist liberalism. On the contrary, even when Bellamy and the Nationalist clubs, and the various other socialistic elements, elaborated a "practical program of step-by-step nationalization," a program that coincided in part with the People's Party's platform, allowing the radicals to march for a time with the Populists, they still maintained their distinct identity. When they recognized the limitations of their allies, they parted company with the Populists. Unlike their liberal allies, they intended that the nationalization of the railroads and other monopolies lead to the

21. Louis Hartz, *The Liberal Tradition in America* (1955), p. 233.
22. *The Nationalist* 2, no. 6 (January 1891): 407.

total collectivization of the economy, not merely constitute bulwarks to preserve property.[23]

Organization for the Unorganizable: The Utopia of Atomistic Collectivism

Merely to have found in the state the collective power greater than the sum of their own individual powers with which to turn back the plutocracy and restore to the "producers" their rightful place in American society, was not sufficient for the reform movement. The middle class still faced the problem of its inability to organize for the kind of collective political and economic action needed to transform the state—an inability that stemmed from the very individualistic, atomized nature of their existence as a class.

For the middle-class readers of *Looking Backward*, Bellamy's utopia with its theory of self-socialization of capital offered a collectivist solution tailored to an individualistic psychology and outlook. In classical liberal theory, society consisted of a collection of atomized individuals, for whom "the common interest was only the sum of individual interest," and "the common welfare was to be attained through the pursuit of each of his individual welfare."[24] Individual freedom and reason were anchored in the widespread distribution of property. With the disintegration of the material underpinnings of the liberal theory of society, that is, with the disintegration of the old, propertied, middle classes and the concentration of capital which, in turn, brought into being a permanent class of propertyless proletarians, the theory itself became more untenable and it therefore became necessary to find a means of reconciling the undeniable collectivist tendencies of society with the old individualistic liberal values. For any solution to remain within the limits of the old liberal middle-class outlook, however, meant that it had to attempt to build upon the kind of asocial or atomistic individualism that was characteristic of the middle class.

Bellamy's "unitary democracy" discussed in the previous chapter was one solution within the limits of this atomistic outlook. Bellamy hoped through the "religion of solidarity" to reduce society to pure individuals—individuals unfettered by other bonds. The atomization of

---

23. Quint, *The Forging of American Socialism*, ch. 7, on Socialist-Populist relations.
24. R. M. MacIver, *The Web of Government* (New York: Macmillan, 1947), p. 187.

all social relationships would pave the way for "all existence under the sole aspect of the one universal and the many individuals."

Thus Bellamy's version of socialism solved the riddle of "organization" that confronted the middle class by constructing a collectivism premised upon its asocial or atomistic individualism. Necessarily it was a nonpluralistic, atomistic collectivism. In the framework of this atomistic-collectivist solution, the question of social order in a society without private property would be solved by the erection of a total bureaucratic state and the elimination of all intermediate associations. All that would remain would be the individual on the one side, and "society" on the other. Community would derive from the relationship of all individuals, equally, to the impersonal state, rather than in and through free association with other individuals. The individual would be "free" in the negative or laissez faire sense. At the same time, people would not need to be powerful, for in the establishment of a totally harmonious society run by a bureaucratic elite, the whole basis or need for a free public life would have been abolished.

Sylvester Baxter, close collaborator of Bellamy and a founder of the Nationalist movement, summed up the essential elements of this atomistic-collectivist outlook in an article that first attempted to define Nationalism. With the complete nationalization of the economy, Baxter wrote,

> we shall . . . reach the higher and perfected simplicity. The intricate complexity of multitudinous industrial antagonisms, keeping the national body in a chronic state of disease through the incomplete working of its various functions, will be reduced to simplicity by bringing all the diversified interests into harmonious and mutually helpful action under one central authority, while preserving the many separate fields of action suitable to differing individual capacity. An industrial army, more completely organized and disciplined than is the best of war today, will thus be necessitated for the operation of the vast national service.
>
> With all transactions confined to the individual on the one side and the nation on the other, the individual is thus dealing with himself in the higher aspect—the great entity composed of himself blended with all his fellows.[25]

The bearing of these ideas upon the dilemma of organization and reform is clear when considered in connection with Bellamy's theoretical postulate of the automatic emergence of the new noncapitalist order

25. Sylvester Baxter, "What Is Nationalism?" *The Nationalist* 1, no. 1 (1889): 11.

through the self-socialization of capital. The organizational demiurge would bring ultimate salvation for the individualistic middle class rather than ruin and destruction. The very process that produced the clotting of society into aggregates was inevitably establishing the basis for a new kind of collectivist community: a "community" composed solely of atomized individuals, in which the individual could lay down the burden of political association and individual freedom.

Looking Backward's theory offered the middle class a magical way out of their disheartening situation. Rather than being crushed between capital and labor, rather than being a class without a future, as the radical socialists claimed (and as events seemed to confirm), Bellamy pointed to a road by which they might triumph. The theory of the self-socialization of capital and of the general movement toward a stronger and all-embracing state, offered salvation without the difficult and perilous effort to organize a political movement to transform the present order. For, even if organization of the middle class had been possible, there was always the danger that in creating a popular political movement the workers might become an independent force not dependent upon the middle class. While they were in theory willing to admit the workers into the camp of the "producers" and to form alliances with workers' organizations, it was only on condition that they subordinate themselves.[26]

The state was conceived of both by Bellamy and the new liberalism to be an institution above particular classes. The more powerful the state grew, the more it could act as a counterweight to those classes and interests whose capacity for the organized pursuit of their narrow class interests threatened to tear society apart. Thus, those who had demonstrated their capacity for organization would be reduced to the same state of relative impotence as the middle class.

Implicit in this conception of a neutral, nonclass state was the idea that its growth would be marked by the gradual emergence of nonpartisan, expert administration, representing the interests of the "community," as over against politics, which to Bellamy, as well as to many middle-class readers, was the product of class conflict. And, as the state was forced to take on more functions, to absorb class conflict, the unorganized individual would benefit from more and more "organization."

26. See Chester McArthur Destler, *American Radicalism, 1865–1901* (1966), chs. 8 and 9, on labor-Populist relations in Illinois.

Even if the middle class could not or would not achieve organization through its own efforts, then, even if it could not or would not cohere together in the kind of mass organizations made necessary under the changed conditions of industrial capitalism, it would nevertheless gain salvation from above by the strengthening of the overall social organization, the state.

Bellamy's socialism from above thus magically bypassed the dilemma of self-organization, and it also got rid of the politics that were so hateful and burdensome, while averting the danger of the development of a movement for social change involving or issuing from the workers.

Paradoxically the more highly organized society became—as it "reached toward the higher perfected simplicity" described by Baxter— and as the partial and special associations were absorbed into the general association, the state, the "freer" the individual would become. A contemporary observer of Nationalism noted this central component of its doctrine:

> The progress of civilization has been through association to produce greater liberty and responsibility. The Nationalists believe that the extension of this principle will continue to produce greater liberty and responsiblity on the part of the individual, and thus tend to the perfect individuality of the individual citizen. . . . the principle involved in all these schemes, the principle operating in all the imperfect methods of today, must ultimately organize itself in some form of a State where the power now centralized in parties, capital, monopolies, will be thoroughly decentralized and diffused throughout the nation.[27]

The perfect individuality of the individual citizen: here lay the promised land of *Looking Backward*. The individual would be released from the anxiety of individual existence through the creation of a totally organized society, and yet remain an "individual." The final outcome of the gradual socialization of society would cure the powerlessness of the unorganized individual because, rather than some classes having the advantage of organization, all would be organized, equally. Paradoxically, once all were organized, none would be organized. The need for selfish partial associations would be eliminated by the fact that every person would have the place and the function accorded to him by merit. If capitalism represented imperfect organization, a semi-anarchic state of

27. H. H. Brown, from the *Christian Register*, reprinted in *The Nationalist* 2, no. 4 (1890): 145.

affairs in which the isolated individual did as well as he could for himself, while those who could organize furthered their selfish ends, then in the new order no one would be left unorganized. Through the simultaneous dissolution of society into its constituent atoms and the creation of the omnicompetent bureaucratic state, every individual would stand united with all, and yet with no one or others in particular.

Moreover, with the interest of every individual made theoretically the same and with the proletarians who were engaged in the vital productive work of society specifically excluded from any voice in determining how society would be run, there was no possibility for individuals to coalesce into separate selfish groups or classes. Hence, there would be none of the "politics" that was (by definition) the expression and necessary outcome of such organized class selfishness. In this way, the unity of every individual atom with all, within the framework of the total bureaucratic state, combined with the elimination of or need for democratic control and participation from below—a participation made possible only through the kind of associative activity that was so difficult and perverse from the standpoint of the middle class—would raise every individual to the same level of organization while at the same time relieving him of any need or chance of assuming the impossible burden of associational activity. The breakdown of the "average citizen" that Henry Demarest Lloyd had worried about would not be a problem in an atomistic-collectivist society that had abolished the possibility and the need for a democratic public life.

Thus Bellamy's anticapitalist utopia attempted to weld the atomized individual of the older liberal society into a collectivist framework and thereby appealed to the undersoul of a frightened and fragmented middle class. The more difficult it was for the middle class to organize itself in order to restructure a political system that favored the rule of the "plutocracy" and the "bosses," and the more probable it seemed that there would occur an ugly, destructive upheaval from below by the increasingly mutinous working class, the more attractive Bellamy's collectivism from above must have seemed to an anxiety-ridden middle class.

N. B. Ashby, a leading Populist organizer, enthusiastically embraced Bellamy's utopia for precisely these reasons. Ashby had been a key figure in the struggle to establish the National Farmers' Alliance in the 1880s, and was perhaps best known for his widely read book *The*

Riddle of the Sphinx (1890)[28] analyzing the economic and political situation of the farmers. In it Ashby offered an explicit argument for Bellamyism as the only remedy for the organizational dilemma of the middle class, particularly the farmers.

"The characteristic of the present epoch," Ashby lamented, "is organization and centralization." The downfall began with the "organization of capital and its centralization." In self-defense, "labor was compelled to organize." Now the farmers' turn had come: they must also organize if they were to survive. And yet, Ashby acutely observed, the farmers' capacity to organize, to discipline themselves in the face of superior forces, was low or nonexistent.[29]

Pessimistically, Ashby admitted that to the degree "reform is imperatively demanded," as indeed it was, given the pressures which the farmer-producers faced from big capital and the labor movement, there could be "no adequate reform" achieved "without the concentrated efforts of those who are in need of the reform."[30] Here the dilemma of middle-class reform is captured in a few words: only the "mystic power of organizations" may achieve such reforms.[31] But, as Ashby despairingly realized, organization is the weak point of the middle class. Rather, it is their enemies who are able to summon up the "mystic" ability to organize and thus to forward their class interests. The inability to solve this dilemma, to overcome the contradiction that faces them, has the most dire consequences:

> Equilibrium in the distribution of the profits arising from productive toil has been destroyed by well-organized and well-disciplined forces among the classes which draw their subsistence from the farmer, working for a common purpose while the farmer has been unorganized. The conditions which oppress the farmer are the results arising from these well-organized efforts having appropriated too large a portion of the profits arising from the capital invested in and the labor expended upon the farm. The organized effort outside the farmer, having men to counter movement from the farmer, has imposed burdens upon the farmer that should have been borne by other classes. These well-disciplined organizations of capital and handlers have forced the farmer to sell his products to them at prices fixed by themselves, and to buy his commodities of them at prices again fixed by themselves.[32]

28. N. B. Ashby, *The Riddle of the Sphinx* (1890).
29. Ibid., p. 233.   30. Ibid., p. 388.   31. Ibid., p. 390.
32. Ibid., p. 388.

The immediate solution which Ashby urged upon his readers was the formation of producers' cooperatives. But the plutocracy's superior efficiency and economies of scale arising out of centralization, not to mention its capacity to organize, led Ashby to conclude that the only real solution for the middle class in the long run was Bellamy's Nationalism. The present attempts to organize the farmers could only be "for the purpose of restoring the equilibrium" that had been upset by the concentration of capital. "It is a strife—a necessary strife, under prevailing conditions" which the farmers must undertake, if only to prevent their immediate obliteration. But insofar as it merely aims "to set all in equilibrium," it is a solution that cannot succeed because the superior organized force of capital will soon reassert itself. Nationalism, in contrast, did not seek to restore the lost equilibrium between parasitic capital and the producing classes, but proposed instead "to put all in harmony."[33]

That harmony could only be achieved through the dissolution of all partial class organization and the constitution of Bellamy's atomistic utopia:

> Nationalism recognizes the beneficence of organization and centralization. It is a protest against the clash of private interests. *It would organize and centralize to the extreme limit of organization and centralization*, but with a perfect adjustment which would bring the varied and conflicting interests into a grand harmony. *For the selfish and individual centralization of the present, it would substitute the State.* It would destroy political government and substitute industrial government; or, rather, it would make politics the science of government, instead of the art of party management, and the science of government the science of properly developing the industries of the country. Nationalism is scientific State Socialism.[34]

Ashby here succinctly reveals the spirit and the real meaning of Bellamy's anticapitalist utopia and the reasons for its appeal. The only way out of its dilemma for the atomized middle class in the new era of industrial capitalism is the abolition of political government—that is, of democracy itself. Nationalism will do away with the possibility and need for self-organization on the part of those classes and individuals who find such efforts beyond their ability, by reducing *all* to the atomized state of the middle class. The very fact of organization on the part of any group or class is evidence of an imperfect, inharmonious society. Now, however, all intermediate organizations will be dissolved into the one grand

33. Ibid., pp. 235, 236, 237.   34. Ibid., p. 235.

organization, the State. In this vision of a "unitary democracy," the Populist publicist Ashby correctly understood the secret of Bellamy's message as did thousands of others readers of *Looking Backward*. They found in it the secure, authoritarian social order in which the individualism and negative freedom of capitalist society that had become so burdensome could be buried.

Bellamy's views were not the isolated expressions of a lonely novelist. Gronlund, Lester Ward, and many others marched to similar tunes.[35] Ward, a key figure in the elaboration of the new, statist liberalism, condemned capitalism in terms similar to those espoused by Bellamy and Gronlund. At the center of Ward's opposition to capitalism was a hatred of its unplanned and chaotic character. His "sociocratic" solution embodied the same atomistic-collectivist vision and expressed the same hostility to politics and politicians as Bellamy's utopian tract. Rejecting democracy, Ward projected a new social order that would be run by an elite of Comtean-style sociologist-scientists. Under the rule of the sociocrats, Ward proposed that "an educated mankind will necessarily think and act only for the welfare of the social whole. Classes, parties, and all self-interest groups will vanish; there will be left only the individual on the one side, and society on the other, interacting in the interests of a harmonious sociocracy."[36] Ward's views make it clear that this extreme anti-individualistic, antidemocratic reaction was in the air, and it is hardly to be wondered at that Bellamy's skill in "sugar-coating" this message elicited a sympathetic response from those who felt themselves excluded from organization.

Bellamy's vision of a collectivist utopia in which society would be composed solely of atomized individuals is thus also the utopian counterpart of the reformers' demands for direct legislation and the various proposals for "nonpartisan" government and civil service reform.[37] Both were designed by middle-class reformers to wrest government from the

35. Henry Steele Commager, *The American Mind* (New Haven: Yale University Press, 1950), ch. 10. Richard Hofstadter, *Social Darwinism*, chs. 4 and 6. Hofstadter notes that Bellamy and Gronlund were both aware of Ward's work, and that the latter drew upon it for his own books (pp. 114–115). See also Ralph Henry Gabriel, *The Course of American Democratic Thought* (New York: Ronald Press, 1940), p. 222. Gabriel characterizes Ward's views as "non-Marxist socialism resting on a foundation of democracy."

36. Charles H. Page, *Class and American Sociology: From Ward to Ross* (New York: Dial Press, 1940), p. 64.

37. See Hofstadter, *Age of Reform*, pp. 259–263.

hands of the bosses by strengthening the position of the unorganized—
the middle class—at the expense of those classes or interests whose capacity for organization was superior or whose numbers were greater.

Advocates of direct legislation, for example, saw this device as a
way of returning to unorganized individuals the power stolen by those
organized conspiracies, the political parties—"organized" and "conspiracy" being, of course, almost a redundancy for them. Rather than form
their own political parties, or even enter into the existing parties and
attempt to fashion an instrument that would be a collective, organized
means for the restoration of democratic self-rule, the proponents of direct legislation directed their efforts toward the dissolution or weakening
of existing political parties and the negation of the advantages of permanent political association. This was the meaning of the movement for
such panaceas as the initiative and the referendum.

This strategy became popular among discontented and disaffected
middle- and working-class elements in inverse relation to their ability to
play a role in organized party politics. Thus, as Hicks has noted, the
"middle-of-the-road" Populists, that is, those who had opposed fusion
with the Democratic Party, believed the People's Party had been stolen
from them by "politicians" and other supposedly corrupt elements from
within their own ranks, and became enthusiastic supporters of direct
legislation as the single solution to the helplessness of the "individual"
and his incapacity for organized political action.[38] Similarly, the proponents of various conceptions of "nonpartisan" government—whether
they advocated direct legislation or consciously counterposed it to the
latter—solved the problem of reestablishing the role of the "individual"

---

38. Hicks, *The Populist Revolt*, p. 408. This is not to suggest that there is something
inherent in the farmer's condition that made them incapable of effective organized class
action. This passage refers only to the consequence of their experiences of political frustration, without discussing the particular sociological circumstances that made them politically
subordinate to other classes and their political representatives. In this regard, the discussion
in S. M. Lipset, *Agrarian Socialism* (1950) is very illuminating. Among other things, Lipset
points out, the wheat farmers of Saskatchewan who were successful in organizing themselves were an especially homogeneous group, with little internal competition, and a clearly
recognizable dependency on the world market which made the formation of a clear program especially easy. See Lipset, pp. 47–48, 67 and 70. See also Hicks, *The Populist Revolt*,
p. 147, on the Farmers Alliance in the Northwest, which was able, for similar reasons, to
organize effectively for its goals. Cf. Schwartz, *Radical Protest and Social Structure*, on the
Southern Alliance, to see how the opposite conditions produced organizational incompe-
tence and oligarchical control (pp. 277–278).

by proposing to sharply restrict the sphere of public life in which partisan politics could play a role.[39]

In his conception of a utopia for the middle class, Bellamy drew upon the hatred and fear of organized politics and politicians and the feelings of impotence that underlay the demand for direct legislation. And he combined its appeal for a return to the unassociated individual with the idea of a society in which politics and public life would have been eliminated. In this respect, Bellamy's early ideas were much closer to the more conservative reformers who advocated a strengthened civil service, government by "experts," etc., as the antidote to the rule of the plutocracy. Later, in *Equality*, in which Bellamy presented a less authoritarian vision of utopia, he added provisions for the exercise of the referendum. This alteration was motivated by an accommodation on Bellamy's part toward democratic rule. However, political associations of any kind still were not to be allowed to play any role in utopia. Such a system of plebiscitarian rule by dissociated individuals, a kind of "polling democracy," would not be incompatible in the least with a bureaucratized society, presided over by a technocratic elite.

Conclusion

Bellamy's message—that the tide of organization contained its own immanent solution to the dilemma of the middle class—was an overwhelmingly hopeful vision which did not require that one accept Bellamy's collectivism in its entirety. The increasing recognition by large sections of the urban and rural middle classes that state intervention was necessary on behalf of the "individual" and small property was an admission that the individual of the older liberal ideal could no longer hold his own without some kind of collective power coming. Why not, then, share for a moment Bellamy's dream of a collective power that would rescue them without requiring them to do what had proven so difficult— to attempt to organize themselves into a political party for the purpose of transforming the political structure and reforming society? In the same fashion, some twenty-four years later, a leading Progressive wrote of a utopia in which the middle class would be saved by a social reformer

39. Lloyd fell into this category, as did a whole wing of the socialist movement of the 1890s, the so-called "nonpartisan" socialists. Many of these were Nationalists and most of them opposed the founding of the Socialist Party. For an account of these currents, see Quint, *Forging*, ch. 8.

who, after abolishing all parties and politicians, makes himself dictator in order to institute the program of the new liberalism.[40] The goals were somewhat different, but the same feelings of political impotence on the part of the same type of people underlies both utopian fantasies. Above all, in a time when the situation of the individual seemed to be so perilous, threatening both from above and "below," how could they fail to pay attention to a message that pointed to a way of regaining by collectivist means a community composed solely of individuals?

Clearly, Bellamy's message foreshadowed tendencies in modern American statist liberalism: the subordination of the individual to a bureaucratic state, and the elimination of individual reason and freedom were the essence of the new liberalism too. If Bellamy resorted to the idea of a bureaucratic state to hold together his "classless" society in which the workers were to be locked up under the tight discipline of a technical-industrial elite, and in which "administration" by experts took the place of politics and democratic decision making, he was only reflecting the development of statist and antidemocratic tendencies within liberalism. To save the individual from the twin evils of big capital and big labor, the new liberalism bowed down lower and lower before the bureaucratic state, convinced that the instrument it was forging was capable of being "neutral" and above politics. "One of the ironic problems confronting reformers around the turn of the century," Richard Hofstadter observed, "was that the very activities they pursued in attempting to defend or restore the individualistic values they admired brought them closer to the techniques of organization they feared."[41] The status of "prophet" accorded to Bellamy by many liberals has its foundation in the bold and unequivocal way in which he seized upon these "techniques of organization"—the corporation, the trust, and the bureaucratic state—and found in them salvation for the middle class.[42]

Certainly Bellamy's authoritarian and antidemocratic doctrine, al-

40. See Col. Edward Mandell House's novel, *Philip Dru: Administrator* (New York: Huebsch, 1918).

41. Hofstadter, *The Age of Reform*, pp. 5–6.

42. See Thurman Arnold's statement in *The Folklore of Capitalism* (New Haven: Yale University Press, 1957), p. 221, that Bellamy was the forerunner of the National Recovery Administration because he saw in the corporation a step toward "socialism." In A. N. Holcombe's defense of the N.R.A., *Government in a Planned Democracy* (New York: Norton, 1935), a book concerned to find some foundation for "the ascendancy of the middle class in a class-conscious state," there is an explicit discussion of the need that the middle class has,

luringly set forth in the dream world of *Looking Backward*, as well as the popular response to it, was, at very least, indicative of a drift toward an authoritarian politics on the part of substantial segments of the middle class. It was a solution toward which such elements were most strongly drawn, of course, when their situation looked darkest. Yet what was at most a mood among discontented middle-class people at large, was a strongly developed element in the Nationalist movement itself.

---

if its hegemony over American society is to be maintained, for a bureaucratic elite to stand between it and other classes. Holcombe writes:

> Experience with the N.I.R.A. has clearly shown the importance of a competent body of technical experts and public business administrators for executing a middle-class program in American politics. . . . the assistance of a body of technicians and administrators is invaluable in maintaining the balance between the upper and lower classes which the practitioner of middle-class politics seeks to establish. Properly organized and directed, such a body can stand against an undue preference for upper or lower-class interests, if the special representative of either class fail to supply the appropriate check upon the other. It can help to stabilize the equilibrium of classes, even if the balance between them is not exactly struck by the measures of the program. In short, an impartial body of competent technicians and administrators is certain to be a favorite instrument of middle-class politics in a class-conscious age. (p. 147)

The similarity of Holcombe's outlook, expressed here, with that of Bellamy is too obvious to require discussion. It should be noted that Holcombe, like Bellamy, when forced to cite some model for the organization of a planned society under the domination of the middle class, cites the General Staff of the Army (p. 153).

4 ORGANIZING FOR NATIONALISM

Unsure of his newly assumed role as an open opponent of American capitalism and an advocate of a collectivist social order, Bellamy had cast his message in the form of a romance, one that was consistent with his reputation as a minor but well-regarded novelist and author of popular magazine short stories. Many reviewers shrugged off *Looking Backward*'s message, but others instantly understood the seriousness of Bellamy's purpose and responded favorably to his condemnation of the viciousness of capitalism and the description of the new collectivist order which would replace it.[1] A sympathetic writer for the *New York Tribune* praised Bellamy for "describing a thorough reorganization of society without demanding the least concession to unpractical fancy." Bellamy's ideas, he enthused, were anything but far-fetched, "for they are introduced and accounted for as to seem to flow naturally and inevitably from the whole tendency of modern evolution."[2] Reviews such as this, which recognized the practical yet conservative nature of Bellamy's views, must have helped the novice social reformer to resolve the ambivalence he felt toward his new public role.

Certainly the novel's astonishing sales strengthened Bellamy's self-conception as a reformer. By the end of 1888, it became an underground best-seller: 210,000 copies had been bought and some 10,000 copies were being sold each week. By the middle of 1890, over 325,000 copies of *Looking Backward* had found their way into the hands of eager readers, causing contemporary conservatives to complain loudly that there was a veritable "Bellamy craze" afoot in America.[3] And most important of all in the transformation of Edward Bellamy was the organization of the Nationalist movement, which at its peak consisted of a loose federation

1. For a summary of contemporary reviews see Arthur E. Morgan, *Edward Bellamy*, pp. 245–246; and "Critical Reviews of *Looking Backward*," in Bellamy Papers.
2. "A New Utopia," *New York Tribune*, February 5, 1888, quoted in Morgan, *Edward Bellamy*, pp. 245–246.
3. Allyn B. Forbes, "The Literary Quest for Utopia," (December 1927): 184.

of 165 clubs with five or six thousand members.[4] The shy and rather reclusive resident of Chicopee Falls found himself and his ideas the subject of intense interest and comment as he somewhat diffidently assumed the mantle of practical prophet and critic of existing society.

If Bellamy at first had toyed with the idea of launching his scheme anonymously, fearful of its reception or the way in which his transformation from a novelist to political propagandist might affect his life, the flow of letters from enthusiastic readers alone must have been greatly reassuring and made him even more conscious of the personal and psychological break that had occurred. "I have just finished the perusal of *Looking Backward*," one Californian wrote Bellamy, "and tho' a stranger I cannot refrain from writing you. Your book has the stamp of Immortality. I had rather have written it than to be the Author of *any* work, contemporaneous with, or preceding it. It is the full and complete realization of the hope . . . that some 'Apostle of Humanity' would arise, capable of showing the people the way and of making the righteous path plain. When the Golden Century arrives . . . your name will receive the homage of the human race of that period as being the only writer of the 19th Century capable of seeing, feeling, and portraying the 'better way.' "[5] And from E. B. Lewis, editor of "Plain Talk," whose motto, "do right, fear God, and make money," must have amused as much as encouraged Bellamy, there came the assurance that *Looking Backward* "breathes, to me, the spirit of a glorious hope for our race."[6] Whatever his hesitations had been, Bellamy quickly became aware of his new role: "I am engaged very seriously in this social reform business," he wrote to his cousin, Will Packer, late in 1888, "and there are many points I want to talk to you about."[7] That his former life as a novelist was finished, Bellamy made plain in a letter to Horace Scudder, editor of the *Atlantic*, in refusing an offer to write a serialized story: "It would indeed be a delight to me to revert to those psychologic studies and speculations which were the themes of my earlier writings. But since my eyes have been opened to the evils and faults of our social state and I have begun to

4. The estimate of membership given by Cyrus Field Willard in 1889 was "over six thousand." In California alone there were from 3,000 to 3,500 members. Arthur E. Morgan, *Edward Bellamy*, pp. 251, 256. See also Everett McNair, *Edward Bellamy and the Nationalist Movement, 1889 to 1894*, ch. 2.

5. E. D. Cooke to Bellamy, August 29, 1889, Bellamy Papers.

6. E. B. Lewis to Bellamy, June 16, 1889, Bellamy Papers.

7. Bellamy to Will Packer, September 26, 1888, Bellamy Papers.

cherish a clear hope of better things, I simply 'can't get my consent' to write or think of anything else. As a literary man I fear I am 'a goner' and past praying for. There is a sense in which I am very sorry for this, for I had much work laid out to do, and should have greatly enjoyed doing it. There is one life which I should like to lead, and another which I must lead! If only I had been twins!"[8] By 1893, Bellamy told Scudder "as for a story I doubt if I could write one now if I tried. I am more hopelessly gone on social reform than ever and have to own to a total lack of interest in anything else. Trusting that you may yet get the fever as badly as I have it. . . . "[9]

By the time sales of *Looking Backward* approached nearly 500,000 in 1891, it was clear that his strategy of employing the form of a utopian romance to sweeten his political views was a stroke of genius. It was equally clear to contemporary observers that *Looking Backward* had tapped an enormous, previously undetected reservoir of anticapitalist discontent by its stinging indictment of the iniquities of the contemporary social order.

The significance of a political tract which boldly advocated a radical break not only with private property and the hard-hearted slogans of social Darwinism, but with basic democratic institutions as well, did not escape the notice of Bellamy's contemporaries. Edward Everett Hale, a fellow writer of utopian fictions and an early supporter of the Nationalist clubs, observed with a mixture of surprise and pleasure that the success of Bellamy's book proved that the American people were willing to "consider very large possible changes in the administration of affairs."[10] These changes in government, Hale admitted, struck at what had hitherto been regarded as the foundation of democracy in America. Bewildered somewhat by the seemingly paradoxical combination of radical anticapitalism and conservative opposition to democracy, a combination which was to confuse subsequent writers who attempted to place Bellamy's politics in conventional categories, Hale wrote approvingly of this new development in American public opinion:

> Oddly enough, the suggestions made [in *Looking Backward*] were suggestions which approved themselves to the most conservative

8. Bellamy to Scudder, August 25, 1890, Bellamy Papers.
9. Bellamy to Scudder, Sept. 5, 1893, Bellamy Papers.
10. *Lend a Hand* 6, no. 1 (January 1891): 1–5. The authorship of this unsigned note on *Looking Backward* is assigned to Hale, its editor, by Morgan.

people quite as much as they did to the most radical. . . . To speak of a single instance, the book coolly swept away universal suffrage, which has been supposed to be one of the panaceas in which the public at large was most interested. If the book has shown anything, it has shown that universal suffrage is by no means the fetish which it had been regarded, and that the people of America, by and large, have learned that men influence their government and carry on their affairs by the weight of their own personal influence swaying things three hundred and sixty-five days in the year much more than by the weight of their ballots which are given only on one day.[11]

Well before Bellamy's utopia began to find popular favor, however, the first impulses which culminated in the launching of the Nationalist movement were making themselves felt. Later commentators have, for the most part, deprecated the importance of Bellamy's manifestly undemocratic politics. Yet, however the hundreds of thousands who read *Looking Backward* may have interpreted it—as an imaginative fairytale, or as a serious critique of capitalist society—those who founded the Nationalist movement regarded Bellamy's indictment of capitalist society, as well as his specific proposals for its reorganization along collectivist lines, as a political manifesto which would be used as the basis for the construction of a movement. "Like the introduction of the electric current into some chemical combination," wrote one of the movement's founders, *Looking Backward* "precipitated the floating ideas, held in the saturated solution of the minds of men, into a concrete and visible reality. That the ideas advanced in this book were eminently feasible was the natural conclusion of the unbiased reader."[12]

From the beginning of the Nationalist movement, all agreed that Bellamy's chief contribution was the idea of the military organization of labor. Thus, the first organized expression of the collectivist politics found in *Looking Backward* occurred in Boston among a group of retired army officers who had banded together in a reading club. According to Cyrus Field Willard, who played a key role in the founding of the Nationalist movement and was the first editor of *The Nationalist*, the magazine of the new movement, it was precisely the idea of "military regimentation" that had "made a great impression on the retired army

11. Ibid.
12. Cyrus Field Willard, "The Nationalist Club of Boston: A Chapter of History," *The Nationalist* 1, no. 1 (May 1889): 16.

officers who composed the reading club."[13] This group included Thomas Wentworth Higginson, noted abolitionist and leader of the first Black regiment in the Civil War, who had also been sympathetic to Fourierism earlier. They wrote to Bellamy in September, 1888, proposing to form an organization which would actively seek to realize the social vision contained in *Looking Backward*. After obtaining Bellamy's approval, the "Boston Bellamy Club" was formed.[14]

At about the same time that the retired Boston army officers were becoming acquainted with Bellamy's scheme, in 1888, Cyrus Field Willard, Sylvester Baxter, and William Dean Howells wrote to Bellamy separately suggesting that an organization or association be formed to draw together those who wished to work for the realization of a new collectivist order.[15] Howells had learned about socialism from Laurence Gronlund's *The Cooperative Commonwealth* and was, moreover, acquainted with Bellamy as a promising novelist.[16] Both Willard and Baxter, who had never met and were only brought together through their correspondence with Bellamy, were Boston newspaper reporters. Both were members of the Theosophical Society. This last fact was of critical importance in the development of the Nationalist movement. The rapid spread of the Nationalist clubs, and their later decline, as well as the hostility to politics and organized political action that characterized the first stage of the Nationalist movement, stemmed in part from the role which the Theosophists played in its history.

Bellamy gave his approval to Willard and Baxter's plans, but took no active role at first, beyond putting the leaders of the "Boston Bellamy Club" in touch with them. Together with the retired military men, Edward Everett Hale and others, they formed the First Nationalist Club of Boston at the end of 1888.[17] The president was Captain Charles E. Bowers, who had been chairman of the now-merged Bellamy Club, and Bellamy was its first vice-president, with General Arthur F. Devereaux, Willard and Baxter taking the other offices.[18] Insofar as the Nationalist

13. Morgan, *Edward Bellamy*, p. 248.   14. Ibid., pp. 248–249.

15. Ibid., pp. 247–248.

16. Ibid., pp. 260–261; see Joseph Schiffman, "Mutual Indebtedness: Unpublished Letters of Edward Bellamy to William Dean Howells," *Harvard Library Bulletin* 12 (Autumn 1958): 363–374.

17. Morgan, *Edward Bellamy*, pp. 248–249; Everett McNair, *Edward Bellamy*, pp. 41–52.

18. Willard, "The Nationalist Club of Boston," pp. 16–20; McNair, *Edward Bellamy*, pp. 41–52.

movement ever had a central organization, it was the First Club of Boston which played that role. In May, 1889, the First Club launched *The Nationalist*, placing the ideas of Nationalism before the general public. Within a year, however, a second club was launched that would be more concerned with "practical" Nationalism.[19]

The philanthropic orientation of the Nationalist movement and the belief of its founders that they were an elite who would lead the ignorant and incompetent masses into the new collectivist society was stamped upon the movement from its inception. In replying to one of Willard's letters concerning the formation of the clubs, Bellamy wrote: "I thoroughly approve of what you say as to directing your efforts more particularly to the conversion of the cultured and conservative class. That was precisely the special end for which *Looking Backward* was written."[20] Bellamy's advice coincided with Willard's Theosophist doctrines. By appealing to the "highest class of citizens," according to Willard, they were following the injunctions in the *Bhagavad-Gita* that "That which is done by the most excellent of men in time is done by all others."[21]

The Nationalists' aim of converting only the "cultured" and highest class of persons, in contrast to the policy of the existing socialistic groups which appealed to the working class and exacerbated class conflict, was consistent with *Looking Backward*'s "evolutionary" and "practical" nature. Rather than damn the capitalists, as the radical socialists did, the Nationalists would convert them, along with the members of the middle class who could understand the need for improving the miserable lot of the workers on ethical grounds, and as a matter of practicality understand the need for heading off the impending destruction of society, whether by a plutocratic usurpation, or an elemental outburst of the brutalized workers. *The Nationalist* in 1889 reprinted an editorial from the *Boston Post* which it affirmed had pinpointed the Bellamyite strategy:

> In one respect the Nationalists and the Christian Socialists who are attempting practically the same work, are right. They are applying to the advance of their reform the system which long and painful work has shown to be the best; they are beginning at the top, and their propaganda is to be carried on, not among the humble and suffering, where it would, at best, but foster a futile discontent, but among the favored classes, who by virtue of their advantages, should

19. McNair, *Edward Bellamy*, p. 76.
20. Willard, "The Nationalist Club of Boston," p. 17.
21. Quoted in *The Nationalist* 1, no. 6 (October 1889): 222.

be the readiest to hear and the promptest to act. It is *noblesse oblige* now, as ever, and their battle cry has the ring of high-minded endeavor, the touch of self-abnegation which has never yet failed of a response.[22]

Similarly, *The Nationalist* called upon the rich to make a wiser use of their possessions. Rich men who heaped up their wealth not for themselves but for their children ought to see that only by improving social conditions could they guarantee their children a "far brighter future" than individual wealth could give to them. "In no better way could this end be reached than by using such power to hasten the day of the triumph of the principles for which Nationalism stands—a triumph that is inevitable."[23]

The immediate task which the budding Nationalist movement set for itself was the winning over of the "educated" middle class and even the higher-minded capitalists themselves. This meant that the organization could not be a political movement, at least not in the ordinary sense of that term. For as *Looking Backward* had made clear, to play at politics and to intensify partisanship meant giving one's approval to the organized expression of individual and class selfishness that led inevitably to the disorder, conflict, and self-seeking of capitalist society. If the final Nationalist goal was truly to be the absorption of all classes into the organic nation, and the breakdown of all partial relationships which stood between the individual and the state, then the way to begin was by minimizing class and group conflict through an appeal to the "higher" impulses of individuals. For this purpose, it was necessary to formulate a program and to adopt an organizational strategy which men of all classes and parties who were imbued with the correct ethical outlook could agree upon; neither the program nor the strategy, if it were to be consistent, could in any way suggest the setting of class against class. Thus in attempting to put these principles into practice, the Nationalists were determined from the first only to engage in "practical" as opposed to political activity. But the meaning of "practical politics" became increasingly fuzzy under the impress of internal and external developments. Its final breakdown signaled a crucial turn in the outlook of the Nationalist movement.

Bellamy's fatalistic theory logically required no activity. Whatever might be conceived as the purpose of the organization of the clubs and of

22. *The Nationalist* 2, no. 2 (January 1890): 73.
23. Ibid.

the propagation of *Looking Backward*'s message, the furthest thing from the Nationalists' minds was to stimulate a popular movement. Not only was it not required if the victory of Nationalism was inevitable, but on the contrary it was positively undesirable, for its only consequence could be to impel the working class into motion. At least until the ground had been thoroughly prepared by those who would steer the inevitable evolution of society into its proper channels, which itself first required the recruitment of a Nationalist vanguard from among the educated, any connection between the Nationalists and a popular movement involved in immediate issues was at best futile, and at worst likely to be dangerous. The method of organization and the kind of persons who were to be appealed to were discussed in great detail by Bellamy himself in his letter to Thomas Wentworth Higginson:

> I am sure you will agree with me that in view of the impending industrial revolution, and the necessity that the American people should be properly instructed as to its nature and possible outcome, a profound responsibility is upon the men who have the public ear and confidence. No doubt somehow or other the revolution will get itself carried out but it will make a vast difference as to the ease or peril of the change whether or not it is led and guided by the natural leaders of the community or left to the demagogues. It was the peculiar felicity of our countrymen in their revolt of 1775 that their natural leaders, the men of education and position, led it. I hope and confidently trust that the same felicity may attend them in the coming industrial and social revolution and assure an equally prosperous course and issue for the great transformation. As for our politicians they will only follow not lead popular opinion. It belongs to the literary classes to create and direct that opinion.[24]

Bellamy's prescription for a Nationalist elite composed of intellectuals drawn from the educated middle classes became the basic formula for the organization, the method of work and social composition of most of the Nationalist clubs throughout the country. The clubs and their spokesmen proudly emphasized this aspect of the Nationalist movement. Reviewing the progress of the movement at the end of its first year, Cyrus Field Willard noted that the parent club, the First Club of Boston, had deliberately limited its membership to 250 persons to avoid "too unwieldy an organization," but far more importantly, because they had wanted "to pick our members and indirectly encourage the formation of

---

24. Quoted in Joseph Schiffman, ed., *Edward Bellamy: Selected Writings on Religion and Society.* pp. 138–139.

other clubs in different sections of the city."[25] Willard's defensive reaffirmation of this distinctive characteristic of the Nationalist movement reveals that it had not been ignored by their critics:

> We have been unjustly criticized on the ground that we were too exclusive or felt too good to mix with the common people, were "rose-water revolutionists" and so on, simply because we desired to pick the best material for effective work and not admit any and every person who came along with a burning desire to reform the world or join a club for the sake of joining. As has been said by Henry A. Ford of Detroit, "The Nationalist Club is not a cave of Adullam for the debtor and the 'malcontent.'" Some of the men who founded the first club had had experience in trying to change social forms before *Looking Backward* was written and they had often been told that it was the unsuccessful man, the ignorant and the violent, who desired a change. Therefore, it was made an unwritten law that this new club should be composed as much as possible of men who had been successful in the present fierce competitive struggle. They were not the weak, crying for mercy; they were the strong, demanding justice. They were not the crank or uneducated foreigner, importing ideas declared to be "exotics"; they were men of position, educated, conservative in speech and of the oldest New England stock. In fact one prominent newspaper accused them of being the Brahmin caste of New England. There were among the charter members ministers and authors, whose names are household words, clear-headed practical newspaper men who had fought their way up to positions of influence in their profession, lawyers, doctors, business men and soldiers who ranked high among their fellows as men of sense. . . . [26]

The strong strain of nativism, revealed in the remark about the "uneducated foreigners," hardly surprising in a native-as-apple-pie socialism, stemmed from the fear of an urban proletariat increasingly made up of immigrants. In no small degree, the presence of these unAmerican elements with their foreign doctrines and "exotic" beliefs, together with their alleged penchant for violence, or at least violent rhetoric, was to the Nationalists' way of thinking only one more reason why the change to the new order had to be guided wisely from above by persons like themselves. Thus the monthly reports of the clubs throughout the country which were regularly published in *The Nationalist* constantly stressed that theirs was

25. Cyrus Field Willard, "A Retrospect," *The Nationalist* 2, no. 1 (December 1889): 38–39.

26. Ibid.

not a movement "composed of the ignorant or 'dangerous classes.' " Unlike these elements, with whom the public associated socialist doctrines, the "men and women in the new club command respect." The "prestige of their social position and the force of their intellect" gave to the new dispensation of Bellamy and his followers an audience among the conservative middle class which no party or group based on the working class could possibly obtain.[27]

Typical of the clubs were the Chicago Nationalists. One hundred and fifty members and guests gathered at a meeting at the Palmer House to which "those only were admitted who had received written invitations." Consistent with their exclusive principles, they decided to continue to meet bimonthly by invitation only. Presumably in this way contamination by the lower classes could be avoided and the membership of the club restricted to members of the middle classes.[28]

The leadership of the First Boston Club, the parent club and the publishers of *The Nationalist*, stressed that their movement was one which embraced *all* classes, in keeping with the ideological beliefs expounded by Bellamy. Yet this line was perfectly consistent with their effort to restrict membership in the clubs to a middle-class elite, for it was only in conjunction with the rare membership of a labor leader in the movement such as P. J. McGuire, secretary of the American Federation of Labor, that the editors felt constrained to stress the all-inclusive character of the movement. Willard noted that Terrence Powderly, head of the Knights of Labor, and Samuel Gompers had praised Nationalism, and that McGuire had organized activities on behalf of Nationalism in New Jersey, but felt compelled to point out in the same breath to readers of *The Nationalist* that "not alone from labor organizations do we derive strength. Our movement takes in all classes."[29] The Nationalist movement, Willard was pointing out obliquely, was not a socialist movement of the working-class variety, such as the American public had come to associate with anticapitalist groups.

Even allowing for a tendency to stress respectability, the regular club reports published monthly indicate that workers were not sought after and did not, in fact, belong to the clubs. When workers did join, they were usually segregated in clubs of their own. The formation of clubs in other sections of Boston indicates the relationship which the

27. Ibid.
28. *The Nationalist* 1, no. 5 (September 1889): 174.
29. Ibid.

Nationalists thought would be the proper one between middle-class reformers and those who were the object of their reforms. In Los Angeles, with some three dozen clubs, there was one workingmen's club: "That it was considered desirable to organize a special club for workingmen was a reflection on the composition of most of the regular Nationalist societies, which recruited their membership primarily from middle-class come-outers of whom a large proportion were women. But it also indicated that the Los Angeles Nationalists were willing to welcome the affiliation of working-class members, a condition not always existent elsewhere."[30] Such a policy of segregation, combined with the Nationalists' reluctance to support elementary demands of the organized labor movement such as the eight-hour day,[31] and their general disdain for the efforts of the trade unions—not to mention their plan for regimentation of the workers—obviously did little to endear them to class-conscious workers.[32]

On the whole the Nationalists were successful both in keeping out unwanted elements and in recruiting members primarily from the ranks of the educated middle classes. William Morris's assertion that the ideal of life embodied in *Looking Backward* was a reflection of the ideals of the "industrious professional middle-class men of to-day"[33] was borne out generally by the social composition of the Nationalist Clubs.

Organization reports of the clubs as well as those of more objective observers consistently noted the predominance of individuals from the professions and the educated middle classes in the ranks of the Nationalists. Lawyers in particular abounded, while clergymen, doctors, teachers, journalists, and an assortment of "literary" people were most often mentioned. From Washington, D.C.: "Our club numbers about sixty members, of both sexes, among whom are doctors, lawyers, divines, as well as a good sprinkling of literary and artistic people."[34] From Chicago: "The membership of the club is composed of lawyers, bank officers, merchants and other persons of the middle classes."[35] From Portsmouth, New Hampshire: "[Membership includes] four teachers, a

30. Howard Quint, "Gaylord Wilshire and Socialism's First Congressional Campaign," *Pacific Historical Review* 26, no. 4 (November 1957): 328.

31. See Willard, "The Eight-Hour Day," *The Nationalist* 2, no. 2 (January 1890): 48 for an expression of the Nationalists' attitude toward the labor movement and the eight-hour day.

32. See Quint, *The Forging of American Socialism*, ch. 3.

33. William Morris, *The Commonweal*, June 22, 1889.

34. *The Nationalist* 1, no. 1 (May 1889): 26.

35. Ibid.

merchant, three master iron workers, an artist, several ladies, and the public librarian."[36]

The social composition of the First Boston Club is of special interest because of the key role it played in the history of the movement. Like the clubs throughout the country, the First Club had a substantial number of professional men—lawyers, doctors, and journalists—and a large number of women, some of whom were writers, teachers, or of that class of fairly well-off, educated Boston women who had played a prominent role in various American reform movements, from women's rights and child-labor protection to temperance and other movements of spiritual uplift.[37] Although few of the Boston Club's members could qualify as Brahmins, contrary to the newspaper reports cited by Willard, a surprisingly large number of those who founded the club and carried on its activities in the early period were related to old New England families, probably much like Bellamy's own family. Willard himself was a journalist, and the son of an "old aristocratic Boston family." At the founding meeting, Willard claimed, "hardly a person in that room . . . but was the descendant of early New Englanders."[38]

Although disputing Willard's claim that the First Club could boast a sizable number of businessmen as members, Nicholas Paine Gilman, a severe critic of Bellamy and the Nationalists, admitted that the Nationalists attracted to their ranks elements drawn from the professional middle classes. By direct observation at Nationalist meetings, Gilman noted only one businessman, but numerous clergymen, and many physicians, journalists, and lawyers, plus some twenty-six women whose occupations he did not attempt to classify. The greatest audience for *The Nationalist* he believed to be among the "literary" classes.[39]

Similar conclusions were reached by other independent observers. In California, where the Nationalists were the most numerous, one

36. Ibid.

37. The membership of the First Boston Club included among the women Frances Willard (Cyrus F. Willard's cousin), who was President of the Women's Christian Temperance Union; Mary A. Livermore, leader of the women's suffrage movement; Abby Morton Diaz, President of the Boston WCTU; Anna Whitney, a sculptress; Lucy Stone, editor of the *Women's Journal;* Helen Campbell and Constance Howell, both novelists; and Julia Ward Howe's daughter, Maude Howe Eliot. (Morgan, *Edward Bellamy*, pp. 247–251.)

38. *The Nationalist* 1, no. 5 (September 1889): 174.

39. Nicholas Paine Gilman, *Socialism and the American Spirit* (1893), pp. 197–199 and "Nationalism," *Quarterly Journal of Economics*, October 1889.

writer noted that the most striking thing about the movement was the "strength of . . . [the Nationalists] among the middle classes. For the most part they are people connected with literature and the professions."[40] Comparing the impact of the Nationalists with that of the Socialist Labor Party, Richard T. Ely observed that the Nationalists had had a great deal more influence with "the professional classes of the country, and particularly the clergy."[41]

The social background and careers of the leading spokesmen for the Nationalists were very similar to those of the members of the clubs. Bellamy, Gronlund, and Burnette G. Haskell,[42] for example, were all middle-class intellectuals possessing a relatively high degree of formal education, who found it very difficult to find occupations offering material security which were at the same time suited to their education and talent. All began as lawyers. Not one of the three, however, found they could earn a satisfactory income in legal practice. Perhaps, too, like Bellamy, they found the concrete realities of law ethically distasteful. Each drifted out of the law into journalism as one of the few occupations open to persons with formal education who wanted a professional career not too closely involved in commerce or business. Sylvester Baxter and Cyrus Field Willard were also professional journalists, employed as reporters on Boston newspapers.

Clergymen also figured prominently in the leadership of the Nationalist clubs. As an occupation, the ministry, like law and journalism, was a profession to which educated middle-class persons with no particular bent, or opportunity for business, and who may have felt some antipathy for commerce, could turn. A minister enjoyed a regular, if low, income and standing in the community.

On the whole, then, the social composition of the membership and immediate supporters of the movement was urban and middle class. Occupationally, the bulk of the members were engaged in the liberal and intellectual professions: doctors, lawyers, clergymen, artists, teachers, journalists, and a mixed collection of occupations which the Nationalists,

40. F. I. Vassault, *The Overland Monthly* 15 (June 1890): 559–561.

41. Richard T. Ely, *Socialism and Social Reform* (1894), p. 71.

42. On Haskell, see Chester McArthur Destler, *American Radicalism*, (1946), pp. 78–104; Henry David, *The Haymarket Affair*, (1958), pp. 146–149; Caroline Medan, "Burnette Gregory Haskell: California Radical" M.A. thesis, University of California, Berkeley, 1958).

in the terminology of the period, usually referred to as "literary folk"—
i.e., declassed intellectual and/or educated persons living in the inter-
stices of an industrial and urban America, earning their livelihoods (or
trying to) at one or another of the jobs open to, and regarded as suitable
for, persons with a better education than the ordinary man, and some
legitimate claim to culture and intellectual standing. In addition, the
Nationalists attracted, especially in New England, people who were of
modest wealth and whose background was that of the established old
middle classes who had been socially and politically dominant before the
Civil War, but whose position had been severely undermined by the rise
of industrial capitalism. One can speculate that this second grouping
probably best describes the large number of women who were drawn to
Bellamy's message of social reform from above, particularly in Boston,
and to a considerable extent probably describes the social origins if not
the actual situation in the 1880s and 1890s of many of those in the first
group. Bellamy himself would, of course, be an excellent example of an
individual who fell into both categories.[43]

Nationalism's immediate influence was most directly exercised
among elements who had in common characteristics which, when taken
together, permit us to treat them as a relatively distinct social stratum
within the middle class. Bellamyites were not, on the whole, property
owners nor small businessmen actively engaged in production, trade, or
farming. Instead, they were drawn either from the traditionally "independent" professions or from the new, dependent, salaried occupations and
professions which were in large part, although not entirely, the product of
large-scale industrial capitalism and of the concomitant trend toward "collectivism" in American society upon which Bellamy had predicated his
utopia. The relationship of both the independent professions and of the
salaried occupations to the economic and social conditions making up the
 world of the old propertied middle class, which had hitherto dominated
American society, was tending to become more similar under the impact
of industrialization and economic concentration. In the case of the former,
the relationship to small property was being radically altered and made
highly tenuous, at least for certain professions, while for the latter the new

43. For a portrait of the aristocratic reformers in Boston, see Mann, *Yankee Reformers
in an Urban Age.*

"collectivist" society of which they were largely a product was pulling them further and further away from the values, aspirations, and social outlook of the propertied middle class, although, at the same time, they were not reconciled to their new existence.[44]

Thus, although it is important for certain analytical purposes to distinguish the independent professions that, historically, had been tied to the entrepreneurial middle class in American society, from those occupations directly divorced from property and entrepreneurial activity—that is, the so-called "new middle class" of salaried employees and professionals—it is descriptively useful and theoretically valid to group them together and to characterize them as members of an "intellectual class" or a native-born intelligentsia. For to do so underlines the point that such elements were not only increasingly divorced from individual property relations, whether formally self-employed or not, but even more important, from the standpoint of explaining the content and direction of their political and social views, both groups together made up the rapidly expanding stratum of relatively well-educated middle-class persons for whom an advanced education rather than property as such was becoming the primary means for personal advancement. Indeed, it was the only way they could maintain themselves in the "middle class"—that is to say, keep from falling into the ranks of the ordinary working class. Harold Lasswell has drawn an incisive portrait of this class as it has developed within modern capitalism:

> The growth of the vast material environment in modern society has been paralleled by the unprecedented expansion of specialized symbolic activity. Medicine, engineering, and physical science have proliferated into a thousand specialties for the control of specific aspects of the material world. Those who master the necessary symbol equipment are part of the intellectual class whose "capital" is knowledge, not muscle. There is a sub-division of the intellectual workers, the "intellectuals" in the narrow sense, who specialize in the symbols connected with political life. The growing complexity of modern civilization had created a vast net of reporters, interpretors, pedagogues, advertisers, agitators, propagandists, legal dialecticians, his-

44. See Samuel P. Hays, *The Response to Industrialism: 1885–1914* (Chicago: University of Chicago Press, 1957), pp. 73–74 for a succinct description and analysis of the circumstances and outlook of these elements in this period. See also Richard Hofstadter, *The Age of Reform* and C. Wright Mills, *White Collar* (1951), chs. 1–3 for a brilliant survey of the decline of the old middle class and the rise of the new.

torians and social scientists who compete among themselves and
with all other classes and sub-classes for deference, safety and material income. . . .[45]

Clearly this is the picture of a class which, at the time of the Nationalists, was a class in the process of formation—with half its roots in the
world of the old middle class and the other half in the organizational
revolution initiated by corporate capitalism. Its transitional character in
this period is crucial to understanding the attraction which the politics
and social ideal of Nationalism held for persons drawn from this class.

The degree to which the typical Nationalist club member or supporter was a member of a relatively privileged minority in American
society of the 1880s and 1890s may be seen from the fact that in 1880 the
average American had less than four years of education.[46] Most of the
Nationalists, on the other hand, especially those in the professions, may
be assumed to have attended and perhaps to have been graduated from a
college or professional school or, at the very least, to have been the
beneficiaries of a secondary education.[47] Yet the fact that they felt it
necessary, as we have seen, to constantly call attention to their superior
education and to assert, somewhat uncertainly, their claim to be the
bearers of "culture"—an assertion made most frequently in connection
with their efforts to distinguish their brand of conservative anticapitalism
from that of the radical democratic politics of the working-class–oriented
socialists—suggests that the opportunities that they believed education
ought to have opened up and the privileges it should have conferred
upon them were far from being realized.

The Nationalist movement thus succeeded in attracting to itself the
very elements which Bellamy had designated as the natural leadership of
the movement that was to introduce the new collectivist order from
above, and to occupy a special and privileged position in the new order.
The technical and scientific professions, of course, were to serve in the

45. Harold Lasswell, "The Psychology of Hitlerism," (July-September 1933): 376.
For a theoretical discussion of the modern intelligentsia and the function of education in
creating a "class" which, because of its frequently diverse social derivation and the nature
of its training and function, seems—especially to its members and ideological spokesmen—
to be "relatively classless," see Karl Mannheim, *Ideology and Utopia* (New York: Harvest,
1936), pp. 154 ff. and the same author's *Man and Society in an Age of Reconstruction* (1940),
pp. 98–107.

46. Arthur M. Schlesinger, *The Rise of the City, 1878–1898* (1933), pp. 171–172.

47. Ibid.

industrial army but their talent and education made them the bureaucratic administrators of the state apparatus, rather than mere privates. In
contrast, the liberal professions and the intellectuals who did not participate directly in the management of the economy were to be excused
from service in the industrial army and would not therefore be permitted
to occupy the office of the commander-in-chief of the industrial army or
state. They could, however, be given the right, unlike those who were
consigned to the industrial army, to vote for the president along with the
guilds of retired workers. Given the total abolition of democracy and
representative government, such a concession is important as an index of
Bellamy's special attitude toward these elements. Bellamy's collectivist
utopia thus assured the intellectuals that only the ordinary and common
workers would be subjected to the discipline of the army of labor. They
would enjoy a privileged position because the educated middle class was,
of all the groups in capitalist society, somehow most capable of rising
above mere self-interest and thus above politics and partisanship. The
belief that the intellectuals or educated portions of the middle class were
in some mysterious way "classless," and hence that their political and
social views could promote the interests of all segments of society—of
the organic Nation—was a critical element in Nationalist ideology. For
within the context of Bellamy's utopian politics, as in Plato's *Republic*, it
was logically required that there exist some force or body of men not
corrupted by capitalist society and immune to the selfishness which was
its essence. The belief in the disinterested character of these elements,
then, provided a *deus ex machina* in the form of living men who could
guide the evolution of Society into the new order from above. At the
same time, it indicated just which stratum within society could and
would provide the nucleus of the new noncapitalist ruling class to rule
over the socialist society drawn to Bellamy's specifications.

5 THE SOCIALISM OF THE EDUCATED CLASSES

Why did members of the educated middle classes, some of them intellectuals in the narrow sense of the term, but all of whom were engaged in the "intellectual occupations," find the political and social vision contained in Bellamy's utopia so attractive? On one level, the answer is obvious: Bellamy offered a socialism in which the educated (or "eddicated" as Engels caustically referred to the Fabians and their Nationalist cousins) middle class would gradually evolve into a new ruling class. Bellamy's bureaucratic state socialism was thus an alternative to the radical democratic collectivism of the working-class socialist movement as well as a solution to the equally undesirable fate many of these elements saw awaiting them with the development of monopoly capitalism. In either case they faced the loss of their superior status over the workers and their eventual amalgamation with them. If a collectivist society was inevitable, then Bellamy at least promised that the talented and educated elite of the middle class could and would create their own kind of socialist society: a hierarchical, bureaucratic social order in which they and people like themselves would best be fitted to come out on top, just where they knew they belonged. Bellamy's ideal of rule by a supposedly unselfish and incorruptible elite or, in our own time, by managers or intellectuals, is as old as Plato's Republic and as new as the latest model of 1984 advocated by the proponents of a "technetronic" society. At bottom, it is the dream of eliminating social conflicts conservatively from above, so that the privileged position of the middle ranks may be preserved from the democratic demands of those classes below them. In the case of the Nationalists, what was clearly at stake in the closing decades of the nineteenth century was the privileged position of those groups whose capital consisted of a monopoly of knowledge and culture, threatened alike by plutocracy and proletariat. As will be shown, the evidence to support this explanation of Nationalism's appeal to discontented members of the educated middle classes may be found readily in the literature of the movement, especially in Bellamy's and Gronlund's writings. A significant parallel is to be found in Europe in this same period. Authoritarian, antidemocratic collectivist movements and ideologies sprang up which appealed primarily to professionals, intellectuals, and other educated or semi-educated persons located in what came to be termed the "new middle class."[1] The enthusiastic reception accorded Bellamy's utopia among members of these strata, one that was no less astonishing in its depth and extent than it had been in America, offers additional evidence of the class nature of Bellamyism's appeal.[2]

Yet, *why* at this particular historical juncture did this mode of anticapitalist thought attract such elements in the first place? Only if one assumes that intellectuals and other members of the educated middle classes have some necessary and natural affinity for socialism of an authoritarian variety as the result of some invariable psychological or sociological law whose operation leads them inevitably to try to impose their rule, is it possible to leave the question at this point.[3] Thus, for example, Lewis Feuer has argued with considerable force that the two souls of the socialist movement emanate "from two basically different psychological sources . . . the desire of the intellectuals to be the ruling class [and] the

1. For the general ideological background of such movements, see J. Salwyn Schapiro, *Liberalism and the Challenge of Fascism* chs. 13–15. There are a number of specific studies, primarily of Germany, which deal with the anti-Semitic parties and various nationalist groupings and ideologies, all from the standpoint of attempting to explain later developments in the 1920s which aided the growth of the Nazi movement. See also George L. Mosse, *The Crisis of German Ideology* (New York: Grosset & Dunlap, 1964). Much of Mosse's description of the several elements of the "German ideology," especially that which deals with the mystical, health-faddist, and nature movement, provides important parallels to Bellamy's Nationalism with its strong Theosophical current (see below) and its close intellectual and social relationship to other seemingly marginal expressions of middle-class anxiety such as Christian Science, spiritualism, and most important of all, antipolitical authoritarianism cloaked in "utopian" ventures. There are two excellent studies which tie anti-Semitic parties with their anticapitalist rhetoric to specific historical and sociological analysis: Paul Massing, *Rehearsal for Destruction*, esp. pp. 75–76, 135 ff. for the new middle class; Peter G. J. Pulzer, *The Rise of Political Anti-Semitism in Germany and Austria*. See especially Pulzer, ch. 29, on the social composition of the various anti-Semitic movements.

2. Sylvia E. Bowman et al., *Edward Bellamy Abroad* (1962) is a survey of Bellamy's foreign impact which, despite the intentions of its editor, indicates quite clearly that aside from the right-wing Social Democrats, Bellamy's tract was the inspiration for a number of individuals and movements that can with accuracy be regarded as the forerunners of the fascists.

3. A summary of such theories together with a critical discussion may be found in Daniel Bell, "Two Roads from Marx," in *The End of Ideology* (New York: Collier, 1961). See also Lewis S. Feuer, "Marx and the Intellectuals," (October 1963): 102–112.

desire of the working class for a society of equals."[4] Yet, as Feuer him-self admits, members of the intellectual class have at times rejected or sloughed off their elitist politics and adopted the democratic viewpoint of the working-class socialist movement. What accounts for this develop-ment? It need hardly be said that an explanation cast in the form of an invariable psychological desire for domination or even a natural affinity for the preservation of class privileges cannot satisfactorily answer this question, however descriptively accurate it may be in particular histori-cal periods. More important, it cannot account for the authoritarian sympathies and politics of the working class itself at different points in its history.[5]

Once again, the case of the early Fabians comes quickly to mind because of their similarity to the Nationalists. The proclivity of the leading members of the Fabian Society for bureaucratic forms of social-ism and their strong aversion to democratic participation was widely recognized by their many critics in the era before World War I. William English Walling, for example, with deadly accuracy accused the Webbs of favoring a socialism in which the intellectuals and the higher levels of skilled workers would rule over the masses.[6] Yet, in the prewar period, before the depth of the inner crisis of capitalism had manifested itself fully, the authoritarian tendency of Fabianism was attenuated by a grow-ing, vigorous, and optimistic Labour Party with its expanding working-class support which created a strong pull in the direction of democracy and egalitarianism. As a result there was a powerful tension within Fabianism itself.

After the war, and especially after the onset of the general crisis of world capitalism in 1929, when the Labour Party proved unable to offer a powerful solution, many of the leading Fabians and other British intel-

4. Feuer, "Marx," p. 112. See also Robert Michels, *Political Parties* (Glencoe: Free Press, 1958).

5. Edward Bernstein, *Ferdinand Lassalle* (1893) is an outstanding example of a Marx-ist analysis of "working class authoritarianism" in the nineteenth century. Michels' treat-ment of Lassalle in *Political Parties* (p. 101), using the very same materials as Bernstein in which Lassalle calls for the submission to his iron will, should be compared with Bern-stein's as an example of why Michels' ahistorical method distorts the evidence in favor of the essentially metaphysical "iron law of oligarchy" which depends, in the last analysis, on a postulate of an invariable drive for power.

6. William English Walling, *Progressivism and After* (New York: Macmillan, 1911), pp. 241–246.

lectuals of a similar persuasion drifted to overtly totalitarian collectivist politics. Some supported Stalin's regime, although others, like Bernard Shaw, also flirted for a time with that other totalitarian cure for the ills of capitalism, fascism. Stalinism was especially attractive to these "moderate" Fabian intellectuals precisely because it was authoritarian and antidemocratic. It provided evidence that the idea of a regime of socialist bureaucrats, or as the Webbs called it, a "civil-service state," was a practical reality. The intellectuals had, in Orwell's words, at last gotten "the whip-hand" over the workers. Gronlund and Bellamy had only been able to visualize such a utopia in an undeveloped form, basing their views on the best models available to them. But in the 1930s, the Webbs and Shaw and other fellow-travelers of the Communist Party—and in America many liberals who did not bother to style themselves socialists—had the advantage of finding a working model of their paradise in Stalinist Russia, one that proved, to their joy, that the workers could not rule themselves and had to be carefully civilized from above by their betters. Of course the existence of the Stalinist state and the Stalinist movement throughout the world introduced a qualitatively new historical factor into the situation. Nevertheless, as the example of the Webbs and other fellow-travelers demonstrates, to the degree that there was already a strong current of socialism-from-above present within the socialist movement, the power of totalitarianism derived in part from its ability to crystallize these tendencies. Or, to put it more accurately, it freed them from the previously effective restraints imposed by a strong, democratic, mass working-class movement.[7]

This example points to the need to examine the specific historical and sociological context in which such ideologies arise in order to assess their function and account for their appeal. In the case of Bellamyism one must view the problem not in static or fixed categories, but in terms of the relationship between existing classes and the "cumulative historical experiences" that shaped the outlook of the kinds of educated middle-class persons attracted to Looking Backward's message.

Only in this way, too, can one grasp the reasons for, and the meaning of, the tension between the authoritarian and democratic traditions in the socialist movement and understand the underlying dynamics

7. See Neal Wood, Communism and British Intellectuals (1959), and David Caute, The Fellow-Travellers (1973).

of the process by which one or the other becomes dominant, if only for a time. In this last, it is the historical perspective which is of special importance. As Paul Massing has noted in a similar context, the study of a sociological phenomenon such as authoritarian politics in historical depth serves not only to demonstrate the many and varied functions it may serve at different times and under different circumstances, and thus to reveal the different forces which may sustain it, but at the same time, "history also shows the forces which resisted it and the circumstances which hindered its growth. Any fruitful analysis . . . therefore, must be concrete and sensitive to its varied and often contradictory manifestations."[8] From this perspective, to explain the appeal of Bellamyism requires an examination of the objective circumstances and the specific historical context which shaped the consciousness of these elements, making them receptive to Bellamy's bureaucratic utopia.

Emergence of the New Class

Although the major thrust for reform in the 1890s came not from the urban middle class but from the farmers, a molecular process was simultaneously taking place among the former in the 1880s and 1890s which was later to be crystallized in the amorphous but powerful Progressive movement. The Nationalists in the early 1890s served as the urban wing of the Populists in the East and the West. As critics of laissez faire capitalism and advocates of state intervention they became the catalyst not only for the nascent socialist movement but also helped to crystallize the urban middle-class discontent and social awareness that found expression in the Progressive movement.

The social background and general outlook of the members of the Nationalist clubs were similar to those patrician reformers whom Richard Hofstadter aptly characterizes as the "Mugwump" type—individuals from the old established middle class who, along with the other members of their class found that they had been, or were in the process of being, ousted from their positions of social and political dominance by the new capitalists of finance and industry.[9] The Mugwump reformers of the

8. Massing, *Rehearsal for Destruction*, p. xvii.
9. Hofstadter, *The Age of Reform*, chs. 4–7. This section, as throughout the previous chapters draws heavily upon Hofstadter's insights about the character of the reform movement, particularly chapter 7 on "the struggle over organization." Since its publication many critics have attacked the empirical basis of Hofstadter's notion of the "status revolution"

1870s and 1880s were "the old gentry, the merchants of long standing, the small manufacturers, the established professional men, the civic leaders of an earlier era,"[10] who found that they were being "overshadowed" and edged aside in the making of basic political decisions.[11] They were not victims of economic hardship, nor did they lack opportunity in some absolute sense, but were, in their view, excluded from opportunities "of the highest sort for men of the highest standards." Thus, while the composite type Mugwumps were not growing poorer as a class "in a strictly economic sense," yet "their wealth and power were being dwarfed by comparison with the new eminence of wealth and power. They were less important and they knew it."[12] Certainly the tenor and content of Edward Bellamy's own complaints against the vulgarity of the rich and their corrupting influence on moral and political standards illustrates the way in which the resentment of these elements could easily find its outlet in demands for reform—reform of a conservative kind, of course.

It is not necessary to accept Hofstadter's disjunction between status and wealth and the notion of "status politics" which follows from it to find in his superbly drawn portrait of the Mugwump reformer a type that may be clearly recognized among the Nationalists—especially in

---

(ibid., pp. 135–166), pointing out that the class derivation of the conservative anti–Progressive politicians was little different than their Progressive counterparts. See, for example, E. Daniel Potts, "The Progressive Profile in Iowa," *MidAmerica* 47 (October 1965), and Richard B. Sherman, "The Status Revolution and Massachusetts Progressive Leadership," *Political Science Quarterly* 78 (March 1963). It is true that the disjunction between "status" deprivation and economic position, which is the basis of Hofstadter's paradoxical thesis that the classes from which the Progressive leadership stemmed were not economically threatened but only felt their status diminished in relation to the plutocracy (hence the characteristic qualities of Progressive politics) cannot be sustained on theoretical and perhaps not on empirical grounds. Status and class situation are inseparably bound together; and it is only on the basis of a kind of inverted crude economic determinism which looks to "self-interest" in the narrowest sense as the wellspring of political motivation rather than *class interest* and the perception of that interest by members of a given class, that Hofstadter's approach makes any sense. For this reason, among others, the argument over Hofstadter's "status revolution" is, I think, misdirected. But the validity—or at least the value—of Hofstadter's contribution does not rest upon this distinction and it has therefore been possible to draw upon his argument here without accepting it in toto. On the period of urban Progressive reform, see also Robert Wiebe, *The Search for Order* (1967), chs. 1–7; and Martin J. Schiesl, *The Politics of Efficiency: Municipal Administration and Reform in America, 1880–1920* (Berkeley: University of California Press, 1977).

10. Hofstadter, *The Age of Reform*, p. 137.
11. Ibid.   12. Ibid.

Boston, the home of nearly every indigenous upper-middle–class reform movement. Indeed, some of those individuals who became active in Nationalist clubs, as well as some of those who provided ideological inspiration for Nationalism's advocacy of a bureaucratic state to replace politics and politicians, had their roots in the tradition of upper-middle–class reform which gave rise to the Mugwump revolt in the 1870s and 1880s.[13]

However, Nationalists, on the whole, belonged to the next generation of reformers that came to maturity in the closing years of the nineteenth century and provided intellectual and political leadership for the era of urban middle-class reform, the Progressive era. These elements, Hofstadter points out, began to become involved in the new wave of reform sentiment in the 1890s; generationally and occupationally, they were very similar to the social grouping from which the Nationalist movement drew its support. The Progressive reformer, Hofstadter contends, was part of the transitional generation that had moved "sideways" in the class structure. For, rather than entering business or commerce, as their parents probably had, they instead had been forced to look for opportunity in the various professions and especially in the intellectual and semi-intellectual occupations in the new middle class that were rapidly increasing both in number and variety, for which education was a prerequisite.[14]

"Conditions varied from profession to profession," Hofstadter observes, nevertheless "all groups with claims to learning and skill shared a common sense of humiliation and common grievances against the plutocracy."[15] Between 1870 and 1890, the independent professions—medi-

---

13. Both Henry Demarest Lloyd and Eltweed Pomeroy began their political careers as supporters of the Liberal Republicans. A careful analysis of Gronlund's *Cooperative Commonwealth* demonstrates that his authoritarian views on democracy and the need for administration are, unquestionably, one hundred percent American insofar as they draw upon the writings of such Mugwump reformers as George Washington Curtis and Albert J. Stickney. Advocates of civil-service reform to cure governmental corruption, they were equally strong critics of democracy. Their ideas, particularly Stickney's, supplemented Gronlund's own authoritarian vision of socialism perfectly. It was Stickney, for example, whose statement, made and repeated in a number of works written from the mid-1870s on, that "Democratic government as I understand the term, means government by the people's brain. . . . It means government by the best men," who Gronlund was echoing in his own definition of democracy as nothing more than good administration. (Albert J. Stickney, *The Political Problem* [New York: Harper Bros., 1890], pp. 73–74.)

14. Hofstadter, *Age of Reform*, pp. 148–163.

15. Ibid., p. 149.

cine, law, dentistry, etc.—more than doubled in size, even though the population as a whole increased by only sixty-two percent.[16] Doctors outnumbered other professionals, although by 1890 there were nearly as many lawyers as doctors.[17] The expansion of the semi-professional self-employed stratum gives an even better indication of the changes in American society that were taking place in a period of rapid industrialization and urbanization. The number of persons who were classified by the census as artists, art teachers, sculptors, and photographers, for example, grew four times in the same twenty-year period—from some 11,772 in 1870 to approximately 42,500 in 1890.[18]

Individuals attracted to the professions now were probably those who in an earlier generation would have entered business or gone into farming. But the successive business crises of the post–Civil War decades, the increasingly precarious position of the independent farmer, and the squeezing out of small manufacturers and merchants by the new concentrations of capital—all of which contributed to a relative decline of the old middle class—meant that the prospect of independence through self-employment was diminishing. This decline in the old opportunity made the possibility of entering a profession with traditional independence more desirable than ever before to those who were anxious to maintain their position in the middle class.[19]

At the same time, the emergence of a new stratum of salaried, propertyless employees and professionals had parallel consequences for the independent professions, making them also more dependent upon the new "collectivism" of corporate capitalism that was undermining the world of small property. Some professionals began to work in an institutional or bureaucratic setting, as employees. This meant both a relative loss of economic independence as well as social and political standing in comparison to that which the old middle class had enjoyed. Now they either sold their services directly to big business or they were forced to compete in an increasingly impersonal urban labor market.[20]

These tendencies are particularly well illustrated in the case of the legal profession, from whose ranks so many Nationalists were drawn.

16. Computed from Alba Edwards, *Comparative Statistics for the United States, 1870 to 1940* (U.S. Government, 1940), Table 8, pp. 104–112 et passim.

17. Ibid.   18. Ibid.

19. See Chapter 3, above.

20. Hofstadter, *The Age of Reform*, p. 155 ff.

Traditionally, law in the United States had been, and still was, an occupation which appealed to young men on the make who lacked the necessary family connections or capital with which to advance themselves. Requirements for entry were low: the law schools were poor and, in any case, attendance at one was not even required for admission to the bar in many states.[21]

Although it is not possible to determine in any precise sense whether the legal profession was becoming an overcrowded occupation—between 1870 and 1890 the number of lawyers more than doubled[22]—the changes in its structure and internal composition brought about directly by industrial capitalism and economic concentration indicate that the kind and quality of opportunity which it offered had indeed changed by the end of the nineteenth century. More and more, in the last decades of the nineteenth century, Hofstadter observes, the complaint was heard from lawyers that the law had become too "commercialized," too subservient to the economic and social needs of big business, and less and less a "true" profession.[23] Behind these expressions of resentment was the fact that lawyers as a group were probably more heterogeneous in their make-up by the end of the nineteenth century than ever before.[24] Some tied their fortunes and aspirations to the declining situation of the old middle class in the small towns, while others became the allies and instruments of the new corporate economy. Moreover, the opening of vast new offices—to which the appropriate term "law factories" was very soon applied—in which small armies of lawyers performed specialized tasks for business clients, further divided lawyers between independent practitioners and salaried employees who had little prospect of ever being anything else. Although the salaried lawyers were not typical, their existence was, nevertheless, regarded as a portent of a precarious future—one in which at best there would be no possibility of independence such as there had been in the past, and at worst, the possibility of outright unemployment.[25]

The clergy, although technically a salaried profession, was at the same time one of the traditional professional careers for educated middle-class young men. It too expanded between 1870 and 1890—doubling in size from approximately 44,000 to some 88,000.[26] The clergy suffered from low wages and declining prestige and authority.[27] The rise of the

21. Ibid., pp. 155–163.   22. Idid.   23. Ibid., p. 157.
24. Ibid.   25. Ibid.   26. Ibid., pp. 149–153.
27. Ibid., pp. 150–153.

Social Gospel movement and of Christian Socialism, the latter being closely connected to the Nationalist movement in spirit and personnel, suggests that the clergy were deeply affected in their social outlook by the impact of industrial capitalism, not only on the laity, but on themselves.

Closely connected to these shifts in the situation and psychology of these older professions was the development of the entirely new stratum of relatively well-educated persons who, broadly speaking, made up the "new middle class" of salaried professionals and white-collar employees.

Although it was not until 1910 that the "new middle class" became a majority of the middle class as a whole, as early as 1870 salaried professionals made up a majority of all professionals: in 1870 only thirty-five percent of those in the professions were self-employed.

Thus, even though the circumstances and aspirations of the relatively well-educated people making up the urban middle-class intelligentsia were still closely bound up with those of the entrepreneurial middle class in 1890, they were, as a group, largely divorced from, or not directly involved in, individual property well before the major impact of industrial capitalism had been felt in American society.[28]

However, it was not until after 1870 that the older, traditional professions began to be supplemented by the "new middle class" that was the direct product of modern industrial organization and technology, and of the related trend toward urbanization. These changes in the occupational structure, especially the demand for persons with more education and training to fill the ranks of white-collar workers, were directly reflected in the transformation of secondary education after 1870, as Martin Trow has shown. Increasingly, larger numbers of people were trained to fill the jobs created by the growth of the very organizations which Bellamy and his followers later found to be the salvation of the middle classes. As the rationalization of industry and the growth of organizations to oversee the production and distribution of commodities now produced for a national market increased, "people had to be trained to handle those papers—to prepare them, to type them, to file them, to process them, to assess and use them. The growth of the secondary-school system after 1870 was in large part a response to the pull of the

28. C. Wright Mills, *White Collar*, ch. 1.

economy for a mass of white-collar employees with more than an elementary-school education."[29]

The number of public high schools grew from approximately 500 in 1870 to some 10,000 by 1910. Not only were more people being educated, but the curriculum changed to meet the schools' new function. "Before 1870 the small secondary-school system offered a curriculum and maintained standards of scholarship geared to the admissions requirements of the colleges."[30] After 1870, however, "the growing mass secondary system was largely terminal, providing a useful and increasingly vocational education for the new group of white-collar workers."[31]

Colleges were undergoing a similar transformation in response to these same trends in technological and economic organization. Land grant colleges and special technical institutions that sprang up after the Civil War together with the older colleges which modified their curriculum and turned away from educating a mere gentleman elite, began to offer the advanced training in the natural and physical sciences, theoretical as well as applied, and the other disciplines important to an industrialized society.[32] From 1870 to 1890, the number of college students more than tripled—from some 52,000 to about 157,000. The proportion of these in the entire population who were enrolled in colleges increased steadily from 1.68 percent in 1870 to 3.04 percent in 1890.[33]

Thus, both the independent and the salaried professions and technical occupations showed phenomenal growth after 1870. However, as Table I shows, while the intercensal rate of growth for both groupings was very great between 1870 and 1890, the salaried professionals and technicians showed the greatest rate of expansion. In the 1870s and 1880s, the independent professions grew at a rate of 44.5 percent in each decade. The salaried elements, on the other hand, expanded by some 71 percent from 1870 and 1880, and by around 64 percent from 1880 to 1890. In the decade from 1890 to 1900, the rate of expansion for both independent and salaried groups dropped by almost half, reflecting the serious depression which began in 1893, but while the latter's rate of growth went up again from 1900 to 1910, the independent professions' rate of growth continued on its downward course.

29. Martin Trow, "The Second Transformation of American Secondary Education," (September 1961): 144–166.
    30. Ibid., p. 145.   31. Ibid., p. 146.   32. Ibid.
    33. Ibid.

TABLE I[a] *Intercensal Rates of Growth of Independent Professions and Salaried Professions and Technical Employees, 1870–1910*

	1870–1880	1880–1890	1890–1900	1900–1910
Independent professions	45%	44%	29%	20%
Salaried professions and technical employees	71	64	38	55

[a] Computed from Alba Edwards, *Comparative Statistics for the United States, 1870 to 1940* (U.S. Government, 1940), Table 8, pp. 104–112.

Thus from 1870 to 1890, the stage was being set for a shift in the political atmosphere by the relative decline of the old middle classes and the enormous gain in relative and absolute terms of strata within the middle class for whom education and formal training, rather than property as such, provided the key to occupational opportunity and social mobility. The direction of the shift was determined by the fact that the elements expanding most rapidly were the salaried and dependent strata whose social antecedents, in all likelihood, were the old middle class, but who were themselves the product of and, in any case, closely bound up with the new collectivist social-economic relationships. Similar pressures and corresponding changes within those professions whose occupants were typically free practitioners weakened their traditional independence, and together with the new middle-class elements forced them to look away from private property and the laissez faire state.

One of the key questions that must be answered, however tentatively because of its problematic quality, if we are to assess the content and direction, as well as the intensity, of the political mood of these elements, is: To what degree did the professions and the proliferating new occupations adequately absorb their growing numbers and, at the same time, give them opportunities for advancement commensurate with those that entrepreneurial activity had provided (and still did, but to a diminishing degree) for the previous generation? To what degree was there "overcrowding" in these occupations? How steady was employment and, in the case of both the salaried elements as well as the independent professions, how difficult was it to earn a satisfactory living? Clearly there can be no answer to these questions formulated in absolute terms, for in the very nature of the matter what was adequate or satisfactory must be judged in terms of the historically determined reference points which the individuals themselves used. Here, certainly, the main point of comparison, given their ties to the old middle class and the fact that they lived in a period of transition, must have been the condition and quality of life that the ownership of one's own property bestowed upon the individual. With property, one was independent—but without it, how independent could one be when those who had economic power directly or indirectly determined whether one would be employed or unemployed, a member of the upper stratum of one's profession or one of those who, for example, grubbed a living in a dingy law office? To the degree that being a member of the "middle class" meant, to the members of the middle class itself, being economically independent, rather than working for a salary as a permanent employee of a firm, then their situation as neither manual workers nor members of the old middle class must have appeared anomalous, not to say precarious, to them. How different in their own eyes were the middle classes in their growing dependence upon an impersonal labor market or their subjection to the economic power of the new capitalists, from the ordinary workers? These and similar questions must have occurred to many middle-class people and, in any case as will be seen, they played a considerable role in the Nationalists' views.

It is not possible for us to answer these questions in any but the most tentative and sketchy fashion, both for the obvious reasons and because the kind of evidence available, statistical and historical, is very scanty, and at best offers an impressionistic overview.[34] The census of

34. There is a need for a detailed study based on a critical use of the sources now available of the economic situation, composition, employment, social origins, income, etc., of the professions and the new middle class in the period from 1870 to 1910. Such a study would, as our own examination of Nationalism should make clear, put into an entirely new light the various social, political, and religious movements in this period that so profoundly affected not only the cause of liberal reform in the pre–World War I period, but have left a lasting intellectual and political legacy to this day. See Lewis Corey's *Decline of American Capitalism* (1934), *The Crisis of the Middle Class* (New York: Covici-Friede, 1935), and the same author's article, written in 1945, "The Middle Class," reprinted in S. M. Lipset and R. Bendix, eds. *Class, Status, and Power* (1953), pp. 371–380. The difficulties in using the material available are very great indeed, but they do not seem to me to be insurmountable, especially if one were interested only in assessing the general outline and direction from a sociological standpoint. A succinct summary of the history of the occupational data gathered by the census, together with an account of the various attempts to group individ-

1890 made the first attempt to ascertain the amount and degree of unemployment among various occupational groups. The data suggest that unemployment or, more likely, *under*employment in the "professional services" was fairly high.[35] An article on unemployment published in the *Encyclopedia of Social Reform*, one of the earliest and most valuable attempts made to compile facts about social conditions for the use of social reformers, philanthropic societies and scholars, contended that the Census of 1890 had understated the amount of unemployment because, among other reasons,

> in the middle classes there are an increasing number of persons who do not work in factories, or stores, where statistics of employment are usually sought, but who are often in secret bitterly suffering for lack of remunerative work, caused perhaps by combinations of business offices and discharge of clerks. They have to keep up appearances just as long as possible in order to keep credit and to secure work. Often the bitterest suffering is in this class, of which the general public rarely hears and which statistics rarely reach.[36]

On essentially the same impressionistic level, but probably of far greater weight, and certainly of greater significance from the standpoint of our discussion, were the observations of the leading economist and

---

ual occupations into economically or socially meaningful categories on the basis of historical data gathered by past government censuses, may be found in W. S. Woytinsky, *Labor in the United States* (Washington: Social Science Research Council, 1938), pp. 235–239. Of great interest and use is Paul H. Douglas' classic study, *Real Wages in the United States, 1890–1926* (1930) which contains analysis of data on incomes for various occupational groups which is very suggestive. More recently, Daniel Carson has written on "Changes in the Industrial Composition of Manpower since the Civil War," in *Studies in Income and Wealth* 11 (New York: Conference on Income and Wealth, National Bureau of Economic Research, 1949) in an attempt to reformulate and rethink the problems involved in the use of the historical data available. On Britain, see Gregory Anderson, *Victorian Clerks* (Manchester: Manchester University Press, 1976), and Geoffrey Crossick, ed., *The Lower Middle Class in Britain* (London: Croom-Helm, 1977).

35. *Eleventh Census of the United States*, vol. 2, pp. cxxxvii–cxliii and 448 ff. For example, of those occupations officially listed as "professional service," it was found that among males, 42.26 percent were unemployed in their principal occupation from 4 to 6 months during the year, June, 1889 to May 31, 1890, and 14.18 were unemployed 7 to 12 months (ibid., p. cxxxvii). Without denying the difficulty of interpreting these figures, given the manner in which they were gathered, the definitions used, etc., it would seem clear that the evidence indicates, even if crudely and inaccurately, that employment in these occupations was something less than steady.

36. W. D. P. Bliss, ed., *Encyclopedia of Social Reform* (New York: 1897), "Unemployment," p. 1349.

student of the labor and socialist movement of the period, Richard Ely. In 1894, in the context of a discussion of the appeal of socialism to various classes in American society, Ely noted that:

> from the standpoint of those engaged in the learned professions, socialism is not without its attractive features. Those professions are now overcrowded, largely because many, better adapted to mechanical pursuits, endeavor to push into the learned professions to escape unpleasant conditions attending those occupations for which they are naturally adapted. This might be expected to cease, if agriculture and mechanical pursuits could be rendered more agreeable; and the anxiety for their children, would no longer perplex them by day and disturb their rest at night.[37]

Whatever the objective accuracy of Ely's observations, the subjective belief that the professions were overcrowded, together with the underlying fear of proletarianization were important elements in the doctrines of Nationalism and related middle-class socialist currents of the 1890s. No less significant is Ely's understanding that such elements could find "socialism" attractive. Yet, given the nature of these strata and their fear of radicalism it would have had to have been a socialism of a particular kind.

In a perceptive analysis of the emergence of this "new middle class," Samuel P. Hays has correctly stressed the importance of understanding the transitional nature of the period from 1885 to the beginning of World War I as the key to understanding the state of mind and the resulting political and social views of these elements.[38] They were "not yet reconciled to permanent status as white-collar and wage and salary earners,"[39] Hays notes. The last decades of the nineteenth century were ones of enormous economic and social dislocation, in which the entire world of small property was forced into decline by the concentration of capital. Only from this perspective is it possible to begin to explain the appeal of Nationalism's anticapitalist collectivist ideology. Bellamy's prediction of the inevitability of the total concentration of economic power in the hands of one big plutocratic trust represented an apocalyptic twist to the apprehension that many secretly felt. Certainly the declarations of the Nationalists themselves strongly point to the "shock" experienced by

37. Ely, *Socialism and Social Reform* pp. 141–142.

38. Hays, *The Response to Industrialism: 1885–1914* (University of Chicago Press, 1957).

39. Ibid., pp. 73–74.

members of the salaried occupations and the lower levels of the independent professions as an important source of Nationalism's appeal to them. It is of some importance that the relationship between the rise of these strata in this period and the emergence of anticapitalist collectivist doctrines which a number of present-day historians have noted, was taken for granted by some of the most perceptive contemporary observers of the pre–World War I period. "It must be remembered," wrote the brilliant Marxist theoretician, Louis Boudin, in 1907, "that this new middle class suffers just as much from insecurity of income as the working class, if not more, to which must be added insecurity of position. . . . It is, because of the nature of its social existence, extremely restless, ever ready to change, and ever longing for a change which would finally do away, or at least alleviate, its unsettledness, give it a rest. 'Governmental interference' has no terrors for it. . . . If such a makeshift may be dignified into an ideology, its ideology is State Socialism."[40]

If it was to brands of "state socialism" and other forms of middle-class anticapitalism to which these elements were attracted in Europe, in the United States it was Bellamy's peculiar left-wing version of this ideology to which such elements were drawn as they felt their position threatened and feared that they were being turned into a kind of intellectual proletariat. "Below the upper crust of professionals," writes Alfred Meusel in his classic discussion of this phenomenon, "loom the doctors without patients, the lawyers without clients, and the writers without readers. An intellectual proletarian may be defined as the recipient of a higher educational training who in his later life finds no opening in which to carry on the kind of practice for which he is trained. . . . The gulf between youthful expectations and the disheartening realities of later life has tended to produce in the case of many professional men an intellectual and emotional lesion, in which the natural sense of frustration and rebellion clashes with the remnants of pretensions and ideas implanted in the impressionable years of academic training."[41] Ideological spokesmen for middle-class reform as widely removed in time, but not in spirit, as the populist Ignatius Donnelly and the Progressive advisor to Woodrow Wilson, Colonel Edward M. House, warned that the plutocracy's seemingly imminent

40. Louis Boudin, *The Theoretical System of Karl Marx* (1907), pp. 209–210.
41. Alfred Meusel, "Middle Classes," (1933).

triumph would not only destroy small property but would also turn professionals and intellectuals into lackeys of capital, a position even more degraded than that of the workers because of the distance of their fall and the higher form of their work.[42] The fears which this prognosis reflected became an active element in determining the political and social consciousness of the middle classes and played a crucial role in the special appeal of Nationalism's politics to the professionals and other propertyless elements among them.

The belief that the position of the middle class was declining both relatively and absolutely, which meant that opportunity was being closed off once and for all, and an articulation of the deep resentment which this gave rise to, was a central theme in Nationalism's rhetoric. Even if small property might be able to survive for a while—though the Nationalists vehemently denied the possibility—it could no longer provide the individual with the freedom and independence that it had in the past. In one of his first public speeches, Bellamy told an overflow audience at Boston's Faneuil Hall:

> Socially the vast disparities of wealth afford on every side inhuman contrasts of cruel want and inordinate luxury. The dazzling illustrations of pomp and power, which are the prizes of wealth, have lent to the pursuit of gain, at all times sufficiently keen, a feverish intensity and desperation never seen before in this or any other country. *The moderate rewards of persistent industry seem contemptible in the midst of a universal speculative fever.*[43] (my emphasis)

However, Nationalists did not direct their resentment solely at the relative increase in power, wealth, and status of the new capitalists, nor did they limit themselves to expressions of moral revulsion at the way the plutocracy obtained and used its money and position. They also found that the subservient position of the middle classes brought real economic hardship, and threatened even greater suffering and a much steeper and more precipitous decline in the near future. The concentration of capital, the Nationalists insisted, affected the small manufacturer and tradesman, the businessman as well as the professional man. Both groups were "suffering quite as much and have quite as much to dread

---

42. Ignatius Donnelly, *Caesar's Column* (Cambridge: Harvard University Press, 1962); Anonymous [Edward Mandel House], *Phillip Dru: Administrator.*

43. Bellamy, "Nationalism—Principles, Purposes," in *Edward Bellamy Speaks Again!*, p. 55.

from monopoly as the poorest class of laborers."[44] The entrepreneurial middle class, the "businessman with moderate capital and plenty of wit," who had conducted the majority of the country's business before the rise of the corporation and the trust, was becoming superfluous.[45] But the outlook for the new generation was, if anything, ever bleaker. Fathers who had been set up in business by their fathers could not do the same for their own sons. "There is almost no opportunity left for starting in business in a moderate way; none, indeed, unless backed by large capital," Bellamy asserted.[46] Soon, Bellamy declared, the concentration of capital would be so complete, that there would be "no class between the very rich, living on their capital, and a vast mass of wage and salary receivers absolutely dependent upon the former class for their livelihood." The middle class, Bellamy concluded, was rapidly "being turned into a proletarian class."[47] Society, under these circumstances, would be "divided into a few hundred families of prodigious wealth on the one hand, a professional class dependent upon their favor but excluded from equality with them and reduced to a state of lackeys; and underneath a vast population of working men and women, absolutely without hope of bettering a condition which would year by year sink them more and more hopelessly into serfdom."[48]

This prediction thus projected into the future what was widely thought to be happening to the educated middle classes. One of the immediate consequences of the "closing up of business careers," Bellamy pointed out, was that "the professions are being over-crowded to the starvation point. The problem before young men coming out of school or college, where to find a place in the world, was never so hard as now. Plutocracy is indeed leaving no place for a young man of independent and patriotic spirit save in the party of Radical Social Reform."[49]

Another Nationalist, J. W. Sullivan, in later years a close intellectual advisor to Samuel Gompers, answered the question, "Who are the discontented in America?" by poignantly describing the situation of the educated middle classes:

> Our fathers regarded ignorance as a primary cause of poverty. But to-day the learned professions are over-crowded with needy men. Of doctors there is one (a graduate of a medical college) to every 500 persons in America; the smallest hamlet and the most remote settle-

44. Ibid., pp. 56–57.   45. Ibid.   46. Ibid.
47. Ibid.   48. Ibid.   49. Ibid.

ments have their medical practitioners, while many poorly paid operatives in chemist factories are in possession of the diplomas of medical colleges. Of lawyers, there are at every county bar three times the number to perform the legal work. Of editors, there is so vast a swarm that rich politicians, desirous of building up a public sentiment favorable to themselves by means of the newspapers they own for the purposes, can hire editorial writers like hod carriers to deliver them stents of paragraphs and leaders, the bricks and mortar in the construction of popularity. Of reporters, the *Journalist* says that their salaries average a little more than those of street car conductors. Pulpit work pays preachers on an average less than $500 a year. Everywhere there is a host of educated poor who seek positions as teachers, clerks, writers, and secretaries.[50]

Just as ordinary workers were forced by their poverty to scab on their fellow workers, Sullivan observed, so too, "professional men, maddened by poverty and sick of hope deferred, resort to sharp practices and become a sort of vermin, living on their fellow men." The educated were the "unseen poor" who feared to lose their respectability and for whom poverty meant that they would not even be able to obtain those jobs for which they were eligible because of their shabby appearance: "Discontent? Is the word adequate to express the feeling of humiliation which possesses the educated man when his necessities force him to choose between a mean action and a petition for alms . . . or the chafing in spirit of the young man who, after devoting years to the acquirement of knowledge, asks not for wealth, but only for a chance to earn a livelihood, and asks in vain. . . . "[51]

Along the same lines, but more explicit in drawing attention to the relationship between anticapitalist politics and the situation of the educated middle class, the editor of the *American Fabian*, journal of a small but important grouping which carried on the propaganda work of the Nationalists in the mid-1890s after the demise of Bellamy's *New Nation*, explained the origins of the middle-class native-socialist movement in America:

A large proportion of the two hundred members of the [American] Fabian Society are persons not only of culture, but of experience in the world's affairs. Educated Socialists have themselves felt the stress of competition in their own works. The proletariat who live and toil from hand to mouth and die leaving nothing behind them but offspring to continue the process are not limited today to day-

50. *The Coming Nation*, no. 35 (December 30, 1893).
51. Ibid.

laborers and soldiers of the line. Their ranks include many of the educated and refined. Education does not, as it once did, lift individuals from out of this class.

There is a recognized 'literary" proletariat being formed as a result of the increase in education and the crowding of women into the professions. . . . [52]

The particular value of *Looking Backward,* another Fabian wrote, was to be found in its powerful indictment of the "ignominy of commercialism" that afflicted the educated and was creating the new class of literary proletarians: "What generous mind does not answer promptly to Julian's description of the resentment which high-minded persons felt in his day at having to bring their mental wares to market and degrade them by commercializing their best products?"[53]

Of all the Nationalist writers, Gronlund most systematically developed an appeal to the "talented." In words which when read today are reminiscent of the views of intellectuals and professionals who in the 1930s and afterward looked to the bureaucratic collectivist society created by Stalinism for the positions and rewards denied to them by capitalism, Gronlund explicitly linked the resentment of the educated to the authoritarian collectivist society which the Nationalists counterposed to working-class socialism. The life of the "bright, educated talented man" in the United States, Gronlund wrote in 1897, is thwarted by the lack of opportunity: "Every year how many thousands of such talented youth issue from our educational institutions, fully equipped to make their mark! Now, is it not a fact, that a practical, well-informed man must contemplate this army with absolute dismay, knowing as he does, that the supply far exceed the demand? What terrible disappointment awaits these youth! They had much better have remained menials and clod-hoppers, for their culture will be their curse."[54]

In the absence of a Nationalist system of public control over the "administration of affairs," Gronlund complained, talented and educated youths had no choice but were forced "to go for advancement, for employment, for their living, to private individuals, and to appeal to their private interest, to their favor."[55] With a mixture of moral indignation

52. Prestonia Mann, "The Secret of Fabian Socialism," *American Fabian,* April 1896.

53. Ibid.

54. Gronlund, "The Teaching of Looking Backward" (August 1897).

55. Gronlund, *Our Destiny,* p. 162.

and envy, expressing obvious feelings of impotence and rage, Gronlund proclaimed: "it is precisely the mark of the highest genius and greatest talents that they cannot create their own opportunities, nor sound their own trumpets. This some with the greatest talents and genius will not do, or can not do; they even, frequently, are too shy to appeal to individuals."[56] Gronlund was here giving vent to what must be regarded as an example of the psychology which Erich Fromm has argued is the basis of the "authoritarian character structure."[57] The applicability to Gronlund's case of Fromm's analysis is further suggested by Gronlund's vision of Nationalism as total communion or the obliteration of the individual in order to release him from the impossible demands of individual freedom.

Even when the educated and talented managed to find private employment, Gronlund noted that they were required to be obedient to these same private individuals and loyal to their private interests. Gronlund's objection was not based on democratic or egalitarian grounds. Obedience to private interests—that is with any and all interests having to do strictly with the needs of the individual rather than of society—was by definition immoral. Moreover, Gronlund wrote, "if the employer be, as often is the case, an inferior person, it is doubly immoral."[58] Obedience to superior persons representing the interests of "society," was obviously highly moral. The result of subordinating young men of talent to their inferiors—inferiors in everything except their power to command—was that by age forty, they, who "had such grand dreams," would have to be "very happy if their mere living is secured to them, in return for daily drudgery."[59]

As for the rebels among the "superior minds" who rejected their fate, Gronlund declared that they would find they were "on the slippery, steep incline that leads to the social *Inferno*—they either are in the abyss, or perilously suspended above it, scorned by the 'prominent' and looked down upon by their comrades."[60] Was it any wonder, Gronlund asked, that "with talent and ability thus positively crushed down, that we seem a nation given over to the cult of base-ball and prize-fighting? With the prizes of life handed over to coarse, cheeky, vulgar and superficial men—the Fulkersons and Dreyfooses—and geniuses neglected, can

56. Ibid.
57. Fromm, *Escape from Freedom*, ch. 4.
58. Gronlund, *Our Destiny*, p. 163.
59. Ibid.　　　60. Ibid.

we wonder that we appear to foreigners 'a commonplace and essentially slight people'?"[61]

By implication as well as by explicit admission, then, the anticapitalist appeal of the Nationalists promised the "educated and wise" a reorganization of society on the basis of merit rather than egalitarian and democratic society which could only—if it were attainable at all—complete the process of leveling begun by the concentration of capital. In place of the plutocracy—"coarse, cheeky, vulgar, and superficial"—the meritorious would rule. Unlike capitalism every person would be accorded a place and a function befitting one's true talents. Or, as Gronlund put it in his surprisingly direct fashion, Nationalism would place "the round man in the round hole, ability having the leadership, not as a matter of chance or of personal favor, but as a matter of right, with loyal seconders, participating in government by his function; sure of his place and his due maintenance as long as he performs his duty."[62]

Bellamy was no less emphatic than Gronlund in his insistence that Nationalism would not do away with social stratification based on systematic differences in power and status between individuals, and just as aware also that his doctrine appealed to the educated middle class because it promised to reward real talent with the privileges of position and power. Strict economic equality would prevail. Yet, in the absence of economic differentiation, Bellamy wrote, one of the central motives necessary to "inspire diligence under Nationalism will be the desire of power, authority and public station, the wish to lead and direct instead of being led and directed."[63] Demonstrating sensitivity to the fears and desires of his audience that had made him such a successful spokesman for them, Bellamy went to the root of their objections to the anticapitalist politics of the socialists which, prior to the publication of *Looking Backward*, they had been accustomed to regarding as the only kind of collectivism. "Let us suppose," he wrote, "a system of industry under which superior diligence not only secures various and immediate minor advantages of preference and privilege, but should offer the sure and single way to all positions of authority, of official rank, of civic honour, and of social distinction, of which the express purpose would be to open the career to talent as it never was opened in human affairs before, in

61. Ibid.   62. Ibid.
63. Bellamy, "What Nationalism Means" in *Edward Bellamy Speaks Again!*, pp. 82–83.

order that the strongest and ablest among the people might find themselves at the head of the nation."[64]

Conclusion

For an educated class which felt itself without opportunity of the
right kind as well as insufficient opportunity, and saw itself slipping out of
the proper station in life to which its education and culture ought to have
entitled it, there was an obvious attraction in a collectivist ideology which
openly proclaimed that the new collectivist order which was permeating
capitalism and would inevitably replace it need not be one which displaced them from their position of privilege. They would lead the movement for its attainment, and also hold the lower orders in check. The
absence of democracy and self-government would bestow upon the meritorious and talented the very right to command and to make decisions
which both the socialists and the plutocracy denied to them.

In the long run, the apocalyptic fears of the educated middle class
at the end of the nineteenth century proved exaggerated. Their apprehension was not, however, unreasonable, given what they could see and
know and the historical context in which they measured their circumstances. If the crisis of American capitalism did not reach the state it did
in Europe, and no authoritarian movement with mass support from the
middle classes developed in America, at least not on anything like the
same scale, it was not because of some mysterious American genius for
softening social conflict and resolving economic contradictions. Bellamy's
generation viewed the future from where they stood in American society
at the end of the nineteenth century. The old middle class from which
they had sprung remained their ideal. They saw the guarantee of individual freedom in the wide dispersion of property—even for those without property. But industrial capitalism was undermining their very existence. Suspended between two worlds, educated middle-class people
gravitated toward the anticapitalist politics of Nationalism. Unlike the
entrepreneurial elements, the most important segment of which, farmers, owned property, and whose politics were designed to use the state to
restore and protect small, independent property against big capital, the
new, dependent, middle class of professionals and salaried employees
had only their education and their pride.

64. Ibid.

Bellamy's bureaucratic society offered them "opportunity"—opportunity for the talents ignored by a capitalist civilization enslaved by
commercial values. But opportunity on this level was only an aspect of
Bellamyism's appeal: it was just as much, if not more, the chance to
become part of something, to find a place and function in the social
organism, and to end the uncertainty of existence under capitalism. It
was neither the opportunity of the old middle class, to base one's liberty
on property, nor the new individualism of a democratic collectivism, that
Nationalism promised, but rather the vision of a secure collective existence of men who, frightened of individual existence, yearned for some
means to cope with their anxiety and loneliness.

6 OBLITERATING THE SELF: NATIONALISM AND THE NEW COMMUNITY

The centrality of *Looking Backward*'s authoritarian politics may have escaped later historians but astute contemporaries had no difficulty in recognizing that Bellamyism was antidemocratic to the core. Albert Schäffle, whose opinion is especially valuable because of his conservative views, contrasted Bellamy's ideas to those of the proponents of working-class socialism. Unlike them, Bellamy was a proponent of an "Aristocratic Communism." Bellamy, Schäffle observed with an acuity not possible among generations of American historians blinkered by Progressivism, "is not a Democratic Communist, he is no Social Democrat. He is an aristocrat and authoritarian of the strictest order. His notion is of a society of mandarins, medallists, and labour officers, such as no Democrat could tolerate, and which I myself . . . assuredly could not accept, although I regard a purely Democratic Collectivism as practically and forever impossible."[1]

The most pervasive aspect of Nationalism's authoritarian message and the core of its appeal is the complex of ideas embodied in "communionism." Communionism provided the cement which held together the various strands of Nationalism: the military model of socialism; the emphasis upon efficiency and planning as ends in themselves; the rejection of class and political conflict and the parallel insistence on seeing the "Nation" as a mystical community to which the individual had to subordinate his private needs and desires; the denial of legitimacy to intermediate associations; the view of Nationalism as a "non-political" movement, transcending "selfishness" and aiming at an authoritarian, "non-political" state—that is, all of those specific elements in Bellamy's political ideology which made it authoritarian and antidemocratic had their doctrinal and psychological roots in the communion theme and in

1. A. Schäffle, *The Impossibility of Social Democracy* (London: Swan Sonnenschein, 1892), p. 413.

the peculiar kind of psychic reaction against capitalist society of which it was the intellectual and ideological expression.

The communion pattern underlies the Nationalist opposition to capitalism and is the central element in the formulation of positive prescriptions for the collectivist reorganization of industrial society. Thus, Gronlund's vision of the "cooperative commonwealth" rested on the idea that the anarchy of capitalism would end when the individual was immersed in the fully organized State and the "self" dissolved into the collectivity. Gronlund's view that absolute identity of opinion was the "natural" state of human affairs and that socialism, as opposed to the anarchistic organization of capitalism, would realize such total unity, flowed directly from his organicist theory of socialism, as did his definition of democracy as the rule of the "competent" minority—the "brains" over the majority—the "hands" of the social organism.

At the same time, Bellamy's personal and intellectual biography demonstrated that his inability to make a place for himself in the new world of industrial capitalism that was undermining the economic, social, and political foundations of the older middle classes, as well as his moral revulsion at the commercialization of life, produced strong feelings of anxiety and self-doubt together with a nearly unbearable sense of loneliness, impotence and insignificance. In reaction, Bellamy denied the reality and worth of individual personality and of the self, and held forth the promise of relief in the form of a mystical state of "solidarity" or communion in which "impersonal consciousness" would obliterate the individual's sense of being a separate, unique personality. Immersed in an impersonal universe that was greater and more powerful than the individual or even the sum of individuals making up mankind and which leveled all the barriers produced by the false sense of self, the individual would no longer feel utterly alone and without power nor would he need to be concerned over his inability to master the external circumstances that molded his life.

Bellamy's "religion of solidarity" and the inner yearning for the eradication of the personality and its subordination to some all-embracing collective power which it expressed was translated into the indictment of capitalism and the positive vision of a harmonious, efficient collectivist society. Individualism was seen as the cause of the chaos, conflict, and disorganization that made one living under capitalism weak and alone. The only cure possible required the suppression of man's innate antisocial character—the valued "individualism" of liberal society—which in turn made necessary the abolition of democratic self-government and the evaporation of any meaningful public life.

Here then was a deep-going revulsion against individualism in all its forms—not merely against the asocial, egotistical "individualism" apotheosized by the Spencerians, but against the entire liberal-humanist and democratic tradition as well. Rather than a new community within which individualism could be anchored in a new, noncapitalist setting, ending alienation, the Nationalists proposed to solve the problem of the individual in modern society by the suppression of individuality and personality in the warm embrace of a bureaucratic society. Paradoxically, the individual would remain an isolated, impotent atom so far as his ability to determine the events and decisions shaping his life was concerned; but the vicarious identification with the organic state and the fact that all individuals, rather than just some of them, would be reduced to this state of atomized individuality provided the solution. In the Nationalist utopia, the sense of loneliness and utter powerlessness would vanish as the individual was immersed in the great noncompetitive bureaucratic organism that would envelop all society. Such total organization from above, together with the elimination of private property and all intermediate relationships, would make the powerlessness of the individual irrelevant.

Loss of Self and Anticapitalist Collectivism

Erich Fromm's classic study of the social-psychological foundations of modern authoritarian movements and ideologies, *Escape from Freedom*, helps to illuminate the meaning of the communion theme in Bellamyism and provides an important link between its underlying psychological appeal and that of later totalitarian movements. Fromm argues that the isolation and impotence of the individual under modern capitalism predisposes large and significant segments of the highly exposed and disintegrating middle classes, who feel their status and material security threatened simultaneously by big capital and the organized workers, to seek a solution outside of the "normal" framework of bourgeois democratic politics. Unable to prevent the doom of small property, lacking the capacity for self-organization and collective action, internally divided as a class in their interests and outlook, and above all concerned for the retention of their superior position in relation to the working class, the middle classes yearn for a solution from above: a party, a leader, or some force that will decide and act for them. What is required is an omnipotent force to which they may submit themselves passively and which will, in turn, come to their rescue without an individual effort on their part—by magic, as it were—giving them a sense of power not through efforts of their own but through vicarious identification with and submission to its power.[2]

Individuals may attempt to relieve their inner anxieties, Fromm argues, by escaping from the "negative freedom"—the isolated individualism—of capitalist society through identification and support for authoritarian social and political movements in which the individual gives up "the independence of one's individual self" and fuses "one's self with somebody or someone outside of oneself in order to acquire the strength which the individual is lacking."[3] Fromm contends that Hitler's character structure strongly embodies these authoritarian characteristics and to that degree Hitler successfully articulated the inner longings of the dispossessed German middle classes, embodying these strains, with all of their contradictions, in the doctrine of Nazism—of which his own writings, of course, form the core expression.[4]

The communion theme as it has been presented here was, on an ideological plane, akin to the authoritarian response described by Fromm. Of course it is not possible for us to analyze directly the psychological characteristics of the strata from which the Nationalists drew their support. However, there is an overwhelming similarity in the content and form of both Gronlund's and Bellamy's ideological formulations and the

2. Fromm, *Escape from Freedom*, p. 141.

3. Ibid., chs. 5 and 6. For an extremely interesting psychoanalytic view of what has been termed here the communion pattern as it applies to modern American expressions of mysticism, see Dr. Peter Hartocollis of the Menninger Clinic, "Mysticism and Aggression: An Object Relations Point of View," unpublished paper delivered at the midwinter meeting of the American Psychoanalytic Association, New York, December 1971. There can be no doubt that the desire for obliteration of the self plays an important role in the contemporary revival of interest in "Eastern" religions and provides additional evidence of the powerful urge to "escape from freedom" among certain, largely middle-class, elements produced by the decay of capitalist society. The admiration during the 1930s of Russia and in the 1970s of Chinese Stalinism expressed in similar terms (see fn. 22 below) is simply another expression of this syndrome.

4. Fromm, *Escape from Freedom*, p. 141.

expressions of their own personal anguish, as well as in the doctrines of Nationalism, to the general configuration of the psychology and ideological expression of authoritarianism described by Fromm. Certainly the fatalistic evolutionary theory of Nationalism—the magic helper which rescues those who feel powerless to deliver themselves—is obviously one such expression of an ideology designed to appeal to the weak and impotent middle classes. Not only can Fromm's analysis point the direction to an understanding of the social-psychological basis of Nationalism's appeal, then, but by the same token the pervasiveness of this aspect of Nationalism also suggests a link between the underlying reaction tapped by Bellamyism in the 1890s and the rise of similar non-working–class anticapitalist collectivist movements. It is relevant at this point to briefly explore some of these later expressions of the communion theme to establish this link as well as to help illuminate the pervasiveness of this pattern in twentieth-century anticapitalist movements.

The tendency of students of the appeal of authoritarian political movements has been to limit their analysis to the "right." This has obscured the important role that the type of reaction described by Fromm has played in the appeal of anticapitalist currents on the "left," especially to the supporters of modern-day totalitarian Communist movements. There is no reason, however, why Fromm's analysis must be limited to right-wing movements, unless we allow ourselves to be misled by the sterile use of these political categories. Both Nazism and Stalinism tapped, at different times and under different circumstances, the same reservoir of anticapitalist political sentiment existing among large sections of the middle classes. This antagonism to big business, to the "commercialization" of life, was equally antagonistic to any form of democracy and democratic collectivism.

Before the First World War, right-wing movements such as the anti-Semitic political groups and parties in Imperial Germany, appealing to the lower middle classes, rejecting democracy and the values of individual freedom, offered an anticapitalist program that was conceived of as a national, as opposed to class, socialism. At the same time, there were similar currents on the left, such as the Fabians and Robert Blatchford in England during the rise of social imperialism.[5]

5. Paul Massing, *Rehearsal for Destruction;* Bernard Semmel, *Imperialism and Social Reform.*

Nationalism shared many of the characteristics of both of these types of anticapitalist currents. Had it arisen in Germany, it would undoubtedly have been of the right, given the prior organization of the working class into the Social Democratic party and its formal commitment to class struggle and Marxism. But in America, with a politically undeveloped working class and a virtually nonexistent socialist movement among native-born workers or intellectuals, *any* anti–laissez faire program was automatically seen by its opponents as a doctrine and a movement of the left—even though in Bellamy's and the Nationalists' case, they vehemently asserted their abhorrence of democratic radicalism. The point is borne out by the fact that *Looking Backward*'s reception in Europe transcended the conventional categories of "right" and "left." Depending upon the circumstances, Bellamy's doctrine became identified with the middle-class anticapitalist, antisocialist tendencies, while in other places it became the rallying point of both the right and the left, simultaneously.[6] This seemingly anomalous ability of Bellamy's vision to arouse the enthusiasm of both democratic and antidemocratic currents, socialist and antisocialist, which Edward Everett Hale had noted at the time of its publication, underscores the point that to make sense of Bellamyism, indeed of modern politics, one must disregard the conventional use of "right" and "left" and focus instead upon what is common to the authoritarian precursors of modern totalitarian collectivist movements: opposition to democracy, representative government, and to all the values of individual freedom shared historically by democratic liberalism, combined with hostility to capitalism. Whether this anticapitalism is real, as it was for the Nationalists and other nineteenth-century expressions of middle-class protest, or demagogic, as in the Nazi case, is not crucial: the lower middle-class masses who supported the Nazis believed their anticapitalist rhetoric and at least one section of the Nazis was genuinely hostile to the continued existence of private property.

To get a firmer grasp of the essential outlines of the communion pattern and to establish the continuity it demonstrates between the type of authoritarian socialism of Nationalism and later totalitarian currents, it will be useful here to examine briefly some latter-day expressions of this theme in connection with the Communist movement.

6. Sylvia E. Bowman et al., *Edward Bellamy Abroad* (1962).

An excellent starting point for identifying and classifying the anti-capitalist impulse is provided by a perceptive article by the old-time socialist, Max Eastman.[7] Published in 1938, Eastman's article appeared at a time when it was just becoming apparent to many socialists that among the fellow-travelers of the Communist Party, not to speak of the Party itself as well as other wings of the socialist movement, and even among professedly nonsocialist liberals, a new and distinctive political tendency had begun to crystallize. Sparked by the crisis of world capitalism and the disintegration of bourgeois democracy in Europe, the special and puzzling character of this new current that first struck opponents of the Communists and of Stalinist Russia, was that its adherents were utterly impervious to criticisms directed against the Communists from a democratic liberal or revolutionary socialist standpoint. Impervious, however, not because of any lack of knowledge about the totalitarian nature of Stalin's regime, but precisely because they consciously believed in the necessity and desirability of a "socialism" from above that extirpated all institutions of democratic self-rule and enslaved the working class.[8]

Analytically, Eastman distinguished between three main groups of motives which historically had impelled people into the socialist movement: "[First,] the rebels against tyranny and oppression, in whose motivation the concept of human freedom formed the axis; second, those yearning with a mixture of religious mysticism and animal gregariousness for human solidarity—the united-brotherhood pattern; third, those anxious about efficiency and intelligent organization—a cerebral anxiety capable of rising in times of crisis to a veritable passion for a plan."[9]

To illustrate the "united-brotherhood" or communion pattern, Eastman cited the example of Harry F. Ward. Ward was not a member of the Communist Party, but an example of that anomalous species, a "totalitarian liberal" whose main credentials as a fellow-traveler were that he was a Professor of Christian Ethics at Union Theological Semi-

7. Max Eastman, "Motive Patterns of Socialism," (Fall 1939): 45–55. On the emergence of this current see the important articles by Irving Howe, James Fenwick, and Hal Draper in the *New International*, April 1944, as well as the article by Lewis Coser and Irving Howe, "Authoritarians of the Left," *Dissent* 2, no. 1 (Winter 1955): 40–50.

8. Eastman, "Motive Patterns," p. 45. Coser and Howe deal almost entirely with the third tendency mentioned by Eastman. Their emphasis is correct, I think, for contemporary "left-authoritarianism."

9. Ibid., p. 50.

nary and, more significantly, had been a Christian Socialist for many years.[10]

Even a casual examination of Ward's writing provides numerous examples of the communion theme. Thus, for example, in *The Soviet Spirit*,[11] written in 1944, Ward explains that the key to the Soviet spirit is the "socialized individual" produced by Communist society: "The aim of all this education and social pressure is the socialized individual, one who finds himself by losing himself in the service of the common good. Thus there comes into being the individualized society, one that finds its life in collectively seeking the fullest possible development of each individual."[12] And:

> To secure the socialized individual, and thus to draw the motivation of life from a more powerful center than the egoistic self, is the underlying purpose in Soviet education. The Communist is not deceived by the myth of the separate individual which has muddied the thinking of the western nations. . . .
>
> The extent to which this is actually being done in the Soviet Union constitutes an historic phenomenon of the first importance. The creative desires are being exalted over the possessive appetites by abolishing the possibility of acquisition, limiting ownership to purely personal property, and opening to the initiative of the masses such engrossing tasks that success in achieving social ends becomes more important than personal rewards. The initiative thus created is being guided by a discipline which both represses the ego and enlarges the social self.[13]

The same pattern is to be found in the reaction of Dr. Frankwood E. Williams, editor of *The Journal of Mental Hygiene*, to his experience in Russia in the early 1930s. According to Lewis Feuer, "[he] found the Soviet Union a mental hygienist's paradise. Here one could escape, he wrote in 1932, the 'atmosphere of competition and rivalry that vitiates everything from the start and at every step.' Here was no patchwork of clinics and hospitals to serve as refuges from a competitive order; the whole Soviet society was a mental hygiene clinic. Squeezed in a Moscow

10. Albert T. Mollegen, in his article "The Religious Basis of Western Socialism" in Egbert and Persons, *Socialism and American Life* (1952), pp. 99–123, lumps Ward with George D. Herron and characterizes their views as examples of "Christian scientific socialism"—an unexplained and unexplainable category which provides one more illustration of the abysmal intellectual level of most of the work on American socialism—not a few examples of which are to be found in the same volume.

11. Harry F. Ward, *The Soviet Spirit*, (New York: International Publishers, 1944).

12. Ibid., p. 150.   13. Ibid., pp. 150–151.

street-car which made the New York subway seem like a half-empty football stand, Dr. Williams had a sense of mystic communion: 'for the moment we are just one body.' "[14]

As in Bellamy's case, the communion idea, especially among fellow-travelers who preferred to defend totalitarianism using terms drawn from the liberal-democratic tradition, was closely linked to the rejection of politics, partisanship, and democracy. The ideological appeal to "unity" and harmony in contrast to the supposed anarchy and self-seeking nature of political life under even the most democratic capitalist regime was reflected in the justifications of one-party rule as a new, and higher, type of democracy. For example, one prominent and widely read Communist sympathizer of the 1930s, who called his book *Russia without Illusions*,[15] explained that the absence of opposition parties or other institutions associated with democratic rule under capitalism was due to the fact that "The USSR is such an organic unity that every measure is the product of the collective comments of thousands of people; every measure can be carried out in practice only when it has the effective and active agreement of millions."[16] Under the circumstances, "parliamentary politics as we know the game cease to exist. For once we have a united people, behind a single leadership, working for a common aim, there is no longer a basis for different parties fighting one another."[17]

Perhaps the most explicit example of the communion theme in connection with the vision of Stalinist Russia as a utopia occurs in *The Man Inside*,[18] a novel written in 1936 by the iconoclastic and erratic editor of the socialist magazine *Modern Quarterly*, V. F. Calverton. It is an especially significant example because Calverton was not a simple fellow-traveler. He was instead a severe if inconsistent critic of both the Party and Stalin's Russia. And yet, despite these political reservations, Calverton was inexorably pulled toward Stalin's totalitarian order because it was a model of a noncompetitive social order in which the "illusion" of individuality would once and for all be destroyed. "Individuals," Calverton wrote, "are very much like the dots and dashes that make up a telegraphic code; they have no reality in themselves as dots

14. Lewis Feuer, "American Travelers to the Soviet Union," (unpublished manuscript, 1960).

15. Pat Waters, *Russia Without Illusions* (New York: Modern Age Books, 1938).

16. Ibid., p. 186.   17. Ibid., p. 187.

18. V. F. Calverton, *The Man Inside* (1936).

and dashes; it is only in terms of the whole code, as all the dots and dashes are rendered coherent by means of codal transcription that they acquire meaning at all."[19] In order to destroy the illusion of individuality, it was necessary to destroy the fear of death. Calverton, speaking through the novel's central character, a scientist who uses hypnosis to cure the human psyche, saw in Russia the only hope by which the mass of men, and not merely the exceptional persons, could shake off this unfortunate illusion:

> Soviet Russia, at the present time, is my only social hope. They do not employ the word life-force there. They describe themselves as ultimate materialists—dialectical materialists. . . . What they are doing in Soviet Russia is a close approximation to what I want to see done all over the world. They are teaching individual man to see that he has no independent existence outside society. Instead of employing the word life-force, the Soviets use the word "society" or "socialism." Which word one uses is unimportant. The important fact is that individual man is being reborn into the group; the illusion of individuality is being destroyed and replaced by the reality of the group and ultimately of the race. They are teaching individual man to see that he has no independent existence outside of society.
>
> That is why socialism is the first step in the remaking of a humanity. Every intelligent man must be a Socialist.[20]

In content and function, then, the Stalinist utopia served Calverton's socialist politics as the Industrial Army did Bellamy's. It was a means to solve the dilemma posed to the utopian by the recalcitrance of the masses caused by capitalism's corruption of human nature; a way to mold men from without, forcing them to give up the illusion of individuality which prevented the construction of a harmonious society. The political conclusion of *The Man Inside* is an explicit statement of the utopian mentality and provides an excellent illustration of the convergence between the impulse of the utopian reformer and totalitarianism:

> It was possible to change the entire reaction pattern of the world. The only trouble was he could not get the world to sit before him, or any one else. . . . If that could ever be achieved, the world could be made over into whatever we wished, people changed into whatever we wished. If we could but get hold of the radio, the news-

19. Ibid., p. 179.

20. Ibid., p. 181. I was led to Calverton's book by a reference in Daniel Aaron's *Writers on the Left* (New York: Harcourt, Brace, 1961), p. 333. Aaron refers to it there—glowingly, of course—as akin to Bellamy's *Religion of Solidarity*. Unconscious of what he is saying, Aaron is nevertheless absolutely correct in noting the similarity.

papers, the schools, the churches, and all the agencies of social hypnosis, we could do the same thing to the whole world in a miraculously swift manner. That was what, he added, the Russians were doing, except that he didn't like certain of the methods the Russians were using since Lenin died and Trotsky had been exiled.[21]

Similar expressions of extreme anti-individualism and of the communion theme crop up in later totalitarian enthusiasms. Communist China until recently replaced for many the Soviet Union as the world's leading example of a society whose socialism is based on the obliteration of individual personality. "The fight against bourgeois ideas in our own heads, [and] the fight against 'self' is much the same thing," one American participant in the cultural revolution told the writer, William Hinton. "The 'self' within us is like this omnipresent glue which persistently tries to twist each of our thoughts into something useful to it. Only by continuous struggle against this glue and constant vigilance as to its tricks can we ourselves keep moving forward on the road to revolution. The enemy knows very well it is the 'self' which is our Achilles heel. . . . To rid ourselves of our own 'self' is not merely our own personal task, but also our responsibility to the revolution. . . . Whenever our subjective thinking starts from self-interest we are blind to the real objective world. . . . With hundreds of millions of people 'fighting

---

21. Calverton, *Man Inside*, p. 242. In John Desmond Bernal's *The World, The Flesh, and the Devil*, written in 1929, the following passage occurs which illustrates perfectly an authoritarian yearning for communion that is strongly reminiscent of Bellamy's "religion of solidarity" as well as his short story (see ch. 1, above) about a country of mind readers, "To Whom This May Come." Bernal, later to become a fellow traveler of the Communist Party advocated the making of an artificial man which would result in the creation of a "complex mind," linking together many individual minds into one. In this way, he explained, "the individual brain will feel itself part of the whole in a way that completely transcends the devotion of the most fanatic adherent of a religious sect. . . . It would be a state of ecstasy in the literal sense. . . . Whatever the intensity of our feeling, however much we may strive to reach beyond ourselves or into another's mind, we are always barred by the limitations of our individuality. Here at least those barriers would be down: feeling would truly communicate itself, memories would be held in common, and yet in all this, identity and continuity of individual development would not be lost. It is even possible, even probable, that the different individuals of a compound mind would not all have similar functions or even be of the same rank of importance. Division of labor would soon set in: to some might be delegated the task of ensuring the proper functioning of the others, some might specialize in sense reception and so on. Thus would grow up a hierarchy of minds that would be more truly a complex than a compound mind." (Quoted in Neal Wood, *Communism and British Intellectuals*, p. 139.)

self' . . . mass consciousness in China is on the verge of an extraordinary leap, the consequences of which can scarcely be estimated."[22]

Communionism also runs through organicist theories of the state. Such theories as the basis of anticapitalist collectivist ideologies are not, of course, peculiar to the period of modern totalitarianism. In this connection William English Walling's analysis of the "state socialists" and the emerging statist liberalism in the pre–World War I period must be noted, because of all the currents in the socialist movement at this time, it stands closest to Bellamyism—indeed, in the United States, "state socialism" may be viewed as its lineal descendant. Walling pointed out that the state socialists saw "society as God," and based their politics on an organic theory of the state which implied that "the activities of the state are of infinitely greater moment than the self-development and self-government of citizens who see the state as their tool."[23]

Here then is an ideological strain in the socialist movement that elicits the support of people on the basis of its promise to immerse the individual in society or the state. Through this immersion they will gain a sense of unity or oneness with others and be granted a release from the anxieties and sense of loneliness imposed upon them by the conditions intrinsic to capitalist society. As Irving Howe has noted, it was this sentiment that the nineteenth-century anarchist Michael Bakunin crystallized in the remark, "I do not want to be I, I want to be We," and which the authors of twentieth-century "anti-Utopias" have correctly fastened upon as expressing the essence of the underlying psychic appeal

22. Quoted in William Hinton, *Turning Point in China: An Essay on the Cultural Revolution* (New York: Monthly Review Press, 1972), pp. 102–104. See also Felix Green's article "China—Free to be Human," *Issues in Radical Therapy* 2, no. 4: 18–19 as another example of the discovery of this pattern in a totalitarian society. "The Chinese are showing us that the concept of individuality which has been developed in the West under capitalism is really not freedom but another kind of imprisonment. It is the imprisonment of 'me' within myself. . . . It is this 'me-ness' which is the prison, and in the very depths of our consciousness we know this. And how we hate it! . . . A cooperative society develops an entirely different kind of ethic, a wholly different concept of freedom—and this is what I learned in China. What we all long for, surely, is to be part of a society that doesn't divide us from one another, which releases us from the prison, the small, boring world of me; which allows us to be members of a community in which we do not have to push ourselves." Here, as in Bellamy, we have (in almost identical language) the reaction against personality and individuality, seen, of course, by Green as identical to the self-seeking, asocial and atomistic "individualism" of capitalist society.

23. William English Walling, *The Larger Aspects of Socialism* (1913), p. 122, and ch. 6, passim.

of modern totalitarian ideologies to people who cannot bear the burden of freedom in capitalist society.[24]

In characterizing it as an ideological current which made the state into God, Walling caught its essential similarity to certain mystical-religious views—ones very similar to Bellamy's "Religion of Solidarity." Rather than unity in communion with God, however, society is made a fetish: it alone is real while the individual and his relations with other individuals are derivative. Indeed, the communion theme may be seen as the political ideological counterpart of the "oceanic" feeling underlying religious-mystical beliefs referred to by Freud in *Civilization and Its Discontents*—the feeling described by his correspondent as "a sensation of 'eternity,' a feeling as of something limitless, unbounded, something 'oceanic'. . . ."[25]

The communion theme highlights the difference between the status the individual occupies in authoritarian socialist thought and in the democratic or libertarian tradition associated historically with classical liberalism and democratic socialism. Eastman clearly formulated these two tendencies struggling for the "soul" of socialism:

> There can be no truce between libertarians and those whom the fraternal or gregarious impulse renders tolerant of totalitarianism. This does not mean that human freedom as a concept excludes a moral attitude, or even an evangel, or universal friendliness. . . . But those who want to see men really free, each to enjoy the values of his own life in his own fashion, will have to abandon the religion of the collective will. *They will have to decide whether by socialism they mean individualism generalized and made accessible to all, or whether they mean a general surrender to some authoritarian concept of the collective good.*
>
> . . . I have not the glimmer of a desire to lose my identity in a collection, nor would I wish this loss upon a single workman. The essential meaning of the [Russian] revolution to me was the liberation of individuality, the extension of my privilege of individuality to the masses of mankind. . . . [I endorse] the words of Trotsky . . . 'The revolution is, first of all, an awakening of human personality in those masses heretofore assumed to be without it.'[26] (My emphasis)

24. Irving Howe, "The Fiction of Anti-Utopia," *The New Republic* (April 23, 1962): 13–16.

25. Sigmund Freud, *Civilization and its Discontents* (New York: Anchor, 1959), p. 2.

26. Eastman, "Motive Patterns," p. 54. Cf. Plekhanov's statement that the "kingdom of reason" remains but a dream, but "it begins to approach us with seven league strides only when the 'crowd' itself becomes the hero of historical action, and when in it, that colourless 'crowd', there develops the appropriate consciousness of self." *The Development of the Monist View of History* (Moscow: Foreign Languages Publishing House, 1956), p. 278.

In brief, then, "communionism" in the context of an authoritarian socialism must be contrasted to the idea of wedding the liberal conception of individualism to a democratic reorganization of society. In the latter, the abolition of private property and the social ownership of the means of production is conceived of not as an end in itself, but as a means by which individualism and "personality" can be "generalized and made accessible to all." In contrast, all of the examples of communionism, whatever their other important differences, have in common a rejection of this aim which flows from the same kind of reaction against capitalism we have observed in Gronlund's and Bellamy's politics. Capitalist society is condemned for its disorganization, and the cause of this disorganization, as revealed in the competetive, conflict-ridden nature of life under capitalism, is located not in the structure of the system, but in the self-seeking, egocentric propensities of human nature—i.e., in "individualism" or "selfishness."[27]

The positive vision of an authoritarian collectivist utopia and the concrete politics developed for reaching it take their content from this moralistic theory. The only way to resolve the contradiction between the needs, interests, and desires of the individual and those of society—a contradiction which cannot be resolved through the rational pursuit by each individual of his self-interest—is to *dissolve the individual in the community*, by constructing a "community" composed of atomized people welded together only at the center of society, through the state. What follows from this is a socialism characterized by less, not more, individualism; less, not greater, opportunity for participation and control over society and hence over the individual's own circumstances; total harmony, absence of competition between groups and even of groups themselves, as the natural state of society.

In their quest for such a utopia, Ward, Williams, Calverton and others of the totalitarian-liberal persuasion were offered by Stalinist Russia a vision which Bellamy could only conceive of in terms of a model based upon the military bureaucracy—a functioning, not imaginary, super-organic social system in which the individual found his place in society as a subordinate, but secure, part of the whole. This utopia was placed by all of them in opposition to the anarchy, planlessness, and unrestrained pursuit of individual goals which they understood to be the

27. See, e.g., Paul Sweezy, "Peaceful Transition from Socialism to Capitalism," *Monthly Review* 15, no. 11 (March 1964): 269–290.

essence of capitalism. Ward, Christ's physician for the soul, Williams, modern psychiatry's healer of the mind, and Calverton's reformer through hypnosis, all saw in such a society a utopia where the individual would no longer be troubled by feelings of loneliness and impotence, or even the fear of personal annihilation in death, because men would have been stripped of the "illusion" of individual existence or of a personality separate from society. The reform of human nature from above by Stalin's totalitarian dictatorship, achieved through creation of total political unity and the abolition of private property, guaranteed that the average individual, particularly the workers, who in the mass had always managed to elude the control of those who believed they knew what was good for them, was at last being properly educated to subordinate his personal, selfish needs to those of society.

Nationalism: Socialized Individualism

Bellamyites could only conceive of a harmonious social order in which the interest of the individual would coincide with the general interest if the ineradicable asocial individualism celebrated by the exponents of laissez faire capitalism was suppressed, forcing the people to subordinate themselves to the interest of the social organism. Order, efficiency, and planning were clearly part of this vision, as they were for the Fabians, but the difference in emphasis led the Fabians—to appropriate Durkheim's terms—to see a bureaucratic order as a means of achieving a kind of mechanical solidarity, whereas Bellamy's bureaucratic society was conceived of as providing an organic solidarity in which the individual would fit, more as a cell in a living organism, than as a cog in a Fabian machine. "*Looking Backward*," Bellamy wrote Howells, "contemplates the nation as a vital organism, a moral being, the industrial organization being an incident and consequence of that fact and not the main thing in itself. . . . If there is any particular merit in the plan of *Looking Backward*, it is that it provides the principle of cohesion and of solidarity by making every citizen's maintenance depend on his membership in the nation."[28]

The Declaration of Principles of the First Nationalist Club of Boston echoed Bellamy's approach. Constructed around the Theosophist-inspired slogan of the "Brotherhood of Humanity," the Declaration mir-

28. Bellamy to Howells, June 17, 1888, Bellamy Papers.

rored Bellamy's moralistic theory of capitalism: "The principle of competition is simply the application of the brutal law of the survival of the strongest and most cunning." Taking at face value this social Darwinist justification of capitalism and accepting its claim to explain the dynamics of the system, as had Bellamy, but then rejecting its moral implications, the Nationalist Declaration argued that the practical application of their views meant "those who seek the welfare of man must endeavor to suppress the system founded on the brute principle of competition and put in its place another based on the nobler principle of association."[29]

The Declaration emphasized the Nationalists' opposition to any "sudden or ill-considered changes" or to attacking individuals, not even the capitalists who had "accumulated immense fortunes simply by carrying to a logical end the false principle on which business is now based." The motive power for change was not the conscious struggle for political and social power by a class, which was implicitly only another example of the "false principle" of selfishness behind capitalism, but the true principle of the evolutionary socialization of capital or association: "The combinations, trusts, and syndicates of which the people now complain, demonstrate the practicability of our basic principles of association. We merely seek to push this principle a little further and have all industry operated in the interest of all by the nation—the people organized—the organic unity of the whole people." As long as competition continued to be the "ruling factor in our industrial system," and was not replaced by the "Brotherhood of Humanity" (the organic unity of the whole people), then "the highest development of the individual cannot be reached, the loftiest aims of humanity cannot be realized."[30] Yet, for the Nationalists the highest development of individualism did not entail the development of personality and individuality within a collectivist framework. It meant the suppression rather than the development of human personality and the subordination of the self to the great, organic collectivity. In the mystical language of Theosophy in which the Declaration was written, the terms "brotherhood" and "individualism" had specific meanings consistent with the communion framework of *Looking Backward*. The "highest development of the individual" in Theosophical terms meant "the re-

29. *The Nationalist* 1, no. 1 (May 1889).
30. Ibid.

nunciation of one's personality,"[31] while the "brotherhood of human-ity," or "universal brotherhood," was equivalent to the idea of solidar-ity in Bellamy's terminology. The relationship between the two was by no means accidental—Bellamy's earliest short stories embodying the communion theme had come to the attention of the Theosophists some years earlier. Bellamy himself may be regarded, in the period before the publication of *Looking Backward*, as a philosophical fellow-traveler of the Theosophists.[32]

The same type of anticapitalist reaction runs through much of Nationalist literature. Frequently the two types, the plannist and the communion strain, are crossed as in the case of the Nationalist author who wrote that: "it is evident that it is not Capital alone which is responsible for the present state of things, but merely disorganization, which always was the cause of all the trouble the world ever saw. Let us combine, organize, more and still more. We can never have enough of it. . . . What plan or scheme of salvation has so much in store? Nay, what else is there that can be the material and moral savior of the race? Disorganization is misery and death. Organization is comfort and life."[33]

The vision of a warm brotherhood through efficiency, together with the use of the idea of "organization" concretized as the trust or the corporation, as a new basis for human community and solidarity ex-pressed in the previous passage was reflected in one Nationalist's plea that "The trust is a bad thing to be outside of and a good thing to be inside of. Let us all get inside."[34] The persistence of this Elton Mayo-like view in the Bellamyite current throughout the decade of the 1890s even found poetic expression in a piece entitled "Organization," which ap-peared in *The Coming Nation:*

31. Blavatsky, *Key to Theosophy* (London, 1889), p. 19; on the Theosophical origins of the Declaration, see Quint, *Forging of American Socialism*, p. 81, and Morgan, *Edward Bellamy* p. 261. Edward Stanton [Huntington's] *Dreams of the Dead* (Boston: Lee & Shepard, 1893) is a theosophical-utopian treatise by "a sincere believer in social and industrial reform and an ardent disciple of Edward Bellamy" (ibid., p. 16), in which the communion pattern emerges as the central theme. In the highest stages of development of the new order, "regard of separate personality has been resigned in favor of the pure condition of the Universal" (ibid., p. 54). Huntington had been a founder of the First Nationalist club.

32. Morgan, *Edward Bellamy*, pp. 66, 260–275.

33. Henry M. Williams, "Palaces and Hovels," *The Nationalist* 1, no. 7 (November 1889): p. 251.

34. *The New Nation* 2, no. 20 (May 14, 1892): p. 307.

Workman, spare the trust,
Restrain thy frantic cries;
Our foolish anger is unjust
To the men who organize;
The Trust is Reason's child,
Destined to lead the way,
Through storms and tempests wild;
It's [sic] march we cannot stay.

Its birth, too long delayed,
We hail as fruitful days;
It will stay the hydra head
of vile unordered ways. . . .

* * *

'Tis narrow love now rules,
And Ego owns the throne;
Our ignorance makes us fools,
In Pluto's grasp to groan,
Forward the coming trust,
Which will include all men.
Let every act be just,
Crowned with love's diadem.[35]

Certainly the rank-and-file Nationalist who wrote to the editor of *The Nationalist* to suggest a beehive as the emblem of the Nationalist clubs had captured the essential spirit of Nationalism.[36]

Perhaps the most dramatic expression of the radical anti-individualism underlying the appeal of Nationalism was voiced by Burnette G. Haskell, whose career began with the authoritarian, elitist International Workingmen's Association and led with perfect consistency through the Kaweah Colony to the Nationalist movement in California where he played an important role in the formation of the clubs.[37] Explaining "why I am a Nationalist," Haskell hailed the state as an organism with a "collective personality." The inevitable evolution of the perfect Nationalist state meant that the doctrine of "individual right" would be

35. *The Coming Nation*, no. 407 (March 16, 1901).
36. *The Nationalist* 3, no. 1 (August 1890): p. 45.
37. Haskell, like Gronlund, was notable for spelling out the assumptions of his belief in socialism from above. In the IWA, "the masses of working men," he discovered, "were densely ignorant, cowardly and selfish, and thus disinclined to learn, to act or to aid others in acting." Hence "the great mass of people" must be "properly led and played upon" by a secret, conspiratorial elite. ("Shall Red and Black Unite?" reprinted in Destler, *American Radicalism*, pp. 83–84.)

put aside. "Let us sink self in the State," Haskell pleaded, "let us toil that our children may be free from pain; let us do as the red disks of the blood do when duty calls . . . These disks are independent cells, instinct with life. . . . They dance with helpful joy through every artery of the body. But let their State be threatened . . . they crystallize into army line; they hasten to the point of danger; they throw themselves in uncounted millions into the breach. The clot of blood that forms and bars death out of your bleeding body is made up of literal dead, who immolated themselves to save their fellows and the State." The individual thus immolated, Haskell saw a vision of Nationalism: "The silver voices of heroic bugles, the sweep of collective armies, with 'broadening front clearing to the outer file,' the million gleaming bayonet points of the marching hosts of heaven above, the orderly pulse of the unseen atom, the absolute harmony of universal law; all these teach me that I am myself too little to be an 'Anarchist' and boss the world; and so, perforce—or no! by choice—I whisper: 'Not *rights* but duties,' and behold, I am a 'Nationalist.' "[38]

Nationalists who started with the same problem of recalcitrant and selfish human nature as had Bellamy were not, of course, prevented from attempting to improve upon Bellamy's scheme for reconciling the self-centered individual with the needs of society. In Solomon Schindler's utopian novel, *Young West*,[39] written as a sequel to *Looking Backward*, the hero is the son of Julian West. "Young West" enlists in the sewer division. There he makes his mark by discovering a method for sanitizing and deodorizing human excrement that would otherwise be wasted. Transformed into bricks for ease in packaging and transporting, the bricks supply a new source of fertilizer for agriculture. On the strength of its overwhelming success, Young West is elected President and the plan is installed throughout the land.

Schindler's political views anticipate the "socialized" individualism of his fellow clergyman, Ward, or of V. F. Calverton, and even directly foreshadow the basic idea in the psychologist B. F. Skinner's authoritarian utopia, *Walden Two*.[40] In the old utopian tradition, Schindler places special emphasis upon the important role of state education under Nationalism. From the age of three, the child is separated from his parents and placed in a nursery. This is not presented as a transitional measure

38. Haskell, "Why I Am a Nationalist," *Twentieth Century*, May 15, 1890, pp. 5–7.
39. Solomon Schindler, *Young West* (1894).
40. B. F. Skinner, *Walden Two*, (New York: Macmillan, 1948).

by Schindler, as a means of training the child for life in the new order. Not at all. The implicit assumption is that the tendency of the individual to assert his "selfish" interests is ineradicable and must be controlled permanently. For this purpose the children are closely observed by a hypnotist. His function is to discover the "talents and vices slumbering in every child," and to give instructions for developing the child's talents while, at the same time, ordering the "vicious inclinations" he observes "be eradicated" through hypnosis.[41]

By isolating the children from their parents, constantly shifting them about from place to place in order to isolate them from one another, and by imposing military discipline upon them from the earliest age, Schindler seeks to prevent the "formation of lasting alliances" among people, which would, inevitably, disrupt the harmony of the social order.[42] At the same time that the child is kept from forming any permanent interpersonal relationships in order to ensure his total loyalty to society, the process of socialization through hypnotic control begun in nursery school continues into the elementary grades. Young West speaks glowingly of this aspect of education in the new Nationalist order:

> The fact that we were always under the eye of someone and that no deed could be perpetrated in secret, accounts for the rare occurrence of any action on our part that could be called bad. Some teacher was always observing us and no sooner were any evil tendencies in our character discovered than they were uprooted either by moral instruction and rational expostulation, or in obdurate cases by the medical advisor who was attached to an official staff of every school.[43]

To emphasize that Nationalism meant a radical break with all of the values of liberal individualism, Schindler devised an ironical twist to Bellamy's story. In Schindler's version, the secret diary of Julian West is discovered after his death. He reveals that after his first enthusiasm for the new order, he found life in a collectivist society utterly unbearable. Not because of any flaw in it, but rather because of a flaw within himself. Unable to shed the acquisitive, individualistic psychology which he brought with him into the twenty-first century, he soon began to feel oppressed by the socialized behavior of individuals in the new order. To the self-centered man of the nineteenth century the denial of personal

---

41. Schindler, *Young West*, p. 43.
42. Ibid., p. 73.   43. Ibid., p. 43.

needs and the lack of any sense of self apart from the social organism soon becomes a hell from which he cannot escape. "I yearn for death," Schindler's Julian West cries out, "because I am not fit to live in the present age on account of my early education, and am unfit to live again in the past on account of the lessons which the present has taught me."[44]

Clearly, whatever difference there is to be found between Schindler's advocacy of a kind of brainwashing via hypnosis to eradicate antisocial behavior on the part of the individual, and the totalitarian nightmare of Orwell's *1984* or Zamiatin's *We,* is not due to any difference in the basic spirit of Schindler's utopian wish, rather only to the fact that Schindler optimistically believed deviant tendencies could be purged early enough in childhood so that the state would not be required to apply constant, direct coercion. Schindler, however, had no objection in principle or in practice to the construction of a police state to re-educate and control those already corrupted by the old order for the purpose of making a successful transition to Nationalism. Yet, as a man of good hope, he did not, of course, portray the new society as one in which extensive coercion would be required. Caught in the utopian's dilemma of denying that men as they were could begin to act on their own behalf and could, to a degree, transcend their own personalities through the act of self-emancipation, Schindler found an external force that would keep people from destroying what they had not themselves been capable of choosing voluntarily.

The most important example of the communion pattern in Nationalist thought is Gronlund's *Our Destiny,* subtitled, *The Influence of Nationalism in Religion and Morals.*[45] Serialized in a slightly abridged form for over six months in *The Nationalist,*[46] frequently filling more than half of its pages, and then published as a separate work alongside the newly revised edition of *The Cooperative Commonwealth,* it undoubtedly reflected the sentiments of many members and sympathizers of Nationalism. Its influence can only be guessed at, of course. But it was widely advertised in socialistic and radical periodicals in the 1890s (including Bellamy's *New Nation*), and it constantly reappeared on lists of socialist works recommended to the uninitiated by these same publications. *Our Destiny*

44. Ibid., p. 279.   45. Gronlund, *Our Destiny.*
46. *The Nationalist* 2, nos. 4, 5, 6, 7, and 8.

thus was of great importance in the education of the native radical public of this period.

In *Our Destiny*, Gronlund argued, much as he had in *The Cooperative Commonwealth*, that socialism or Nationalism was consistent with the true moral foundation of society. The basis of all morals, Gronlund contended, was to be found in man's innate desire to subordinate himself and his needs to society, to "cooperate," as Gronlund put it, with his fellow men. In a word, "the germ of morals is, in its very essence, obedience. Man is truly made to obey, and to feel remorse if he does not obey."[47] The "immorality" of capitalism stemmed from the strong emphasis placed upon individualism; such an emphasis had led to the erroneous belief that men were rebellious and undisciplined by nature, and did not desire to obey.[48] On the contrary, Gronlund insisted, "there is in all of us a natural disposition to obedience; it is certain that we are all of us more or less disposed to respect any real superiority, especially intellectual and moral in others."[49]

Only under Nationalism could man's natural yearning to obey be properly realized because only then would obedience have as its object "true" authority rather than the "sham" authority exercised by the capitalists. True authority was authority which was in harmony with the collectivist "trend of social evolution": authority conferred upon individuals because of their superior moral and intellectual capacity, rather than because of their ability to get money. Obedience to true authority was, therefore, moral because it was consistent with submitting oneself to history itself. Thus, Nationalists, unlike anarchists and other radicals who wished to "abolish or discredit authority," instead "exalted authority."[50]

As the new socialist order evolved out of the old, its progress could be measured by the degree to which the posts of authority in industry and government were filled by men of intellectual achievement. Under capitalism, success went "to the cunning, the unscrupulous, the worthless, the impotent, rather than to the worthy."[51] Under Nationalism, both as it would ultimately triumph, and as it would evolve out of capitalism, "the direction of affairs" would belong more and more to the "capable."

47. Gronlund, *Our Destiny*, p. 47.
48. Ibid.   49. Ibid., p. 48.
50. Ibid.   51. Ibid., p. 58.

Gronlund's views on authority are a classic expression of the authoritarian pattern described by Fromm.[52] Subordination to authority and obedience to the capable are the moral foundations of the coming Nationalist society. To deny this, and "to regard subordination as a humiliation," Gronlund insisted, was "surely a mark not of spirit, but of base disposition, subversive of everything worth having in life."[53] Contrary to those who would abolish all authority, "to obey a real superior is a great blessing, essential to achieving anything great . . . 'command and obedience stand at the very entrance to life. The tacit assumption that it is a degradation to give one's will to that of another is the root of all evil.' "[54]

The aim of Nationalism, Gronlund explained, is a society of total harmony achieved by suppressing the "private self" and putting in its place the "social self," while at the same time making sure that public opinion, divided and anarchic under capitalism, would be turned into a "collective Conscience."[55] The great trouble under capitalism, Gronlund complained, "is that public opinion is at sea on all moral questions and therefore neither speaks nor claims to speak with authority on any."[56] Through the action of Nationalism's collective conscience, human nature would be drastically altered so that rather than the "divided public opinion" that characterized anarchic capitalism, the new collective conscience would be "consciously unanimous."[57] Under the pressure of this new morality, duty to society would become an obligation, because the unanimity of opinion so created would "imperatively, with authority, with a sense of being infallibly right, point out to all the welfare of the aggregate, the solidarity of the social organism, as the end of morals."[58] Once "our common destiny becomes a universal of faith what a pettiness will be infused into all mere private ends!"[59]

Within this context of total unity, the private self will be replaced by the "social" self, the higher part of man's nature. It alone is the "true" self, for "it is only as a member of society that the individual is at all real."[60] Denouncing Spencer for claiming that society was the abstract while the individual alone was real, Gronlund affirmed that on the contrary, "society is the real and the individual is the abstract."[61] The lower self, which is "of ourself" rather than of society, was therefore the false

52. Fromm, *Escape from Freedom*.
53. Gronlund, *Our Destiny*, p. 116.
54. Ibid.   55. Ibid., pp. 91, 61.   56. Ibid., p. 61.
57. Ibid.   58. Ibid., p. 58.   59. Ibid.
60. Ibid., p. 91.   61. Ibid., p. 92.

self, the product of capitalist society: narrow, selfish, and private. On the other hand, "the 'social self' accounts for our Personality: it accounts for Conscience as being the objective mind, self-conscious in the individual, the voice of the whole in the breast of each citizen, the utterance of the public spirit of the race in each social self. . . ."[62]

Nationalism, the society of perfect communion, would in Gronlund's peculiar use of the term make "self realization" possible. For "Morality is self realization; realization of the true, the real self, which . . . [is] the social self, self as a member of society, of humanity, in contradistinction to the private self."[63] Upon this ethical foundation Gronlund's entire indictment of capitalism and his support for Nationalism rested. In words removed in years but not in spirit from those of the Professor of Christian Ethics, Dr. Ward, Gronlund explained that:

> the mischief of the present social order is, that this private self is even with 'moral' men virtually the exclusive self, because we are made, COMPELLED, by the prevailing system to look out for our private interests first of all; but Nationalism will so repress this private self that men will refuse any longer to identify themselves with it; they will so live in the lives of others, will find humanity so involved in their own very essence, that their social self will be all to them; they will acknowledge this alone, this divine part of them, as their real personality, and be concerned only about that.[64]

Gronlund's exposition of the moral implications of Nationalist doctrine is a pure example of the communion pattern. Together with *Looking Backward*'s message and Nationalist politics, it offered its largely middle-class audience a way to "escape from freedom," into the arms of an authoritarian collectivist society. It is unneccesary, indeed, to look any further than Gronlund's own words to see how well Fromm's description of the authoritarian response to the breakdown of capitalism fits Nationalism: "WHO, in these anarchic times of ours, has not in his secret mind often felt how sweet it would be to obey, if he could have the rare privilege of assigning burdensome responsibility for his conduct to wise guidance?—a feeling, in fact, strongest in those best fitted to rule."[65]

To understand precisely how Nationalism proposed to realize Gronlund's wish to lay down the intolerable burden of individual freedom, one must turn to the politics and theory of Nationalism and especially Bellamy's military model of socialism.

62. Ibid., p. 93.   63. Ibid., p. 202.
64. Ibid., pp. 202–203.   65. Ibid., p. 48.

7 THE POLITICS OF NATIONALISM

"It is the distinguishing quality of Nationalism, and one on which its near success largely depends," wrote Bellamy in 1889, "that it places the whole subject of industrial and social reform on a broad National basis, viewing it not from the position or with the prejudices of any one group of men, but from the ground of a common citizenship, humanity and morality. Nationalism is not a class movement; it is a citizen's movement."[1] The claim to be a movement of the entire nation, one standing above particular social classes with their selfish interests, was basic to the Nationalists' open antipathy to organized political conflict and political parties. And, in turn, their "non-partisanship" was an essential part of the Nationalists' posture as a conservative movement. To call forth a political movement would stir up class antagonisms and undermine the kind of "brotherhood" or sense of organic communion between men of all classes for which the Nationalists were striving.

Above all, the refusal of the Nationalists to see themselves as a political movement stemmed from the very practical fear that it would set into motion the people of the abyss against the possessing classes—against the very class upon whom the stability of society and the present safety of the middle classes rested. From the latter, the Nationalists hoped for the broad, self-denying philanthropic outlook which would make the transition a painless and nonviolent one. Bellamy emphasized the Nationalists' determination to avoid any "denunciation of the wealthy in the supposed interests of the poor." "Nothing could be more unjust and senseless" because it was "the system that is to be attacked [rather than] . . . individuals whose condition, whether riches or poverty, merely illustrates its results."[2] Although there were many rich men who had gotten rich by "vicious methods" and deserved condemnation, Bellamy argued that "there are probably more to whose enterprise and leadership the community owes much of the little wealth and comfort it has. It is a very barba-

1. Bellamy, "Looking Forward," in *Edward Bellamy Speaks Again!* p. 176.
2. Ibid., pp. 175–176.

rous and wasteful sort of leadership to be sure, and one for which we hope
to substitute a mode of organizing industry infinitely more humane and
efficient. But meanwhile let us not fall into the mistake of those who rant
against capitalists in general, as if, pending the introduction of a better
system, they were not,—no doubt selfishly, but yet in fact—performing a
necessary function to keep the system going."[3]

In rejecting attacks on the rich, Bellamy was also making it clear
that Nationalism was an elitist movement different from that advocated
by radical socialists. The transition could be made only from above—
through the tutelage of the "educated" and conservative middle-class elite
that was not partisan to labor or capital. "Evolution, not revolution,
orderly and progressive development, not precipitate and hazardous experiment" was the "true policy" of Nationalism. "No party or policy of
disorder or riot finds any countenance from us" the Nationalists boasted,
hoping to gain "the confidence of the law-abiding masses of the American people," for whom their peculiar brand of conservative anticapitalism was primarily designed.[4]

To attain their goal and at the same time maintain their stance as a
supra-class movement hostile to politics and political parties, Bellamy
had called for a "national" party rising above politics in the ordinary
sense and striving for the creation of a nonpartisan collectivist movement.[5] The very name of the movement, Sylvester Baxter pointed out,
had been adopted precisely because Nationalists wanted to distinguish
their doctrines from the partisan collectivism of the socialists. Nationalism, "unlike socialism as commonly understood, is not a class movement
but for the whole country."[6] To the Nationalists the struggle of the
workers and the organized labor movement was "not more unselfish in
basis, though much more justifiable in its grounds, than a capitalistic
movement for better returns. . . ."[7] The "present industrial agitation" on
the part of the workers represented a "narrow, selfish and clannish spirit
of self-seeking—each trade and class for itself. . . ."[8] It was fortunate,
therefore, when the Nationalists discovered "the masses of workers are

3. Ibid.   4. Ibid., pp. 177–178.
5. See ch. 4 above. Cf. Quint, *The Forging of American Socialism*, ch. 6 et passim on
the phenomenon of "non-partisan socialism" in the 1890s.
6. Bellamy, "Why the Name Nationalism?" in *Edward Bellamy Speaks Again!*, p. 29.
7. *The New Nation* 1, no. 20 (June 13, 1891), p. 310.
8. Ibid.

rapidly coming to recognize, in common with the professions and business classes, that no radical improvement in the social situation can be
accomplished on class or trade lines, but must be undertaken as a citizens' movement composed of and appealing to all classes, in the interest
of all alike."[9]

A social order that could be described as a family or in terms
drawn from plant physiology obviously excluded methods for its attainment that depended upon the exacerbation of class conflict or disorder.
An organic growing together of the various elements in society required
the cementing over of class antagonism and in particular of its expression, politics and partisanship. Their disappearance and the gradual substitution of the representative organ of all society, the state, was both the
means and the precondition for the "orderly and progressive" development of Nationalism: "Nationalism is the evolution of the nation, or, if
you please of the state, whereby it is destined to carry into the industrial
organization the principle of all for each and each for all without respect
of persons which principle is already illustrated in the political, military,
judicial and other forms under which the national idea has thus far
attained realization."[10]

Despite the Nationalists' reluctance to use the term, people insisted
on viewing Nationalism as a type of socialism, thereby forcing the Nationalists to constantly reiterate the difference between their doctrines
and those of the radical socialists. On the one hand they rejected
"anarchism," which they believed to be the most numerous and powerful
section of the socialist movement.[11] In England, the Nationalists saw
William Morris, whose anti-Bellamy novel, *News from Nowhere*, had just
been published, as a representative of the "anarchist" wing of the socialist movement. Morris was, of course, by this time a revolutionary socialist and a Marxist, and their indictment of what they termed "anarchism"
reflected, in fact, their objections to revolutionary socialism.[12] Thus the
"anarchists" not only aimed "at an anarchic or unorganized social state as
the ultimate ideal," which the Nationalists regarded as impossible and
undesirable, but also expected "to attain it by violent and revolutionary
methods."[13] The views of the "Marxists" were also unacceptable because

9. Ibid.   10. *New Nation* 2, no. 9, p. 130.
11. *New Nation* 1, no. 46 (December 12, 1891), pp. 725–726.
12. E. P. Thompson, *William Morris* (New York: Monthly Review, 1961).
13. *New Nation* 1, no. 46 (December 12, 1891), pp. 725–726.

their ultimate goal was "a sort of confederation of industrial guilds, each controlling for its own benefit some province of industry."[14] Clearly the Nationalist understanding of Marxism as well as anarchism was wanting.

To these other socialisms, the Nationalists counterposed their own doctrine, but they found it impossible not to make the very terminological concession which Bellamy had so strongly resisted at the first. Nationalism, "the latest phase of socialism . . . called by some the American socialism," they argued,

> differs utterly from anarchistic socialism, both as to ends and means. Its social idea is a perfectly organized industrial system which, by reason of close interlocking of its wheels shall work at a minimum of friction with a maximum of wealth and leisure to all. This end it would not attain by revolution but by an orderly evolution of the republican idea of the equal interest of all in the state. . . . From state socialism, so far as its program has been defined, nationalism differs vitally though less completely than from anarchism. State socialism, while undoubtedly favoring a great reduction of social disparities, does not postulate the economical equality of citizens or sexes.[15]

In a word, Morris's revolutionary socialism was judged too utopian for wishing to do away with the state, while the "utopian" socialism of the Bellamyites, which instead wanted to abolish government while retaining the state, came down in practice to an authoritarian state socialism similar to that advocated by German "socialists of the chair" as a policy directed against the Social Democrats.

Yet, anticipating critics who would point to the subservient position of the individual in relation to the organized state, a position clearly indicated by this definition of Nationalism, the Bellamyites were capable of conceding that the ultimate goal of the "anarchists," a noncoercive social order, might well be the same as their own. But this was a purely formal concession which had little practical meaning for Nationalism as a movement. It was a concession made, in large part, with the same logic and the same spirit as those justifications of despotic rule and coercion in the present which rest their case upon the promise that only in this way can a desirable goal of freedom be reached at some vague point in the future. This kind of reasoning was inherent in the utopian politics of Nationalism and it permeated the movement's ideology. Thus, for example, the *New Nation* published an article by Henry S. Salt, prominent

14. Ibid.   15. Ibid.

member of the semi-Fabian British organization "Fellowship of the New Life," prefaced by an editorial note which indicated their approval of its conclusions, that was a model of this type of justification.[16] Salt, addressing himself to Spencer's argument that socialism was slavery, denied that socialism meant the end of individuality. He did not deny, however, that its introduction necessarily entailed coercion by a minority and that, therefore, it would have to be introduced from above. The only question of importance for Salt was whether the socialists advocated state intervention "for pure love of what Prof. Huxley calls 'regimentation,' " or whether it was "with the purpose of using regimentation in the present as a means toward complete freedom in the future?"[17] Obviously the answer was that it was not the former but the latter goal which was the "ultimate tendency" of socialism, even if there were, as Salt conceded, many socialists who "in the hurry and bustle of political crusade, do not, perhaps cannot, look beyond the immediate object they have in view" and thus who had stressed, or seemed to stress, regimentation for its own sake. Yet, these "short-sighted socialists," Salt argued, only see today, while the "far-sighted anarchists" can only see the future. When one understood that "anarchism is the further horizon, the ideal of socialism," then the apparent contradiction between the two vanishes and "one and the same man may, with perfect consistency, be a state socialist as regards the politics of today, and an extreme anarchist in his forecast of tomorrow. . . . "[18]

Precisely what it meant to be a "state socialist" during the long period before the ultimate goal would somehow be attained, Salt spelled out in terms which were not foreign to Nationalists: "Let us suppose," he explained, "that an army has to be marched through two passes, or, to take a more homely metaphor, that a pig has to be driven through two gates. Both passes, or both gates, must in each case be kept open; and the advance guard that is detached to do the further duty is co-operating, even if it be unaware of the fact, with the main army that devoted itself to the nearer one; the time of the one is the present, of the other the future, that is the sole difference between them."[19] The idea of freedom and individuality in the far-distant future, after having passed through regimentation in the present, an idea which the Nationalists were to

---

16. Ibid., pp. 729–730.   17. Ibid., pp. 729.   18. Ibid.
19. Ibid., p. 730.

develop as part of their theory of how the transition to the new order would come about was, of course, what made them, in truth, men of good hope or more accurately, *utopians* in the scientific sense of the term: utopians whose sure knowledge of the passes which lay ahead entitled them to drive the swinish multitude into the promised land.

The Nationalists' belief that they were truly a party above parties, individuals wholly free of class interest, was not consciously hypocritical, of course. But it was an illusion contradicted by the reality of their own organization, by the activity which they set in motion, and above all the hard fact of a society divided into classes, driven by opposing and conflicting interests and needs. The Nationalist denial of class politics was merely a different mode of class politics. However susceptible the workers might be for a time to such a political claim, the capitalists whose property was to be taken away could not and did not regard the Nationalists in quite the favorable way that was expected of them, even when their higher and unselfish motives were appealed to by the Nationalists. The contradiction posed to Nationalism's nonpolitical politics by the reality of a class society and the obduracy of the capitalists came out into the open within a very short time after the movement began to attract attention and followers and impelled the movement in a direction different from the one it had originally determined upon.

The Theory of Nationalism

The critical reaction to both *Looking Backward* and the Nationalist movement required an elaboration and development of Nationalist politics far beyond the confines of the scheme laid down in *Looking Backward*. As the clubs spread, the question of a specific program outlining the practical steps to achieve Nationalism came to the fore. On this point, *Looking Backward* had been at its vaguest, even though the line of march had been made clear enough. The task of defending and extending Nationalist doctrine fell upon Bellamy's shoulders, although several others, especially Gronlund, contributed to Nationalist thought. In assuming the new role of an ideologue, Bellamy abandoned forever his career as a novelist.

The fundamental theoretical postulate of Nationalism was Bellamy's view that the achievement of the new collectivist order would evolve through self-collectivization of capitalism. No separate political movement and party in the ordinary sense was necessary. "In order to realize in due time the Nationalist idea," wrote Bellamy in 1889, "it is only necessary to take judicious advantage of the contemporary tendency toward the consolidation of capital and concentration of business control. The 'Ship of State' is already being borne onward by a current which it is only needful to utilize in order to reach the desired haven. The progressive nationalization and municipalization of industries by substituting public control for the public advantage, in place of already centralized forms of corporate advantage, is at once the logical and the inevitable policy in Nationalism."[20] Here the same emphasis upon Nationalism as the inevitable outcome of the present, as "the wave of the future," may be observed. And yet, to "utilize" the current of evolution, to have a "policy" for Nationalism, implicitly introduced an element of choice, and suggested the possibility of historical alternatives. But if the new society was inevitable, what room was there for choice or for alternative paths of historical development? What could be the role of an organized movement or, for that matter, what was the point of writing *Looking Backward* itself? Troubled by this paradox of being a conscious, active advocate of the inevitable, Bellamy offered a contradictory and faltering explanation: "A book of propaganda like 'Looking Backward' produces an effect precisely in proportion as it is a bare anticipation of what everybody was thinking and about to say. Indeed, the seeming paradox might almost be defended that in proportion as a book is effective it is unnecessary. The particular service of the book in question was to interpret the purpose and direction of the conditions and forces which were tending toward Nationalism, and thereby to make the evolution henceforth a conscious, and not, as previously, an unconscious one."[21] In seeking to extricate himself from this contradiction, Bellamy could only conclude lamely: "The Nationalist who accepts that interpretation no longer sees in the unprecedented economical disturbance of the day a mere chaos of conflicting forces, but rather a stream of tendencies through ever greater experiments in concentration and combination towards the ultimate complete integration of the nation of economical as well as political purposes."[22] The admission of the possibility of alternative paths which particular individuals or classes, whether out of perversity or selfishness or ignorance, might choose for the develop-

---

20. Bellamy, "Looking Forward," *Edward Bellamy Speaks Again!*, p. 173.
21. Bellamy, "Progress of Nationalism in the United States," in *Edward Bellamy Speaks Again!*, pp. 136–137.
22. Ibid.

ment of society constituted an intolerable ideological break with the fatalistic evolutionism of *Looking Backward*. A purely ideological contradiction, however, would have meant little for the course of Nationalism's development. More important was the opposition from the capitalists and others who were vigorously opposed to social reform which later led Nationalists to alter their original views. The Nationalist movement, no less than the writing of *Looking Backward* itself, were thus both contradictory: once achieved they began to be altered by the very forces they had set into motion.

Bellamy's fatalistic theory, like all "quasi-miraculous" solutions,[23] reassured middle-class elements, frightened and impotent in the face of the corporation and the trust, and yet whose position made them incapable of helping themselves, that they did not have to fear for their future. The overt thematic recognition of these feelings of despair and impotence in Nationalist writings is marked, and its connection to the "optimistic" discovery of the self-collectivizing wave of the future is often explicit: "The rise and spread of Pessimism is a fact of great interest and significance. A strange protest, surely, that, in these days when the jubilant chorus is loudest, the note of desolation and despair has broken in as a discord that suddenly finds acceptance, first of all, among the fortunate classes—a philosophy affirming the nullity of all things and asking: Is life worth living? . . . In spite of experiencing as much as any one the hardships of the established state of things . . . I know that this is the threshold of the Golden Age, and feel that it is a high privilege to live now . . ."[24] In the same vein Bellamy wrote, "Like the children of Israel in the desert this new and strange peril causes the timid to sigh even for the iron rule of a Pharoah. Let us see if there be not in this case a promised land, by the prospect of which faint hearts may be encouraged."[25] The Bellamyite answer was positive. There was indeed a force not dependent upon the isolated individual's capacity for struggle or self-organization, in fact one somehow not even dependent on human effort or choice at all, that was bringing salvation: "Today it matters

23. See Hans Gerth, "The Nazi Party: Its Leadership and Composition," in Merton et al., *Reader in Bureaucracy* (Glencoe: The Free Press, 1952), pp. 100–113. Cf. Fromm, *Escape from Freedom*, pp. 174–179 on the psychology of the "magic helper."

24. Gronlund, *Our Destiny*, p. 11.

25. Edward Bellamy, "Plutocracy or Nationalism—Which?" in *Edward Bellamy Speaks Again!*, pp. 37–38.

little how weak the voice of the preacher be, for the current of affairs, the logic of events is doing his work and preaching his sermon for him."[26] In giving the individual something more powerful than himself to hold to and to trust to save him, the fatalistic theory of inevitable collectivism was, despite its claim that it relied upon an impersonal force, only an echo of Gronlund's belief that it would be sweet to obey, and to surrender individual responsibility to "wise guidance."[27]

A second critical function of Bellamy's theory of inevitable salvation was to obviate the need for a political social movement or organization, and avoid the danger of pushing the masses into motion. Here again the theory broke down logically and then in practice—aided by strength of the opposition and the success of the movement in arousing people.

Practical Utopianism: Nucleation

Pressed to explain exactly how the transition to the new society would take place, almost three years after *Looking Backward* had been published, Bellamy finally specified the "First Steps toward Nationalism."[28] Nationalism was not only a "theory dealing with the ultimate possibilities of human development," it was also "a proposition tending to immediate action or practical results."[29] Indeed, the first steps were known, and the rest could be indicated: "Stated in general terms, the policy proposed by nationalists is the successive nationalizing or municipalizing of public service and branches of industry, and the simultaneous organization of the employees upon a basis of guaranteed rights, as branches of the civil service of the country; this process being continued until the entire transformation shall have been effected."[30] Bellamy called for nationalization of the telephone, telegraph, railroads, coal, the express business, and all public utilities, bringing over two million workers in the public service. "Here will be consumers enough to support the beginnings of national productive industries, both manufacturing and agricultural, together with a system of distribution, for the exclusive supply of those in the public service."[31]

The transition to a full-blown Nationalist society would come

---

26. Ibid., pp. 42–43.   27. Gronlund, *Our Destiny*, p. 48.
28. Bellamy, "First Steps Toward Nationalism," in *Edward Bellamy Speaks Again!*, pp. 105–119.
29. Ibid., p. 105.   30. Ibid., pp. 105–106.   31. Ibid., pp. 118.

about through creation of these collectivist enclaves within capitalism. Once a nucleus of state or municipally owned industry had been established, and the workers made functionaries, then the "object lesson" of its success would convince the majority to take the next logical steps. Each industry thus nationalized would "truly . . . be a bulwark against capitalism, against corporate usurpation, against industrial oppression." In brief, *"Here would be a mighty nucleus of the coming industrial army"*[32] (my emphasis). The passage of the last trust into the hands of the state, and the incorporation of the last group of workers into the national service, would mark the completion of the evolutionary process.

If the new order could be created within capitalism, and if each bit of state ownership constituted a nucleus of the coming industrial army within capitalism, no conscious majority of the people need be won over to the Nationalist cause, nor was it necessary to call into existence a mass political movement. The new order would surround them. The Nationalists' awareness of the relationship between the form of organization assumed by the clubs, the undesirability of moving by "political" means, and this nucleation theory is confirmed by their frequent proclamations that their movement was a "conservative" movement. The first steps to the attainment of Nationalism outlined by Bellamy involved "no revolutionary measures, no letting go of the old before securing a hold on the new; but an orderly progress, of which each step shall logically follow the last, and shall be justified to the most shortsighted by its immediate motives and results, without invoking any consideration of ultimate ends."[33] In this fashion, the Nationalists believed, the new collectivist order could be brought in through the back door by a determined elite, without any necessity for the workers to struggle (hopelessly) for "small immediate improvements in their condition," and most importantly, according to Bellamy, "absolutely without a risk of derangement of business."[34] If there was no need to create a conscious mass movement, in fact, it was perfectly consistent to believe that Nationalism might be introduced, or at least helped on, by a closed conspiracy of men strategi-

32. Bellamy, "Nationalism—Principles, Purposes," in *Edward Bellamy Speaks Again!*, p. 66.
33. Bellamy, "First Steps Toward Nationalism," in *Edward Bellamy Speaks Again!*, pp. 117–118.
34. Bellamy, "Nationalism—Principles, Purposes," in *Edward Bellamy Speaks Again!*, p. 70.

cally placed at the levers of power. Gronlund's "American Socialist Fraternity," formed during his association with the Nationalist movement, was just such an attempt to create a conspiratorial elite, and there is evidence that Bellamy was repeatedly asked to help form such a group.[35]

The Politics of Antipolitics

With the idea of an unconscious "socialism" stealing upon the nation with the inevitable growth of public and private collectivism so central to the politics of Nationalism, neither Bellamy nor the Nationalists in the early period were concerned with political mechanisms nor, of course, did they wish to identify the transition in any way with the expansion of democratic controls. The conservative nature of Nationalism promised that the emergence of the new order would be kept in the right hands. Once the statification of industry was complete, the state would in effect be identical with the industrial army. And whatever other differences of opinion there were among Nationalists, there was unanimity that the state would lose its political function and become solely an instrument for the efficient bureaucratic administration of the economy and the regimentation of the working class.

Each step toward the statification of the economy, every substitution of bureaucratic administration for "politics," was a step toward the ultimate goal of Nationalism. Who or what class controlled the state and precisely how the process of statification and bureaucratization came about was of no interest within the framework of Nationalist politics. Whether the state was controlled by Czarist or Prussian despots, or was the existing American state, the assumption of some segment of industry by the state was hailed as a step toward Nationalism.[36] Under these circumstances, even capitalists could help to introduce the new order. "Many of the capitalists who have secretly favored Nationalism for some time," Cyrus Field Willard wrote in 1890, "are now openly advocating it."[37] Their open advocacy of Nationalism—specifically here the nationalization of the railroads—did not, it is clear, require a belief in any other changes in the social order, and least of all a transfer of political power. The prominent Nationalist, Rabbi Schindler of Boston, travelled abroad to Europe in order "to convince the 'lazy and torpid masses' that social-

35. Mason Green, "Edward Bellamy," in Bellamy Papers, p. 179.
36. See, e.g., The New Nation 1, no. 42 (November 14, 1891): 662–663.
37. The Nationalist 2, no. 7 (June 1890): 274.

ism could work."[38] In 1889, Schindler "wrote glowing reports about Bismarck's social welfare state. What 'we . . . call in America National- ism . . . may be studied best here in Germany,' [wrote Schindler]. The government-owned railroads, telegraph, schools, post office, war facto- ries, and express business were more prosperous than he previously had known it. Germany was truly on the road to a 'communistic Brother- hood.' "[39] Schindler, like Lincoln Steffens some thirty years later, had seen the future and it *worked;* most important of all it worked within the framework of the Prussian police state. No lazy and torpid masses could prevent Bismarck from introducing Nationalism, or, as Schindler idealis- tically characterized it, a "communistic brotherhood." Only later, begin- ning in late 1890 or early 1891, were some Nationalists to begin to raise the question of who was to control the state which concentrated all economic power in its hands, and to suggest, hesitatingly, that the ques- tion of democracy could be relevant for Nationalists. But on the whole it was far more natural for the Nationalists to discover that Kaiser Wil- helm, under the pressure of the socialist workers, was ready to introduce socialism under the auspices of the Prussian state.[40]

Only once did an article in *The Nationalist* publicly raise the ques- tion of political power and challenge the equation of statification with "nationalism." Revealing himself either as a fugitive Marxist or perhaps someone who had gravitated toward Marxism from Nationalism, the author began by citing Engels' denunciation of the "bogus socialism" of Bismarck and others which had sprung up toward the end of the cen- tury. He did so "for the benefit of those optimistic nationalists who think they discover evidences of nationalism and a realization of their ideals in every step or effort of governments—whether American or foreign, na- tional or municipal,—to assume ownership of one or the other indus- tries."[41] He urged those Nationalists to ponder Engels' words, "who hail in every advocate of the nationalization or municipalization of this or that industry a brother nationalist," especially those "who are inflated with the belief that in the nationalization of what they term 'natural monopo- lies' . . . lies the whole solution of the stupendous social problem." As

38. Arthur Mann, *Yankee Reformers in an Urban Age* (1954), p. 60.
39. Ibid.
40. *The New Nation* 1, no. 42 (November 14, 1891): 662–663.
41. Max Georgii, "State Ownership of Industries," *The Nationalist* 3, no. 7 (Febru- ary 1891): 466–470.

long as the state was a capitalist state, then even if "all the producing and serving agencies were thus transferred to this class-state, think you that such class would not find in it the amplest means of riveting your fetters still closer?" The only solution, he concluded, was to take political power and to prosecute the class struggle with the goal in mind not of nationalization by itself, but of the capture of state power.[42] Certainly Engels' warning, repeated by the article's author, that "the state owner-ship of the means of production is not the solution of the conflict, but . . . the formal means, the lever, to the solution," could not have been more alien to original Nationalism.

Superficially, the Nationalists' conception of the state may appear similar to the liberal or reformist-socialist view of the state. But unlike either of these political currents, for the Nationalists the representativeness of the state which was to assume full control over the economy did not rest on the premise that nationalization had to take place under the auspices of a "democratic state," as, for example, Bernstein advocated in his revisionist theory. Whatever the ultimate implications or contradictions in Bernstein's or other reformist theories of socialism in regard to the state, they did not envision the dissolution of political parties and contraction of democratic political controls in connection with statification of the economy. Trade unions, a mass social democratic party or parties, some kind of system of representation, including universal suffrage, of course—in short, a free and active public life—were all taken for granted as the sine qua non of social-ism, even in the most right-wing theories which like Bellamy saw socialism arriving through the gradual, piecemeal nationalization of industry by the existing state. The state was to be purified not of democratic institutions, as the Nationalists envisioned, but only of the restraints upon democracy inherent in capitalism itself. Illusory or not, this critical difference meant that Nationalism was something quite different from simply an American version of European reformist socialism, contrary to what so many histori-ans of American radicalism have suggested.

Essentially, Bellamy's and the Nationalists' belief that the state was a supra-class institution was ultimately based upon a kind of metaphysi-

42. Ibid., pp. 467, 469–470. For another contemporary Marxist's hostile views on Nationalism see Philip S. Foner's valuable introductory essay, "Friedrich Adolf Sorge: 'Father of Modern Socialism in America,' " in Foner and Chamberlin, eds., *Labor Movement in the United States* (Westport: Greenwood Press, 1977) pp. 34–36.

cal reasoning that simply posited the identity of interest between the state and the citizen as a matter of definition. Such a mystical, authoritarian conception of the state similar to that found in Gronlund's *Cooperative Commonwealth* was prominent in Nationalist writings. One of *The Nationalist*'s editors, thus, proclaimed Nationalism to be the realization of the Hegelian idea of the state.[43] Expressing surprise and disappointment at the noted American Hegelian W. T. Harris's attack on *Looking Backward*'s ideal as potentially "more repressive to individual development than any despotism of which we have any knowledge in recent times,"[44] the editor replied that the state, as the Nationalists viewed it, was the fulfillment of man's destiny: "From its birth in a State in which the individual lived in unthinking submission to a central will power, its course has been and will continue through one civilization after another, onward, upward and outward, till in its fulness it shall inspire a State in which the individual shall feel, that his life in its conscious purpose and devotion is in perfect harmony with the purpose and life of the State, and in this total abnegation of selfish struggling the ideal man and the ideal state shall bless the world."[45]

The End of Democracy

Given the radical organicist theory of the state which was basic to Nationalism, it followed that the freedom of the individual lay in the highest development of the state. The question of democratic self-government and individual liberty apart from the needs and goals of the state was simply irrelevant. Indeed, insofar as democracy and its concomitant, associative political activity, were nothing more than the reflection of individual or class "selfishness," their existence within such an organic society was not only irrelevant, but the very demand for the right to participate in making the decisions affecting one's own interest and circumstances could only be regarded as evidence of a selfish hostility to society—a failure to submit which, as in Bellamy's proposed treatment of the criminal or deviant, would be worse than any actual crime. By extension, politics and partisanship became at least akin to a crime to

43. J. Foster Biscoe, *The Nationalist* 1, no. 7 (November 1889): p. 271.

44. For Harris's criticism see "Edward Bellamy's Vision," *The Forum* 8 (October 1889): p. 207.

45. Biscoe, *The Nationalist*, p. 271.

the degree that their persistence prevented the creation of the Nation as an organic unity of the entire people

How clearly the Nationalists, or at least their leading spokesmen, understood that the realization of their ideal social order entailed the elimination of democratic self-government may be demonstrated not only by the role of the military model in Nationalist ideology, which will be explored in the next chapter, but also by the enormous popularity of Gronlund's *Cooperative Commonwealth* which emerged in its revised format as one of the most widely read expositions of Nationalist-style socialism. Side by side with it was Gronlund's specifically Nationalist book, *Our Destiny*. In it he reiterated the earlier book's view that democracy had nothing to do with "counting of heads."[46] A few years earlier, in 1887, in writing an article on the American socialist movement, Gronlund had broken whatever slight connection he had with Marxism by denouncing Marx for failing to understand, as every all-American socialist did, that the "democracy of the future" which would accompany the nationalization of industry, entailed "government by the most competent, the most industrious and the wisest," rather than the counting of votes.[47] In *Our Destiny* Gronlund announced that Nationalism, which was the organized embodiment of the American-style socialism he had been advocating in his works, saw that "true democracy" required that the "direction of social affairs belong to the capable, and secondly, that all citizens must participate in that direction by their intelligent cooperation."[48]

Rabbi Schindler's book, *Young West*, similarly rejected democracy. Schindler was one of the most prolific propagandists for Nationalism, next to Bellamy and Gronlund,[49] and had translated *Looking Backward* into German. In numerous articles, published between 1889 and 1895, many appearing in the influential reform magazine, *The Arena*, Schindler advocated Nationalist ideas to a wide non-Nationalist audience.[50] Al-

46. Gronlund, *Our Destiny*, pp. 79–80.
47. Gronlund, "Le Socialisme aux Etats-Unis" (1887), p. 123.
48. Gronlund, *Our Destiny*, p. 80.
49. The main source of information about Schindler is Arthur Mann, *Yankee Reformers*, ch. 3.
50. The most important of these articles were: "Nationalism Versus Individualism," *Arena* 3 (1891): 601–607; "What is Nationalism?" *New England Magazine* 7 (September 1892): 56; "First Steps to Nationalism," *Arena* 13 (January 1895): 29. In addition, Schindler published his novel, *Young West*, and in 1889, according to Mann (*Yankee Reformers*, p. 66), wrote special reports as their European correspondent to the Boston Globe.

though Schindler "hated war . . . he admired the efficiency and discipline of the Prussian military force; hence Bellamy's industrial army,
working for peaceful ends, appealed to him."[51] For this reason, he favored the growth of trade unions, because they would "train the workers
in the discipline necessary for the industrial army."[52] His vigorous activity on behalf of the Nationalist movement led to dismissal by his conservative congregation and forced him to eke out a meager existence for the
few remaining years of his life as a writer and lecturer on Nationalism.

Schindler's utopian novel, *Young West*, which we have already
touched upon, was conceived of as a reply from an orthodox Nationalist
to the critics of Nationalism. In it, Schindler asserts the disillusionment
with politics and democratic self-government that pervades *Looking Backward*. For years, nations under the yoke of monarchy and despotism
dreamed of self-government, of "a government of the people, for the
people, and by the people."[53] Yet, Schindler observed, "After a brief
experience they found to their sorrow that these hopes, too, were delu-
sive. Instead of by one monarch or despot they were now ruled by
hundreds of political bosses or by moneyed corporations, syndicates, and
monopolies too numerous to be counted. The very representatives whom
they elected to transact the public business betrayed them, and the iron
hand of despotic majorities rested more heavily upon them than had in
previous ages the hand of an irresponsible tyrant."[54] When reformers
"tried to reach the will of the sovereign people" they discovered that it
was all in vain. They concluded that: "Let alone that political equality
cannot exist unless social and economical [sic] equality support it, their
axiom, that the 'majority must rule' was a fallacy, if not in itself at least
in its execution."[55]

At last, Schindler explained, as a result of the reformers' disillusionment with the ability of the masses of men to take the true path to
social betterment, "the honest and thinking classes came to the conclusion that their whole system of electing a government was a failure and a
farce; they objected to serve any longer as voting cattle and to hurrah for
some scheming politician, who, by shrewd machinations or by the depth
of his bar'l, had succeeded in capturing a nomination."[56]

51. Mann, *Yankee Reformers*, p. 64.
52. Ibid., p. 69.   53. Ibid., p. 64.
54. Schindler, *Young West*, pp. 209–211.
55. Ibid., p. 210.   56. Ibid., pp. 210–211.

The discovery of this truth required Nationalism to do away with elections and politics. In an explicit defense of Bellamy's system against those who found *Looking Backward*'s plan to be undemocratic, Schindler replied:

> When the social order which we enjoy at present hove in sight, its framers evolved a constitution so different from that of their ancestors that a great many of their supporters even doubted its feasibility, and feared that instead of enhancing liberty it would destroy it, because the new order went almost to the extreme and reduced what was formerly called "the expression of the public will," "the safeguard of liberty," to a minimum. That they had not been mistaken, that they had discovered at last the most effective method of good government, is known to us, and although our children may yet improve certain details, it is our hope that in its main features the constitution of our days will be able to satisfy in its execution the remotest generations."[57]

By the time Schindler had written these words (1893–1894), Bellamy as well as many other Nationalists would have probably not openly agreed with him (which explains Schindler's reference to the doubting supporters of Nationalism), but his rejection of democratic political institutions in the contemporary social order and in a fully developed Nationalist utopia was faithful to the original doctrine of Nationalism as outlined by Bellamy in *Looking Backward*. In place of democracy—"the expression of the public will" as Schindler so bluntly put it—there would be the disciplinary power of the industrial army which would constitute the framework of the Nationalist state.

57. Ibid., pp. 211–213. Arthur Mann's comment on Schindler's antidemocratic ideas offers an example of the kind of contradictory statements which even excellent historians get into when confronted with Bellamyite-style politics. Thus, Mann writes, "Because he [Schindler] accepted without qualification the American democratic creed that the people is the government, he saw no dichotomy between authority and liberty— between those who governed and those who were governed." (*Yankee Reformers*, p. 64.)

⑧ BARRACKS SOCIALISM AND THE INDUSTRIAL ARMY

Looking Backward's most distinctive and unique idea, whose adoption decisively separated Nationalist-style socialism from the radical democratic ideas of the working-class movement, was the industrial army, a bureaucratic model on which the collectivist organization of the economy could successfully be based. Bellamy's army mirrored the organization of a modern nineteenth-century army in every respect: it concentrated power with those at the top of a hierarchical system of grades or ranks; it explicitly excluded democratically elected represented bodies, political parties, trade unions, or any other mechanisms by which the people could directly participate in or affect the politics of the state. The officers of the industrial army would also be the officials of the state, for in time the evolution of collectivism would make them one.

Historians who dismiss Bellamy's choice of the military model misunderstand the central feature of his ideology. Bellamy's authoritarian socialist views were an historical precursor of totalitarian collectivist ideological currents because he insisted that a private, atomized existence was all that his utopia could allow to the masses of people, and even that was to be highly circumscribed. Organic unity within the confines of the state was the overriding principle and in this sense it is correct to speak of the industrial army as a "technique for welding together an effective working force and making the nation one economic organism."[1] But to so weld the workers into an army left no room, by design, for democracy of any sort. Bellamy turned Marx's vision of the withering away of the state upside

---

1. Daniel Aaron, *Men of Good Hope*, p. 111. On the impact of war and militarism on conservative post–Civil War reformers, see George M. Frederickson, *The Inner Civil War*, whose discussion of the "moral equivalent of war," ch. 14, touches briefly but insightfully upon Bellamy (pp. 225–228). To understand the conservative nature of Bellamy's adoption of the industrial army model it is necessary to see it in the context of the democratic antimilitarist tradition as well as the antipathy to the use of the army and the militia to break strikes. See Arthur A. Ekirch, Jr., *The Civilian and the Military* (1956), esp. chs. 7 to 11; Robert Reinders, "Militia and Public Order in Nineteenth-Century America" (1977): 81–101; Barton C. Hacker, "The United States Army as a National Police Force" (April 1969): 255–264.

down, proposing instead the absorption of society into the state, leaving the latter free to emerge as an all-embracing, all-powerful institution.

It is true that Bellamy's use of the military model and his admiration for the military had little or nothing to do with a love for "militarism" in a narrow sense of glorification of war and its attendant violence. It was modern military *organization*, seen as a model bureaucratic system, not dependent upon profit for its motive power and possessed by a sense of supra-individual purpose which bound privates and officers together, that attracted him. The military was capable of imposing discipline over the ranks to accomplish its task efficiently, without conflict or disorder, all in contrast to the selfishness of capitalism. In the industrial army the masses would discover an impersonal, unselfish goal for which they would gladly strive. The army model proved that there could be a noncapitalist ruling class; one rewarded by honor and sense of duty rather than money; it was "classless" and egalitarian only in the sense that merit, not wealth, would be the sole basis for power and status.

Contemporary critics had no difficulty in understanding the central importance of the military model to the politics of Nationalism. How obvious it was to anyone who had paid attention to the Bellamyites' doctrine was plainly revealed when, in 1891, some Nationalists, including Bellamy himself, who had vigorously and consistently defended the idea of the industrial army, began to hedge and back away. Commenting on this new development in Bellamyite doctrine in the widely read reform periodical, *The Arena*, Reverend Minot J. Savage protested that Nationalism without the industrial army ceased to be a distinctive political current. "Dreams are old and common; but when this book appeared, people shouted 'Eureka.' We have found the way. This is the fulfillment of our dreams! Now we are told, on authority, that it is not. And we are just where we were before."[2] Nationalism, Savage pointed out, could not "consist of an indefinite confession that the industrial condition of the world is not all that one could wish, and an equally indefinite dream, or hope, or trust in evolution. If that be nationalism, then, of course, we are all nationalists. The nationalist clubs have platforms, declarations of principles, statements of aims and methods. The only value of Mr. Edward Bellamy's book—beyond mere entertainment—was in its clear

2. Minot J. Savage, "The Tyranny of Nationalism," *The Arena* (August 1891): 312–313.

statement of an *end to be reached in certain definite ways*. Take this feature away, and there is no nationalism even left to talk about"[3] (emphasis in original).

Criticism from many quarters compelled the Nationalists to reply to the charge that they glorified military discipline and opposed individualism. "It is a plan that attracts unthinking men, and dazzles superficial minds, but carried out in practice, it would reduce this country to the condition of the military-ridden nations of Europe, except that our standing-army of laborers would be compelled to serve for twenty-four years, while the standing-army of Europe serve for seven years only," wrote one Baltimore magazine. "We must say that his theories on the labor question cannot be realized, for the laborer himself would be unwilling to accept the condition of a mere Government machine."[4] In the course of their response to charges such as these, the original conception of an industrial army underwent a subtle but important change. At first the notion of a "civil service" or a "public service" began to be used interchangeably with the industrial army. But this shift in terminology was more a protective reaction in response to the popular antipathy to militaristic ideas than a real change in content. Only after a few years did the disappearance of the term "industrial army" coincide with a shift toward a less authoritarian viewpoint on the part of Bellamyites.

Well over a year after the first Nationalist club had been organized by retired army officers, Bellamy insisted in his article, "Why I Wrote *Looking Backward*," that the industrial army was to be taken literally as the "prototype" of the future organization of labor.[5] The industrial army, just as it had been described in *Looking Backward*, Bellamy affirmed, is the "destined corner-stone of the new social order."[6] That Bellamy insisted on this point suggests that many readers had not understood—or had not wanted to—the literalness of Bellamy's message about the military organization of the economy.

The charge of "militarism" annoyed Bellamy, however. Defensively and somewhat contradictorily, he explained that his choice of the

---

3. Ibid., p. 313.

4. *No Name Magazine* (Baltimore), May 1890. "Critical Reviews of Looking Backward," in Bellamy Papers.

5. Bellamy, "Why I Wrote Looking Backward," in *Edward Bellamy Speaks Again!*, p. 202.

6. Ibid.

military had nothing to do with any desire for war or for creating a war-like nation, except in the sense that a nation prepared for war possessed the "moral unity" which could overcome the selfishness, individualism, and antagonism between classes typical of capitalism. The virtues he saw in militarism were its authoritarian and bureaucratic aspects. Thus, in response to the prominent Belgian historian of socialism, Professor Emile de Laveleye, Bellamy reaffirmed his enthusiasm for "the gigantic contemporary illustrations of the possibility of elaborately organizing vast populations for united action to a common end, which are afforded by the military systems of the great European states."[7] And, once again, he took his critics to task because they failed "to see, in these wonderful examples of what method and order may accomplish in the concentration and direction of national forces, prototypes of the industrial system of the future."[8]

Yet, increasingly aware that his enthusiasm for an institution which most American liberals, socialists, and democrats of all kinds regarded as anathema to a free society had placed him in a vulnerable position, Bellamy felt it necessary to frequently deny any militaristic sympathies. "It should be unnecessary, but to avoid possible misapprehension, it is perhaps desirable, to point out just here, that the analogy between the national military organizations of Europe and the coming armies of industry in no way extends to the details of the organization of the respective bodies. Except as to the principle of a common duty and the desirability of order, of system, of complete cooperation, and of a central oversight and direction, the conditions of industry and those of war are very dissimilar."[9] He did not propose that there be "any stricter discipline for the members of the army of industry than is customary to any well-conducted industrial establishment today," and promised that except during work, "the citizen will be, in all respects, as much his own master as at present, and for that matter, much more so."[10] With the exception of Gronlund's criticism, made from the standpoint of his own authoritarian system, there is not the slightest evidence that any of the rank and file or the leadership of the Nationalist movement took public exception to the military model or even complained about the lack of

    7. Bellamy, "What Nationalism Means" (1890), in *Edward Bellamy Speaks Again!*, p. 92.

    8. Ibid., pp. 92–93.   9. Ibid., pp. 93–94.   10. Ibid.

democracy in such a system. The industrial army was simply taken for granted as the foundation stone of Bellamy's Nationalism. The Reverend Alexander Kent, President of the Washington, D.C. Nationalist club, undoubtedly reflected the views of many of the ordinary Nationalists when he confessed that he had always regarded socialism as a "castle in the air" until *Looking Backward*.[11] The problem of making business compatible with Christianity, Reverend Kent observed, required the construction of a "system in which the individual will consciously do his whole life work in the service of his brother—the service of humanity." However, "the defect of all Equalization theories in the past has been their failure to present any practicable working plan under which the cunning and ambitious could be prevented from using power for personal ends, and the lazy and thriftless prevented from shirking the law of reciprocal service." *Looking Backward* had found the answer: "Mr Bellamy's proposal to apply to our entire industrial interests the principle of military service, opened to me a new and blessed vision of glorious possibilities," testified Reverend Kent enthusiastically. Because it was so practical a solution to so difficult a problem, "Mr. Bellamy's little book must . . . be the chief missionary document in this pioneer work." The practicality of its proposal for the military organization made *Looking Backward* especially useful, Reverend Kent concluded, because such a solution appealed to "men of every class."[12] "Every day or two brings to me some fresh evidence of its conquering and convincing power. Businessmen, lawyers, merchants, ministers, are daily being captivated by it. It is the most effective gun yet fired in this holy war. Let us keep it to the front and in action."[13] Kent, of course, did not include the workers among those classes "captivated" by the efficacy of Bellamy's scheme for the military organization of labor. The enthusiasm of the gentlemen from the other classes for his scheme provides additional evidence of how well understood the reactionary nature of Bellamy's model was, at least among those who chose to understand *Looking Backward* as Bellamy had intended.

As their critics' attacks on the military form of organization were stepped up, however, a substitute model naturally suggested itself to the

11. Alexander Kent, "Mr. Bellamy's Industrial System," *The Nationalist* 1, no. 6 (November 1889): 238–239.

12. Ibid., p. 239.   13. Ibid.

Nationalists: the civil service. As early as 1890, Bellamy began to use the idea of the civil service interchangeably with the industrial army.[14] Less jarring to the democratic ear than the idea of an army, and thus a definite concession to traditional American notions of the opposition between military organization and individual liberty, this was only a formal shift in terms, for in no way was the content any more democratic.

The idea of organizing the workers into an "industrial civil service" had the additional virtue of meshing directly with Bellamy's specification of the evolutionary steps which were to begin the transition to the new collectivist social order. As the nucleus of the new order was formed by the statification of industry, workers would become "civil servants." His description of the organization of this civil service made clear that here was the industrial army under a new name (he even called it "the nucleus of the coming Industrial Army"):

> The manner of the organization of this industrial civil service is vital to the plan of nationalism, not only on account of the rights it guarantees to employees, but by its effect to prevent their intimidation or control for political purposes by government. Upon the nationalizing or municipalizing of a business, the employees in it would be taken bodily over into the public service. The force would then be strictly graded, and would be kept up exclusively by admissions to the lowest grade, with subsequent promotions. Admissions would be restricted to persons meeting certain prescribed conditions of fitness strictly adapted to the duties to be discharged, and selections for vacancies would be made from among competent candidates, not by appointment, but either by lot or in order of filed applications. Promotions would be a matter of right, and not of favor, based on merit as shown by record, combined with a certain length of service and upon proof of qualifications for the higher rank. No employee would be dismissed except for cause, after a hearing before an impartial tribunal existing for the purpose. Suspension of subordinates pending trial would, of course, be allowed to the management, with full control otherwise of the operation of the force. . . . It is proposed by nationalists that this radical and only effectual plan of civil-service reform be immediately applied to all existing national, state, and municipal services.[15]

Obviously the shift in terms did not involve any change in the content of the idea behind the industrial army. All authority would explicitly reside

14. See, for example, Bellamy, "First Steps toward Nationalism," (1890), *Edward Bellamy Speaks Again!*, pp. 105–106.

15. Ibid., pp. 116–117.

in the hands of the managers while their power over the workers would be unchecked by any form of independent workers' organizations. There is not even the hint here, as there was not in *Looking Backward*, of any democratic rights or of any mechanism in the society at large which might be utilized by the workers to defend themselves against the arbitrary and unlimited power of the office managers. Trade unions, of course, simply vanished, much to the relief of Bellamy's followers.

Sylvester Baxter, one of Bellamy's closest collaborators, echoed Bellamy's connection between the military organization of labor and the new model of the civil service. Writing to the Conference on Civil Service Reform which met in Boston in 1889, Baxter revealed the Nationalist way of advancing "true civil-service reform":

> Our Civil-Service is the great army of peace, of industry. When war shall have been made impossible by the very might of its instruments . . . the military branch of the national service [will] give place to the civil. The Civil-Service therefore deserves the highest honor, and it should have the same permanency of organization, the same principle of promotion for merit, and be imbued with the same sense of duty or *esprit du corps* that are now essential features of the Army or Navy.[16]

These were all practical proposals for reform made to the existing state and were not regarded as measures to be undertaken in the distant future, under the allegedly ideal circumstances of Bellamy's harmonious utopia. The civil service, purified of corrupt political practices, and injected with the spirit of military discipline, was to be part of the nucleus of the coming collectivist society, another step in the organic evolution of the state leading to its eventual merger with the industrial army.

Consistent with the blueprint contained in *Looking Backward*, neither Bellamy nor any of the Nationalists in this period contemplated any role for trade unions, either in the present or the future society. On the contrary, not only were the workers to be subjected to the complete control of their superiors within their particular organization, but consistent with the belief that the new or perfect state could not be saddled with partisanship, politics, and the other attributes of representative government in a democracy, the "great force of public employees" which would compose the nucleus of the industrial army was "to be placed

---

16. Sylvester Baxter, "How to Advance True Civil-Service Reform," *The Nationalist* 1, no. 5 (September 1889): 162–163.

beyond the power of politicians and administrations to use for partisan purposes."[17] Nationalists, Bellamy consistently pointed out, proposed a "plan for organizing and maintaining all public departments of business that shall deprive parties or politicians of any direct or arbitrary power over their membership, either as to appointment, promotion or removal."[18] The workers were to occupy the position of privates in any army, lacking any independent organizational recourse as a potential counterweight to the power of their superiors over them. Because of their superior conditions of work as well as the more important fact that the workers employed in nationalized industries would regard themselves as servants of the state, when "the public conduct of business shall take the place of the present system of private enterprise, strikes will become unknown."[19]

Precisely what the Nationalists understood the industrial army to mean in everyday life, how they translated it into a practical, hard-headed proposal to rid the country of the troublesome labor organizations and their strikes, and what would happen concretely if the Nationalists had their way when the workers persisted in upsetting the stability of society, was made completely and unmistakably clear in the response of Bellamy's New Nation to the Scottish Railway Strike of 1891. Noting that as a result of this prolonged and violent strike of Scottish workers, a proposal had been introduced into Parliament which would organize "the railroad workers of that country upon a public basis as the servants of the people as well as the corporations, and holding them to a military responsibility for insubordination or desertion," Bellamy and the editors of the New Nation hailed this action as nothing less than a direct step toward Nationalism.[20]

Equally encouraging to the Nationalists was support by the New York State Arbitration Board for the British scheme: "Railroad employees should no longer merely be hired but enlisted like soldiers, under rules and regulations made by the state and constituting a part of the law, and . . . men leaving duty during the period of enlistment should be punished as mutineers. On the other hand, as a necessary condition of

17. Bellamy, "Nationalism—Principles, Purposes," in *Edward Bellamy Speaks Again!*, p. 64.
18. Ibid.
19. *The New Nation* 2, no. 15 (April 9, 1892): 227.
20. *The New Nation* 1, nos. 2 and 3: 30, 44–45.

such a system, the men are to be guaranteed certain hours, pay, rates of promotion, with protection against arbitrary dismissal, to which should of course be added provision for pensions in case of accident or superannuation."[21] The *New Nation* concurred enthusiastically: "The fact that this idea of an industrial army, which a couple of years ago was ridiculed as a Boston 'fad,' should now be brought forward in the British Parliament, advocated by a state board of arbitration and favorably discussed by the most conservative portion of the press, is extremely significant of the manner in which men, in spite of themselves, are being forced to seek in the plan of nationalism the protection of society."[22]

In welcoming the proposal to draft the striking railway workers as the first step toward the creation of the industrial army (the second step would be the nationalization of the railroads), the editors of the *New Nation* were merely following out their position to its logical conclusion: the unruly workers and, by extension, the entire lower class as well as all of those persons whose resistance to the new order marked them as not part of the elite, could be, if it became necessary, marched into the Nationalist utopia at the point of bayonets. If they still remained discontented despite the improvement of their conditions, then there would be no reason not to treat them like mutinous soldiers in any other army. This, then, was Bellamy's evolutionary utopianism translated into practical terms: terms which revealed his own and his followers' utopian fantasy transmuted into the base metal of authoritarian politics.

The Nationalists' reaction to the railway workers' strike demonstrated that the immediate appeal of the industrial army was its efficacy as a device to tame the rebellious workers whose actions threatened the stability of society. By arguing that the "protection of society" required the "conservative classes" to choose the nationalization of industry and the drafting of the workers into military formations, the Nationalists reaffirmed their stance as a conservative anticapitalist movement which understood that the main danger to social order was from below. The plutocrats, in contrast, were few in number and, even if never convinced of the need for the new order, would be absorbed by the tide of collectivism. But the workers obviously posed a more difficult problem. They were, as Bellamy had pointed out, numerous, organized, prey to radical demagogues preaching foreign doctrines, and although possessing the

21. Ibid.   22. Ibid.

ballot were fundamentally incapable of doing anything by their own efforts toward the elimination of capitalism—not, that is, in any way which would be acceptable to middle-class folk.

H. B. Salisbury's *The Birth of Freedom*, a novel serialized in *The Nationalist* throughout late 1890 and early 1891, reveals the Nationalists' intense fear of workers.[23] It was very similar in plot, style, and political message to Ignatius Donnelly's *Caesar's Column*. The novel's central character is a Nationalist-type reformer who is conducted under blindfold to a secret meeting of workingmen in order that he may observe the range and depth of their discontent. Many of the workers give speeches advocating a violent revolutionary *coup* to overthrow the capitalists. The Nationalist hero, shocked by what he hears, speaks out against violence and any attempt to overthrow the capitalists. The desperate workers disregard his advice and plan an uprising. Unfortunately, it turns out that an *agent provocateur* informs the Pinkertons who set off a premature uprising which the workers are forced to continue. The provocation is successful, the workers are defeated, and the Nationalist himself is condemned to the Alaska salt mines by the triumphant plutocracy. He languishes there for years until by some unexplained development, the plutocracy is overthrown and the cooperative commonwealth takes its place. The new order does away with politics, politicians, and representative government. Just as in Donnelly's novel, Salisbury preached that the intolerable conditions of the lower orders must be corrected from above—if not by the plutocracy then by the middle classes—or else a revolt would occur which would inevitably fail, and provide the plutocracy with an excuse to establish its tyranny over all classes.

The fantastic picture of the workers and their readiness for violence held by middle-class Nationalists was conveyed in scenes such as this one describing the workers' meeting:

> A sorrowful, dejected-looking man of about fifty years next began with a question: 'Say, how are ye goin to get control of the government?' . . . How are you goin to manage the first surprise? . . . How are you goin to win? The ballot-box is no good. It leaks and is rotten. ('Hear, hear.') The police and the militia are all under capitalists' order. I am in for anything,' he shrieked, 'if you will show how it is to be done. Anything is better than what we have now. ('You're right!') . . . I have neither shame nor fear, and I don't care

23. *The Nationalist* 2, nos. 4–9 (November 1890 through March-April 1891).

how desperate a plan you have. I am in for anything.' (A tumult of shouts.)[24]

Or, describing the workers' response to the plan for the uprising, which will if necessary entail the use of dynamite, Salisbury wrote: "Gleams of hope, the fire of fanaticism, wild exultations of caged tigers suddenly seeing a door opening to freedom seemed to leap from the dullest eyes. Had the word of command been given to carry out the plan detailed, every man was ready to do his part or perish in the attempt."[25]

To the extent that the Nationalists accepted lurid stories such as this one as an accurate portrayal of the workers, it is not hard to understand why they would be reluctant to move politically, except in the most conservative and cautious fashion, avoiding at all costs the unleashing or stimulation of mass movement. The Nationalists' attitude toward the working class was, of course, a crucial variable in the determination of their political stance: the authoritarian content of their politics varied directly with their perception of whether the "barbarians from below," or those from above, the plutocracy, posed the greatest menace to their aims. Once the movement was launched and the middle-class reformers began to have actual contact with workers' groups and their leaders, the kind of fantasy reflected in this story began to lose its hold upon them. To that extent they became less fearful of activity and actions which would stimulate a mass movement. But until this second phase of Nationalism became a reality, the problem as it appeared to the Nationalists at the beginning was to keep the workers in line and yet satisfy their legitimate grievances without at the same time encouraging or seeming to encourage the formation of a mass movement or political party from below.

Solving the "labor question" and making the transition to the new collectivist society without an upheaval from below, and without a popular political movement or party, was addressed, in theory, by the idea of nucleation. The absorption of class conflict and the preservation of social stability would both be served by this method of creating nuclei of the coming industrial army within the shell of the old world. Best of all, the Nationalists felt the immediate benefits would recommend the creation of these islands of collectivism even to non-Nationalists; conservative people who, although not agreeing with the aims of the Nationalist elite,

24. Ibid., vol. 2, no. 5 (December 1890): 317–318.
25. Ibid., p. 320.

would go along because their fear of a militant, even revolutionary, working class was even greater than their belief in the sanctity of private property. Once having taken this fatal step, the "logic of events," pushed on by the immanent collectivist tendencies in industry, would convince the conservative middle classes of the necessity of more such steps. For the time being, however, it was sufficient for them to accept the more limited purpose of appeasing and controlling the workers.

For the fully committed Nationalists, the creation of the nuclei of the industrial army had another function. From the standpoint of practical utopianism, it was legitimate to advocate that the existing state draft the workers into the industrial army, because human nature in the mass being what it was, all changes had to come from above. Yet at the same time, if it was true, as one Nationalist writer observed, that "the chief obstacle to Nationalism will be found in the personal passions of the human heart which oppose the equal distribution of force and crave personal supremacy"[26]—another way of saying what Bellamy meant when he explained the capitalist system to be the expression of selfishness—then it was necessary to do more than merely march the workers into the nucleus of the industrial army. Otherwise, given the unfitness of mankind in general to live under the higher conditions of the coming collectivist order, the system would not work without the continuous application of external coercion. In short, the industrial army was not a far-off dream, but a practical way of achieving "moral unity."

Even though the need for some system of coercion was implicit in the model of the industrial army as it was presented in *Looking Backward*, the element of external discipline as a means of social control was played down. Instead, Bellamy emphasized the importance for the individual to internalize the norms of the new order so that he would no longer crave "personal supremacy" or desire any goals at variance with organized society. To the extent such lower, selfish tendencies were permanently rooted in human nature, as Bellamy believed they were,[27] the collectivist society would have to be organized so that they would have no societal avenue for expression. Obviously, Bellamy, the utopian idealist and the man of "good hope," could hardly have regarded his plan as a satisfactory solution to the world's problems, had it required any suggestion

26. J. Campbell Ver-Planck, "The Future of Nationalism," *The Nationalist* 1, no. 6 (October 1889): 214.

27. See Bellamy, "Looking Backward Again," *Edward Bellamy Speaks Again!*, p. 189.

that force and the threat of force, or even constant institutional pressure, would alone be the means of social control. The goal was to make the individual conform out of his own free will—to force him to be "fraternal," not merely because he was externally disciplined but primarily because he felt an inner compulsion to obey and to subordinate himself to "society." To create this sense of unity or communion, Bellamy insisted in a letter to Thomas Wentworth Higginson, had to be one of the primary aims of Nationalism:

> Not only is it the Nationalist idea that the Nation should become an economical organism, but a *moral* organism as well. Before this last point I would lay extraordinary stress. This is, of course, necessarily an economic reform but its most important aspect is that of a moral movement for uplifting, enlarging and enabling the individual life by making every individual contribute his efforts first and directly to the common or national wealth, and himself dependent for his livelihood upon his equal chance in it, so he is rich as the nation is rich and poor as his fellow citizens are poor and never otherwise. Then all the issues of life will be first from the individual to the nation, then from the nation back to him. As the hand profits not directly by what it seizes nor the mouth by what it devours, but only by sending its booty to the common treasury to be nourished in return by red blood from the heart, so the members of the coming nation will serve and live in constant remembrance and realization of their common life and mutual dependence. The great heart will beat in the pulse of the smallest member.[28]

It was one thing, however, to recognize in abstract terms the importance of the spirit of communion to the Nationalist scheme, and even to incorporate it in the design for the new order, but something else again to be able to outline in concrete detail the practical steps which would get to that ideal society from the present, given human nature as it actually was—or as it appeared to be to the Nationlists. Here we see the central dilemma of utopian politics. If the nucleus of the new society were to be created within the framework of the old, then it was still necessary to find some method for changing men—for socializing them—even *before* the structure of the new order had been completed. Marching them into the industrial armies and requiring them to perform their duty on pain of being treated as mutineers only solved the most obvious problem—the problem of desertions to the society outside and of maintaining order. The Nationalists still had to answer the charge of their

28. Quoted in Morgan, *Edward Bellamy*, p. 409 (no date or source given).

critics who pointed out, as Jesse Cox, leader of the Chicago Nationalists admitted, that "men are not fit for it [Nationalism] at present; that they are brutalized and demoralized, and could not be made use of under its conditions."[29] Even if Bellamy's belief that the vicious characteristics of men were the reflection of their circumstances and, therefore, under better conditions the higher or better side of human nature would flourish, was granted, the problem of offering a concrete plan of where and how to begin the process of socialization still remained. An elite was obviously required, but locating and training it only answered the question of where the generals would come from. Its solution would still leave unsolved the problem of reforming the character of the privates— the wretched human material produced by capitalism who were hardly fit to participate in a society that required the individual to willingly renounce any craving for "personal supremacy" and to give up all private needs at variance with those of society.

In providing the way out of this dilemma, the idea of the industrial army as the immediate, practical form which the nucleus of the new order was to take—as opposed, for example, to the model of a voluntary colony—performed its second critical function in Nationalism's down-to-earth utopianism. Besides suppressing the conflict between capital and labor and thereby performing the immediate function of ending all open manifestations of class conflict, it would immediately begin the process of socializing the workers—of using military discipline to bring out the "higher" side of human nature in order to make it possible for the masses to live in the collectivist future which the Nationalists had planned for them.

An explanation and defense of the industrial army which explicitly pointed to this function of the military organization of labor in nationalized industry was offered by Jesse Cox. Cox argued that it was the brutalization and demoralization of the masses which made Nationalism an entirely practical proposal. Nationalism and Nationalism alone, he maintained, could take men as they were, and still solve the problems of existing society:

> It is the present system which can make least use of these
> men. It, rather than the proposed nationalist system, requires per-
> fect men. If all men were perfect in wisdom, in physical and mental
> qualities, and in moral nature, all might possibly be well under our

29. Jesse Cox, "Objections to Nationalism," *The Nationalist* 2, no. 5: 325–330.

present unorganized industrial society. But because men are not so, it becomes necessary, in order to make the best of these imperfect men, that they should be placed in an organization where their imperfections may be aided by the systematic help of their superiors in wisdom, morality, and ability. Organization is civilization.

When raw, untrained, or barbaric men are taken into an army, they are made part of the military organization, and trained to act in unison with it. In this way only can they be made effective. No intelligent officer would think of leading an untrained mob of such men against an enemy. But this is exactly what the present industrial system does. It expects its untrained and demoralized barbarians to act without organization, order, or even leaders, in bringing the untamed forces of nature into the services of man.[30]

The dual functions of the nucleation theory—the creation of a collectivist society without the need to call into existence a mass movement, and the civilizing function of the industrial army nucleus—were thus just two aspects of the same thing: a device for introducing an authoritarian socialist society from above.

The explicit avowal of this idea stood out boldly in Nationalist literature. In the one article published in the entire history of *The Nationalist* which purported to be a "workingman's view of Nationalism,"[31] the author reported that he had become a convinced Nationalist upon discovering that Christianity, trade unions, and the ballot were all "inefficient" remedies for social problems. The "inefficiency" of Christianity and of political action were due to their reliance upon "voluntary" adherence when what was needed, the worker-Nationalist opined, was an "all-binding system" such as the Nationalists proposed. He rejected the trade unions for the same reason. They were too committed to the wage system to be able to attack the problems of society in a fundamental way. Only "that more radical and perfect form" of socialism, "known as Nationalism," could offer any chance of successfully helping the workingmen because it rejected voluntary methods and proposed instead a solution by which the requisite discipline could be effectively brought to bear upon the unwilling, corrupted majority in order to force them to enter the new society. The system of equality dictated by the Nationalist elite would, he promised, "teach men in time a wise use of the ballot,

30. Ibid., p. 329.
31. Michael Lynch, "A Workingman's View of Nationalism," *The Nationalist* 1, no. 4 (August 1889): 106–109.

would extend that unity and discipline which Trade Unionists sigh for; and being based upon the golden rule of Christianity would go more than half way to make that rule a ruling thing."[32] It was just such a worker who looked to the imposition of strong external discipline from above by the Nationalist ruling class so that "in time" the workers would be capable of being free, who would be welcomed to the Nationalist cause.

The only Nationalist of significance to reject Bellamy's collectivist military model was Laurence Gronlund. He objected to the "love of militarism, equal wages, and appointments by retired functionaries," as "decidedly unsocialistic notions [which] belong exclusively to Mr. Bellamy. . . ."[33] However, Gronlund's objections and his own peculiar plan for the organization of a socialist society were no more democratic than Bellamy's. Gronlund's special contribution to the Nationalist theory was the idea of building a mass movement, using the workers as a battering ram in the hands of an elite to subvert capitalism. He warned Nationalists to "beware of becoming all officers and having no privates. An army of mere generals is worthless."[34] Fortunately, Gronlund argued, the Nationalist elite would find "the privates are ready at hand; that is one of the great signs of the times."[35] Organized workers were already obedient and submissive before authority, true authority, the authority of the capable.[36] The trade unions had performed the civilizing function which most Nationalists assigned to the nuclei of the industrial army. Disciplined, and submissive to authority, the workers were ready for the new society now. All that they needed were leaders. The Nationalist elite, Gronlund promised, did not have to be afraid of calling into existence a mass movement made up of such workers.[37]

Thus, like Bellamy, Gronlund believed that the workers could not and should not achieve Nationalism by their own efforts. Like the Nationalists, he thought that their permanent subordination to a ruling elite was a precondition for the kind of collectivist society which he and Bellamy both envisioned.[38] Gronlund's advocacy of the idea of building

32. Ibid., p. 109.
33. Gronlund, *The Cooperative Commonwealth* (1890), p. viii. See Bellamy's reply to Gronlund's ideas as a whole in *The New Nation* 1, no. 38 (October 17 1891): 598–599.
34. *Our Destiny*, pp. 215–216.   35. Ibid.   36. Ibid., p. 48.
37. Ibid., pp. 215–218, passim.
38. It is clear that at no point did Gronlund, like the older utopians, envision the subordination of the workers to their rulers as a precondition to some kind of democratic self-governing society. In this he was at one with the Nationalists.

a mass movement below was compatible with Nationalist ideology, even if not necessarily accepted, because it was offered as one way of accomplishing the same task that the theory of nuclear evolution was designed to do: to introduce the new collectivist society from above.

Contemporary criticism of Nationalism naturally centered about the idea of the industrial army and the practical proposals to induct the workers into a conscript army of labor. The liberal and even conservative attack on Bellamyism rested not merely on a defense of capitalism but at least as much, if not more so, was based upon a rejection of the manifestly authoritarian and antidemocratic character of Bellamy's collectivist politics. Nicholas P. Gilman criticized Nationalism as a departure from the traditional American values of liberty and democracy:

> The ideal state of "Looking Backward" is a hard and fast bureaucracy, "a society of mandarins, medallists and labor officers," as Dr. Schäffle says, "such as no Democrat could tolerate," the *personnel* of which, once instituted by a popular vote would perpetuate itself in the closest routine until overthrown by a revolution. The power of appointment in each grade of the industrial army being in the officers of the grade above, the advantages of monarchical and democratic rule would be equally absent. . . . Such an institution cannot be expected to appear soon in a country which has always repudiated the model on which Mr. Bellamy has constructed it.[39]

As vehement as Gilman in their denunciations of the Nationalists' collectivist politics as antidemocratic were two critics who were well to the left of Gilman—perhaps classifiable as semisocialists. B. O. Flower, editor of the influential magazine, *The Arena*, which was sympathetic to populism and to reform causes generally, carrying many articles by Gronlund, Schindler, and other partisans of Nationalism, attacked *Looking Backward* and the Nationalists' doctrine in an editorial, characterizing them as inimical to human freedom and nothing less than proposals for the new slavery.[40] And, in the pages of the same journal, a liberal

---

39. Gilman, *Socialism and the American Spirit*, pp. 209–210.

40. *The Arena* 3 (May 1891). Flower's editorial provoked a reply from Bellamy's cousin and fellow Nationalist, Francis Bellamy. It was in turn answered by M. J. Savage's article (see below). Thaddeus B. Wakeman then replied to Savage. See: Francis Bellamy, "The Tyranny of All the People," *The Arena* 4 (July 1891): 180–191; and Thaddeus B. Wakeman, "Emancipation by Nationalism," *The Arena* 4 (October 1891): 591–603. The controversy was very significant because both Francis Bellamy and Wakeman, especially the latter, retreated before Savage's criticisms of the undemocratic nature of Nationalism, which allowed Savage, as we showed in an earlier quotation at the beginning of the chapter, to expose them for inconsistency. Wakeman's article was reprinted in the *New*

reformer, the Reverend M. J. Savage, sympathetic to Christian socialism, denounced the "tyranny of Nationalism."[41] "Military despotism
such as Mr. Edward Bellamy advocates," Savage wrote in reply to one of
Bellamy's defenders, "would only be another name for universal despotism in which the individual, if not an officer, would only count for one
in the ranks. It would be a paradise of officialdom on the one hand, and
helpless subordination on the other."[42]

Of course, the various spokesmen for the Nationalist movement
were not silent in the face of attacks such as these, coming as they did
from fellow reformers who spoke for an important segment of the intellectuals and reform-minded middle-class persons in Boston, New Haven, and New York. On the whole, the Nationalists' replies only confirmed the charge of the critics that the plan for the industrial army of
labor was consciously antidemocratic, authoritarian, and, in general, at
violent odds with the tradition of democracy and individual rights in
American life.

John Storer Cobb, for example, who was an editor of *The Nationalist*,
coolly answered General Francis A. Walker's denunciation of Bellamyism
which had appeared in the *Atlantic* by frankly stating that although the
ordinary "end of military discipline is an evil [i.e., war], the discipline
itself is good."[43] All that this meant was that the Nationalists were not
admirers of war and violence. Nationalists were, however, as Cobb's reply
made equally clear, for the application of such discipline to the problem of
constructing a collectivist society, and far from rejecting the industrial
army's disciplinary power because it was inimical to individual freedom
and democracy, regarded it as a welcome change from the undisciplined,
anarchic behavior and institutions which typified capitalism.

In the first issue of Bellamy's own journal, the *New Nation*, Capt.
Edward S. Huntington (Ret.), a Theosophical Nationalist, aggressively

---

Nation, with a supporting editorial note. In giving up the essential elements of original
Bellamyism, as Savage correctly pointed out in his rebuttal, Wakeman's article provided a
definite sign that the new phase of Nationalism meant a break with the original Nationalist
doctrine as it had been laid down in *Looking Backward*.

41. M. J. Savage, "The Tyranny of Nationalism," *The Arena* 4 (September 1891):
311–321.

42. Ibid., p. 320.

43. John Storer Cobb, "General Walker and the Atlantic," *The Nationalist* 2 (March
1890): 135–138.

defended the good name of military discipline—the very discipline to which the workers were to be subjected under Nationalism.[44] Huntington had been one of the original group of retired army officers living in Boston who had been inspired specifically by *Looking Backward*'s program for the military organization of a collectivist state—or, as Huntington called it in this article, a "Grand Army of Peace"—to form the Boston Bellamy Club. Huntington vociferously denied the charge by Reverend Savage and others that the Nationalists' program for imposing military discipline upon the workers meant that they favored "military despotism." Nationalists did not favor military despotism, he replied, and in any case his critics did not understand that military discipline was not despotic but only represented the application of order and efficiency to the task of coordinating large numbers of men. Counterattacking, Huntington asked if the critics of Nationalism sincerely believed "the wage-earning producers so happy . . . under the system we (the Nationalists) have so truly depicted that they fear so slight a beneficent discipline as would exist under an order founded on regularity and exactness?"[45] Just as the apologists for slavery had attempted to do a few decades earlier, Huntington proceeded to defend the Nationalists' military solution to the labor question by accurately describing the hardship and sufferings of the free wage workers under the rule of capitalism. The implication, which Huntington did not hesitate to spell out, was that the "beneficent discipline" of the industrial army together with the material security it gave the workers was more than a fair exchange for their unhappy and precarious existence under capitalism, free though they might be to form unions or parties of their choice.

Huntington made it clear that the Nationalists did not propose that the workers exchange their situation under capitalism for anything resembling greater individualism or that there would be an expansion of democratic control and participation as the result of the Nationalists' method for the statification of the economy:

> There need be but little said regarding the necessity of strict methods of discipline in all departments of this ideal army of industry, for such a requirement is self-evident. As in military organizations . . . the first requisite for our army of production must be a

44. Edward S. Huntington, "The Grand Army of Peace," *The New Nation* 1, no. 1 (January 31, 1891): 16–17.
45. Ibid., p. 16.

perfect drill in duties to be performed by these soldiers of industry, with a rigorous system of exact discipline in the fulfillment of all orders.

There is a mistaken idea in the public mind that army discipline is only a slightly mitigated form of despotic abuse; that the members of the rank and file of an army are subjected to steady, petty tyranny. Any fair-minded officer or private who attends to his necessary duties never calls in question the justice of systematic arrangements which insure the orderly performance of military duties, no matter how arduous, even dangerous such duties may be. The humblest soldier of our present army can but say that the discipline under which he serves does not suppress his true individuality; on the contrary, he will declare with truth that his personal nature is continuously enlarged and improved by association with his fellows in the close comradeship of army life and by the methodical habits engendered through systematic discipline. So we have good reasons for a belief that the order and necessary discipline of the army of industry will increase the capacities of each individual worker—not only in his powers for production of economic goods, but also it will enlarge his mental and physical faculties for large enjoyment of all life's blessings.[46]

Huntington's views cannot be described as a "mistake" or a failure to understand the implications of the organization of a socialist society along these lines. If he was able to find "true individualism" arising out of military discipline, it could only mean that by "individualism" Huntington meant exactly what Bellamy meant in the *Religion of Solidarity*—the shedding of the personal and private side of the person's existence, the substitution of institutional reason and authority for that of the individual, and the immersion of the person and the personality in an organic society designed to do away with both the need and the desire for individual freedom. Once again, it may be seen, we have come back in the course of our discussion of the industrial army to the most pervasive theme of Nationalism—communionism.

The emergence of the Nationalist movement and of Bellamy's politics was not merely the birth of a new version of the old utopianism, although it was closely related to it in its spirit and intellectual premises, but represented instead the appearance of a new and different breed of socialism: a hybrid which combined a passion for collectivization and planning with an equally strong antipathy to democracy and democratic

46. Ibid., p. 17.

collectivism as proposed by the advocates of working-class socialism. It is this apparently contradictory and paradoxical crossing of supposed opposites which produced a new and distinctive species of socialism that must be kept firmly in mind in order to correctly understand the organized utopians of the Nationalist movement and to see their significance for developments in the twentieth century.

⑨ AWAY FROM UTOPIANISM: THE SECOND PHASE OF NATIONALISM

In reviewing *Looking Backward*, William Morris noted that "the really distinctive part" of Bellamy's anticapitalist tract was its fatalism and social passivity. Neither conflict nor struggle, class warfare nor the effort to organize a conscious political movement or party, Morris recognized, were necessary to Bellamy's scheme. To Morris, Bellamy's reliance on the evolutionary self-collectivization of capital and the growth of the state was illusory—and worse yet, dangerous in its implications. It was a "far better hope", Morris replied, "to trust . . . that men having once got it into their heads that true life implies free and equal life, and that it is now possible of attainment, they will consciously strive for its attainment at any cost."[1]

Morris's criticism of Bellamy's fatalism and his counterposition to it of the necessity of a conscious struggle from below for the attainment of socialism challenged the very heart of Nationalism's authoritarian doctrine. Even as Morris wrote, however, the contradiction inherent in Bellamy's fatalistic theory of social change was coming to the fore as the organization of the Nationalist movement progressed. The very act of organizing the movement had itself posed the contradiction in its post-paradoxical form. If Nationalism was the inevitable result of forces beyond the control or desire of men, why organize a movement that strived for its attainment? Bellamy very quickly was brought face to face with this paradox and although he could recognize it, he was unable to find a satisfactory answer to it.

This contradiction would have remained a purely formal one, however, without any consequences for the actions and beliefs of the Nationalists had it not been for the completely unexpected rapid growth in Nationalist membership and influence which transformed Bellamy overnight into the leader of a political organization and his followers into an

1. Morris, *The Commonweal* (London), June 22, 1889.

apparently potent moral and political force. Moreover, the enormous wave of social and economic protest among farmers and workers in the 1890s, which took political form with the formation of the People's Party in 1891–1892, and the bloody outbreaks of class warfare, symbolized by the Homestead steel strike of 1891, profoundly reshaped both Bellamy and the Nationalist movement. Ironically, the Nationalists had contributed to this upsurge and in turn were swept up by the force of the movement. The Nationalists were forced to confront their elitist premises and as a result part of the original Nationalist grouping moved away from the doctrine and mode of organization with which they had started.[2] There began to emerge a political strain that involved the Nationalists, unwittingly at first, in an active struggle for social and economic change. These pressures led them to begin to attempt to resolve the ideological contradiction posed by Bellamy's theory of an automatic collectivist future by placing greater and greater emphasis upon the need to build a popular movement and to stimulate action from below. Although this was at first only an adjunct to their elitist strategy, in the sense that Gronlund had called for the use of the workers as a battering ram to bring the socialist elite to power, nevertheless it too had consequences neither predicted nor desired by most of the Nationalists.

At the same time, Bellamy's conception of the new order—the bureaucratic collectivization of the economy by the state organized within the framework of the industrial army—began to be tacitly questioned by some Nationalists, including Bellamy himself. Internal tensions within the Nationalist club which resulted pitted those who adhered to an "ethical" Nationalism against those members who advocated and practiced organized "partisan" political activity directed against the plutocracy. Out of the tension between these two tendencies or wings was born the second

2. Cf. Howard Quint's explanation of the disintegration of the Nationalist clubs:
    Nationalism was a movement which exploded in all directions at the
    same time. That was its principal weakness. Its energies were never channel-
    ized. It had little organization, less leadership, and almost nothing in the way
    of a co-ordinated program. After the first flush of enthusiasm had passed, it
    failed to attract new converts and lost the services of several able men who
    had initially been its sponsors. Even its utopian objectives lacked those ele-
    ments of imminent expectation and of ultimate fulfillment that won countless
    thousands over to Marxist ideological doctrines which, in the last analysis,
    were no less utopian. Perhaps all of this was inherent in the original nature of
    the movement. Yet Nationalism, organizationally considered, was not de-
    stined to fall, for it might have gone the way of British Fabianism, to which
    it was so similar. (*The Forging of American Socialism*, p. 101.)

phase of the Nationalist movement. Nationalism became a movement with a divided soul, committed on the one hand by the conditions of its origin and the content of Bellamy's doctrine to the vision of a bureaucratic socialist society and fearful of democracy, while at the same time increasingly caught up in an actual struggle for its program through a popular, democratic movement.

From Philanthropy to Politics

The contradiction between the actual organization of a movement, elitist and philanthropically inclined as it was, and the doctrine of inevitable passive evolution into collectivism through the trustification of society, was resolved at first by a distinction between "practical" steps to forward the new order, and political action. The latter was prohibited, while the former was encouraged as consistent with the Nationalists' claim to be an "ethical" movement, above parties and class interests. But the distinction between the two was always cloudy, and as the movement expanded, attracted new converts, and drew the fire of many of those from the middle classes whom it expected to win over, rank-and-file Nationalists began to do their practical work in a political manner.[3]

"Practical work" in the vocabulary of Nationalism meant the attempt to wrest collectivist concessions in the form of public ownership from the state. "The growth of Nationalism can best be forwarded by the most practical action on the part of Nationalists," advised the editors of *The Nationalist*. "We must encourage every tendency in that direction, and bear in mind that the movement can only advance step by step." Concretely, these steps included the nationalization and municipalization of the utilities, railroads, insurance offices, etc. An essential part of the program was the proposal "to increase the efficiency, training and scope of the civil service, *which is the present basis of the industrial army*,"[4] (my emphasis).

These practical steps to establish the nuclei of Nationalism were not to be accomplished through the organization of a political movement, nor by actions that might suggest that Nationalism was a class movement, rather than a movement of the entire Nation, one above parties

3. Cf. Quint, "The broad theoretical generalizations of the Nationalist leaders failed to satisfy the rank and file. The former considered themselves primarily as interpreters and teachers; the latter was more interested in action" (ibid, p. 93).

4. *The Nationalist* 1, no. 7 (November 1889): 265; also, vol. 3, no. 2 (September 1890): 109–110 and vol. 1, no. 3 (July 1889): 95.

and partisanship. The mode of organization that this conception entailed has already been indicated: small, exclusive meetings were to be held at which the elite that was to lead the Nationalists could be reached and any suggestion that the "dangerous classes" might be set into motion could be avoided.[5]

Every club was strongly advised to make itself the center of such practical work. And, in keeping with the Nationalist ideal of a functionally rationalized society, the readers of *The Nationalist* were reminded that "the key-stone of practical nationalism is efficient organization. That which we seek to see the nation become must serve as a model for the building up of the nationalist movement."[6] Even if the model of the industrial army was not always explicitly called upon, there is no doubt that it was this—or rather its officer cadre—which the editors had in mind. "We must use our best efforts to base it upon the most efficient instrumentality possible, working with the least possible friction and waste of energy. By our own processes we must illustrate the correctness of the principles we advocate."[7] The Nationalist clubs thus were seen as a vanguard but a vanguard which neither wished to create a broad popular movement to attain its ends, nor to take into its ranks or educate the masses of people to its principles. Far from being a weakness of the movement, Bellamy carefully explained, its character as a movement of the elite was its positive virtue: "We like to think that not one in a hundred who more or less fully sympathize with us, is a member of a Nationalist club or probably will be until the nation becomes the one Nationalist Club."[8]

Theosophy and Nationalism

The full meaning and significance of the Nationalists' antipolitical, philanthropic mode of organization and style of politics requires an understanding of the role played by the Theosophists in the formation and spread of the movement.[9]

From the beginning, the Nationalist movement had close ties with

5. *The Nationalist* 1, no. 7 (November 1889): 265.
6. *The Nationalist* 3, no. 2 (September 1890): 109.
7. Ibid.
8. Bellamy, "Progress of Nationalism in the United States," in *Edward Bellamy Speaks Again!*, p. 138.
9. The subject of the Theosophist movement is difficult to deal with because there exists no objective study of its origins, doctrines, and impact. It was, nevertheless, one of the more important of a number of similar spiritualist-mystical cults that sprang up among

the Theosophists. Of the founding officers of the First Nationalist club, half were members of the Theosophical Society. Sylvester Baxter and Cyrus Field Willard, who were probably the most important leaders apart from Bellamy in the early stages of the movement, were both Theosophists, as were John Ransom Bridge, Secretary of the First Club, Henry Willard Austin, and John Storer Cobb—the last two being editors of *The Nationalist*.[10] As the publication of the First Club, *The Nationalist* generally expressed the views of the Theosophically oriented Nationalists.[11] Although Bellamy was not a member of the Theosophists, his "Religion of Solidarity" expressed many of the same sentiments to be found in Theosophist doctrine.[12]

Baxter and Willard, who first proposed the formation of the Boston Nationalist club to Bellamy, saw in *Looking Backward* the working out on the material plane of the harmony and brotherly love that Theosophy preached. Willard regarded Bellamy's elitist and authoritarian approach as entirely consistent with Theosophist doctrine because of their mutual emphasis on the role of an enlightened elite in lifting men from the abyss.

---

middle-class elements in the late nineteenth century which were closely symptomatic of great psychic distress on the part of these social strata in the face of large-scale industrial capitalism. Christian Science, Unity, the "New Thought" movement are all closely related to it. The most readable document of Madame Helena Petrovna Blavatsky, its founder, is *The Key to Theosophy* (London, 1889). It is comparatively free of references to lost continents and other mysteries. Alvin Boyd Kuhn, *Theosophy: A Modern Revival of Ancient Wisdom* (1930) is an able but biased account of Theosophical doctrines. The only scholarly work that has attempted to describe Theosophy in America, inadequately, is Charles Braden, *They Also Believe*. Informative articles on theosophical doctrine are to be found in *The Encyclopedia Britannica* (11th ed.), vol. 26, pp. 789–791, "Oriental Theosophy"; and Schaff-Herzog, "Theosophy," in the *Encyclopedia of Religion*.

The most important convert was made by Madame Blavatsky, and the best-known connection between Theosophy and the socialist movement was Annie Besant, a Fabian and collaborator in *The Fabian Essays*. Besant became the world leader of Theosophy after Blavatsky's death and played an important role in the struggle for Indian independence. See Arthur H. Nethercott's *The First Five Lives of Annie Besant* (Chicago: University of Chicago Press, 1960) and its sequel, *The Last Four Lives of Annie Besant* (Chicago: University of Chicago Press, 1963). Both Besant and Blavatsky are treated in Warren Sylvester Smith, *The London Heretics, 1870–1914* (New York: Dodd, Mead & Co., 1968). The lasting influence of Bellamy on Besant is demonstrated in her Theosophical-socialist tract, *The Changing World and Lectures to Theosophical Students* (1910), in which large helpings of Bellamy are used, with and without attribution, to describe the Theosophist utopia on earth.

10. Morgan, *Edward Bellamy*, pp. 260–261.
11. Ibid.   12. Ibid., p. 264.

Official endorsement of Bellamy's views was first received from William Q. Judge, editor of the American journal of Theosophy, *The Path*. He wrote to Bellamy early in 1889 expressing approval of Nationalism's principle of universal brotherhood: "I thus conceive of it as closely linked to Theosophy, and a desirable means whereby Theosophists may assist in the ethical advancement of the race, substituting brotherhood and co-operation for competition, and do good work on the practical plane. Hence I desire to popularize Nationalism. . . ."[13]

The endorsement by the leader of Theosophy, Madame Blavatsky, apparently upon the urging of Judge, gave *Looking Backward* and Nationalism its real foothold among Theosophists. This endorsement, plus the one which Judge published in *The Path*, stimulated Theosophists throughout the country, particularly in Southern California, to order *Looking Backward* and to organize, under the direction of the First Club in Boston, new Nationalist clubs.[14] While the Theosophists were by no means entirely responsible for the rapid spread of the Nationalist movement, they undoubtedly played an important role.[15]

From the content of its beliefs and the composition of its supporters, it seems clear that the Theosophist movement sprang very much from the same kind of displaced and anxious middle-class elements to whom Nationalism appealed. According to Madame Blavatsky, Theosophy was "essentially the philosophy of those who suffer, and have lost all hope of being helped out of the mire of life by any other means."[16] In Theosophist doctrine the earth was hell—"Avitchi": a place "to which soulless men are condemned on this physical plane."[17] Avitchi was "a long drawn out dream of bitter memories—a vivid consciousness of failure without volition, or the power of initiative—a dream of lost opportunities and futile regrets, of ambitions thwarted and hopes denied, of

13. Judge to Bellamy, Feb. 18, 1889, Bellamy Papers.

14. Morgan, *Edward Bellamy*, pp. 262–275.

15. Morgan probably overstressed the role of the Theosophists proper. Both from internal evidence as well as studies of California radicalism, it seems clear that while the Theosophists were an important factor, they were by no means the only one. "Unity" was a split-off from Theosophy. Both Unity and Theosophy were discussed frequently in *The Coming Nation*. The Unity magazine was published by Charles Kerr, who was later to become the chief Socialist Party publisher.

16. Blavatsky, *Key to Theosophy*, p. 37.

17. *Theosophical Glossary* (London, 1892).

neglected duties, abused powers and impotent hate; a dream ending ultimately in the oblivion of utter annihilation."[18]

Like Bellamy and the Nationalists, Theosophists believed that the cause of this living hell, of which capitalism was only the expression, was the "selfishness" of men. "We Theosophists . . . say that 'Good' and 'Harmony' and 'Evil' and 'Dis-Harmony' are synonymous. Further we maintain that all pain and suffering are results of want of Harmony, and that the one terrible and only cause of the disturbance of Harmony is selfishness in some form or another."[19] The ultimate solution to the state of intense personal anxiety was the attainment of Karma—or complete harmony on the spiritual plane. Karma required "the entire renunciation of one's personality."[20] Clearly the Theosophist solution was only one more expression of the desire to escape from the burden of individual freedom through immersion in an all-embracing something—in this case a mystical-religious experience similar to that described by Bellamy in "The Religion of Solidarity."

Yet, the Theosophists were not devoted to spiritual reform alone. While they did not consider themselves a political organization—rejecting politics on the same grounds as the Nationalists did, as one more expression of selfishness—nevertheless they did not stand aloof from the material or "practical" social questions which plagued capitalist society and resulted in misery for the masses of workers. The active philanthropic orientation of Theosophists was constantly reiterated in its literature. "All Theosophists," Madame Blavatsky declared, "are only too sadly aware that, in Occidental countries, especially, the social condition of the large masses of the people renders it impossible for either their bodies or their spirit to be properly trained, so that the development of both is thereby arrested. As this training and development is one of the express objects of Theosophy, the T.S. is in thorough sympathy and harmony with all true efforts in this direction."[21]

Theosophists regarded Nationalism as a "true effort" for reform on the physical plane because like Theosophy it strived for communion and attempted to raise the masses from above. The utopian character of Bellamyite politics fitted in perfectly with the Theosophist view that the

18. St. George Lane Fox-Pitt, "Oriental Theosophy," *Encyclopedia Britannica*, 11th ed.

19. Blavatsky, *Key to Theosophy*, p. 207.
20. Ibid., p. 19.   21. Ibid., pp. 232–233.

precondition for the betterment of the condition of the masses was a change in the human spirit which could only be brought about by the Theosophist elite. It was this ethical-philanthropic outlook that lay behind the Theosophists' rejection of politics. "To seek to achieve political reforms before we have effected a reform in human nature, is like putting new wine in old bottles."[22] Only when selfishness was abolished in individuals, could there be a just social order—a society of total harmony such as that described in *Looking Backward*. The misery of the lower classes and their spiritual sickness could only be relieved by the Theosophical practice of true brotherhood. Out of this would come "the real human solidarity which lies at the root of the elevation of the race. . . ."[23] Through progressive reincarnation, aided by the spiritual and material ministrations of the Theosophists' vanguard, all men could move from the lower to the higher plane of spiritual development, gradually finding complete inner harmony through the elimination of the extrinsic personality. In the process a more perfect social order, "a higher plane of being," for all humanity would be created.[24]

For the Theosophists, like the Nationalists, the motor force of the process of spiritual and material progress for the masses was located in evolution—not evolution as the social Darwinists taught but rather an organic fatalistic evolutionary process similar to that which Gronlund and Bellamy looked to for social salvation. "True evolution" according to the Theosophical doctrine, taught "that by altering the circumstances of the organism we can alter and improve the organism; and in the strictest sense this is true with regard to man. Every Theosophist is bound to do his utmost to help on, by all the means in his power, every wise and well-informed social effort which has for its object the amelioration of the condition of the poor. Such efforts should be made with a view to their ultimate social emancipation, or the development of the sense of duty in those who now so often neglect it in nearly every relation of life."[25]

It was on this point of the reform of human nature as the precondition for the spiritual and material uplift of the masses that the Theosophists' philanthropic reformism coincided with Bellamy's vision of the progress of the human race through increasing control by the State over

22. Ibid., p. 231.   23. Ibid., pp. 233–234, 235.
24. Ibid., pp. 235–237.   25. Ibid., p. 235.

men. The democratic idea of men struggling for their own freedom and in the course of this struggle altering themselves, throwing off reliance on "superiors," was rejected by these utopians of the material and spiritual world alike. For both it was the mass of mankind as it was, corrupted by the selfishness of the present order, which was the major obstacle to progress. A new society, Annie Besant later explained, "must be planned by wisdom, not by ignorance, and brought about by the love and sacrifices of the higher, and not by the uprising of the lower. Mobs can make revolutions; but they cannot build a State."[26] The State was "the father-mother" of its citizens, "the Protector of all."[27]

Thus whatever the formal contradiction—whether in the last analysis human nature had to be completely altered as the Theosophists maintained or the selfish antisocial side of human nature suppressed by new institutional arrangements as the Nationalists believed—did not matter, except in the long run. However, because of this doctrinal difference, Blavatsky's endorsement of Bellamy's utopia expressed some reservations as to its perfection:

> The organization of Society, depicted by Edward Bellamy in his magnificent work, 'Looking Backward' admirably represents the Theosophical idea of what should be the first great step towards the full realization of universal brotherhood. The state of things he depicts falls short of perfection, because selfishness still exists and operates in the hearts of men. But in the main, selfishness and individualism have been overcome by the feeling of solidarity and mutual brotherhood; and the scheme of life there described reduces the causes tending to create and foster selfishness to a minimum.[28]

Despite these differences, Theosophists were urged to take part in the effort to realize the goals of Nationalism: "In the constitution of all their clubs, and of the party they are forming, the influence of Theosophy and of the Society is plain, for they all take as their basis, the first and fundamental principle, the Brotherhood of Humanity as taught by Theosophy."[29]

As long as Nationalism was a practical movement by which a philanthropic elite could liberate the masses from above, and did not move toward politics, the Theosophists could support Nationalism. Pre-

---

26. Annie Besant, *Theosophy* (n.d.), p. 75.
27. Ibid., p. 74.
28. Blavatsky, *Key to Theosophy*, p. 44.
29. Ibid., p. 45.

cisely what the distinction between practical work and political action meant to ordinary rank-and-file Theosophist-Nationalists, was revealed in the words of one of them, recorded some years later:

> The Nationalist clubs were strictly non-political and adhered to the spirit of Mr. Bellamy's *Looking Backward* in not allowing class antagonisms in their discussions. . . . Our principal speakers were city and county officials, judges, school board members, etc., all elected on the Republican ticket and opposed to radicalism. . . .

> It is of particular importance that the Theosophical Society should in no way be connected with any political party or with anything that promotes class or sectarian distinctions.

> The charm, the universal drawing power, of Edward Bellamy's *Looking Backward* was the absence of "class consciousness." The emphasis was placed upon the transition from the nineteenth century condition to the ideal state without class conflict, hate or injustice. It seems to me that this point cannot be overemphasized.[30]

The contradiction of actually organizing a movement, running their own candidates for public office, supporting the candidates of other parties, or participating in pressure-group campaigns for specific demands, was a clear sign that there had begun a process of drift away from the advocacy of a socialism from above that had been the hallmark of Nationalism at its founding and which had been the basis of the Nationalists' claim to be a conservative anticapitalist movement. It initiated a process of revision in the Nationalists' political beliefs and in the very goals of the movement. In time the revisions resulted in the retirement of the industrial army as the model of a collectivist society and some genuine but ambiguous concessions to the idea of democratic participation.

The history of the Fabian Society which was similar in more ways than one to the Nationalists sheds light on these changes.[31] William Clarke, one of the Society's founding members, explained that the Fabians went through three successive stages before the form of organization and political activity emerged which came to be regarded as characteristic of the Fabians in the 1890s. Each stage was the unintended consequence of the preceding one. The first, according to Clarke, was the "self-forming" stage during which ideas were discussed privately among its members without any intention of seeking a wider audience. Then

---

30. Abbott Clark, cited in Morgan, *Edward Bellamy*, pp. 268–269.

31. William Clarke, Introduction to the American edition of the *Fabian Essays in Socialism* (Boston: Shaw Publishing Co., 1911).

came an "educational" phase in which the Fabians undertook to educate others from their own class. Philanthropic and elitist, they did not intervene in politics or spread their ideas to any group beyond select audiences of well-disposed middle-class folk. Out of this period, however, quite contrary to their intentions, came a third phase: the phase of "practical politics," which, Clarke writes,

> was not undertaken without some misgivings. On the principle that you cannot touch pitch without being defiled, I confess I doubted whether, until the people had been far more educated in these ideas, it was wise to enter the somewhat dirty political arena. But the intense desire to be doing something, to translate these ideas into facts, to organize the people, to help in shaping the actual progressive movement in England, and above all to weaken and destroy the individualist wing of the Liberal party—these and other motives acted with cumulative force, especially as members of the society began to find that they had acquired influence over little groups of workmen here and there.[32]

Through such activity, the Fabians, like the Nationalists, started many persons on the road to socialism and in the process the conflict between the "two souls" of Fabianism intensified. In the case of the Nationalist movement, the contradiction between its original intentions and the actual life of the movement as it gathered momentum, was more extreme because they relied much more on a fatalistic theory of unconscious evolution than did the Fabians.

Try as they might to restrict the movement to an elite of intellectuals and professionals, of responsible and educated persons only, the Nationalists, even the Theosophists, were faced with results that they had not foreseen and certainly never intended. In November 1889, Willard had declared that the problem for the movement was to decide which "practical step the more conservative will most readily support first."[33] Holding small meetings to train a "splendid corps of men and women" who would be prepared, in Willard's words, to "push with tremendous force all along the line,"[34] the Nationalists were so successful that it undid their hope of restricting the movement to the more conservative middle-class elements. Pushing and exerting force attracted not only a following, as it had for the Fabians, but it also called forth opposition

32. Ibid.
33. Willard, *The Nationalist* 1, no. 7 (November 1889): p. 265.
34. Ibid.

from many of the same conservative elements whom the Nationalists had naively hoped would help them, once convinced of the truth. This led, in turn, to the need for new allies, especially when the opposition was felt from the railroads, utilities, and insurance companies marked for nationalization.

Disappointed by the capitalists, the Nationalists began to sound more and more like advocates of organized conflict than of class harmony. The Theosophist-oriented First Club of Boston attempted to secure a bill from the Massachusetts legislature in 1889 to allow municipalities to own their own electric and gas utilities.[35] In keeping with the conception of practical, nonpartisan Nationalism, they were deliberately low key, and hoped to avoid any charge of radicalism. They testified before the state legislature and mounted pressure campaigns among notables and other middle-class sympathizers rather than engaging in associative political action.[36]

These activities engaged them in a struggle for their program, and carried them away from their original stance. The Declaration of Principles had promised that Nationalists would not make war on individuals, nor would they "censure" the capitalists who had reaped immense fortunes from their businesses. But as early as April 1889, the Boston Nationalists learned from their legislative lobbyist, Arthur Hildreth, battling to secure the desired municipal enabling bill: "The infant Hercules [i.e., the Nationalist movement] was compelled to strangle in his fists the great snakes that Juno sent against him. No sooner was the Club born than it was called upon to contend with snakes still greater—the gas companies—enormous, slippery reptiles with tails of limitless length. We may fail in our attempt to get a grip, but sooner or later we will stretch these monsters on their backs."[37] Hildreth vehemently denounced the representatives of the gas utilities:

35. For a detailed account of this campaign, see Everett McNair, *Edward Bellamy*, pp. 69–76.

36. The "good citizen" approach of the Nationalists is illustrated in the following advice to the Nationalists of Boston. In the primary elections, they were to "see that only the best men are selected. Exact solemn promises to correct present abuses. Question the candidates closely and publicly. Get their pledges to insist on the most rigid scrutiny, regulation, and control of corporations." (Arthur Hildreth, "Monopolies of Muncipal Service," *The Nationalist* 1, no. 1 [May 1889]: 228–232. An address delivered to the April 1889 meeting of the Nationalist club.)

37. Ibid., p. 228.

> These positions [of the opponents] are so monstrous that we are led
> to ask how it comes about that a man can arrive at such conclusions.
> The liberty that Mr. Russell cares about is not the liberty of the
> people; no such thing. What he is concerned about is the liberty of
> toll gatherers to keep possession of the bridges, and support them-
> selves by taxing the public. The liberty that Mr. Russell cares about
> is not the liberty of the people, but the liberty of a few favored
> citizens. . . .[38]

As for the Massachusetts legislature, it was "the most incompetent and
corrupt body that ever sat in the State House."[39] Such statements undoubtedly made many conservatives, once favorably disposed to Bellamy's views, wonder whether the Nationalists' profession of nonparti-
sanship and belief in the spirit of brotherhood was not a false front for
more sinister, more radical, motives. Statements which seemed to verge
on the incitement of class hatred, little different in temper and content
from those made by the radical, working-class socialists, reinforced this
alarm. The corruption of the legislature was due, the Nationalists proclaimed, to "vast moneyed interests wielding the power of their wealth
to their selfish advantage, and . . . private corporations, created to
render public service, but seeking to control the law-making power and
tax the Public for their own profit. To attain these ends they scruple at
nothing."[40]

The sudden growth of the movement and the discovery that the
bastions of capitalism would not be taken by love, pushed the Nationalists
in new directions. In December 1889, just one year after the founding of
the First club, John Ransom Bridge, its secretary and a Theosophist,
apologetically revealed the club's removal to larger headquarters because
of its astonishing success.[41] "If in the past few months," the Nationalist
club "had had the quarters and the money, it could have done an amount
of work scarcely exceeded by the National Committee of one of the great
political parties during an active campaign."[42] Uncomfortable with the
comparison which had come so quickly to mind, Bridge reminded the
Nationalists that their unexpected success had not, however, turned them
into a political party. "Such a comparison," he admonished his readers, "is
not intended as an indication that in any sense is the Nationalist club a
political organization. While this notice of change of location is not an

38. Ibid., p. 229.   39. Ibid., p. 231.   40. Ibid.
41. *The Nationalist* 2, no. 1 (December 1889): 36–37.
42. Ibid., p. 36.

exposition of the principles of nationalism, it may not be out of place to say that the Club is in no way tainted by party politics. It is rather the point of crystallization for a moral revolution against the glaring defects in our present social life which threaten to further widen the already dangerous breach between capital and labor."[43]

Bridge reminded his fellow Nationalists that organized politics and partisanship were undesirable because they prompted class warfare and were unnecessary in any case. Monopolies were growing rapidly and their evolution was the best basis of the kind of progress that Nationalism stood for. Rather than self-defeating attempts to enter politics, Bridge cautioned the Nationalists to stick to the conservative policy laid down by the founders. Yet, it was clearly just this policy that Bridge and his co-thinkers now felt to be threatened by the success of the movement: "The Nationalists fully recognize that but one step in advance at a time can be taken and that each advance must show the direction for the next step. This is not Anarchy or extreme Socialism that would despoil those who have been able to take advantage of present social conditions. It is good 'common sense,' if an unselfish conception of something better than the present with its want, misery, and crying distress, means anything. The ethics of Nationalism are at bottom the principle of unselfishness. . . ."[44]

The tide had already begun to run swiftly in the opposite direction, however. The formation of a second club in Boston, clearly more oriented toward practical Nationalism than the first and taking into its ranks less conservative elements, was an alarming signal to the original Bellamyites that the movement had gotten out of their control.[45] And, worst of all from their standpoint, it seemed clear too that Bellamy himself was increasingly sympathetic to the active and aggressive tactics expressed in these organizational developments. By the summer of 1890, impatient with the abstract, philanthropic orientation of the publishers of *The Nationalist*, Bellamy had decided to break with the self-styled orthodox Bellamyites and to launch his own periodical, the *New Nation*. "I am anxious to get things on a working basis as soon as possible," he wrote to a friend. "I am full of steam and shall explode if I don't get to

43. Ibid.   44. Ibid.
45. See McNair, *Edward Bellamy*, pp. 76–84 on the formation of the Boston Nationalist Club Number 2 and the increasing emphasis on the "practical," "non-partisan" work of the movement.

work pretty soon."[46] Undoubtedly, the practical success of the work of the Second Boston club had had its effect upon Bellamy, as it did upon other Nationalists throughout the country. "These two Boston clubs were prototypes of movements in other cities," Mason Green, Bellamy's aide and biographer, recalled. "The First Nationalist was strong on theory and doctrine, and the second Nationalist was more particularly identified with 'first steps.' At the meetings of the first club one would hear much about 'Evolution' and 'Environment,' the 'solidarity of the race,' the 'Enthusiasm of humanity' and so on; while at the second club government ownership of railroads and telegraphs and municipal tenement houses and the public conduct of the liquor traffic were the sort of subjects that held the boards."[47]

Club reports to *The Nationalist* reveal clearly that by late 1889 many of the clubs throughout the country were also groping their way toward practical politics and the tension between the views expressed by the orthodox Bridge and those of the political actionists was growing. By mid-1890, even before the formation of the People's Party, the Nationalist clubs had already definitely entered the political arena as an independent force, much to the distress and confusion of many of the founding Nationalists.

The history of the Nationalist clubs in Cleveland and Cincinnati typifies the process by which the clubs moved toward political action.[48] They had begun, as had the First Boston Club, with small meetings at which members read papers concerning social problems. Quite naturally the "intense desire to be doing something, to translate these ideas into facts" that had seized the like-minded Fabians, impelled the Ohio clubs to exchange discussion for action. At the start, "the clubs acted as a sort of pressure group usually in purely local matters."[49] Applying pressure as "good citizens" for municipal ownership of utilities and good sewers, they were quickly forced to engage in state politics, although they continued to act only as a pressure group rather than as an independent political tendency. But when this proved ineffectual, they looked for some other mode of operation. Their opportunity was provided in 1891 by the founding of the People's Party. The Cincinnati convention of the Popu-

46. Mason Green, *Edward Bellamy*, p. 96, Bellamy Papers.
47. Ibid., p. 86.
48. Zornow, "Bellamy Nationalism in Ohio," (April 1949): 152–170.
49. Ibid., p. 157.

lists in February, 1891, was attended by an Ohio delegation heavily weighted by Nationalists. Of one hundred delegates from Hamilton County, nearly all were Nationalists.[50] The Ohio Nationalists played an important role in founding the Ohio People's Party and gradually assuming its leadership, although at first they had been cautious. In Ohio, California, Massachusetts, Rhode Island, New York, New Jersey, and other eastern states, the Nationalists also pushed toward independent political action, flowing into the People's Party. The new party thus became the main focus for their activity.

In New York City, Rhode Island, California, Michigan, and elsewhere, Nationalist clubs nominated candidates for public office. Rhode Island's nomination of a slate of candidates for state office was quickly followed by the clubs in New York City.[51] In New York, Nationalists set up ward clubs in July and August of 1890,[52] as a "prelude to entering the political field, which it is intended to do prior to the forthcoming elections."[53] A circular sent out to "labor, trade and radical organizations" in New York City proclaimed that the Democrats and the Republicans had "outlived their day." Conditions called for "a new, vigorous party; a party conscious of the needs of our age, and resolute to carry out the demands."[54] It seemed to the New York Nationalists that a veritable "political revolution" was a possibility, at least in New York.[55]

In February, 1890, the Detroit Nationalists gleefully reported their political successes: "Right under the noses of the old politicians of Wayne County is growing a political movement that may play hob in the near future with their fine drawn schemes."[56] The Nationalists had

50. Ibid.

51. *The Nationalist* 2, no. 8 (July 1890): 346.

52. Ibid., vol 3, no. 1 (August 1890): 43.

53. Ibid.

54. Ibid., vol. 3, no. 2 (September 1890): 112–113.

55. Ibid., vol 2, no. 1: 43. On the New York developments, see McNair, *Edward Bellamy*, pp. 102–111; McNair also discusses at length the role of the S.L.P. in not only the New York movement but its relationship to the Nationalists as a whole (ibid., pp. 102–128). It seems clear both from McNair's account as well as from the pages of the *Workmen's Advocate* that some segments of the S.L.P. regarded the newly formed Nationalist clubs as an arena for their own activity and although the exact weight of their role is impossible to assess, the internal tension within the Nationalist movement and the drive toward political involvement were obviously independent of the S.L.P. This is borne out by the fact that the same process of bifurcation took place throughout the country, leading to the entry of the political Bellamyites into the People's Party—a step certainly not approved of by the S.L.P.

56. *The Nationalist* 2, no. 3 (February 1890): 119.

organized "social clubs" where the ideas of Nationalism were preached. The clubs sent delegates, in turn, to Ward Clubs, and these then sent representatives to Congressional Clubs. "Thus the machinery of a political party is forming that, if rightly handled, cannot fail to change the political complexion of some sections of Wayne County, and may even place the election of Congressmen in the hands of a minority party."[57]

But, as the reports of the New York clubs revealed, this shift toward political action had had a divisive effect: "There is within the city and state a strong and influential detachment, opposed to taking political action at present, and the resolution of the central committee that the time is now ripe for taking steps to overthrow the present political parties has been severely condemned by these. The indications are, however, that the opponents are in a minority, and that political action will be inaugurated."[58] The reporter's assurance that feelings associated with the "Brotherhood of Humanity" would nevertheless not be breached by any "difference of opinion as to method of immediate procedure" within the movement was something less than convincing.[59]

The antagonism which these new developments aroused in the minds of those club members who continued to believe in old-style Nationalism as they had first learned it from *Looking Backward* and *The Nationalist*, was most apparent in one of the key strongholds of Nationalism, Southern California, where Gaylord Wilshire ran for Congress as the candidate of a "Nationalist party."[60] Wilshire's campaign produced a sharp and irreconcilable split among the Nationalist clubs. Wilshire's campaign against the use of government troops against strikers in defense of private property antagonized conservative, antilabor Nationalists. As in New York, however, the main issue in the split was opposition to independent political action—although, of course, this was directly related to a conservative hostility to anything that smacked of a class movement.[61]

The editors of *The Nationalist* were torn by the success of the movement and the promise of realizing their aims within the coming decade or two. One editor boasted that although the Nationalists might be sentimentalists, they were "sentimentalists who are capable of accom-

57. Ibid.   58. Ibid., vol. 3, no. 1, pp. 43–44.

59. Ibid., vol. 3, no. 1, p. 44.

60. Quint, "Socialism's First Congressional Campaign," *Pacific Historical Review* 26, no. 4 (November 1957): 327–340.

61. Ibid., pp. 335–337.

plishing a great deal of work in a very practical way." But it was clear from his added boast that in California "the nationalists are making themselves felt more and more as a power in the government of the state,"[62] that the older philanthropic idea of practical action had been forced to make concessions to the demand for political action.

Bellamy himself gave hesitant but increasingly open approval to these steps toward active involvement in independent political action during 1890, bringing him into direct conflict with Nationalists, especially of a Theosophical persuasion, who, after wavering a bit, had become more and more hostile to remaking Nationalism into a political movement.[63]

Bureaucratic Plebiscitarianism

In the transitional period of Nationalism, during 1890–1891, in which divisions had not yet produced an open break, the orientation toward political action was tolerated to preserve the spirit of "Brotherhood," and uphold Nationalism's theory of a nonpolitical politics, more specifically, of a "non-partisan socialism," as it came to be called during the 1890s. This stance led in practice to a plebiscitarian conception of politics which was the logical political complement to the Nationalists' practical program of building a collectivist social order from the top down through the bureaucratic statification of the economy. If neither mass consciousness nor an independent political organization to instill that consciousness and to counterpose itself to the other parties were required, Nationalists could have the best of both worlds: an atomized movement of "the people," rather than of any single class, led by a Nationalist elite, giving to the latter sufficient voting force to carry out their program against the nonphilanthropic plutocrats without the danger of an independent movement from below. Though this formula was designed to reconcile the two tendencies within the movement, it only increased the tension

62. *The Nationalist* 3, no. 2 (September 1890): 111.

63. See Bowman, *The Year 2000*, p. 130 ff. and Aaron, *Men of Good Hope*, p. 106. Aaron's discussion of the split between the Theosophists and Bellamy, while interesting, is no more enlightening than the rest of his discussion of Bellamy. He writes that Bellamy found the Theosophists too nonpolitical, and the latter had no interest in Nationalism as a "practical political movement." All of this is true, but misleading since Bellamy had shared their peculiar antipolitical mode of politics at first, and in this respect the Theosophists' resistance to the politicization of the movement was consistent with Bellamy's original doctrine. It was Bellamy who was inconsistent.

between them. It indicated that the movement was coming to a fork in the political road, and also revealed the latent plebiscitarian content in Bellamy's bureaucratic socialism.

The editors of *The Nationalist* at first reacted to political action by attempting to combine the goal of a collectivist social order with the method of plebiscitarian politics:

> The Nationalists are very busy in New York, organizing, circularizing, lecturing, and spreading the doctrines among all classes. The people are fast becoming interested in the movement; they see that it is not a class movement; is not exclusively for the laboring class, or the wealthy or the middle classes, but for all classes, and they see this fact precludes the possibility of corruption which is inevitable when "parties" get control of the government. The nationalists are not rallying around a banner whose principal motto has been "to the victor belong the spoils," but they elevate a banner on whose folds everybody can read "Purity."[64]

This contradictory formula for a nonpolitical party or organization bringing into being the Nationalist utopia of a nonpolitical state, served to make the political activities of the clubs formally compatible with the original doctrines of Nationalism. As long as the new party stood above classes, political activity was acceptable. Such a party, representing the organically united interests of the entire Nation, rather than the selfish interests of particular classes, was not, strictly speaking, a political party at all and was therefore the perfect instrument for the construction of a functionally rationalized social order based on a mass of atomized individuals.

The notion of such a "national party" had been implicit in the form of organization and style of political activity adopted by the Nationalist clubs at their founding. Yet the nature of a party above parties had not been spelled out concretely either by Bellamy in *Looking Backward* or by other spokesmen for the movement. With the growth of the clubs and the increasing involvement of the Nationalist membership with day-to-day political questions, the need for a detailed conception of the appropriate forms of political action became more pressing. Out of this search came a solution which was consistent with the premises of original Nationalism and at the same time gave the proposed course of action a populistic coloration which could also satisfy the wing of Nationalists moving toward direct political involvement. The answer was to create a plebiscitarian system of "direct democracy" which would simultaneously outlaw as

64. *The Nationalist* 3, no. 2 (September 1890): 112.

criminal conspiracies all forms of organized political association and provide for the incorporation of politics and political activity into the state.

Thaddeus Wakeman, leading Nationalist from New York and later
an important figure in the Populist movement, led the way.[65] Parties
were an unnatural and undesirable growth upon the American political
system, Wakeman announced. They had corrupted the body politic contrary to the original, wise intentions of the Founding Fathers. George
Washington, Wakeman pointed out, had warned against the danger to
the nation of permanent "factions" or parties, but the American people
had tragically failed to heed his advice. Parties had been permitted to
come into existence and the result, Wakeman lamented, echoing a long
line of antiparty thinkers in America, was the social and political impasse
in which Americans now found themselves. The individual could not
make his political will felt. Only the party, organized and cohesive, with
its ability to mobilize the mob as voting cattle to support its goals,
blindly and without reason, had the power to shape events. "The political party with its Machinery and Boss . . . has . . . captured and an-
nexed the whole government to itself. The people are utterly powerless
except to change one political despot for another. . . . As the Trusts and
the Monopolists consolidate, the Parties will be their dependents."[66]

Although Wakeman formulated his views from the standpoint of
the Nationalists' opposition to democracy, and here expressed the deep
feelings of political impotence which had made Bellamyism such an
attractive doctrine to the middle classes, the content of his indictment of
party and of democracy was a reflection, in an anticapitalist mirror to be
sure, of the attacks on party by those among the Nationalists' contemporaries who were committed to the maintenance of private property and,
like the Nationalists, fearful of the propertyless masses.[67] Conservative
doctrine was thus joined to a collectivist perspective.

65. Wakeman, "Politics and the People," *The Nationalist* 2, no. 1 (December 1889):
11–17.

66. Ibid., pp. 12–13.

67. The antiparty tradition and its role in American political thought, particularly
in the political reform movement which begins in the 1870s and culminates in the Progres-
sive-era changes in the structure of the party system, the most important of which was the
direct primary, has been dealt with by Austin Ranney, *The Doctrine of Responsible Party
Government* (1962), and idem, *Curing the Mischiefs of Faction* (1975). See also Richard Hofstadter, *The Idea of a Party System: The Rise of Legitimate Opposition in the United States, 1780–
1840* (Berkeley: University of California Press, 1970).

Wakeman, true to Bellamy's own antidemocratic and authoritarian views attacked party government as government by "the mob." It was an "unwieldy Monster, more potent in the tail than in the head, and . . . hardly stimulated to action but by the garbage or trash, thrown to it by the base, or the weak, for base and weak purposes."[68] Counterposing "the people" to "the mob," Wakeman made it clear that the people, those to whom Nationalism appealed and to whom his own proposal was directed, were the traditional middle classes—the farmers, small businessmen, merchants, artisans, professionals, intellectuals, all of native birth. The mob, the "garbage or trash," was made up of the urban working class, particularly the swelling number of non-English–speaking immigrant workers: an alien, propertyless, rootless mass whom the professional politicians exploited and upon whom they built the Machine.

But although Bellamy in his fantasy had been able to advocate openly the abolition of universal suffrage and political democracy, Wakeman, like the political reformers of the last decades of the nineteenth century, was forced by the very impracticality of such a course of action to find a way to put power back into the hands of the responsible middle classes—"the people"—without directly attacking universal suffrage.[69] To take the political power out of the hands of the mob it would be necessary to take it out of the hands of the professional politicians and organized parties: to create, in the lexicon of conservative procapitalist reformers, nonpartisan government which would make the right kind of people powerful without at the same time formally taking the suffrage away from the masses—at least not until the first nuclei of the coming administrative state were brought into being and the workers gradually removed from any participation in politics. Anticipating the political reformers of the Progressive era, the substance of democracy had to be changed while the form and especially the term itself was retained. For people afraid of political associations they could not control, for whom the dilemma of organization was an expression of their own inability to act together effectively, the logical solution was the forced atomization of

68. Wakeman, "Politics and the People," p. 17.
69. The consequences of these changes in the "rules of the game" entailed in the strategy of undermining mass suffrage through various reforms to "purify elections," such as the personal registration laws and the Australian ballot, have been dealt with by Walter Dean Burnham, in "The Changing Shape of the American Political Universe," *American Political Science Review* 59, no. 1 (March 1965): 7–28, and later book, *Critical Elections and the Mainsprings of American Politics* (1970).

the electorate and the reduction of the suffrage itself to its purest plebi-scitarian form. Wakeman cogently posed the dilemma facing the National-ists: "Can the *initiative*, the moving and controlling power of the Govern-ment, be taken from the outside political party managers, and restored to the primal democratic assemblies of the people, and to their *legal* represen-tatives? Can political action be included within the governmental action, or shall it remain an extraneous, extraconstitutional mob-power, the pos-session of which in the end, by the monopolists, will give them completely the government itself? Unless the people can combine their government and politics, is it not certain that Politicians will own their voters? . . . Equally certain is it, that no effective civil service reform is possible as long as the chance to get an office and to keep it depends upon party interests and party managers."[70]

Wakeman's solution was to create by law small districts in which direct personal participation by each voter would be possible. All citi-zens would be required to attend meetings of the district organization under penalty of law. But to prevent this direct democracy from becom-ing the instrument of either the mob or the politician, as well as to guarantee the Nationalist goal of substituting bureaucratic administration for politics—"a true civil service"—it was absolutely imperative, Wake-

70. Wakeman, "Politics and People," pp. 13–14. The idea of including "political action . . . within the governmental action" and the proposal for outlawing all forms of private association is a key not only to understanding the politics of Bellamyism but of the entire direction which political reform in the United States took in the absence of—or rather in opposition to—the emergence of a labor party. Ostrogorski, old-fashioned nine-teenth-century liberal and democrat, noted that "the idea underlying the form of regulation resorted to—that of incorporating political parties into the state—was fundamentally wrong. . . . A political party is by its very nature a free combination of citizens acting solely of their own will, so far as it does not offend the law of the land. Their relations to the State and to public authorities are just the same as any number of citizens lawfully uniting for this or for that purpose. Party as such is quite unknown to a State which respects the fundamen-tal rights of citizens. The State has no right to ask the members of any group what their political ideas are or what is their political record. . . . In no free country has such an interference been attempted. Russia alone has recently hit on the idea of 'legalizing political parties.' . . . The American State suppresses no party but interferes with all." (Ostrogorski, *Democracy and the Party System in the United States* [1910], pp. 427–428). The direct primary, unique to the United States, as well as the prior "reforms" of the Australian ballot required the granting (and by implication the denial) of legal status to political parties and direct intervention by the state into their internal affairs with the result being registration rather than membership as the basis of the party system. See Austin Ranney, *Curing the Mischiefs of Faction*, pp. 144–150. The most important single article on this topic is H. G. Nicholas, "Political Parties and the Law in the United States" (1954): 258–270.

man argued, to outlaw organized political activity and freedom of political association. "The holding or attempting to hold political caucuses or conventions, State or National, should be severely punished as criminal conspiracies against the Liberties and Welfare of the people. No political action should be permitted except through the District Assemblies and the nominating conventions [for Senators and Congressmen] and [through] the Legislatures and Congress elected; . . . These simple arrangements would sweep out the whole political party and election machinery as we now have it, abolish all the "Halls" and "primaries" and save the people an immense amount of money, time, worry, disappointment, corruption, and deviltry of nearly every description."[71]

This proposal for "direct" government and the statification of the political process in place of voluntary political associations, together with its concomitant, the illegalization of organized politics, flowed logically from the Nationalist theory of the step-by-step evolution of society toward the organic bureaucratic community composed of atomized individuals which Bellamy had portrayed in *Looking Backward*. It was an approach which completed the theory of nucleation for it provided a definite method by which to begin the piecemeal evolution toward the Nationalist goal of a nonselfish "politics": the substitution of bureaucratic administration by experts for the exercise of the suffrage and the functioning of elected, representative bodies. Wakeman spelled out these conclusions with unusual clarity. With the new system installed, he explained, "*Civil service* could then be established practically and in good faith, instead of being a hypocritical mockery as it is now, and always must be under party government." The evolution to the new order would then begin: "To such a civil service under the control of a State and National Executive with proper Industrial Departments, all of the public administration necessary to secure the general welfare of the people, such as transportation, and the production and distribution of the common means of living, could be very soon safely committed. Then Corporate Franchises and Monopolies, the Money King, and finally the Landlord, would be replaced by *Uncle Sam*, or someone under him or the State, holding and working for the benefit of all."[72]

The coupling of plebiscitarianism with the idea of an increasingly

71. Wakeman, "Politics and the People," pp. 13–14, 16.
72. Ibid.

powerful bureaucratic state apparatus—essentially the program of the Progressive era liberal reformers who spoke in the name of "direct democracy"—reduced those classes or groups with the capacity for self-organization in the political or economic realm to the unorganized state of the middle class. Here then was the perfect method for the introduction of the new collectivist order from above. Party government was government by the "mob," and the Nationalists hated the mob just as much as the capitalists did, except that the latter had been able, unlike the middle class for whom the Nationalists spoke, to make use of them for their ends through the organized party and the "machine." The only way the reform-minded sections of the middle class could rule, as Wakeman and the other advocates of direct democracy in the 1890s and the early twentieth century understood, was through a plebiscitarian system of direct democracy in which the "natural leaders" of society would overcome the power of the plutocracy and lead the workers from above. As Herbert Croly correctly observed in 1914, the entire array of plebiscitarian devices such as the initiative and referendum were instruments of minority rule, giving those minorities a means to harness "popular action" to their political program.[73]

73. Herbert Croly, *Progressive Democracy* (New York: Macmillan, 1914), p. 306 et passim. Hofstadter's discussion of the direct primary and the entire set of direct democracy reforms of the Progressive era is, on the whole, insightful (*The Age of Reform*, pp. 254–269). On the conservative consequences of municipal reform see Samuel P. Hays, "The Politics of Reform in Muncipal Government in the Progressive Era," *Pacific Northwest Quarterly*, October 1964, pp. 157–169. The argument set forth here that these reforms, including the much-vaunted initiative and referendum, were designed to *prevent* participation and entailed a kind of sham, plebiscitarian, conception of democracy, rests on the premise that participation requires not the ratification by plebiscite of policies, programs, and candidacies initiated by a well-placed elite, but the possibility of joining organized, mass membership political parties, democratically structured and committed to ideas and issues rather than to persons. This is the only sense in which one can speak of democratic participation in modern society. Effective democratic participation in politics requires effective democratic political *organization*. Whatever breaks that down—as the reforms of the Progressive era did—leads to the plebiscitarianization of politics. If there is an iron law of oligarchy, indeed, it is the iron law of *non-organization*, and this is precisely what the reformers from the Mugwumps, from whom Wakeman borrowed his ideas, to the Progressives desired. The incorporation of the parties and politics into the state was—as Ostrogorski dimly recognized—just one more logical step toward the undermining of democracy, and in this sense anticipates the reforms of the Watergate era. It is not accidental that the "public financing" of parties is first heard of in the pre–World War I period (see the interesting discussion by Ostrogorski, *Democracy and the Party System*, pp. 430–431, of this idea and its attempted application in Colorado in 1910), and in this sense Wakeman's bureaucratic

In joining the methods of plebiscitarianism to the goals of anticapitalist collectivism, the Nationalists closely resembled authoritarian movements of the "left" and "right" in Europe in the pre–World War I
period. The most important parallel is the case of Robert Blatchford,
editor of the *Clarion*, one of the most widely read socialistic newspapers
in England between 1890 and the outbreak of the World War.[74] Like
Bellamy, who undoubtedly influenced him greatly, Blatchford's socialism entailed an openly avowed admiration for military order and discipline, a model which he used for his idea of socialism. Rejecting the class
struggle and the necessity of independent working-class parties, Blatchford made the unity of all classes within the organic "nation" the object
of socialism. Hating liberalism and rejecting the institutions of liberal
democracy, Blatchford, as Bernard Semmel has pointed out, "set the
ideal of the nation as a family against the atomistic cosmopolitanism of
the liberals."[75] Like the Bellamyites, Imperial Germany provided Blatchford with his model of socialism. Universal military training had made
"the German nation . . . an army," while Britain, softened by liberalism, was "a mob of antagonistic helpless atoms."[76] "Fairly early in his
journalistic career," Semmel notes, "Blatchford described himself as no
Republican but a 'Democrat'. . . . His 'Democracy' had a Rousseauian
flavour. He had no use for parliaments or for parliamentary action
which, he felt, 'is not worth the trouble and expense it will entail.' He
sneered at manhood suffrage. 'For some reason not present to the practical Radical mind,' he wrote, 'votes seem to produce only representatives
who are not representatives, or carpetbaggers—with nothing in their
bags.' If he [Blatchford] did not 'care a cigar stump for elections, nor for
Parliament,' he was a strong advocate of a system of Initiative and Referendum. Only in that way could the clear collective voice of the nation be
heard and the will of Britons be done in Britain."[77]

Paradoxically, although the Nationalists' adoption of the politics of
plebiscitary democracy was the logical complement of its authoritarian

---

viewpoint permitted him to take what was only an implication of the legalization of the
parties to its logical antidemocratic conclusion. For a history and discussion of these issues
see Lipow. "Plebiscitarian Politics and Progressivism" (unpublished paper, American Historical Association, 1973).

74. The following discussion of Blatchford's views is based on Bernard Semmel's
excellent work, *Imperialism and Social Reform* (1960), pp. 222–233.

75. Ibid., p. 232.   76. Ibid.   77. Ibid., pp. 229–230.

vision of an organized nation of atomized individuals—the unitary democracy yearned for by Bellamy from his earliest days—and although it
also represented a practical solution to the problem of generating sufficient pressure from below to bring about Nationalism from above, still
its adoption also represented an important transitional phase for the
movement, toward a less authoritarian conception of Nationalism. For
Nationalists and native socialistic elements who clung to authoritarian
utopianism down through the 1890s, plebiscitarianism became the core
of Bellamyism, one that was emphasized more and more toward the end
of the decade when the threat of a socialism oriented toward independent
working-class political action became prominent.[78] On the other hand,
however, Nationalists equally committed to Bellamy's doctrine gradually
abandoned his fatalistic theory with its authoritarian implications and
threw themselves into political activity which aimed at the transformation of society from below. For this wing of Nationalism, one that to a
degree included Bellamy himself, the demand for direct democracy represented an attempt to find a political position that would transcend the
authoritarian utopianism with which they had begun.

Two Roads From Bellamyism

The internal tension generated by the shift of the Nationalist clubs
toward political action exploded after the 1890 fall elections. The vigorous espousal of independent politics by some Nationalists alienated those
who had joined the clubs on the condition that it remain safely nonpolitical. The Populist unheaval enormously strengthened the political action
tendency in Nationalism. In October, 1890, *The Nationalist* learned that
"the interest in the movement does not abate one particle. It seems to
plough its way through the country. It is manifesting itself by the
people's taking a keener interest in local government, in the granting of
public franchises, in the character of men who are chosen to govern or
represent them in a legislative capacity, and in the character of the
persons who are selected to educate their children."[79] In California especially, the Nationalists had succeeded in forcing Nationalism to the
front, with all that it meant in "purer politics, better government, wiser
education, and reform in industrial occupations."[80]

78. Quint, *Forging of American Socialism*, pp. 249–250. See *The Coming Nation*, esp.
after 1896 for the expression of this view.
79. *The Nationalist* 3, no. 3 (October 1889): 208.
80. Ibid., vol. 3, no. 3: 209.

The editors of *The Nationalist* in their reaction to the activities undertaken by the clubs, attempted to avoid the pitfalls inherent in an endorsement of political action. Their insistence that "it was not generally considered well for the clubs, as organizations, to take any part in the elections, and thus become appendages to either party,"[81] hardly squared with the actions of the New York, Rhode Island, Ohio, and California clubs described previously. Nor did it accurately reflect Bellamy's current views. Nevertheless, as long as the antipolitical Nationalists could maintain the fiction that the members might function as a party above parties, conservative Nationalists could tolerate the foray of the clubs into matters of practical reform, including electoral politics.

But not very well concealed beneath the conservative Nationalists' endorsement of the clubs' efforts on behalf of individual candidates from the two major parties who had "announced themselves unequivocally . . . prepared to go to the greatest distance in the promotion of legislation along Nationalist lines"[82] was an uneasy feeling that they were coming perilously close to the kind of political involvement that would set class against class, arouse the slumbering masses to a destructive outburst, and violate the spirit of "universal brotherhood."

Seizing on the encouraging results of the 1890 elections as evidence of how "quietly and effectively nationalism [is] taking hold of the minds of thinking people," *The Nationalist* nervously announced "the battle is over, and we have conquered."[83] It was time, therefore, to withdraw into the "real" work of the movement. Far from having conquered, of course, withdrawal from political activity was motivated by a fear of being conquered. Nationalists were warned that it was "love of self rather than love of our principles which has caused so friendly a manifestation of feeling on the part of the professional politicians and the established political party."[84]

Even more dangerous, clubs and individual members found their initial forays into politics congenial and relatively effective, offsetting the revulsion and fear of organized politics inherent in Nationalist doctrine. The emerging confidence that middle-class people in politics could act effectively led conservative Nationalists to issue stronger warnings against "entangling alliances" at the beginning of 1891.[85] "Pure National-

81. Ibid., vol. 3, no. 5 (December 1890): 352–353.
82. Ibid., vol. 3, no. 5 (December 1890): 353–354.
83. Ibid.   84. Ibid.
85. Ibid., vol. 3, no. 6 (January 1891): 414.

ism," the editors of *The Nationalist* insisted, must not be contaminated by
the old parites or become identified with "side issues," even if such
issues concerned real injustice. Their solution would best await the advent of the Nationalist utopia. In the meantime, if Nationalists persisted
in embracing these specific issues of social reform, "the only result will
be to create a needless prejudice against our movement, and retard its
progress."[86] Politics of this kind would clearly put the Nationalists on
the side of the victims of injustice and set them aggressively against the
perpetrators. Conservatives demanded a return to pure Nationalism and
a withdrawal from conflict-generating political activity: "We must keep
solely to the plain lines of nationalism, as laid down in the progressive
nationalization of industry, together with the municipalization of community services; and also the preliminary work of perfecting the mechanism of government, the protection of the interests of the nation's
workers, and the improvement of our system of public education by
making it in reality the democratic institution it claims to be. Here, then,
is a field broad enough to occupy all our energy, and there is no need of
going outside of it."[87]

Conservative Nationalists had gone along with the attempt to
broaden the movement's base of support through active involvement in
the current struggles for social reform, only as long as it seemed that they
could ride the movement from the top and could use whatever popular
enthusiasm existed to exert pressure for changes. Once, however, it became clear that the movement would not necessarily be subject to their
dictates, reawakening in the minds of the Nationalists their fear of disorder and chaos, it became necessary to call for a hasty retreat—if it was
still possible—back to the conservative, elitist mode of organization that
would allow them to institute their plan without unintentionally provok-
ing the independent intervention of the lower classes. Conversely, for
Nationalists who became involved in the building of a popular movement,
the view of themselves as the bearers of *the* plan to save the people began to
lose its hold upon them.

Antipolitical Nationalists renewed their emphasis upon Bellamy's
fatalistic evolutionary theory. Nationalism, the old guard once again
reminded people, was "a natural product of the times, an inevitable
sequence in a series of evolutionary stages, and as assuredly an element

86. Ibid.
87. Ibid., vol. 3, no. 6 (January 1891): 414.

of many sequences and stages that are yet to come."[88] The task of "pure" Nationalists was to enlighten—not stir up—the educated middle classes whose fears were aroused by participation in politics, and to rely on enlightened individuals such as the mayor of Boston or the governor of Massachusetts, who supported Nationalism because it advocated the municipal ownership of utilities.[89]

Significantly, the most explicit formulation of the antidemocratic outlook underlying the orthodox Bellamyites' hostility to any attempt to turn the Nationalist clubs into a political movement came in the last issue of *The Nationalist*, published in the spring of 1891. Even as it appeared, Bellamy's own venture into Nationalist journalism, the *New Nation*, was placed before the public and formalized the division between the two wings of the movement. If Bellamy and the other Nationalists who had begun to lean toward the idea of tying Nationalism to a political movement were not fully conscious of the direction in which such a concession might carry them, then the directness with which the issue was put to them by the author of "Nationalism and Politics,"[90] Stansbury Norse, who had been active in the movement from its inception, must have hastened the process of political self-clarification which would lead to the emergence of the other side of Nationalism. Norse noted correctly that the shift in the outlook of the "political" Nationalists was the direct consequence of the unexpectedly sudden success of the movement. He admitted that he as well as the rest of the founding members of the Nationalist clubs had believed it would be necessary and, of course, desirable to spend at least a decade in pure "educational" work. Yet, at the end of only three years, it had become apparent to all of them, according to Norse, that "within a few years undreamed of success becomes a possibility."[91]

This belief in the possibility of imminent success together with the fact, ruefully conceded by Norse, that the "majority of nationalists seem to have decided the question of political action in the affirmative,"[92] convinced the Nationalists of Norse's persuasion that the original doctrine of Bellamy and the founders had been betrayed. Confronted within their own ranks by heresy, antipolitical Nationalists like Norse reaf-

88. Ibid., vol. 3, no 5 (December 1890): 352–353.
89. Ibid., vol. 3, no. 7 (February 1891): 448–491.
90. Ibid., vol. 3, nos. 8–9 (March–April 1891): 558–560.
91. Ibid., p. 558.   92. Ibid.

firmed the authoritarian premises of orthodox Nationalism's objection to political action in a starker and less ambiguous fashion than would have been possible if no challenge had ever arisen. Without first invoking the usual rhetoric of "love" and "brotherhood" which had served to diffuse the authoritatian content of Nationalism's hostility to politics, Norse bluntly stated the major premise of the practical utopians' objection to the new direction of the movement. "Our movement," he reminded his fellow Nationalists, "is not that *of* the proletariat, but *for* the proletariat."[93] He warned that even if the erring Nationalists did not realize it at this stage, the consequences of their actions would inevitably carry them toward the methods of radical, democratic change from below—methods that were incompatible with Nationalism's conservative anticapitalism. This was a development, Norse pointed out, which would make Nationalism indistinguishable from the very kind of democratic radicalism of the socialists against which Bellamy's authoritarian collectivist utopia had originally been directed and which had given to it its peculiar appeal. Nothing could be more disastrous, Norse explained:

> The socialist and labor organizations are proletarian; and it is at the almost invisible line of demarcation that so many hesitate and are swerved in the wrong direction. Why the wrong direction? Because the proletaire never can right matters. Because the people regard any attempt on his part to be what it, alas, too often is, an effort to level society downward. Nationalism is the converse. Its aim is to level upwards, always upwards, by educating the people in the principles of the brotherhood of humanity. . . . Upon that foundation alone . . . we wish to build a structure into which the reforms we propose shall have been incorporated as a political necessity. Until the foundations have been securely laid it is surely unwise to begin our edifice.[94]

Norse urged the Nationalists to return to the fundamental principles of *Looking Backward* and to spread the ideas of Nationalism from above until they "permeated every grade of society" and not just the discontented but dangerously incompetent workers. Nationalists had to remember these principles and, for his part, Norse was not hesitant to remind them just what they were:

> The structure must be built by the educated and the wise, because it is based upon equity, cemented with justice, and constructed by

93. Ibid., p. 559. Emphasis in original.
94. Ibid.

love, and has for its broad dome the golden ties of fraternity. These are the concomitants of this class alone. The rich are too busily engaged in their worship of the golden calf, and the very poor have no leisure to study equity or justice, and even for thoughts of love and fraternity they have but fleeting moments. When they strike for justice they are apt to use a boomerang. Our mission is to teach them to conquer by wise and peaceful measures.[95]

Norse's article came too late. The Nationalists who followed Bellamy were moving too fast down another road to pay any heed to his warning.

95. Ibid., p. 560.

⑩ THE NEW NATIONALISM

Bellamy recognized in retrospect that the launching of The *New Nation* marked a new and qualitatively different phase in the ideological development of Nationalism. In the last issue of The *New Nation*, forced to suspend publication for financial reasons and because of Bellamy's failing health, he observed that "up to three years ago, when this paper was started, our program, save in one Congressional district, had not taken on a political character. Since then the Nationalists have become the advance guard of a national party which has accepted our immediate program as its platform and a large part of whose million voters, with the vast populations behind them, cherish our social ideal as their own. Never before in the history of the nationalist movement did the work so glow as now, never has the promise, the opportunity and the appeal to workers been so great."[1]

The transition to the new Nationalism had not, however, at first appeared as a sharp ideological break with the old Nationalism. Bellamy and his supporters attempted to keep the old line Nationalists like Cyrus Field Willard within the fold. But the attempt failed because the conservative, especially the Theosophically oriented, Nationalists perceived, perhaps more clearly than Bellamy himself, that the clubs were moving in a radically new direction and that the philanthropic-authoritarian character of Bellamy's politics which had won them to Nationalism in the first place was jeopardized by the attempt to find active support for their program and to broaden the movement itself. Theosophical Nationalists such as Henry Willard Austin, first editor of *The Nationalist*, sorrowfully believed that Bellamy had ignored the wishes of his "truest friends" and had "permitted himself to quit his proper sphere, essay editorship, and play at politics. . . ."[2] Cyrus Field Willard explained that "the Theosophists were obliged to drop the Nationalist movement when Bellamy alienated the members of the Nationalist Educational Association and started his own paper under the influence of Mason

1. Bellamy, *New Nation* 4, no. 5 (February 3, 1894): 50.
2. Quoted in Morgan, *Edward Bellamy*, pp. 269–270.

Green and such corrupt politicians as I knew [Henry] Legate [Massachusetts lobbyist for the club] to be."[3] Rather than becoming ensnared in the corrupting influence of politics, Austin, Willard, and the other Theosophists preferred to devote themselves once more to the Theosophical movement.[4]

Even the least discerning reader or sympathizer could not miss the broad differences between the new orientation of Bellamy in the *New Nation* and the antipolitical stance of *The Nationalist*. The new direction was most apparent in the format of the *New Nation*. *The Nationalist* had been a dully colored monthly which tried in its appearance and style to project the abstract, genteel and philanthropic orientation of its founders, an approach which by design could not appeal to a mass audience. In contrast, the *New Nation* was a weekly journal of opinion and topical comment, patterned after Godkin's *Nation*. Although it contained theoretical articles, some of them not too different in style and content from the old *Nationalist*, it also covered a wide range of current events which it viewed from the perspective of the new Nationalism. As a lively and highly political journal, it was obviously intended to reach an audience far greater and broader than its predecessor and although its circulation probably never exceeded 8,000,[5] the turn which Bellamyism had taken was clear enough.

Certainly the greatest impact of the establishment of the *New Nation* was on Bellamy himself and it marked the full emergence of the lonely utopian author into a new role which was to indelibly alter the man and the ideas first set forth in *Looking Backward*. The process of Bellamy's self-transformation had begun with the founding of the first clubs as he discovered himself playing an active role in the new movement. His interest in a literary career evaporated. Bellamy, his collaborator Mason Green reported, "threw himself into the work of inspiring in others the faith that was in him. He mixed in politics, in newspaper discussions, in anything that would tend to sweep away the cloud of individual selfishness that hung between the masses and the firmament of his visions. He was no longer an academicism [sic]. He had broken from his Arcadia and had become a leader of men. The man of letters was now the man of action."[6]

3. Ibid., pp. 270–271.   4. Ibid., p. 271.
5. Green, *Edward Bellamy*, p. 96.
6. Ibid., p. 86.

Spurred to aid in the founding of the *New Nation*, Bellamy commuted weekly from his small-town haven in Chicopee Falls to Boston to spend from Wednesday to Saturday overseeing the affairs of the paper. His editorship gave the ever-sickly Bellamy "a new lease on life," Green observed. "He became quite a mixer for a congenitally retiring man. He was ready and fertile with practical suggestions in politics when thousands of Nationalists became active in third-party movements. He was a safe councilor in matters of detail, all of which characteristics were a surprise even to himself. He wrote magazine articles, delivered occasional short speeches, composed editorials for the paper, attended conferences, and made and kept appointments when the object was to advance the cause."[7] The fact that the *New Nation's* premises doubled as an editorial office and as a center of the movement accelerated the emergence of the new Bellamy. "In the part of the week when Bellamy was in town . . . the office had the appearance of a continuous caucus. It was a cosmopolitan crowd. All classes and conditions of men were represented—men and women who were with property and those who never had any, the lawyer and the litigant, minister and layman, . . . those who could speak correct English and those who could not, the union labor leader, the scheming politician, [and] the honest folk who only ask a chance to make a living. . . . An immense amount of business was transacted at the office. During a political campaign the arrangements for meetings and the scheduling of speakers were perfected there. And nationalistic petitions were usually left there to be forwarded to the state house or to Washington."[8] Immersed in this highly charged political atmosphere, the ideas which were to modify Bellamy's original views began to take form.

Undoubtedly the key event which influenced the decision of Bellamy and the politically oriented wing of the Nationalists to chart a new course and eventually to begin publication of the *New Nation* was the emergence of the Populist movement. In late 1890, the editors of the *Nationalist* had hailed the Farmers' Alliance program of government ownership of transportation and communication.[9] But its editors had avoided any suggestion that Nationalists themselves might engage in independent partisan political activity. In contrast, the *New Nation* from

7. Ibid., pp. 97, 98.   8. Ibid., p. 97.
9. *The Nationalist* 2, no. 5 (December 1890): 345.

the very beginning called for the formation of a third party and as the People's Party began to take form in late spring 1891, it seems clear that Bellamy and the politically involved clubs saw the farmers' movement as the basis of a new Nationalist party. At the same time, many of the clubs continued to make plans for their own independent political action. The Rhode Island Nationalists announced in March 1891, that they would run a full slate of candidates for state offices in the forthcoming elections.[10] In Chicago, the Nationalist club endorsed the Socialist Labor Party candidate for mayor, Thomas J. Morgan.[11]

By spring 1891, discussion of a third party filled the pages of the *New Nation*.[12] In March, the editors wrote that "it is already apparent that under whatever name the third party may be organized . . . in 1892, it will be organized substantially along the lines and for the ends of nationalism." In May 1891, the Nationalist clubs and various Nationalist publications were invited to send delegates to a Cincinnati convention that month to discuss formation of a third party. The conference led to formation of the People's Party. The *New Nation* urged Nationalists to cooperate and work for a platform that corresponded to the Nationalist program.[13]

Despite their favorable reactions to the new party—reinforced by the friendly reception given their representatives at the Cincinnati conference—the *New Nation* admonished Nationalists to be wary of too deep an involvement in such a party: "We do not believe that the nationalist clubs, as organizations, should turn themselves into campaign clubs. The clubs stand for more advanced principles than any party is likely at once to take up, and it would be unwise policy for them as clubs to engage in any line of work which would compromise the completeness of their doctrine. But individually, and as citizens, we hope and believe that nationalists generally will be found in sympathy with the new party."[14]

10. *New Nation* 1, no. 7 (March 14, 1891): 101, 103.
11. *New Nation* 1, no. 8 (March 21, 1891): 118.
12. See for example, *New Nation* 1, nos. 7, 8, 9 (March 14, 21, and 28, 1891). On the role of the Nationalists within the People's Party and the development of their views see Quint, *The Forging of American Socialism*, pp. 217–222, and Everett McNair, *Edward Bellamy*, pp. 162–201.
13. *New Nation* 1, no. 8 (March 21, 1891): 118–119; vol. 1, no. 14 (May 2, 1891): 220; vol. 1, no. 18 (May 20, 1891): 277–278.
14. Ibid., vol 1, no. 18 (May 20, 1891): 278.

Desire to protect the autonomy of the clubs undoubtedly motivated this warning. But the basic reason for their position was the lingering adherence to the plebiscitarian doctrine of a nonpartisan, nonpolitical "Nationalist" party. The *New Nation* continued to insist that "Nationalism is not a party but a breaking of light. Parties are incidents; light steals upon the world slowly and after a season men find the paths leading to higher ground."[15]

By this standard, even the thoroughly middle-class People's Party did not deserve the full support of the Nationalists. The new party called for a war of the "producing" classes against the capitalists and stressed the necessity of a popular, mass movement to overturn the rule of the plutocracy. Could such a party rise above the corrupting influence of self-interest and class partiality, and be trusted to achieve its aims in the spirit of nonpartisan "brotherhood"? With this question in mind, the *New Nation* observed, just prior to the Cincinnati conference:

> The preponderating class of our population in the conference will be farmers. They have won the right to lead, but they should realize the responsibilities of leadership accordingly. The demands of no class, however large, are a sufficient basis for a national party. Neither can the demands of any two classes. The new party may succeed in making more or less disturbance with a platform representing the demands of a class or classes, but it will never triumph save as a national party, representing the needs of the nation without distinction of class.[16]

Throughout the remainder of 1891, Bellamy and the *New Nation* maintained a friendly but somewhat aloof attitude to the nascent People's Party. Before the Populists met at St. Louis in February 1892, to draw up a platform, the *New Nation* reminded the Nationalist delegates to the convention that "it should be kept in mind that nationalism is a movement and not a party." Its task was to permeate all reform groups, including the People's Party, with Nationalist ideas and, implicitly, to create thereby the sentiment for a nonpartisan movement, or a party above parties, to usher in the new order.[17] Yet, although the expressions of sympathy remained tepid and hesitant prior to the St. Louis convention, the Populist revolt had a profound effect upon the Nationalist clubs. In California especially, but also in Ohio, Illinois, New York,

15. *New Nation* 1 no. 7 (March 14, 1891): 101.
16. Ibid., vol 1, no. 15 (May 9, 1891): 236.
17. Ibid., vol 2, no. 7 (February 13, 1892): 98.

New Jersey, Rhode Island, and Massachusetts, the clubs threw themselves into the role of stimulating third-party sentiment.[18]

A turning point in the attitude of the average rank-and-file club members came with the adoption of a new program at the St. Louis meeting in February 1892. Bellamy found that in contrast to the "timid" utterances at Cincinnati, the St. Louis manifesto was "a ringing denunciation of the whole industrial system logically implying nothing less than an utter breaking with it."[19]

By the Spring of 1892, then, the sympathies of the New Nation were decidedly with the Populists. After the Omaha convention in July, the New Nation fully supported the Populist candidates, virtually becoming a semi-official organ of the new party, especially among its eastern and urban wing.[20] Bellamy himself became a candidate for the electoral college on the Populist ticket in Massachusetts.[21] However, the New Nation, if not the individual members of the Nationalist clubs, continued to regard the People's Party as an imperfect vehicle for Nationalist politics. Following the election, the New Nation editorially summed up the attitude of the Nationalists to the Populists and the future of the party: "We consider the recent democratic national campaign to have been a very valuable preparatory school for a host of voters who are destined within a few years to graduate as full-fledged disciples of Nationalism, which, now partially represented by the people's party, may four and perhaps two years hence, be completely represented and embodied, either in the platform of that or some other party."[22]

The new Nationalism which slowly emerged between 1891 and 1893 moved away from the older authoritarian doctrine which friend and foe alike had considered the essence of Nationalism. This had the effect of blurring the original anti-democratic, authoritarian image of Nationalism—not only in the 1890s, but later. Nationalists, who themselves had feared a mass movement from below, now found the Populists stamped by many conservative middle-class people, whose support they had sought, as inimical to the stability of society as the most violent anarchist

18. Quint, *Forging of American Socialism*, p. 101; Donald Edgar Walters, *Populism in California* (1952), ch. 3.

19. Bellamy, *New Nation* 2, no. 10 (March 5, 1892): 145–146.

20. John Hope Franklin, "Edward Bellamy and the Nationalist Movement," p. 768.

21. Ibid., fn. p. 769; *New Nation* 1, no. 45 (December 5, 1891): 716.

22. *New Nation* 2, no. 47 (November 19, 1892): 685.

or socialist group. Ironically, Bellamy and his fellow Nationalists who supported the People's Party found themselves embracing a company of agrarian radicals. Teddy Roosevelt, expressing a common reaction, believed the Populists were "plotting a revolution and subversion of the American Republic," and could add, with deadly seriousness, that the only way to reestablish law and order was to take twelve Populist leaders, line them up against a wall, "shooting them dead."[23] If the "better people" like TR reacted so violently to a movement of farmers, what hope was there of convincing them to give up their property and privileges even if only to save their own skins? This experience disillusioned the Nationalists, yet their association with the Populists revealed to conservatives as well as to themselves the degree to which they had departed from their original conception of a conservative anticapitalist movement.

A hostile reporter for the Chicago newspaper, the *Inter-Ocean*, contrasted the Nationalists' professions and those of their new-found friends and captured the ambivalence which many Nationalists felt toward the new party. "Mr. Bellamy had his followers" present at the convention,

> but they were the more peaceful dreamers who call themselves the nationalists. They were the brains of the convention, and yet they were theorists. They were college professors, editors, artists, and authors, who are infatuated with the socialism which dreams of uniting the nation into a great family, where all shall be dependent children without independence of thought and action. They want to see Mr. Bellamy's dream in 'Looking Backward' realized. They preach advancement and not destruction. They look with horror upon Donnelly's nightmare and its revolutionary teachings, but they were swallowed up by the revolutionists, and became part of the people's party, preaching destruction and anarchy. After it was over they realized how vain it is for men of peaceful dreams to try to influence revolutionaries.[24]

The Populists' success in mobilizing a powerful mass movement for democratic reform shook the foundations of American politics and transformed the climate of opinion. Even the Nationalists, once enemies of political action, took heart. For urban middle-class Nationalists, aware of the immense social and economic problems of industrial America and yet who had seen no major movement or party challenge corruption in poli-

23. Quoted by C. Vann Woodward, "The Populist Heritage and the Intellectuals," *The American Scholar* 29, no. 1 (Winter 1959–1960): 68–69. William Allen White, of course, made similar statements concerning the Populists.

24. Quoted in *New Nation* 2, no. 29 (July 16, 1892): 454–455.

tics and the immense new power of the captains of industry and finance, the Populist movement was a kindergarten of political education in which they experienced at first hand a mass, social-reform movement. The elemental upsurge of the agrarian radicals had been frightening at the outset, especially for reformers whose stock of political ideas had more in common with the conservative procapitalist Mugwump reformers, particularly in their antipathy to democracy, than with the orations of "Sockless" Jerry Simpson or Mary Elizabeth Lease.

In contrast to the elitist tradition of liberal reform, Populism represented a sizable section of the rural middle class in a political struggle to undermine the power of big capital and its political agents and to institute sweeping democratic reforms in the political system. Flawed as their conception of democracy may have been, the flaws were the product of the social and economic position of the farmers and not the result of some mystical "illiberal" elements inhabiting *all* mass movements.[25] On the contrary, the Populist contribution to the democratic tradition of reform was enormous despite its contradictory program and plebiscitarian leanings precisely *because* it was a mass movement that taught the lesson—even to persons outside their ranks—that involvement in organized politics and social reform was not only possible, but a meaningful way through which even the "average" citizen could improve the circumstances of his life. Events had overtaken Bellamy and the reactionary outlook which had produced *Looking Backward*. The new party, thus, performed two important functions which helped to transform Nationalism. It provided individual Nationalists whose experience had been limited to the exclusive and genteel atmosphere of their clubs with an opportunity to participate in a relatively heterogeneous and popular movement. Second, it provided them with a large and receptive audience for their ideas, one which, in contrast to the mass of atomized, unorganized readers of Bellamy's utopia, was showing an interest and capacity for organized activity. Under these circumstances, Nationalists could reasonably hope to move the Populists to their position or to recruit support from the latter's ranks for a Nationalist party. The imperatives of the Nationalists' new organizational and political commitment imposed upon them the need to defend their point of view, and, in defending it, reshape those ideas most at variance with the democratic values or

25. Cf. Richard Hofstadter, *Age of Reform*, pp. 48–75.

specific programmatic demands of their new friends. A small but revealing sign of the way in which the original utopian-authoritarian premises
of Nationalist ideology were silently set aside was the replacement early
in 1892 of the *New Nation*'s regular column, "The Nationalist Drift,"
with another feature, filling the same space, under the heading "Nationalism and Politics." The former column had topically illustrated Bellamy's theory of the inexorable, unconscious "drift" or evolution of society into the new collectivist order through the self-collectivization of
capital and the statification of economic enterprise. In contrast, the column on Nationalism and politics reported the activities of Nationalists
who were seeking various reforms and engaged in support of the People's
Party efforts. Within a few months whatever reluctance Bellamy and the
editors of the *New Nation* had felt at so closely linking Nationalism with
politics vanished: the new column underwent still another change of
title, emerging now as "Nationalism *in* Politics."

Along with a commitment to organized, partisan politics, Nationalists gradually and haltingly moved away from the contradictory belief in
a nonpartisan politics, above classes and interests. Bellamy and the Nationalists who had followed him down the primrose path of political
involvement ceased viewing their role as reconcilers of class and political
conflict through its absorption from above by an all-powerful bureaucratic state, and began to regard themselves and the Populists as representatives of the masses, locked in mortal conflict with plutocracy. No
longer did Bellamyites call upon the Populists to become a party above
class. Their cause, the *New Nation* wrote early in 1893, was "that of all
against the few, of the masses against the classes, the people against the
plutocrats." They boasted that "we have everywhere put the other side
on the defensive."[26] By the middle of 1893 matters became even clearer
for the Nationalists:

> The fusion of all the conservative elements in a compact opposition
> to socialist ideas, already so clearly foreshadowed in Germany, must
> soon take place in the politics of all nations of the civilized world.
> We are come to a crisis in human evolution, to a parting of the ways,
> to the necessity of a great decision as to the future of the race, on
> which there is room but for two opinions and two parties. The vote
> must be a 'yes' or 'no' one. We do not need to look over the sea for
> proof of this movement in politics. It is already distinctly foreshad-

26. *New Nation* 3, no. 1 (January 7, 1893).

owed, as we have constantly pointed out in these pages, by the attitude of the two old parties in this country toward the newly risen people's party.[27]

The attitude of the Nationalists toward the workers and their political role underwent a similar clarification: "In America labor is very restless, but the sentiment of independent political action is growing rapidly. West of the Mississippi River the workingmen have generally made common cause with the populists. That is, laborer and farmer have joined hands, as was done in New Zealand on a platform strongly nationalistic. East of the Mississippi, it may take a year or two to solidify the wage-workers upon any plan antagonistic to the old parties."[28] Even though its assessment of possible alliance between the urban working class and the farmers proved to be wrong, the new outlook toward independent political action implicitly ruled out the hope that social change could be expected to come from above by philanthropic action or acquiescence of the possessing classes. And in drawing the line between the farmers and workers on the one hand, and capitalists on the other, the Nationalists placed themselves however hesitantly on the side of the struggle of those "below" against those "above." Neither reason nor appeals to brotherhood had convinced the conservative classes of the necessity of change. Experience now taught the Nationalists that only a political organization—composed of "the people"—could undertake the task they had set for themselves.

New Politics for Old

The radicalization of the Nationalist movement and the strain toward a more democratic conception of socialism which presented such a striking departure from Bellamy's original political views is clearly illustrated by the devolution of the industrial army model and the Nationalists' response to the struggles of the organized labor movement during the 1890s. Throughout the first phase of Nationalism, approximately until early 1891, neither Bellamy nor his fellow Nationalists had argued for their collectivist vision on the grounds that it would strengthen and expand democratic institutions. Progress toward Bellamy's utopia lay in a different direction and not only were the Bellamyites hostile to such an idea, but even the very term "democracy" was noticeable by its absence

27. Ibid., vol. 3, no. 26 (July 1, 1893): 322.
28. Ibid., p. 327.

from Nationalist literature and propaganda, just as it had been in *Looking Backward*. The increasing frequency after 1891 with which Bellamy and the Nationalists justified the methods and goals of the movement as congruent with democracy—a trend which culminated in *Equality*, Bellamy's testament to the native socialist movement—was a further sign of the growing tension between the new and the old Nationalism in response to the Populist upsurge. Here was a new and powerful mass movement that had not existed when Bellamy and his followers launched their movement. Its organization together with the enormous political and social ferment which it produced filled the vacuum in which Bellamy's elitist politics had naturally flourished.

As early as March 1891, the *New Nation* felt called upon to deny emphatically that Nationalism was "paternalistic" or that, as some critics charged, it aimed at a despotic, bureaucratic social order similar to the "socialism" of the Incas in Peru. Rather they insisted that "nationalism presupposes a democratic state based upon the equal rights of all."[29] The bare assertion that Nationalism stood for "democracy" without specifying its meaning may have been no more than a verbal concession. Still, the mere fact that the Bellamyites felt compelled to answer in these terms rather than standing their ground with the industrial army as they had always done before was an index of the internal and external pressures to which Nationalism was being subjected.

Gradually, the idea of democracy rather than the mere ritualistic use of the term became a more prominent feature in the ideological defense of Nationalism as the formation of the People's Party proceeded and the Nationalists became more and more deeply involved in active political life. At the same time, of course, the authoritarian strain in Nationalism persisted. But it was attenuated to the degree that the pressures, both internal and external, led to the deepening of the commitment to democracy and, conversely, later tended to reassert itself when the prospect of radical change from below began to wane, making it seem unlikely that an effective solution to the problems confronting them could be found by this method.[30]

29. *New Nation* 1, no. 8 (March 21, 1891): 127.
30. It was precisely at those moments when the hard struggle to forge an instrument for the purpose of attaining reform goals through associative action yielded bitter fruit—most notably, in the 1890s, when the People's Party endorsed Bryan and free silver—that there occurred the resurgence of plebiscitarianism as a panacea together with the reassertion of the bureaucratic evolutionary perspective developed by Bellamy in *Looking Backward*.

Understandably, the question of democracy was raised in concrete terms by the Nationalists' program for statification of the economy and the organization of labor into the industrial army. Merely to assert, as they had, that there was an identity of interests between the state and the individual by definition obviously could not satisfy farmers or workers whom the Nationalists now attempted to win over. The state they saw and had to grapple with had little relation to the metaphysical organic state the Nationalists postulated.

More important, it could no longer satisfy the Nationalists themselves. In the first place, they began to find out very early in their attempts at "practical" reform from above that the existing state or "nation" in whose aggrandizement of power and ownership of the means of production they had placed their absolute faith was in the hands of the plutocracy and the conservative classes who were not about to allow *their* state to be used for attacking the foundations of private property. This discovery had at first reinforced the Nationalists' belief that the only solution to the problem was to do away with politics and representative government altogether—to erect the nonpolitical, bureaucratic state of Bellamy's utopia. Yet, when the Nationalists gave their support to the Populists, they took the fatal step of denying in practice their previous equation of statification and bureaucratization per se with progress toward the Nationalist utopia. For, although they had first joined the People's Party with the intention of making it into a Party above parties, they committed themselves implicitly to the position that it was necessary to win political power before the state nationalized industry and, indeed, before it could be allowed to do it. Statification of industry with the capitalists firmly in control of the state, the Nationalists came to realize, could mean the multiplication of the capitalists' power and the erection of a block to further progress.

Yet, to grant that statification was not a sufficient condition for the establishment of the future Nationalist society still left open the much more vexing question of who should have the political power that was to be taken away from the capitalists. As they moved deeper and deeper into the Populist movement, Nationalists had to answer this question: Did they propose to institute the domination of a new class of bureaucrats over an omnipotent state, as the critics of the Industrial Army had openly charged from the start? Or were they committed to a democratic government that would enable the people collectively to be the masters of the state and its officials? Without explicitly repudiating their former views, the meaning of Nationalism was reshaped to make it more consistent with their new commitments.

Ironically, the Nationalists' metaphysical belief in the state as the unqualified instrument of anticapitalist progress received its first and sharpest blow from the growing practice of using the state militias against striking workers in the 1890s. At the outset, the *New Nation*'s view of the labor question was no different than what it had been in the first years of the movement. In conservative fashion, it pointed to "the tremendous strain of the present situation" created by the discontent of the working classes, and warned that "unless the better elements of the nation unite betimes to carry out the social evolution by measures radical but also gradual and orderly, there will ere long come an outburst which will overwhelm the evil with the good."[31] Thomas Lake Harris called upon the "prudent wise" to reform before it was too late and the terror engulfed them. "There is not here to meet it, as in Europe," Harris warned, "the obedient force of millions of soldiery."[32]

In mid-1891, however, the *New Nation*, without explicitly departing from its conservative anticapitalist posture, criticized an officer of the New York State Militia who revealed that members of labor organizations were not permitted to join the militia.[33] The editors of the *New Nation* charged that union members were excluded from the militia because "it is chiefly for the purpose of repressing labor disturbances and over-awing the laboring classes that the militia is now sustained."[34] The militia's main function was to protect "the interests of capital in its collisions with labor, and the safeguarding of the community from riotous outbreaks resulting from industrial discontent."[35] In shocked response to these comments, a Vermont critic declared that the *New Nation*'s views had convinced him that Nationalists were, contrary to their claims, no different and no less subversive than the "[Johann] Most Anarchists"—here evoking the most dreaded contemporary symbol of bushy-bearded, bomb-throwing workers' conspiracies with which to compare the Nationalists.[36] The *New Nation* defended itself from this

31. *New Nation* 1, no. 8 (March 21, 1891): 123.
32. Ibid.
33. *New Nation* 1, no. 28 (August 8, 1891): 438; vol. 1, no. 42 (November 14, 1891): 661–662.
34. *New Nation* 1, no. 28 (August 8, 1891): 438.
35. Ibid.
36. *New Nation* 1, no. 42 (November 14, 1891): 661–662.

charge by pointing out that their criticism had been intended as a warning against the exacerbation of class warfare, but in fact the Vermont editor had correctly sensed that the Nationalists had departed from their earlier brand of anticapitalism and moved in a radical direction.

By the middle of 1892, the *New Nation* had placed itself on record against the use of militia in the Homestead strike, and openly sympathized with the strikers in their cause.[37] The Nationalists' criticism of the use of the militia was no longer couched in terms of an appeal to the upper and middle classes to show a philanthropic spirit, nor for the state to place the striking workers in an industrial army—a proposal that they had been quite willing to make in early 1891. The use of the militia was denounced as a capitalist attempt to crush the workers by using the machinery of the state. Comparing the Columbus Day Parade in New York in 1892 with repressive demonstrations in Czarist Russia or Bismarck's Berlin,[38] the *New Nation* contended that "the excessive presence of the military feature in these and other recent great public ceremonies has not been without intention."[39] In sharp contrast to the idealization of military discipline and order that had pervaded *Looking Backward* and which Bellamy had unhesitatingly restated for the benefit of the critics of the industrial army in 1889 and 1890, the Nationalists made one of their strongest and most radical attacks on the capitalists:

> The plutocracy which is taking possession of the republic cannot hope to maintain itself except by bayonet rule, and its policy is and will be the fostering of a spirit of militarism whereby the spirit of democracy may be antagonized and suppressed. For this end, as has of late been apparent, every occasion is sedulously taken advantage of to exalt the military idea and revive the barbaric traditions of the sword, which has no place or reason here, unless our experiment of popular government is to prove a failure.[40]

Old-line Nationalists reacted sharply to this radical heresy. Early in 1893, the *New Nation* acknowledged that "we are called to account for sympathizing with strikers." An "earnest nationalist since reading *Looking Backward* in 1889," wrote that he found himself bewildered and troubled by the change in line: "I think the *New Nation* desperately wrong—strangely blind—in its utterances last fall on strike questions. I

---

37. *New Nation* 2, no. 9 (July 16, 1892): 450, 453.
38. "The Shadow of the Man on Horseback," *New Nation* 2, no. 46 (November 12, 1892): 675.
39. Ibid.   40. Ibid.

have not the smallest pecuniary interest in them, but I wonder how any one can fail to see that the spirit that informs and dominates the Labor organizations is everywhere antipodal to public peace and private good will. Is it possible that hate and riot and murder are the apostolate of the Better Times to come?"[41] After sympathetically reviewing the details of the Homestead strike, the protest of the Tennessee miners against the lease-convict system, and other examples of the militia's use against striking workers, the *New Nation's* editors responded:

> Which side in any of these three controversies does he think Jesus Christ would have taken—that of the rich and powerful oppressor, breaking the laws of God and man with the support of the militia, or that of the toiler desperately fighting with the feeble aid of his labor union to protect the scanty wage on which his famlily depends to resist intolerable hardship?
>
> We cannot too strongly emphasize our disagreement with the opinion of our correspondent that the spirit of the labor organizations is inimical to the public welfare. From the point of view of nationalism the program of the labor unions is in many respects narrow and short-sighted, while the mistakes in leadership are many, but on the whole they seem to us to be fighting the common battle of us all against the advancing plutocracy, to which our learned and literary classes are too largely subservient.[42]

In the new conception of Nationalism, Bellamy's most highly prized contribution to American anticapitalism, the industrial army, underwent a sea-change no less drastic than the Nationalists' alliance with the Populists and their acceptance of partisan political action. Specific references to the industrial army began to decline in 1891 and disappeared almost altogether by the end of 1892. At first the model of the civil service began to be used interchangeably with the industrial army— with the clear understanding, however, that the former was merely the primitive form of the evolving bureaucratic, hierarchical, and nondemocratic organization of the future industrial army. But once again, what was at first primarily a verbal concession took on a new and different meaning as the inner contradictions of Nationalism and the impact of external events upon it gave rise to the second phase of the movement. Thus, in early 1892, the *New Nation* argued that the existence of the civil service was evidence on a "large scale" that "the national industrial army

---

41. *New Nation* 3, no. 4 (January 28, 1893): 50–51.
42. Ibid.

is not a dream of the future but a fact of the present."[43] Here, in the absence of any qualifications, and in the presence of firm assurances that the workers in nationalized industries would not be allowed to strike,[44] the comparison to the civil service was only an indication of the discomfort which the military model now created for the Nationalists.

By the middle of 1892, however, substantial changes in the content of the Nationalists' ideas on the organization of labor under Nationalism began to appear. Asked by a reader of the *New Nation* how managers would be selected under Nationalism, they replied:

> no one, so far as we know, has any peculiar and patented plan for the selection of managers of affairs under the new order [*sic!*]. There is no apparent necessity for such a plan. The basis of the new nation will be absolutely democratic, which of course will insure the selection of the heads of the nation by popular choice. In the selection of minor officials, chiefs, heads of departments and so on, there is no reason why the principles already recognized as proper to a reformed civil service should not be adequate.[45]

Here the Bellamyites had rejected the authoritarian-utopian idea of a ready-made plan to be handed down from above. For utopian spirits who had enormous pride in their plan with its every detail, this about-face was remarkable. Yet, now they simply threw out of the window the particular "patented plan" which Bellamy had advocated in *Looking Backward* and in numerous articles and speeches later. Nor was the election of the nation's leaders any more in keeping with Bellamy's and the Nationalists' earlier views.

By the end of 1892, coinciding not accidentally with the Nationalists' support of the People's Party and the idea of building a political party, the military model collapsed altogether. The *American Artisan, Tinner and House Furniture Journal* had angrily charged that "it would be difficult to point out an institution in whose organization and maintenance the principles of nationalism are better illustrated than in that of the military body known as the state militia."[46] The early Bellamy and the orthodox Nationalists who had proposed drafting mutinous railroad workers would have found little to argue with in this characterization of

43. *New Nation* 3, no. 6 (February 6, 1892): 84.
44. Ibid.
45. *New Nation* 2, no. 33 (August 6, 1892): 498–500.
46. "Nationalism Considered in the Light of a Very Odd Objection," *New Nation* 2, no. 42 (October 15, 1892).

their views. Now, however, reflecting the enormous shift which had taken place in the politics of Bellamyism, the *New Nation* agreed with the labor critics that military organization was based on "personal authority" and, even more sweepingly, asserted that military organization was "utterly opposed at all points to the democratic ideas of general liberty and equal rights."[47]

After this devastating criticism of their own earlier views—constituting, in effect, an admission that everything the critics of Nationalism had said about its antilibertarian nature was correct—the *New Nation* had no difficulty in stating that under Nationalism labor would be organized along the lines of the civil service and "in no respect of its military or militia service."[48] "It is the post office, not the militia service, the civil service and not the military service, in which the prototype of nationalism is to be found, and not even there by any means completely until civil service reform shall have had its perfect work . . ."[49] Although this formula contained an element of ambiguity, the *New Nation* made it clear by laying special stress upon democracy that the model of the civil service was not meant to be, as it had earlier been, only the embryonic form of the industrial army: "Under Nationalism the entire organization of the industrial system with its conditions and discipline *will be determined and modified at will by the most absolute democracy that ever existed*, one in which the voters will not only have nominally the same voice but also the same education and an absolute guaranteed economic equality with the mutual independence that implies"[50] (my emphasis).

With the repudiation of the military model of socialism and the affirmation of their belief in democracy, the Nationalists were free to discuss more explicitly than they had before the "panacea"—as Edward Everett Hale had contemptuously termed it—of universal suffrage which only a few years earlier Bellamy had found to be incompatible with an efficient, orderly, and harmonious collectivist society. A few weeks after denying that the military was the "prototype" for Nationalism, the first explicit discussion of elections under a Nationalist regime appeared in the *New Nation*. Managers of state enterprises, the editors announced, would be elected in the new order.[51] Not surprisingly this important concession occurred during the national elections of 1892, the first in

47. Ibid.   48. Ibid.   49. Ibid.   50. Ibid.
51. *New Nation* 2, no. 46 (November 12, 1892): 673.

which the People's Party participated. An election under Nationalism would of course not be characterized by the "heat and venom" of political struggles as they were conducted under capitalism. Instead, they "would be like a friendly council of people having absolutely the same interests but possibly different opinions as to how those interests might best be served."[52] The function of the limited "electorate" portrayed in *Looking Backward* had been restricted to the election, once every five years, of a president chosen from among the top ten bureaucrats who had reached their positions through merit. Now, however, without the slightest mention of this earlier view of politics and participation in self-government under the coming collectivist regime, the Nationalists began to back away. Prefacing the remarks with the caveat that their suggestion was "not necessarily involved in nationalism," the *New Nation* tacitly recognized the radical break with the form of Bellamy's utopia that was involved:

> It is to be hoped that men will in time cease the folly of electing a whole Congress or Parliament at a time, or a president for a fixed term. Eventually we may hope that every election district will, at its own option, change its representative, just as a business firm changes its agent on evidence of incapacity, by simply recalling him and sending a substitute.
>
> Who would employ an agent for a fixed term? He might as well turn over his business to him. The idea of fixed and irrevocable delegation of power to representatives, which underlies our election system, makes popular government a mere empty phrase.[53]

This willingness to specify definite mechanisms of self-government—including, of course, the sine qua non of democracy, universal exercise of the suffrage—provided the link between the people and the government or state in the absence of which previous statements of allegiance to "popular" or "democratic" government had been essentially rhetorical gestures with no real content, resting implicitly upon the mystical-authoritarian equation of the interests of the state with those of the individual. To this extent the statement may be viewed correctly as a significant and potentially definitive break with the old Nationalism. However, in the absence of any further specification of their acceptance of organized participation in the form of political parties under Nationalism, their view of democracy and popular government had a distinctly plebiscitarian ring. On the other hand, there was no call for the abolition

52. Ibid.   53. Ibid.

of political parties or for the illegalization of private associations as there had been earlier and, more important, the Nationalists were now committed to the organization of a partisan political movement. As long as the People's Party seemed to provide a viable alternative, the tension between the democratic and the plebiscitarian elements in Nationalism remained muted; with its collapse, however, the disillusionment with organized politics and parties and the renewed feelings of impotence gave new impetus to the Bellamyites' plebiscitarianism.

Even with these important qualifications, however, the tendency toward a more democratic conception of Nationalism—now frankly labelled by the Nationalists themselves as a "socialistic" current—continued to become more pronounced as the Nationalists sought to increase support for their ideas among the Populists and even among workers. The clubs had consciously excluded workers when the movement was first launched, but in 1893 Bellamy wrote an article on "why every workingman should be a Nationalist" for an official publication of the Boston Building Trades Council.[54] In it he appealed to workers on the grounds that the Nationalists stood for the extension of "popular government, the rule of the people, to industry and commerce."[55] In the same year the *New Nation* replied to the charges of a critic that Nationalism would create a giant bureaucratic organism that would snuff out individual liberty, by insisting:

> The government [under Nationalism] will be far more completely than now, the tool, the agent, and the creature of the people, inasmuch as the economic independence of every citizen and the equal grade of education it implies, will put an end to the power of designing men to pervert the suffrage of the masses through bribery, intimidation or misleading arguments. Does it seem likely . . . that citizens using their suffrage with such independence and intelligence as these, will permit a bureaucracy, with its head center at Washington, having absolute power over every individual, modified by no resource or appeal; a tyranny absolute and unqualified? Does it not seem likely on the other hand that an electorate so much more universal and intelligent than ever one was before, will find ways to protect the liberties and guard the rights of members as human rights and liberties were never protected and guarded before?[56]

54. Bellamy, "Why Every Workingman Should Be a Nationalist," reprinted in *Edward Bellamy Speaks Again!*, pp. 147–150.
55. Ibid., p. 147.
56. *New Nation* 2, no. 3 (January 21, 1893): 34.

Thus the utopian outlook of the author of the authoritarian collectivist plan that had been set forth in *Looking Backward* and the movement which had been organized for the purpose of guiding its introduction from above, had both been profoundly altered, paradoxically, by the very attempt to act in accordance with their ideology and by the success in attracting support for their cause. Even if they were still burdened with the original theoretical equation of "progress" with the bureaucratic statification of the economy—and far more important, even if they had injected this idea of socialism into the embryonic native socialist movement so that it would come to the fore again under different circumstances—Bellamy and the Nationalists had taken the first steps down one fork of the road in the direction of forging a political and moral link between collectivism and democracy.

Yet, in the absence of any firm theoretical basis for such a link it was possible for them to reverse their steps and to revert to the idea of a "socialism from above"—as many Nationalists did at the end of the decade when faced with the formation of the Socialist Party. Nevertheless to have reached the point of perceiving that democracy and socialism were inseparable was a sign that a new and contradictory element had been injected into the development of the indigenous socialist movement. A new and basically different standard for progress was now offered. The *New Nation* now rejected the "state socialism" of Bismarck which Nationalists had previously conceived of as the analogue of Nationalism: "Whether it is desirable from the socialist point of view to put more functions in the hands of a government depends absolutely and entirely on whether the government be a monarch or the people themselves. In the first case no socialist and no democrat would favor any extension of governmental functions. In the second case every socialist must favor such extension because the popular government of industry is the express ideal of socialism."[57]

While the democratic side of Nationalist ideology which characterized this second phase of the movement's existence grew roots strong enough to allow it to constitute an ineradicable part of the Nationalists' legacy to the native socialist movement, the authoritarian ideology did not simply vanish. On the contrary, the tension between these two sides of Nationalist ideology continued, albeit on a new and higher plane, as

57. *New Nation* 3, no. 23 (June 10, 1893): 286.

long as the link between democracy and socialism remained only an abstract ideal based on moral and/or pragmatic considerations alone. In the absence of any broader political and theoretical justification for asserting that the relationship between democracy and collectivization was necessary and not fortuitous—an outlook that required the conviction that only an organized democratic movement from below could achieve a democratic collectivist reorganization of society—Bellamy and the Nationalists could still easily slip back and forth, especially back, between utopian appeals to the philanthropic motives of the enlightened middle classes or capitalists to introduce socialism from above and, sometimes simultaneously, statements which rejected any such expectations as unrealistic. Following a bread riot by workers in New York in 1893, the *New Nation* echoed *Looking Backward* in blaming the outbreak upon "the educated and wealthy classes whose business it was and is to seek the social solution."[58] But the very next week, as if embarrassed by its own naiveté, the *New Nation* shed any illusions about the ruling class: "The people must work out their own salvation; beneficiaries of the present economic system will not do it for them."[59] Still uncertain, even in 1893, Nationalists could regard the order of a judge—whom they openly characterized as a tool of the capitalists—that striking workers be compelled to return to work because of the "public" nature of their occupation, as an opening wedge for Nationalism. Under pressure, it was argued, the owners of other businesses whose workers were similarly compelled to work would eventually "draw out and ask the government to run the factories itself."[60]

In short, without some deeper theoretical basis for rejecting salvation from above other than pragmatic or abstract moral grounds, the kernel of Bellamyism's utopianism remained untouched even though in practice the Nationalists attempted to build a popular political party from below to overthrow capitalism. Though the Nationalists had participated in a popular mass movement, they still thought it impractical to expect a majority of the people to consciously give their support to an organized democratic movement from below. A plebiscitarian methodology that would allow an elite like themselves to operate upon an atomized majority of passive people was the solution. Gronlund's conception

58. *New Nation* 3, no. 34 (August 26, 1893): 403.
59. *New Nation* 3, no. 35 (September 1, 1893).
60. *New Nation* 3, no. 13 (April 1, 1893): 165.

of introducing socialism from above by the use of a mass movement from below was thus only another practical form which utopianism could take, as was the turn by many Nationalists, after the People's Party debacle in 1896, toward "direct legislation" as the means for attaining a Nationalist society.[61] Only when the Nationalists and the embryonic native socialist movement that had learned its socialism from Bellamy and Gronlund committed themselves to a popular democratic movement and began to question whether or not salvation from above was an undesirable method because it was self-defeating, given the nature of their goal, was the stage set for a direct confrontation between the two souls of the American socialist movement.

Until that confrontation at the end of the century when the colonization wing of the Social Democracy of America split with the "political" socialists who formed the Social Democratic Party in 1898, this contest between the utopians, whose supporters lurched from plan to plan designed to achieve salvation from above, and the other elements who were convinced through their experiences that only a democratic movement from below could produce a democratic end, plagued the nascent socialist movement in one form or another.[62] This issue became the Rubicon over which native socialists had to pass before the formation of a modern democratic socialist movement was possible in the United States. The issue between "nonpartisan" and "partisan" socialists or between the communitarians and the politically oriented socialists were all expressions of this conflict. Gronlund's bitter charge, made in the late 1890s,

61. Quint, *Forging of American Socialism*, pp. 329–330.
62. Ira Kipnis, *The American Socialist Movement.* chs. 1 and 2. Bellamy's old Theosophist-Nationalist colleague, Cyrus Field Willard, who had dropped away with the founding of the *New Nation* and had rejected the involvement in politics which the new-style Nationalism represented, became deeply involved as one of the members of the commission selected by the Social Democracy of America "to put into practical operation the ideas of industrial cooperation as exemplified in Looking Backward." Soliciting Bellamy's support, he explained that "the idea of the colonization is to get control of one state politically at a time, so that we may have a commissary department and basis of supply established, which can then feed and supply the people who are willing to enlist in the movement." His description of the approach of the new movement recalled the military metaphors of the early days of Nationalism: "The organization of the Social Democracy is going on at lightning speed, and huge masses of men are being enrolled by competent and skillful officers, and it appears to be in fact the mustering of that industrial room [sic] which you portray." Above all, he assured Bellamy, "I want you and all the rest of the old boys in the Nationalist Movement to realize that this is only the culmination and realization of that movement." (Willard to Bellamy, August 3, 1897, Bellamy Papers)

that Bellamy had become a quasi-Marxist because he had seemed to suggest or imply in *Equality* that as a matter of necessity the working classes emancipate themselves is yet another illustration of this conflict.

Outside of the ranks of Nationalism, among the growing number of radicalized, semisocialistic native-born elements who were beginning to take socialism seriously, the same conflict raged. Eugene Debs, as leader of the Socialist Party, insisted upon the necessary relationship between the self-emancipation of the workers and the goal of a democratic socialism. Yet, Debs, in 1897, almost three years after his conversion to socialism, wrote to John D. Rockefeller asking him to finance the establishment of the Social Democracy of America's utopian colony in a western state to undermine the capitalist system.[63] The collapse of this attempt to build a "pocket edition of the new Jerusalem" also brought the demise of the last remnants of Debs' hopes for salvation from above and, concomitantly, reinforced his commitment to the idea which became the central refrain in his view of socialism throughout the next two decades: "I am not a Labor leader; I do not want you to follow me or anyone else; if you are looking for a Moses to lead out of this capitalist wilderness, you will stay right where you are. I would not lead you into this promised land if I could, because if I could lead you in, someone else would lead you out. *You must* use your heads as well as your hands, and get yourselves out of your present condition; as it is now the capitalists use your heads and your hands."[64] In this form or in its many variations over the next two decades, Debs' statement symbolized the break with the utopian-authoritarian socialism from above inaugurated by Bellamy and Gronlund which the founding of the Socialist Party represented.

Neither the Nationalist clubs nor Bellamy personally ever completely extricated themselves from the contradictory and fundamentally irreconcilable conflict between the authoritarian and the democratic ideological elements with which they had started. Nor did they ever satisfactorily solve the problem of finding an appropriate vehicle for organized political action as socialists. Well before the native socialist movement wrenched itself free of its ties with Populism and rejected the last element of utopian socialism from above in the form of the Social Democracy of America's colonization plan, and committed themselves to build-

63. Ray Ginger, *The Bending Cross*, p. 201.
64. Debs, *Debs: His Life, Writings and Speeches*, (1908), p. 71.

ing a working-class movement, the clubs disappeared. Bellamyism, however, did not disappear nor did it cease to be a distinct political and
ideological current operating for the most part on the left wing of the
People's Party and among the urban middle-class reform movements that
began to emerge as an important force in the second half of the 1890s.[65]

The dissemination of Nationalist politics, aimed for the most part
at a Populist audience, was carried on by the Ruskin Colony's *Coming
Nation* throughout the remainder of the decade. The *Coming Nation*'s
efforts to keep Bellamyism alive were supplemented by the *American
Fabian* whose much smaller circulation—certainly fewer than the
100,000 subscribers which the *Coming Nation* was reported to have—
nevertheless reached an audience of urban intellectuals primarily.[66]

Bellamy carried on the publication of the *New Nation* until 1894,
when the decline of the organized clubs combined with economic difficulties brought on by the depression of 1893 and his own failing health,
forced him to suspend publication. He lived to write *Equality*, the sequel
to *Looking Backward*, but died shortly after its publication. Ironically, his
death occurred just as the native authoritarian-utopian current whose
bureaucratic vision of "socialism" he had inspired and led came to a
parting of the ways with the "political" socialism of Morris Hillquit,
Debs, and Victor Berger.[67]

It is impossible to say how Bellamy would have responded to the
Socialist Party and to the perspective of building a mass political party
committed formally to class struggle and to winning of political power to
create an egalitarian socialist society. The collapse of the People's Party
in 1896 was a critical turning point in the development of the nascent
socialist movement and of leftward-moving labor elements such as Debs,
all of whom, to one degree or another, had regarded the Populists as
potentially capable of becoming a major opposition party representing an
alliance between farmers and urban workers.[68] Bellamy reacted to the
demise of the Populists as an independent political party with sharp
disillusionment—though he did not despair of politics and revert to his
original views as did the *Coming Nation*. Instead he urged Henry Dema-

65. Quint, *Forging of American Socialism*, chs. 5–9.
66. See Quint, *Forging of American Socialism*, ch. 6 on J. A. Wayland and the *Coming
Nation*; on the Fabians, see pp. 120–124.
67. Kipnis, *American Socialist Movement*, ch. 1.
68. Ginger, *The Bending Cross*, pp. 162–164, 187–191.

rest Lloyd and other like-minded middle class socialists to consider the formation of a new, more radical party.[69] But Willard, Gronlund, Lloyd, Pomeroy, and others clustered about the utopian-colonization wing of the Social Democracy of America turned back to the conception of socialism from above with which Nationalism had begun. Just as the Fabians, particularly Shaw, became even more bitterly opposed to independent working-class politics and more violently antidemocratic at the end of the century when they saw their chances of leading the movement slipping away, so too the reactionary side of Bellamyism became most prominent when it had become plain that many of the individuals, groups, and publications which constituted the ill-defined movement of native-born, English-speaking socialists and radicals were in the process of leaving behind the authoritarian collectivist version of socialism taught in *The Cooperative Commonwealth* and *Looking Backward*.

Gronlund's response, *The New Economy*,[70] published in 1898, contained his most consistently antidemocratic ideas. Advocating the colonization scheme of the Social Democracy and bitterly criticizing the "partisan socialism" of Debs and Hillquit, Gronlund called himself a "collectivist" rather than a socialist, because he did not accept the idea, now proclaimed by the new socialist movement, that the working class could emancipate itself.

Henry Demarest Lloyd, deeply and genuinely torn between his democratic instincts and a deep-going pessimism as to the possibility of democracy, died in 1903 without joining the Socialist Party. Lloyd's refusal to join the party stemmed from the fact that by the end of the century he had resolved the tension in his own political views in favor of a nonpartisan, bureaucratic collectivist social order similar to Bellamy's industrial army. Under Lloyd's socialism a permanent ruling bureaucracy would replace all democratically elected officials and representative bodies. This reassertion of Nationalism's bureaucratic anticapitalism made membership in the Socialist party too inconsistent an act for Lloyd.[71]

The disjunction between the utopian socialism of the 1890s and the new socialism of the Socialist Party produced a revealing confrontation

69. Quint, *Forging of American Socialism*, p. 245.
70. Gronlund, *New Economy*.
71. On Lloyd's refusal to join the Socialist Party see Chester McArthur Destler, *Henry Demarest Lloyd and the Empire of Reform* (1963), pp. 449–451.

between one of Bellamy's loyal supporters, Eltweed Pomeroy, and the editor of the semiofficial theoretical journal of the Socialist Party, Algie M. Simons.[72] Pomeroy's Nationalism had early taken a plebiscitarian turn. He had devoted himself through the 1890s to promoting direct legislation as the road to Nationalism by which a small minority of educated, middle-class persons could lead the docile masses into social-ism or Nationalism from above.[73] In 1902, Pomeroy explained that though he had been a "warm friend of Edward Bellamy" and a contribu-tor to his paper, the *New Nation*, as well as a contributor to the host of native, non-Marxist, socialistic periodicals which appeared in the 1890s, he could not join the Socialist Party, as Simons and his fellow former Nationalist, Gaylord Wilshire, and others in the new party had urged. In fact, Pomeroy admitted, he could hardly call himself a socialist any longer because the "partisan" socialists in the S.P. had defined socialism as "nothing but Marxism, revolutionary, class-conscious socialism" which radically altered its commonly understood meaning.[74] By reject-ing Bellamy's discovery that the manual workers would have to be led into socialism from above by the educated and cultured middle classes, Pomeroy argued, the S.P. had forfeited the support of socialists like himself who had been reared in Bellamy's teachings. For a true Bellamy-ite socialist, Pomeroy insisted, there could be "no salvation coming from the working classes." The workers could only "assent to the plans of others . . . they will be the ciphers which will multiply the force of the leaders."[75] The Socialist Party had repudiated the Chicopee doctrine.

Algie Simons responded by challenging Pomeroy's right to call him-self a socialist merely because of his association in the previous decade with Bellamy and the embryonic socialist movement. It was as absurd, Simons wrote, as it would be if a student claimed the right to be regarded as a biologist on the grounds that he had read Linnaeus, Cuvier, and Aggassiz, but was as unfamiliar with the theory of evolution and the work of Darwin as Pomeroy was with Marxism and modern scientific social-

72. Eltweed Pomeroy, "Why I Do Not Join the Socialist Party," *International Social-ist Review* 2, no. 9 (March 1902): 641–648; A. M. Simons, "Reply to Mr. Pomeroy," ibid., pp. 649–653.
73. Quint, *Forging of American Socialism*, p. 249; Pomeroy's views can be followed in the pages of the *Direct Legislation Record*.
74. Pomeroy, "Why I Do Not Join," p. 643.
75. Ibid., p. 644.

ism.[76] Simons did not recognize the double-edged meaning that could be read into his analogy. For by stressing the disjunction in the tradition of American socialism that the founding of the Socialist Party represented, Simons tacitly admitted that the anticapitalist current which stemmed from the Bellamyites had sired the movement to which he now laid sole claim as a "scientific" socialist. The very sharpness of Simons' denial of any relationship between Pomeroy's socialism and that of the Socialist Party can be seen not only as an involuntary recognition of the former's paternity, but also as indicative of the degree to which the new socialism had been and still was influenced by its utopian predecessor.

Equality

Slowly dying of tuberculosis, Bellamy worked feverishly during the last years of his life to complete his last political will and testament, *Equality*.[77] The demise of the *New Nation* left him free to retire from the active political involvement that had reshaped his life and political views and to ponder the meaning of the experiences and events that had followed the publication of *Looking Backward*. Nominally a sequel to *Looking Backward*, written because he had not been able to get into his first book "all I wished to say on the subject," and because "what was left out of it has loomed up as so much more important than what it contained,"[78] the slight fictional form of the utopian novel now disappeared almost entirely. In its place appeared a lengthy, dense tract in which Bellamy presented the political views which had emerged out of his personal evolution from an isolated utopian to a leader and spokesman for an American brand of socialism. Reading it reveals not only how much Bellamy and his ideas had changed from the mid-1880s when *Looking Backward* had been composed, but serves too as an indication of the impact of the great political upheaval and social ferment of the nineties on the emergent native socialist movement.

On one level, *Equality* is Bellamy on Bellamy: not only the Bellamy of *Looking Backward*, but the entire tradition of conservative political thought in which the authoritarian antidemocratic perspective and proposals of *Looking Backward* and the early Nationalist movement had been

76. Simons, "Reply," *International Socialist Review* 2, p. 650.
77. Bellamy, *Equality*. On Bellamy's last years see Morgan, *Edward Bellamy*, pp. 67–71; Bowman, *The Year 2000*, pp. 138–152.
78. Bellamy, *Equality*, p. vii.

firmly rooted. "My experiences since I waked up in this year 2000,"
said Bellamy in the voice of his protagonist, Julian West, "might be
said to have consisted of a succession of instantaneous mental readjust-
ments of a revolutionary character, in which what had formerly seemed
evil to me had become good, and what had seemed wisdom had become foolishness."[79]

In a draft preface which he abandoned, but whose tone and specific
message is contained in the text of *Equality*, Bellamy confirmed the
radicalization of his views. "From the time human beings began to live
together in society," he proclaimed, "they have been, so far as we know,
divided into rich and poor, those who have and those who have not.
This division has always been the real basis of the social organization. . . . To the rich of all lands and nations, all ages, all civilizations
have been the same . . . for in all they have been the masters and have
enjoyed everything that was best and most under the conditions of the
place and period. To the poor, likewise, have all climes and epochs and
institutions been the same in substantial respects, for everywhere and
always they have been the footstools and burden bearers."[80] Now, however, Bellamy found "a most wonderful change has come over the world
in these latter days. By common agreement the largest and most significant fact of the present time is the worldwide agitation, organized and
unorganized, material, intellectual and moral, against the ancient and
existing system of inequality in the distribution of work and wealth, and
the demand for more equal social arrangements." Why, he asked, was
there so suddenly the "tremendous urgency and volume to the cry of the
oppressed and disinherited masses? . . . Why . . . has the revolt waited
so long and why has it come just at this time of all times?" Bellamy's
answer to his own question demonstrated the degree to which he had
departed from the fearful elitist posture of *Looking Backward*: "It is because, thanks to the modern diffusion of knowledge, for the first time
since men were on earth, the masses of the race have, during the last
century in the more advanced countries, begun to be rational beings,
capable of intelligent thought and united action."[81]

Repeatedly, although still frequently contradictorily, Bellamy returns to this newly acquired understanding of the role which the masses of

79. Ibid., p. 211.
80. Original Preface to *Equality*, typescript, pp. 2–3, Bellamy Papers.
81. Ibid., pp. 3–4.

ordinary people are capable of playing in the new democratic epoch. In the most effective segment of the book, the "Parable of the Water Tank," which long remained a staple of socialist propaganda in the twentieth century, he tells the oppressed people: "Now, behold the way out of this bondage! Do ye for yourselves that which is done by the capitalists— namely, the ordering of your labor, and the marshalling of your bands, and the dividing of your tasks. So shall ye have no need at all of the capitalists."[82] And in what can only be understood as a repudiation of his own approach in *Looking Backward*, Bellamy observes that "of course . . . the idea of an integrated economic system coordinating the efforts of all for the common welfare, which is the basis of the modern state, is as old as philosophy. As a theory it dates back to Plato at least, . . . for it is a conception of the most natural and obvious order. Not, however, until popular government had been made possible by the diffusion of intelligence was the world ripe for the realization of such a form of society. Until that time the idea, like the waiting for a fit incarnation, must remain without social embodiment. Selfish rulers thought of the masses only as instruments for their own aggrandizement, and *if they interested themselves in a more exact organization of industry it would only have been with a view of making that organization the means of a more complete tyranny*. Not until the masses themselves became competent to rule was a serious agitation possible or desirable for an economic organization on a co-operative basis" (my emphasis).[83]

Singled out for special attack is the conservative-Tory reformer tradition of opposition to universal suffrage and mass democracy to which Bellamy himself had subscribed in *Looking Backward*. During the period of "negative democracy," before the extension of the democratic idea to the economy, the corrupt and "plutocratic subversion" of government had led many of Bellamy's contemporaries to go "so far as to say that the democratic experiment had proved a failure when, in point of fact, it seems that no experiment in democracy, properly understood, had as yet ever been so much as attempted."[84] Before the revolution which overthrew the older order, "the money kings took no pains to disguise the fullnesses of their conviction that the day of democracy was passing and the dream of equality nearly at an end. As the popular

---

82. Bellamy, *Equality*, p. 202.
83. Ibid., p. 331.   84. Ibid., p. 21.

feeling in America had grown bitter against them they had responded
with frank indications of their dislike of the country and disgust with its
democratic institutions."[85] "Our rankest Tories," observes Julian West,
argued that "from all who had not the economic stake the suffrage should
be taken away. There were not a few of my friends who maintained that
some such limitation of the suffrage was needed to save the democratic
experiment from failure."[86] "That is to say," replies Dr. Leete, "it was
proposed to save the democratic experiment by abandoning it. . . . The
primal principle of democracy is the worth and dignity of the individual.
That dignity, consisting in the quality of human nature, is essentially the
same in all individuals, and therefore equality is the vital principle of
democracy. . . . The raising up of the human being without respect of
persons is the constant and only rational motive of the democratic policy.
Contrast with this conception that precious notion of your contemporaries as to restricting suffrage. Recognizing the material disparities in
the circumstances of individuals, they proposed to conform the rights
and dignities of the individual to his material circumstances instead of
conforming the material circumstances to the essential and equal dignity
of the man."[87]

   If in *Looking Backward* democracy is conspicuous by its terminological and, more importantly, conceptual absence, in the new revised order
which the Bellamy who had passed through the political fires of the
1890s now proposed, it takes the center of the stage although not without
a plebiscitarian overcast and other flaws. Yet its very presence and the
strength of Bellamy's newly found conviction permeate the argument for
a collectivist society in *Equality*. "Democracy," Dr. Leete explains, "logically meant the substitution of popular government for the rule of the
rich in regulating the production and distribution of wealth, . . ." The
new society was plainly "an inference from the idea of popular government" and "one which the masses of people," whom the earlier Bellamy
had feared as much as the "rankest Tory," "were so directly interested in
carrying out."[88] Even more striking by contrast for a utopian planner
(whose scheme and the movement which it had inspired had been so
concerned to avoid any hint of a connection between his conservative
anticapitalist politics and those of the radical democrats) is the explana-

85. Ibid., p. 316.   86. Ibid., p. 25.   87. Ibid., pp. 25–26.
88. Ibid., p. 17.

tion that "the revolutionary party in the great Revolution . . . carried on the work of agitation and propaganda under various names more or less grotesque and ill-fitting as political party names were apt to be, but the one word democracy, with its various equivalents and derivatives, more accurately and completely expressed, explained, and justified their method, reason, and purpose than a library of books could do."[89]

In *Equality*'s new order, "the people hold the reins" of power through elections supplemented by referenda and immediate recall. The symbol of the government of the future is a self-steering windmill. "The mill stands for the machinery of administration, the wind that drives it symbolizes the public will, and the rudder that always keeps the vane of the mill before the wind, however suddenly or completely the wind may change, stands for the method by which the administration is kept at all times responsive and obedient to every mandate of the people, though it be but a breath."[90] And yet, as in *Looking Backward*, parties and forms of organized political association are omitted, with a kind of instant system of polling democracy made possible by the new means of communication, taking their place. "Our representative bodies, corresponding to your former Congresses, Legislatures, and Parliaments, are under this system reduced to the exercise of the functions of what you used to call congressional committees" whenever it seems necessary. "The people not only nominally but actually govern. We have a democracy in fact."[91] Thus the fear of organized, selfish interests which had animated Bellamy's earlier views, had not disappeared. With the "indefeasible, unchangeable, economic equality" of the new system, in fact, it would be possible, Bellamy notes in an aside reflecting a reversion to his older views, "to safely turn over to a selected body of citizens the management of the public affairs for their lifetime. The reason we do not is that we enjoy the exhilaration of conducting the government of affairs directly."[92] Ambiguous and flawed as Bellamy's new view of democracy may have been, however, his political views had clearly taken a quantum leap away from the starkly antidemocratic politics of *Looking Backward*.

In other important respects, however, Bellamy remained true to his middle-class outlook and important elements of the original authoritarian-utopian politics of *Looking Backward* remained in *Equality*. Refusing to

89. Ibid., p. 22.   90. Ibid., pp. 273, 274–275.
91. Ibid., pp. 274–275.   92. Ibid., p. 275.

term his new system "socialism"—although it was in most respects identical to the garden-variety reformist currents within the contemporary socialist movement—Bellamy couched his ideas in conservative terms designed to appeal to middle-class persons still unwilling to call themselves socialists because of its radical associations. "Public capitalism,"[93] Bellamy proclaimed, would replace private capitalism, and the Revolution which would take place would be "an assertion and vindication" of the right of property "on a scale never before dreamed of" through the assurance to each citizen of "a large, equal, and fixed share in the total national principal and income."[94] Certainly to be able to say, with Dr. Leete, that "the Revolution made us all capitalists and the idea of the dividend has driven out that of the stipend" would have appealed to middle-class elements for whom the metaphors of private property were more congenial than those of collective owmerhsip.[95] The terminology reflected Bellamy's unwillingness and inability to understand or to come to terms with the necessity of building a socialist movement from below based on the organized working class.

Although the centerpiece of *Looking Backward*, the industrial army, vanishes in *Equality* (with one exception) to make way for a system of "universal industrial service" in which the system of military organization is not involved, there are no strikes mentioned and certainly no room for independent trade unions of workers. At best, the absolute freedom to move from job to job together with the now restored suffrage gives the individual worker "indirect" control over the conditions of his labor.[96] More ominous, however, is the punishment meted out to those who refuse to do their industrial service. They are not compelled to work, but "as in your day soldiers would not serve with skulkers, but drummed cowards out of the camp," Dr. Leete explains, "so would our workers refuse the companionship of persons seeking to evade their civic duty."[97] In addition to this social pressure and the denial of the right to share in society's material benefits, any adult who "deliberately and fixedly" refuses "to render his quota of service in any way, either in a chosen occupation, or in failure to choose, in an assigned one," would be sent to a "reservation expressly prepared for such persons, corresponding a little perhaps with the reservations set apart for such Indians in your

93. Ibid., p. ix.   94. Ibid., p. 120.   95. Ibid., p. 91.
96. Ibid., pp. 55–56.   97. Ibid., p. 41.

day as were unwilling to accept civilization."[98] In the absence of any discussion of strikes or forms of worker organization and the denial of any system of workers' control, it seems clear that Bellamy envisioned this as one way of solving the strike problem—although in the more perfect order of things, of course, strikes were simply not to occur.

Another aspect of Bellamy's lingering authoritarianism, as well as his racist views, manifested itself in the one point at which the industrial army reappears in *Equality*. "The population of recent slaves was in need of some sort of industrial regimen, at once firm and benevolent, administered under conditions which should meanwhile tend to educate, refine, and elevate its members. These conditions the new order met with ideal perfection. The centralized discipline of the national industrial army, depending for its enforcement not so much on force as on the inability of any one to subsist outside of the system of which it was a part, furnished just the sort of control—gentle yet resistless—which was needed by the recently emancipated bondsman."[99] Here the industrial army reappears to play its original civilizing role for the masses as in *Looking Backward*, although one that formerly had not been limited to the blacks. Now, however, Bellamy had discovered that the white workers for whom he had intended the same treatment were "relatively . . . further advanced,"[100] and not in need of military discipline. But to have admitted the theoretical possibility and, in this case to have made the practical proposal for reincarnating the industrial army, demonstrates the ambiguity that remained at the heart of Bellamy's new collectivist politics.

Even more revealing and far more important in understanding Bellamy's ultimate inability to transcend his authoritarian utopianism, however much his new views represented a shift in the opposite direction, is his portrait of the organized working class and the conception of the way in which the transition to the new society will take place. In his portrait of the organized workers and the expression of his attitude toward strikers, once again Bellamy's views in *Equality* are in part best seen as a commentary on the old Bellamy and on the conservative middle-class tradition out of which *Looking Backward*'s authoritarian solution to the "labor question" had arisen. As the *New Nation* had done in its last years, Bellamy condemned strongly the capitalist government's use of the mi-

98. Ibid.   99. Ibid., pp. 364–365.   100. Ibid., p. 365.

litia and the army for crushing the workers' strikes. The United States was fast "becoming a government by bayonets."[101] As for the strikers themselves, Bellamy, who had called for the crushing of the 1877 strike, noted that "even people who thought they sympathized with the working class shook their heads at the mention of strikes, regarding them as calculated rather to hinder than help the emancipation of labor."[102] But Bellamy's fundamental contempt for the workers had not changed: "The strikers, like the workingmen generally, were, as a rule, ignorant, narrow-minded men, with no grasp of larger questions, and incapable of so great an idea as the overthrow of an immemorial economic order."[103] Nevertheless, the strikers' "pathetic demonstratons of passive resistance for fifty years" aroused the world to the existence of an "industrial question." "It was . . . those despised, ridiculed, cursed, and hooted fellows . . . who with their perpetual strikes would not let the world rest till their wrong, which was also the whole world's wrong, was righted. Once more had God chosen the foolish things of this world to confound the wise, the weak things to confound the mighty."[104] Fortunately in the revolutionary period many "cultured men and women . . . with voice and pen espoused the workers' cause, and showed them the way out." The ignorant but heroic workers then were to be honored as "protomartyrs of the industrial republic of to-day" not because of their efforts on their own behalf but because their strikes "operated to impress upon the people the intolerable wickedness and folly of private capitalism."[105] The labor unions "after twenty-five years of fighting had only demonstrated their utter inability to maintain, much less improve the condition of the workingman."[106]

Under the circumstances it was not from the working class that the revolution to overthrow capitalism would come. "The net result of the industrial civil war," Bellamy concluded, "had been to prove to the dullest working-men the hopelessness of securing amelioration of their lot by class action or organization, or indeed of even maintaining it against encroachments. After all this unexampled suffering and fighting, the wage-earners found themselves worse off than before."[107] Nor was it from the farmers, "the other great division of the insurgent masses," that salvation would come. "Their leagues, although controlling votes by the

101. Ibid., p. 319.   102. Ibid., p. 207.   103. Ibid., p. 208.
104. Ibid., p. 209.   105. Ibid.   106. Ibid., p. 327.
107. Ibid., p. 328.

million, had proved even more impotent if possible than the wage-earners' organizations to help their members."[108]

Inexorably, Bellamy was forced by his conclusion that there was no class capable of carrying out the transition, to fall back on the version of his theory of how capitalism might be overthrown from above, without the organization of a mass movement, which had emerged in the course of the second phase of the Nationalist movement. The answer lay in the theory of creating nuclei of the new order within capitalism. With the prolonged economic and social crisis caused by capitalism would come a "Great Revival," "a tide of enthusiasm for the social, not personal, salvation, and for the establishment in brotherly love of the kingdom of God on earth which Christ bade men hope and work for."[109] In time the new enthusiasm would sweep the entire population, and in the end, in true utopian fashion, even "the greater and better part of the capitalists" would join "with the people in completing the installation of the new order" which men of all classes would "come to see was to redound to the benefit of all alike."[110] The actual overthrow of capitalism would be by a "flanking operation," "one in which an army, instead of attacking its antagonist directly in front, moves round one of his flanks in such a way that without striking a blow it forces the enemy to leave his position."[111] The tactic would be to "municipalize and nationalize various quasi-public services" which would prove the "superior simplicity, efficiency, and humanity of public over private management of economic undertakings."[112] More important, however, this "partial process of nationalization" would "prepare a body of public employees sufficiently large to furnish a nucleus of consumers when the Government should undertake the establishment of a general system of production and distribution on a non-profit basis."[113] Gradually the entire economy would be absorbed into the nationalized industry and the revolution would be complete.

Thus, despite the radical break with his own past and that of the Nationalist movement which the significantly more democratic ideas presented in *Equality* represented, Bellamy failed to be able to conceive of a genuine movement from below, certainly not one based on the workers, through which the transition to the new society might be

---

108. Ibid.   109. Ibid., p. 340.   110. Ibid., p. 345.
111. Ibid., p. 352.   112. Ibid., pp. 353–354.   113. Ibid., p. 354.

achieved. In the end, *Equality*'s vision was deeply divided between the old and the new Bellamyism, between the authoritarian utopian soul of *Looking Backward* and the new, democratic spirit of the emergent socialist movement of the 1890s. The major legacy of Bellamyism, one that became part of the tide of antidemocratic reaction that flowed into the twentieth century, was its conception of socialism from above and its vision of a bureaucratically organized collectivist society. Yet, Bellamy's attempt, faltering and ultimately unsuccessful, to find that historic fork in the road which led in the direction of a more democratic idea of socialism, represented another, much smaller, part of his legacy also.

SELECTED BIBLIOGRAPHY

Note on Sources

The following bibliography includes only the more important sources used in the preparation of this study. Extensive and detailed bibliographies listing all of the books and articles by Bellamy, individual Nationalists, and contemporary critics, together with the numerous articles, reviews, and books which deal directly and indirectly with Bellamy and the Nationalists, may be found in Arthur E. Morgan, *Edward Bellamy* (New York: Columbia University Press, 1944), and Sylvia E. Bowman, *The Year 2000: A Critical Biography of Edward Bellamy* (New York: Bookman Associates, 1958). Bowman has identified the articles which Bellamy contributed to the *Springfield Daily Union* and these are listed in her bibliography. A later bibliographic essay by Bowman, "Edward Bellamy (1850–1898)," in *American Literary Realism*, no. 1, Fall 1967, pp. 7–12, contains additional references of importance. Kenneth M. Roemer's *The Obsolete Necessity: America in Utopian Writings, 1888–1900* (Kent, Ohio: Kent State University Press, 1976), provides an excellent annotated bibliographic guide to studies of utopian ideas as well as a detailed listing and summary of the vast outpouring of utopian literature stimulated by *Looking Backward*. No attempt has been made here to duplicate these sources except to list some of the more important articles which have appeared subsequently. Together with Bowman et al., *Edward Bellamy Abroad: An American Prophet's Influence* (New York: Twayne, 1962), which contains an extensive bibliography and references to sources concerning the worldwide reception accorded Bellamy's *Looking Backward*, and Everett McNair, *Edward Bellamy and the Nationalist Movement* (Milwaukee: Fitzgerald, 1957), these books constitute the basic secondary sources for any study of Bellamy and the Nationalists and ones that are the more valuable because of the extensive quotations and detailed citations which are utilized. Arthur E. Morgan was responsible for gathering together not only Bellamy's private papers and, in many cases, translating Bellamy's almost indecipherable handwriting into typescript, but also a vast mass of other materials, including letters, clippings, reviews, and a number of theses and other unpublished studies, the most valuable of which is Mason A. Green, "Edward Bellamy: A Biography of the Author of 'Looking Backward'." These materials were deposited in the Houghton Library of Harvard University, with additional copies also placed in the collection of the Huntington Library and Antioch College, where Morgan was president for many years. All references to manuscript material, except where otherwise noted, are from the Houghton Library, and have been given the shortened designation of Bellamy Papers. The standard scholarly edition of *Looking Backward*, edited with an extremely insightful introduction by John L. Thomas, has been published by the

John Harvard Library (Cambridge: Harvard University Press, 1967). Thomas uses the second edition, published by Ticknor, annotating it with what are, for the most part, minor emendations taken from the first edition, although in some cases the changes which Bellamy made in the few months between the two editions are of substantial interest. I have chosen, however, because of its wide availability, to cite the Modern Library edition of *Looking Backward*, which is also based on the second edition. The pioneering and still unmatched scholarly treatment of the emergence of the socialist movement in America after the Civil War and of the impact of the Bellamyites on the emergent socialist movement of the 1890s is Howard Quint's, *The Forging of American Socialism* (Columbia: University of South Carolina Press (1953), and I have drawn upon it extensively in trying to pick my way through the maze of organizations and individuals constituting the movement in this period.

Periodicals
American Fabian (Boston, New York). Vol. 1, no. 1, January 1895; vol. 5, no. 7, July 1899.
Coming Nation (Tennessee City, Tenn., Ruskin, Tenn.). Nos. 1–512, April 29, 1893–December 26, 1903.
The Nationalist (Boston). Vol. 1–3, May 1889–April 1891.
New Nation (Boston). Vol. 1, no. 1, 1891; vol. 4, no. 5, 1894.
Springfield Daily Union (Massachusetts).

Books, Articles, and Miscellaneous Publications
Aaron, Daniel. *Men of Good Hope: A Story of American Progressives.* New York: Oxford University Press, 1951.
Ashby, N. B. *The Riddle of the Sphinx.* Des Moines: Industrial Publishing, 1890.
Barkin, Kenneth. "A Case Study in Comparative History: Populism in Germany and America." In Herbert Bass, ed., *The State of American History*, pp. 373–404. Chicago: Quadrangle, 1971.
Bell, Daniel. "The Background and Development of Marxian Socialism in the United States." In Donald Drew Egbert and Stow Persons, eds., *Socialism and American Life*. Vol. 1, pp. 213–406. Princeton: Princeton University Press, 1952.
Bellamy, Edward. *Edward Bellamy Speaks Again!* Kansas City: Peerage Press, 1937.
———. *Equality.* New York: D. Appleton-Century, 1897.
———. *Looking Backward: 2000–1887.* New York: Modern Library, 1917.
———. "The Religion of Solidarity." In Joseph Schiffman, ed., *Edward Bellamy: Selected Writings on Religion and Society.* New York: Liberal Arts Press, 1955.
———. *Talks on Nationalism.* Chicago: Peerage Press, 1938.
Beringause, Arthur F. *Brooks Adams: A Biography.* New York: Knopf, 1955.
Berneri, Marie Louise. *Journey Through Utopia.* Boston: Beacon Press, 1950.

Bernstein, Edward. *Ferdinand Lassalle: As a Social Reformer*. Translated by Eleanor Marx Aveling. New York: Scribner's, 1893.

Besant, Annie. *The Changing World and Lectures to Theosophical Students*. London: The Theosophical Publishing Society, 1910.

————. Review of *The Cooperative Commonwealth*. In *Our Corner* 6 (Sept. 1, 1885): 162–167.

————. *Theosophy*. London: T. C. and E. C. Jack, n.d. [c. 1920s].

Boudin, Louis B. *The Theoretical System of Karl Marx*. Chicago: Charles H. Kerr, 1907.

Bowman, Sylvia E. *The Year 2000: A Critical Biography of Edward Bellamy*. New York: Bookman Associates, 1958.

————et al. *Edward Bellamy Abroad: An American Prophet's Influence*. New York: Twayne, 1962.

Bruce, Robert. *1877: Year of Violence*. Cleveland: Bobbs Merrill, 1959.

Burbank, David T. *Reign of the Rabble: The St. Louis General Strike of 1877*. New York: Augustus Kelley, 1966.

Burnham, Walter Dean. *Critical Elections and the Mainsprings of American Politics*. New York: Norton, 1970.

Calverton, V. F. *The Man Inside: Being the Record of the Strange Adventures of Allen Steele Among the Xulus*. New York: Scribner's, 1936.

Caute, David. *The Fellow-Travellers: A Postscript to the Enlightenment*. New York: Macmillan, 1973.

Chalmers, W. E. "Laurence Gronlund." *Dictionary of American Biography* 8:14–15.

Cochran, Thomas C. and William Millar. *The Age of Enterprise: A Social History of Industrial America*. New York: Macmillan, 1950. Rev. ed. New York: Harper Brothers, 1961.

Corey, Lewis. *The Crisis of the Middle Class*. New York: Covici-Friede, 1935.

————. *The Decline of American Capitalism*. New York: Covici-Friede, 1934.

————. "The Middle Class." In R. Bendix and S. M. Lipset, eds., *Class, Status and Power*, pp. 371–380. Glencoe: Free Press, 1953.

Coser, Lewis and Irving Howe. "Authoritarians of the 'Left'." *Dissent* 2 (Winter 1955): 40–50.

Cross, Ira B. *A History of the Labor Movement in California*. Berkeley: University of California Press, 1935.

Cudd, John Michael. *The Chicopee Manufacturing Co., 1823–1915*. Wilmington, Del.: Scholarly Resources, 1974.

David, C. G. [David Goodman Croly]. *A Positivist Primer*. New York: David A. Wesley, 1871.

David, Henry. *The History of the Haymarket Affair*. New York: Russell & Russell, 1958.

Debs, E. V. *Debs: His Life, Writings and Speeches*. Chicago: Charles H. Kerr, 1908.

————. *Writings and Speeches of Eugene V. Debs*. Introduction by Arthur Schlesinger, Jr. New York: Hermitage Press, 1948.

Destler, Chester McArthur. *American Radicalism 1865–1901, Essays and Documents*. Chicago: Quadrangle Books, 1966.

———. *Henry Demarest Lloyd and the Empire of Reform*. Philadelphia: University of Pennsylvania Press, 1963.

Dewey, John. "A Great American Prophet." *Common Sense* 3 (April 1934): 6.

Dombrowski, James. *The Early Days of Christian Socialism in America*. New York: Columbia University Press, 1936.

Dorfman, Joseph. *The Economic Mind in American Civilization*. Vol. 3, *1865–1918*. New York: Viking Press, 1949.

———. *Thorstein Veblen and His America*. New York: Viking Press, 1934.

Douglas, Paul H. *Real Wages in the United States, 1890–1926*. Boston: Houghton Mifflin, 1930.

Draper, Hal. "Neo-Corporatists and Neo-Reformers." *New Politics* 1 (Winter 1962).

———. *The Two Souls of Socialism*. Berkeley: Independent Socialist Press (2nd ed. rev.), 1961.

Eastman, Max. "Motive Patterns of Socialism." *The Modern Quarterly* 11 (Fall 1939): 45–55.

Egbert, Donald Drew and Stow Persons (eds.). *Socialism and American Life*. 2 vols. Princeton: Princeton University Press, 1952.

Ekirch, Arthur A., Jr. *The Civilian and the Military*. New York: Oxford University Press, 1956.

———. *The Decline of American Liberalism*. New York: Longmans, Green, 1955.

Elsner, Henry. *The Technocrats: Prophets of Automation*. Syracuse: Syracuse University Press, 1967.

Ely, Richard T. *Socialism and Social Reform*. New York: Thomas Y. Crowell, 1894.

———. *The Strengths and Weaknesses of Socialism*. New York: Chautauqua Press, 1894.

Fabricant, Solomon. "The Changing Industrial Distribution of Gainful Workers: Comments on the Decennial Statistics, 1820–1940." In *Studies in Income and Health*, Vol. 2, pp. 3–45. New York: National Bureau of Economic Research, 1949.

Feuer, Lewis. "American Travelers to the Soviet Union 1917–1932: The Formation of a Component of New Deal Ideology." Paper read to the Northern California Chapter, American Studies Association, at its winter meeting, Feb. 27, 1960, San Jose State College.

———. "John Dewey and the Back to the People Movement." *Journal of the History of Ideas* 20 (October-December 1959): 545–568.

———. 'Marx and the Intellectuals." *Soviet Survey* no. 49 (October 1963), pp. 102–112.

Filler, Louis. "Edward Bellamy and the Spiritual Unrest." *The American Journal of Economics and Sociology* 8 (April 1949): 239–249.

Fine, Sidney. *Laissez-Faire and the General Welfare State*. Ann Arbor: University of Michigan Press, 1956.

Forbes, Allyn B. "The Literary Quest for Utopia, 1880–1890." *Social Forces* 6 (December 1927): 179–189.

Franklin, John Hope. "Edward Bellamy and the Nationalist Movement." *New England Quarterly* 11 (December 1938): 739–772.

Frederickson, George M. *The Inner Civil War: Northern Intellectuals and the Crisis of the Union*. New York: Harper and Row, 1965.

Frisch, Michael H. *Town into City: Springfield, Massachusetts and the Meaning of Community: 1840–1880*. Cambridge: Harvard University Press, 1972.

Fromm, Erich. *Escape from Freedom*. New York: Rinehart, 1941.

———. Foreword to *Looking Backward* by Edward Bellamy. New York: Signet Books, 1960.

Gay, Peter. *The Dilemma of Democratic Socialism*. New York: Columbia University Press, 1950.

Gemorah, Solomon. "Laurence Gronlund's Ideas and Influences, 1877–1899." Ph.D. dissertation, 1965, New York University.

Gilbert, James. *Designing the Industrial State: The Intellectual Pursuit of Collectivism in America, 1880–1940*. Chicago: Quadrangle Books, 1972.

Gilman, Nicholas Paine. *Socialism and the American Spirit*. New York, Boston: Houghton Mifflin, 1893.

Ginger, Ray. *The Bending Cross: A Biography of Eugene Victor Debs*. New Brunswick, N.J.: Rutgers University Press, 1949.

Gladden, Washington. *Applied Christianity: Moral Aspects of Social Questions*. Boston: Houghton Mifflin, 1886.

Goldman, Eric F. *Rendezvous with Destiny: A History of Modern American Reform*. New York: Knopf, 1952.

Goodwin, Lawrence. *Democratic Promise: The Populist Movement in America*. New York: Oxford University Press, 1976.

Greenwalt, Emmett A. *The Point Loma Community in California, 1897–1942: A Theosophical Experiment*. Berkeley: University of California Press, 1955.

Grimes, Alan Pendleton. *American Political Thought*. New York: Henry Holt, 1955.

Gronlund, Laurence. *Ça Ira: Or Danton in the French Revolution*. Boston: Lee and Shepard, 1887.

———. *The Cooperative Commonwealth: In Its Outlines: An Exposition of Modern Socialism*. Boston: Lee and Shepard; New York: Charles T. Dillingham, 1884. Second ed. rev. and ann.: Boston: Lee and Shepard, 1890.

———. "Godin's 'Social Palace.'" *The Arena*, May 1890, pp. 691–699.

———. "Le Socialisme aux Etats-Unis." *Revue d'Economie Politique* 1 (1887): 109–124.

———. "Nationalism." *The Arena*, January 1890, pp. 153–165.

———. *The New Economy: A Peaceable Solution of the Social Problem*. Chicago, New York: Herbert S. Stone, 1898.

————. *Our Destiny: The Influence of Nationalism on Morals and Religion*. Boston: Lee and Shepard, 1891.

————. "Socializing a State." In *Three in One: A Trinity of Arguments on Socialism*. Chicago: The Social Democracy, n.d. [1898?].

————. "Une Tournée Missionaire Socialiste." *Revue d'Economie Politique* 10 (1896): 687–695.

Guerin, Daniel. *Fascism and Big Business*. New York: Pioneer Publishers, 1939.

Haber, Samuel. *Efficiency and Uplift: Scientific Management in the Progressive Era, 1890–1920*. Chicago: University of Chicago Press, 1964.

Hacker, Barton C. "The United States Army as a National Police Force: The Federal Policing of Labor Disputes, 1877–1898." *Military Affairs* 33 (April 1969): 255–264.

Hartz, Louis. *The Liberal Tradition in America: An Interpretation of American Political Thought Since the Revolution*. New York: Harcourt Brace, 1955.

Hertzler, Joyce. *History of Utopian Thought*. New York: Macmillan, 1926.

Hicks, John D. *The Populist Revolt: A History of the Farmer's Alliance and the People's Party*. Minneapolis: University of Minnesota Press, 1931.

Hillquit, Morris. *History of Socialism in the United States*. 5th ed. rev. and enl. New York: Funk and Wagnalls, 1910.

Hobsbawm, Eric. "The Fabians Reconsidered." Ch. 14 in *Labouring Men*. London: Weidenfeld & Nicholson, 1964.

Hofstadter, Richard. *The Age of Reform: From Bryan to F.D.R.* New York: Knopf, 1955.

————. *Social Darwinism in American Thought*. Rev. ed. Boston: Beacon Press, 1955.

Hoogenboom, Ari. *Outlawing the Spoils: A History of the Civil Service Reform Movement*. Urbana: University of Illinois Press, 1961.

Howells, William Dean. Review of *Looking Backward*. In *Harper's Monthly*, April 1888, pp. 801–803.

Hughan, Jessie Wallace. *American Socialism of the Present Day*. New York: John Lane, 1911.

Kipnis, Ira. *The American Socialist Movement, 1897–1912*. New York: Columbia University Press, 1952.

Kuhn, Alvin Boyd. *Theosophy: A Modern Revival of Ancient Wisdom*. New York: Henry Holt, 1930.

Laidler, Harry W. *Socialism in Thought and Action*. New York: Macmillan, 1920.

Lasswell, Harold D. "The Psychology of Hitlerism." *Political Quarterly* 4 (1933): 373–384.

Lebovics, Herman. *Social Conservatism and the Middle Classes in Germany, 1914–1933*. Princeton: Princeton University Press, 1969.

Lipset, Seymour Martin. *Agrarian Socialism*. Berkeley: University of Calfornia Press, 1950.

Lloyd, Caro. *Henry Demarest Lloyd; 1847–1903: A Biography*. 2 vols. New York: G. P. Putnam's Sons, 1912.

Lloyd, Henry Demarest. *Man, the Social Creator.* London: Harper, 1906.

————. *Newest England: Notes of a Democratic Traveller in New Zealand, with some Australian Comparisons.* New York: Doubleday, 1901.

————. *Wealth Against Commonwealth.* New York: Harper, 1894.

McHugh, Christine. "Edward Bellamy and the Populists: The Agrarian Response to Utopia, 1888–1898." Ph.D. dissertation, University of Illinois, Chicago, 1977.

McKee, Don K. "Daniel DeLeon: A Reappraisal." *Labor History* 1 (Fall 1960): 264–297.

Madison, Charles A. *Critics and Crusaders.* New York: Holt, 1947.

Mann, Arthur. *Yankee Reformers in an Urban Age.* Cambridge: Belknap Press, Harvard University Press, 1954.

Mannheim, Karl. *Man and Society in an Age of Reconstruction.* London: Routledge and Kegan Paul, 1940.

Marx, Karl and Frederick Engels. *Letters to Americans, 1848–1895.* New York: International Publishers, 1953.

Massing, Paul. *Rehearsal for Destruction: A Study of Political Anti-Semitism in Imperial Germany.* New York: Harper, 1949.

Merton, Robert. "Social Structure and Anomie." In *Social Theory and Social Structure.* Rev. ed. Glencoe, Ill.: Free Press, 1957.

Meusel, Alfred. "Middle Classes." *Encyclopedia of the Social Sciences.* Vol. 10, pp. 407–415. New York: Macmillan, 1933.

Miller, Sally M. *Victor Berger and the Promise of Constructive Socialism, 1910–1920.* Westport: Greenwood Press, 1973.

Mills, C. Wright. *White Collar.* New York: Oxford University Press, 1951.

Montgomery, David. *Beyond Equality: Labor and the Radical Republicans.* New York: Knopf, 1968.

Morgan, Arthur E. *Edward Bellamy.* New York: Columbia University Press, 1944.

————. *Nowhere Was Somewhere: How History Makes Utopias and Utopias Make History.* Chapel Hill: University of North Carolina Press, 1946.

————. *The Philosophy of Edward Bellamy.* New York: King's Crown Press, 1945.

Mumford, Lewis. *The Story of Utopias.* New York: Boni and Liveright, 1922.

Nicholas, H. G. "Political Parties and the Law in the United States." *Political Studies* 2 (1954): 258–270.

Nisbet, Robert A. *The Quest for Community.* New York: Oxford University Press, 1953.

Ostrogorski, M. *Democracy and the Organization of Political Parties.* 2 vols. New York: Macmillan, 1902.

————. *Democracy and the Party System in the United States: A Study in Extra-Constitutional Government.* New York: Macmillan, 1910.

Parrington, Vernon Louis. *The Beginnings of Critical Realism in America.* Vol. 3 of *Main Currents in American Thought.* New York: Harcourt Brace, 1930.

Pelling, Henry. *The Origins of the Labour Party: 1880–1900.* London: Macmillan, 1954.

Pollack, Norman. *The Populist Response to Industrial America.* New York: Norton Library, paper, 1962.

Pulzer, Peter G. J. *The Rise of Political Anti-Semitism in Germany and Austria.* New York: Wiley, paper, 1964.

Quint, Howard. *The Forging of American Socialism.* Columbia: University of South Carolina Press, 1953.

Ranney, Austin. *Curing the Mischiefs of Faction: Party Reform in America.* Berkeley: University of California Press, 1975.

————. *The Doctrine of Responsible Party Government: Its Origins and Present State.* Urbana: University of Illinois Press, Illini Books, 1962.

Reinders, Robert. "Militia and Public Order in Nineteenth-Century America." *Journal of American Studies* 11:81–101.

Rogin, Michael. *The Intellectuals and McCarthy: The Radical Specter.* Cambridge: M.I.T. Press, 1967.

Sadler, Elizabeth. "One Book's Influence: Edward Bellamy's *Looking Backward.*" *New England Quarterly* 17 (December 1944): 530–555.

Schapiro, J. Salwyn. *Liberalism and the Challenge of Fascism.* New York: McGraw-Hill, 1949.

Schiesl, Martin J. *The Politics of Efficiency: Municipal Administration and Reform in America, 1880–1920.* Berkeley: University of California Press, 1977.

Schiffman, Joseph, ed. *Edward Bellamy: Selected Writings on Religion and Society.* New York: Liberal Arts Press, 1955.

Schindler, Solomon. *Young West: A Sequel to Edward Bellamy's Celebrated Novel, Looking Backward.* Boston: Arena Publishing, 1894.

Schlesinger, Arthur Meier. *The Rise of the City: 1878–1898.* Vol. 10 of *A History of American Life.* New York: Macmillan, 1933.

Schwartz, Michael. *Radical Protest and Social Structure: The Southern Farmers' Alliance and Cotton Tenancy: 1880–1890.* New York: Academic Press, 1976.

Semmel, Bernard. *Imperialism and Social Reform.* London: Allen and Unwin, 1960.

Sennett, Richard. *Families Against the City: Middle Class Homes of Industrial Chicago.* Cambridge: Harvard University Press, 1970.

Shaw, George Bernard, ed. *Fabian Essays in Socialism.* Boston: Ball, 1911.

Shlakman, Vera. *Economic History of a Factory Town: A Study of Chicopee, Massachusetts.* Smith College Studies in History, vol. 20, nos. 1–4 (October 1934–July 1935).

Shurter, Robert L. "The Writing of Looking Backward." *South Atlantic Quarterly* 38 (July 1939): 255–261.

Sorge, Friedrich. *Labor Movement in the United States: A History of the American Working Class from Colonial Times to 1890.* Phillip S. Foner and Brewster Chamberlin, eds. Westport: Greenwood Press, 1977.

Sproat, John. *The Best Men: Liberal Reformers in the Gilded Age.* New York: Oxford University Press, 1968.

The Theosophical Movement: 1875–1950. Los Angeles: Cunningham Press, 1951.

Thomas, John L. "Utopia for an Urban Age: Henry George, Henry Demarest Lloyd, Edward Bellamy." *Perspectives in American History* 6 (1972): 135–163.

Trow, Martin. "The Second Transformation of American Secondary Education." *International Journal of Comparative Sociology* 2 (September 1961): 144–166.

Waldo, Dwight. *The Administrative State: A Study of the Political Theory of American Public Administration.* New York: Ronald Press, 1948.

Walling, William English. *The Larger Aspects of Socialism.* New York: Macmillan, 1913.

Walters, Donald Edgar. "Populism in California: 1889–1900." Ph.D. dissertation, University of California, Berkeley, 1952.

Weinstein, James. *The Corporate Ideal in the Liberal State, 1900–1918.* Boston: Beacon Press, 1968.

Wiebe, Robert. *The Search for Order: 1877–1920.* New York: Hill and Wang, 1967.

Williamson, Chilton. *American Suffrage from Property to Democracy, 1760–1860.* Princeton: Princeton University Press, 1960.

Wilson, R. Jackson. "Experience and Utopia: The Making of Edward Bellamy's *Looking Backward.*" *Journal of American Studies* 11 (1977): 45–60.

Wood, Neal. *Communism and British Intellectuals.* New York: Columbia University Press, 1959.

Yearly, Clifton K. *The Money Machines: The Breakdown of Government and Party Finances in the North, 1860–1920.* Albany: State University of New York Press, 1970.

Zornow, William F. "Bellamy Nationalism in Ohio 1891 to 1896." *Ohio State Archaeological and Historical Quarterly* 58 (April 1949): 152–170.

INDEX

Designer: Sandra Drooker
Compositor: Huron Valley Graphics
Printer: Braun-Brumfield, Inc.
Binder: Braun-Brumfield, Inc.
Text: Janson Linotron 202
Display: Helvetica Bold